Why Science and Art Creativities Matter

D1809682

Critical Issues in the Future of Learning and Teaching

The titles published in this series are listed at *brill.com/cifl*

Why Science and Art Creativities Matter

(Re-)Configuring STEAM *for Future-Making Education*

Edited by

Pamela Burnard and Laura Colucci-Gray

BRILL

SENSE

LEIDEN | BOSTON

Cover illustration: Artwork by Diana Scherer (http://dianascherer.nl/)

All chapters in this book have undergone peer review.

The Library of Congress Cataloging-in-Publication Data is available online at http://catalog.loc.gov

Typeface for the Latin, Greek, and Cyrillic scripts: "Brill". See and download: brill.com/brill-typeface.

ISSN 2542-8721
ISBN 978-90-04-42163-9 (paperback)
ISBN 978-90-04-39611-1 (hardback)
ISBN 978-90-04-42158-5 (e-book)

Printed by Printforce, the Netherlands

To future-making educators and their students

∴

Contents

Acknowledgement

With all books are a collective effort, some are more collective than others, and this book is definitively a team achievement. We are, however, deeply grateful and appreciative of the immense efforts and time given to us all by Caroline Maloney, our book administrator, who gave so generously and enthusiastically of her time and patience.

Figures and Tables

Figures

Tables

Notes on Contributors

Ramsey Affifi

is a Lecturer in Science (Biology) and Philosophy Education at Moray House School of Education and Sport, The University of Edinburgh. He is the founder of the organisation Sustainable Laos Education Initiatives and the Sai Nyai Eco-school. His writing and teaching are devoted to fostering flourishing in this great time of need.

Sofie Areljung

is Senior Lecturer in Educational Work at Umeå University, Sweden, where she is engaged with questions regarding science education in preschool and primary school. Her research interests lie within the interface of science education, early childhood education, and the arts. In that interface, epistemology becomes critical (what are valid ways of knowing, according to teachers), casting light on how time, matter, and power matters to science teaching. Sofie is particularly interested in developing science pedagogy and challenging epistemological traditions in collaboration with practitioners. Her research involves early years' transitions, documentation practices, children's relations with the material world, and teachers' professional development in relation to science education. More recently, her research interest has turned towards exploring visual arts as means of expressing and exploring science concepts in the early years, being open to children's non-canonical ways of representing natural phenomena.

Christopher Brownell

(BA, MA, PhD) (Associate Professor, Mathematics and STEM Education, Program Director, Mathematics Education, Fresno Pacific University, USA) is a secondary school mathematics instructor (for 14 years), turned university mathematics education researcher now with 30+ years combined experience in the teaching and learning fields. His primary focus has been on the Mathematical Knowledge for Teaching framework narrowing in on the specialized content knowledge teachers require to be highly effective in their role as instigators of learning. A focus on the human story that is mathematics, and how that story serves to connect students to continued study in the subject has lead him to broaden his focus to the artistic and aesthetic nature of mathematical thought. He is a co-author of the upcoming book, Math Recess: Playful Learning for the Age of Disruption.

Pamela Burnard

is Professor of Arts, Creativities and Educations at the Faculty of Education, University of Cambridge. She is Chair of the Faculty Board and the Arts and Creativities Research Group (https://www.educ.cam.ac.uk/research/groups/artsandcreativities/). She has published widely with 20 books and over 100 articles which advance and expand the conceptualization and plural expression of diverse creativities across early years, primary and secondary school settings, through to higher education, doctoral research practices, and creative and cultural industry sectors. She is co-editor of the journal *Thinking Skills and Creativity*. She publishes widely on future-making STEAM education.

Kerry Chappell

is a Senior Lecturer in Education at the University of Exeter. Her research is focused on the contribution creativity in arts education can make to debates about educational futures; the interdisciplinary study of creativity; and methodologies for participatory research. Her work as a dance-artist with a Devon-based dance lab collective informs her research practice

Laura Colucci-Gray

is a Senior Lecturer in Science and Sustainability Education at Moray House School of Education and Sport, University of Edinburgh. Formerly a Biology teacher, Laura holds a degree in Natural Sciences from the University of Turin (Italy) and a PhD in Science Education from the Open University (UK). Her research focuses on participatory methodologies – from discussion and role plays to arts based methodologies – to deal with complex and contested issues in science and society. Laura has published extensively in the field of science education, environmental education and sustainability education. She is a founding member of the Interuniversity Research Institute for Research on Sustainability (www.iris.unito.it) in Turin, and has held teaching and research appointments at the Universities of Turin, Aosta Valley, Strathclyde and Aberdeen.

Carolyn Cooke

is currently completing a PhD exploring music student teachers' experiences of improvisation as a radical apparatus for troubling enlightenment epistemology at the University of Edinburgh's Moray House School of Education and Sport. Having worked as a music teacher in secondary schools, and more recently as a lecturer across primary, secondary, music and generic education course, she has developed interests in student teacher learning and arts-based pedagogies, as well as writing on musical learning behaviours, music curricula issues, and inclusion.

Kristóf Fenyvesi

(PhD) is a researcher of STEAM Trans- and Multidisciplinary Learning at the Finnish Institute for Educational Research, University of Jyväskylä. He is the Vice-President of the world largest mathematics, arts and education community, the Bridges Organization. In 2008 he started Experience Workshop – Global STEAM Network (www.experienceworkshop.org). Fenyvesi's articles have appeared in several prestigious peer-reviewed journals and he has edited numerous math-art-education handbooks, including *Aesthetics of Interdisciplinarity: Art and Mathematics* (Springer-Birkhauser, 2017). He has been very active in organizing international scientific events, education programs, exhibitions and STEAM workshops and festivals all around the globe.

Erik Fooladi

holds a doctorate in organometallic chemistry from University of Oslo, and is presently associate professor in science education and home economics at Volda University College, Norway. He has an extensive production of teaching resources and popular scientific material in the interface between science and food, most recently as co-author of the popular science book "A Pinch of Culinary Science: Boiling an Egg Inside Out and Other Kitchen Tales". His research interests are education and communication in the intersection between food, science and sense/ory experiences, particularly on inquiry, argumentation, context-based education and epistemic perspectives in transdisciplinary contexts. He is also a musician (percussionist), and collaborates with both researchers, artists and other practitioners to produce multisensory performances and research, including not only what can be heard and seen, but also that can be smelled and tasted.

Catherine Francis

is a doctoral candidate and Lecturer at the University of Aberdeen's School of Education. Previously she was a Chartered Teacher working in the north east of Scotland for almost twenty years and a primary teacher for ten years in England and Germany. Whilst at school, she championed Learning for Sustainability and Global and International Education. During this time, she worked in partnership with many schools from across Europe and in Pakistan. As a teacher and teacher educator, she enjoys learning and teaching in a variety of indoor and outdoor contexts. A love of Nature guided this work and Nature's work is to be found at the heart of her research today. Her research specifically explores the dynamics of children's ecological identities provoked by experiential, embodied learning in Science and LfS outdoors through Art making. In particular, she is intrigued by the nature of knowing and noticing. Through engaging with arts-based methods she hopes to draw out the learning which, perhaps hitherto, has gone unknown, un-noticed and almost certainly undervalued.

Lindsay Hetherington

is a Senior Lecturer in Education at the University of Exeter. Believing that science is fundamentally about questioning and experimentation with the natural world, her research is focused on exploring how learners intra-act with the natural world and how transdisciplinary creative pedagogies can foster young people's understanding of science as creative. She uses new materialist and emergent theoretical and methodological perspectives to engage with the inherent messiness and uncertainty of real-world research.

Anna Hickey-Moody

is a Professor of Media and Communications at RMIT University and an Australian Research Council Future Fellow 2017–2021. Between 2013 and 2016 Anna was the Director of the Centre for Arts and Learning at Goldsmiths College, London and Head of the PhD in Arts and Learning. Anna has also held teaching and research positions at The University of Sydney, Monash and Uni-SA. Anna is known for her theoretical and empirical work with socially marginalized figures, especially young people with disabilities, young refugees and migrants, those who are economically and socially disadvantaged, and men at the margins of society. She is also known for her methodological expertise with arts practice, or practice research, ethnography and methodological invention. She has published 9 books and many articles and chapters.

Christine Horn

has worked in the field of social research, art, design and digital media for several years. She has taught digital and analog art and design including photography, print, typography and illustration. Besides her work with the Interfaith Childhoods projects at RMIT University she has an interest in the cultural approaches to Aboriginal and Torres Straits Islander health. Her previous research aimed to establish the impact and specific use of digital technologies among Indigenous communities in Sarawak, Malaysia. Christine was awarded her PhD from Swinburne University in 2015.

Tim Ingold

is Professor Emeritus of Social Anthropology at the University of Aberdeen. He has carried out fieldwork among Saami and Finnish people in Lapland, and

has written on environment, technology and social organisation in the circum-
polar North, on animals in human society, and on human ecology and evolutionary theory. His more recent work explores environmental perception and
skilled practice. Ingold's current interests lie on the interface between anthropology, archaeology, art and architecture. His recent books include *The Perception of the Environment* (Routledge, 2000), *Lines* (Routledge, 2007), *Being Alive*
(Routledge, 2011), *Making* (Routledge, 2013), *The Life of Lines* (Routledge, 2015),
Anthropology and/as Education (Routledge, 2018) and *Anthropology: Why it
Matters* (Polity, 2018).

Riikka Kosola

is a professional 'mover'. She works with several bodily languages, dance being her core. As a choreographer, dancer and pedagogue, she is interested in
space and its complex structure in the world, linking this to the dynamic structure of the human body. Riikka has a master degree from CNSDM of Lyon in
France in Contemporary Dance and degree in Cultural Anthropology and Performance Art from Lyon 2 University, while currently starting her studies in
Mathematics and in Art History in Helsinki University in Finland. She has a
dance company – *Kustavi Korps* – studying kinaesthetic intelligence through
dance works, and offering workshops to multiple audiences. Riikka is a part of
Maths-in-Motion team through Experience Workshop STEAM Network.

Zsolt Lavicza

(BA, BA, MS, MA, MPhil, PhD) is Professor in STEM Education Research Methods at Johannes Kepler University's (JKU) Linz School of Education. After receiving his degrees in mathematics and physics in Hungary, Zsolt began his
postgraduate studies in applied mathematics at the University of Cincinnati.
While teaching mathematics in Cincinnati he became interested in researching issues in the teaching and learning mathematics. In particular, he focused
on investigating issues in relation to the use of technology in undergraduate
mathematics education. Afterwards, both at the Universities of Michigan and
Cambridge, he has worked on several research projects examining technology
and mathematics teaching in a variety of classroom environments. In addition,
Zsolt has greatly contributed to the development of the GeoGebra community and participated in developing research projects on GeoGebra and related
technologies worldwide. While at JKU he is working on numerous research
projects worldwide related to technology integration into schools; leading the
doctoral programme in STEM Education at JKU; teaching educational research
methods worldwide; and coordinates research projects within the International GeoGebra Institute.

Elsa Lee

is an educationalist with a longstanding interest in environmental issues and connections to place. She started her working life as a secondary school science teacher, teaching in the UK and Mexico; this experience continues to inspire and guide her academic work. Elsa has previously undertaken academic research seeking to understand how children perceive and articulate their connections to place, particularly significance of climate change within this. She now researches community-based waterway rehabilitation projects, as well as exploring how art, artists and children's connections to nature intersect. Elsa has a Bye-Fellowship at Homerton College, Cambridge.

Saara Lehto

(Science Education Coordinator at LUMA Centre Finland; PhD Student in Mathematics Education, University of Helsinki; dancer and dance teacher) works as a Science Education Coordinator at LUMA Centre Finland at the University of Helsinki (UH). She is currently a PhD Student in Mathematics Education at UH and her research falls in the field of embodied mathematics education. Lehto has a Licentiate's degree in Mathematics from UH where she has worked as a researcher, research assistant and a part time teacher during the years 2000–2010. She has a long experience in non-formal mathematics education and she is a co-author (with Björklund et al.) of a book about fun and creative ways to teach mathematics in primary education, entitled *Sukkia ja muuta matematiikkaa* (MFKA-kustannus, 2002). Lehto has a heavy background in dance and has worked as a professional dancer and dance teacher in Helsinki during the years 2010–2017. Her amateur dance group Saara Lehto Equation currently explores connections between mathematics and dance.

Danielle Lloyd

is a third year undergraduate student on the BA (Hons) Primary Education Studies course at Anglia Ruskin University, Cambridge. She has participated in a number of research studies across her degree course, in particular working as a student research intern for a four-week project, the work for which formed the basis of this chapter. Danielle has a range of experience working with children in a variety of settings and hopes to go on to complete a PGCE and become a primary school teacher.

James MacAllister

is Senior Lecturer in Philosophy of Education at Moray House School of Education and Sport, the University of Edinburgh. His recent publications include the book *Reclaiming Discipline for Education: Knowledge, relationships and the birth of community* (Routledge, 2017) as well as various papers on what Scottish philosophers have written about education. He has a PhD from the University of Edinburgh and has taught in Edinburgh primary schools.

Tessa McGavock

is Director of Western Sydney University Early Learning Centre, Penrith, at Western Sydney University. She is currently undertaking research to explore the integration of Indigenous ways of knowing and being into early learning. In her capacity as director, Tessa led and supported the development and implementation of pedagogical responses to the deep hanging out researcher observations in "Naming the World". As the Centre Director Tessa initiated a connection with the Villentarha Preschool in Oulu Finland. This was developed and implemented as "The Finland Project" exploring Finnish and Australian nature in the Goodher Room with children from 4–5 years. She also supported the ongoing evolution of "What can we see outside?", the very exciting and creative project that emerged with educators and very young children from 0–2 years in the Boori Room, and its extension into the 3–4 year old group. This latter project is the focus of our jointly authored chapter.

Karin Murris

is Professor of Pedagogy and Philosophy at the School of Education, University of Cape Town. She is a teacher educator and grounded in academic philosophy, her main research interests are: child studies, school ethics and postqualitative research methods. She is principal investigator of various funded research projects and her books include: *The Posthuman Child* (Routledge, 2016), and (with Joanna Haynes) *Literacies, Literature and Learning* (Routledge, 2018), *Picturebooks, Pedagogy and Philosophy* (Routledge, 2012). She is co-editor of the *Routledge International Handbook of Philosophy for Children* (Routledge, 2017) and Chief Editor of a new Routledge series on Postqualitative, New Materialist and Critical Posthumanist Research.

Lena Nasiakou

is Learning and Development specialist, Founder of Lena's Moves, Olde Vechte Foundation, and believes that working with body offers a space for a deeper understanding and makes learning a joyful process. This is the reason for applying mostly embodied methodologies when she is training teachers, students, youth and adults. She is a Learning and Development Specialist with MSc in Lifelong Learning & BSc in Educational Studies with extensive experience in designing & delivering international educational projects. The topics

Lena makes the greatest difference in, is mathematics, coaching and trainer education through the projects she is involved in.

Edvin Østergaard

is a composer and Professor in Art and Science in Education at the Norwegian University of Life Sciences. His research focuses on the interplay between art and science, with emphasis on educational aspects, and history and philosophy of science, with emphasis on aesthetics and the diversity of forms of knowing. In 2008–2009 he held a position as visiting scholar at Harvard University, Boston and 2016–2017 as visiting professor at Humboldt University, Berlin.

Anne Pirrie

is Reader in Education at the University of the West of Scotland. Her recent book *Virtue and the Quiet Art of Scholarship: Reclaiming the University* (Routledge, 2019) offers a fresh and unorthodox perspective on what it means to be a 'good knower' in a social and educational environment dominated by the market order. In an era characterised by deep and enduring social and cultural divisions, the book offers a timely, accessible and critical perspective on the perils of retreating behind disciplinary boundaries. These issues have a bearing on the ultimate success of the movement from STEM to STEAM.

Hermione Ruck Keene

is an Associate Lecturer in Music Education at the University of Exeter and was previously a Graduate Research Assistant on the Creations Project.

Ruth Sapsed

is the Director of arts and well-being charity Cambridge Curiosity and Imagination (CCI). The charity was founded in 2007 by a group of artists, educators, parents and researchers with a shared passion for how the arts can transform lives. Ruth is particularly interested in how young children's ideas can lead others, their families, friends, neighbours and educators, and their role as crucial community navigators and connectors. Co-creation and collaboration is central to everything she does. www.cambridgecandi.org.uk

Diana Scherer

is a visual artist living and working in Amsterdam. Her work explores the relationship of man versus his natural environment and his desire to control nature. Encompassing photography, material research, plant root-weaving and sculpture, she develops her ideas by working in collaboration with biologists, engineers and designers. Currently, her material research is focussed on the development of a new sustainable material woven from plant roots. More information about her work is available at: http://dianascherer.nl/

Pallawi Sinha

joined the Faculty of Education, University of Cambridge as a postdoctoral research associate in February 2018. She is currently working on a qualitative study jointly funded by the British Academy and Department for International Development under Dr. Aarthi Sriprakash. The study is examining the contexts, practices and costs of early childhood care and education in India to address culturally responsive models.

Margaret Somerville

is Professor of Education in the School of Education and member of the Institute for Culture and Society at Western Sydney University. She is interested in exploring alternative and creative methods of research for planetary wellbeing. Her background is long term engagement and collaborative research with Australian Aboriginal communities, exploring alternative knowledge systems and ways of being and knowing. More recently she has been involved in researching with teachers and schools in relation to experiential sustainability learning. Her current project *Naming the World: Enhancing early years literacy and sustainability learning* addresses the ontological and epistemological problem of the separation of culture (as language) from nature (as world) in early years learning. Drawing on the latest new materialist methods, with a parallel study site in Finland, this project asks: "How can we integrate literacy and sustainability to produce powerful new learning for young children of the 21st century?"

Keiren Stephenson

is a creative early childhood practitioner who engages very young children from 0–3 years. She has conducted a range of innovative projects such as 'the hands project' in which the children learned bodies, representational practices, and naming by creating a mural of their hand prints in bright colours. They learnt to recognise each child's hand prints when the child placed their hand on their print and said their name. The project 'What Can We See Outside', described in this chapter, similarly begins with very young children's curiosities, engagements and sensory pleasures to extend their learning in creative ways.

Carine Steyn

is the project leader for the Govan Mbeki Mathematics Development Centre (GMMDC) National Math Art Competition for Secondary Schools in South Africa and the project leader for the Technology, Pedagogy and Content Knowledge (TPACK) professional development project for Mathematics teachers in the Eastern Cape. She taught mathematics at secondary school level for 24 years before she returned to studying and joined the GMMDC which is an engagement entity under the Science Faculty at the Nelson Mandela University in Port Elizabeth. Carine has a passion for teaching mathematics and exciting learners about learning. She loves finding creative ways in which to encourage teachers and learners to see Mathematics in real life.

Jan van Boeckel

is a visual artist, art educator, researcher and film-maker. His main field of interest is in arts-based environmental education. Currently, he is senior lecturer in visual art education at the Academy of Design and Crafts in Gothenburg, which he combines with working with the Centre for Environment and Development Studies and Climate Change Leadership node in Uppsala. Van Boeckel was professor in art pedagogy at the Estonian Academy of Arts in Tallinn (2015–2018) and has been program director in design theory at the Iceland University of the Arts in Reykjavik (2014–2015). In 2013, he defended his doctoral thesis entitled *At the Heart of Art and Earth* at Aalto University in Helsinki. From 2007 onward, Jan is active member of the international Eco-Art Network. Jan co-produced a series of documentaries on the world-views and environmental philosophies of indigenous peoples. He also made films on the sociologist Jacques Ellul and eco-philosopher Arne Naess. www.janvanboeckel.wordpress.com

Nicola Walshe

is a Principal Lecturer at Anglia Ruskin University in Cambridge. She gained a PhD in glaciology and taught and worked as Head of Geography in three secondary schools in the UK before going on to teach and lead the Geography PGCE course at Cambridge University. She is now Deputy Head of the School of Education and Social Care and Course Leader of the BA Primary Education Studies programme at Anglia Ruskin University. Nicola's research interests include students' understandings of sustainability, environmental and sustainability education, and pedagogies at the intersection of the arts, nature and wellbeing, particularly with reference to children.

Olivier Werner

is the founder and director of the Govan Mbeki Mathematics Development Centre (GMMDC) at the Nelson Mandela University (NMU), Port Elizabeth, South Africa. He held a National Chair in Mathematics Education over the period 2011–2015. His extensive academic background as research mathematician and experience of teaching mathematics from secondary school to PhD level stretches back to 1990. His passion and experience in STEM education is centred in the development, implementation and testing of large scale customized teaching and learning models that integrate technology, pedagogy and curriculum content. His work also includes a strong focus on professional skills development of in-service teachers, promoting the use of GeoGebra and STEAM education to meet some of the challenges posed by 4IR.

Marissa Willcox

is a digital ethnographer currently conducting PhD research in the Digital Ethnography Research Centre at RMIT University in Melbourne, Australia. Her research looks at feminist artists representations of gender and sexuality in digital art on Instagram. Willcox has worked in PR and media-based roles in industry focused jobs, and after shifting to academia, now aims to change the way we teach gender and sexuality in media studies for future generations. She is known for her work with LGBTQIA+ and feminist activist art communities online. As a Research Associate on the ARC funded Interfaith Childhoods project, Marissa works with Chief Investigator Anna Hickey-Moody to leverage creative research methods in art practice, digital technologies, the sociology of religion and gender and sexuality studies to bring a new perspective to ways we understand identity, community and belonging.

Heather Wren

is a PhD student in creative education at the University of Exeter and was previously a Graduate Research Assistant on the Creations Project.

(Re-)Configuring STEAM in Future-Making Education

Laura Colucci-Gray and Pamela Burnard

This book was written against a background of global environmental and political turmoil. Daily reports of the impacts of climate change on soils; on biodiversity; on sea levels are challenging what is known and assumed to be good and true about the world. They demand a renovated activism to address the barriers to the future wellbeing of all living things on the Earth.

Bringing together a range of international contributors engaged in research and practice across the arts and the sciences, the focus is on STEAM for future-making education. Unquestionably, all education is about the future. In writing this book we are concerned with how education across the arts and sciences can move beyond ideas of prescription and enculturation, whereby education is viewed as preparing for a future which may be predicted, feared or simply expected. Instead, we focus on the idea of education as stimulating thinking and practices of *future-making,* by enabling people and communities to respond resourcefully and creatively to ongoing changes. In pursuing this aim, this book will take the lead from the idea of education as a moment of 'participation', a term understood both as *being part of* something and *participating in*, thus occurring every moment and in-the-moment in the complex space of everyday life.

In this scenario, STEAM is considered as a relatively new entry in the field of education, and such 'newness' calls for greater engagement of its role vis a' vis ideas of education and the future. The acronym refers to the combination and synergistic interplay of different subjects, generally identified as science, technology, engineering, and mathematics (STEM) *plus* the arts. Linguistically, STEAM can be seen as an expansion of STEM, which is commonly referred to as the assemblage of scientific and technological disciplines driving the promise of economic growth and human prosperity. The arts may lack a specific collocation and/or definition, ranging from specific forms of visual art (painting, drawing, photography, sculpture, media arts and design), to a variety of arts including visual, performing (dance, music and theatre), digital media, aesthetics and crafts, and widening even further to include the liberal arts and humanities disciplines. If STEAM is seen as a continuation of STEM, adding to

© KONINKLIJKE BRILL NV, LEIDEN, 2020 | DOI: 10.1163/9789004421585_001

the economic drivers supporting scientific and technological developments, the arts are framed as a handmaiden to STEM, to facilitate engagement, to raise interest, to increase appeal.

Such a position is contested on a number of grounds (see Chapter 1, by Annie Pirrie; Chapter 14 by Nicola Walshe et al.): that it denies the intrinsic value of the arts, but also that of the sciences; that it presupposes a hierarchy of knowledge and that it assumes that the arts should necessarily be appealing to everyone. But there is also another line of thinking which forms the basis of this book. The relationship between STEM and STEAM can be seen as an important forum for addressing questions of scientific and technological development vis-à-vis society and the environment. This view seeks further dialogue and experimentation across different fields of knowledge, practice and inquiry to deepen understanding of knowing in the arts and sciences and to widen their purpose and evolution to support prosperity as well as sustainability and wellbeing. It was Ivan Illich (1973) who invoked the need for educational and medical institutions to develop tools for "conviviality", that is, spaces for dialectics, debate and openness to a multiplicity of ways of being and doing in the world. However, conviviality is not an abstract concept. The Earth is the space in which we live and co-exist with others; the only planet which can support us and on which we entirely depend.

1   STEAM as a Knowledge-Practice Construct

Taking the Earth as a point of reference, and viewing education as a process of critical engagement with questions that matter to us, we draw from Star and Griesemer's (1989) tools for policy analysis to refer to STEAM as a "boundary object" (Colucci-Gray, Burnard, Gray, & Cooke, 2019), that is, a "knowledge-practice" construct that can be shared by different communities and networks, as they come to interact with one another. Typically, boundary objects lack definition as they are not entirely part of any one community, but they are dynamic configurations bringing into confluence a multiplicity of discourses and understandings about what is perceived to be significant and worthy of investigation. This book draws upon this inherent and exciting tension which is at the core of our everyday experiences as teachers and learners, as well as citizens and consumers of knowledge in contemporary societies. We do so by seeking to develop the educational space as a site for pluralist dialogue across different fields of practice and inquiry, with the aim of gaining deeper understanding of "STEAM" as "(re)-configurings", that is, as enactments of learning processes drawing together and synthesising different epistemological and methodological approaches.

In so doing, we avail ourselves of concepts and practices ranging from policy analysis, to discourse studies and the philosophy of science and technology to reflect on the multiple uses of STEAM as an umbrella term (Colucci-Gray et al., 2017) lacking any specific characterisation or "model" of practice. It is a term that is often associated with creativity, productivity and innovation, as in the interpretation provided by the Cultural Learning Alliance (2016), promoting the arts in STEM to enhance students' prospects for employability and competitiveness in the job market. In post-industrial societies, where manufacturing industries have been largely replaced by a service economy, STEAM has been endorsed as a means to inspire students to take up an interest in STEM (Isabelle & Valle, 2016), to enable greater synergies and alignment between schools and industry and, in so doing, to renovate the skills and knowledge of the young workforce. However, engaging with STEAM as a pedagogical offering also brings into question a number of other important issues related to the purposes of education, ultimately, by asking how education in the sciences as well as the arts is positioned vis-à-vis *everybody* and vis-à-vis an uncertain future. Hence STEAM is a multi-vocal and dynamic construct, bringing to the fore issues of power and intersectionality which characterise curricula and the landscape of teachers' practices more broadly.

2   What Is New?

Arguably, the idea of STEAM is not entirely new as it draws upon an existing international literature on using the arts in the teaching of science. Common approaches include teaching using dance and drama to better represent and model abstract scientific concepts (Braund & Reiss, 2019; Colucci-Gray et al., 2017). In these accounts, the emphasis shifts from conceptual to kinaesthetic learning, and vice versa, as we move backwards and forwards between the early years and higher education. For example, the "STEAM makers" movement (see Maslyk, 2016) in primary education is gathering particular momentum in the United States. Focusing on the so called twenty-first-century skills of creativity, collaboration, communication and critical thinking, the arts and sciences are integrated in practical problem-solving and design activities, spanning several disciplines and seeking to stimulate children's imagination, storytelling and creativity (Martinez, 2017). The arts are viewed broadly, from visual and performance arts to craft skills, such as cooking or sowing – seeking to value cultural heritage and to develop school–community collaborations (Sousa & Pilecki, 2013). Conversely, moving to higher education, the literature on STEAM appears to have found a niche in the education of future scientists. STEAM is proposed as a way to reconnect scientists with the object of their studies,

developing imaginative and observational skills in scientific inquiry – often using drawing and digital design – to enhance methodological innovation, and to enable scientists to reach out to wider audiences (Segarra et al., 2018).

Generally, STEAM practices appear to develop in liminal spaces, such as informal learning environments or as part of programs devoted to promoting science outreach. In formal school curricula, however, teaching through a combination of subjects, usually as part of interdisciplinary projects, is often viewed as problematic by teachers, who are working within a curriculum and assessment structure that appears to be narrowing, both in terms of subject choices and scope (Shapira & Priestley, 2018; Humes, 2013). In the UK at least, one interesting case is design and technology, spanning arts and design, home economics and technology education (the latter route often being populated by teachers who entered the profession with degrees in architecture and landscape and design and engineering).

Arguably, positioning this subject at the core of the STEAM acronym is a powerful way to bridge the gap between traditional scientific teaching and the desire to engage in real-world learning, taking account of real issues and problems and working together to find a solution. This idea is gaining momentum amongst science educators wishing to re-purpose STEM education from its original emphasis on recruiting excellent students to pursue careers in the sciences and related industries to widening access and participation of disadvantaged groups. In some cases, the preoccupation lies with seeking a better understanding of the interdisciplinary collaboration that is inherent in STEM to enhance students' own learning (Tytler, Prain, & Hobbs, 2019) and to re-examine conventional epistemic practices of disciplinary teaching in science education. Advocates of this approach are concerned with broadening the notion of scientific literacy through greater understanding of scientific inquiry as part of a historical and social context. In other cases, and by endorsing an explicit social justice agenda, the emphasis is put on STEM education as a form of empowerment for children in disadvantaged communities, to enable them to fight inequities by directing science education practices towards meeting their needs (Calabrese-Barton, Tan, & Greenberg, 2017). In this other conception, the arts are not always but may be included to give pupils a voice and offer tangible opportunities for participation in society.

So, from an educational perspective, the genealogy of STEAM education appears to feature several lines of germination; as an extension of the original STEM agenda, the "addition" of the arts is construed instrumentally as a means to compensate for the shortcomings of a curriculum that is still largely subject-based. Another line of development however may be concerned with understanding science and technology education not simply as acquisition of knowledge and skills but as important *activities* with the potential to make a real impact on one's life and one's community. In such case, the problem does not lie simply with interdisciplinary collaboration, and the ways in which academic and vocational areas of the curriculum may integrate, because relationships amongst subjects within the curriculum are decidedly unequal, often confronting teachers with making hard choices about which pedagogy to adopt in order to differentiate on the basis of pupils' different career prospects and abilities.

In order to understand STEAM beyond what may be conceived of as something special or occasional, or even as a remedial action for special categories of pupils (Kirchgasler, 2018), we argue for much greater understanding of the nature and the logics of knowing in the arts and sciences, their different and multiple creativities and how they shape and cultivate the ways in which we experience the world. Importantly, we seek to inquire into not only how arts and sciences purposefully *connect*, as in the manner of putting things together to create a finished product, but how they intra-act, that is, how they stimulate different forms of logics, rationality and affect; how they become part of an inquiry that is embedded within the world.

3 Why This Book?

As Carlson (2015) reports, we live in an age in which the idea of the "democratic" has changed dramatically from enlarged consultation to deconstructing the dichotomies and binary oppositions that have maintained the power relations and inequalities separating some from "others". While current accounts of STEAM have sought to integrate disciplines and approaches, and create bridges among different communities, the focus remains largely concerned with fulfilling the needs of specific "categories" of people and groups. A "discursive performativity" is in place which creates "disadvantage" in contrast to "advantage" and "humans" in contrast to non-humans or less-than-humans, the oppressed who are cast in lower-status roles in the hierarchy of knowledge and power. The emergence of a posthumanist philosophy, which has drawn together feminist and science and technology studies, phenomenological and existentialist accounts, is offering some new readings of social and evolutionary relations, going beyond the limitations of the human-centred view.

In contrast to the "pipeline model" of education, bringing the linear imagery of educational progression as the acquisition of increasing levels of abstract knowledge, a phenomenological understanding of knowing and learning is construed "horizontally", by reinstating sense experience as a prime locus of *sense experience as 'prime locus'*

learning about ourselves and our surroundings; a prime locus of understanding our dependence from others, humans and non-humans. In this view also the relationship between arts and sciences changes from one of alternate subservience to one of close and integrated correspondence, serving the learner by training faculties of perception, attentive observation, and haptic and affective participation in unfolding phenomena "in-the-world" (Dahlin, 2001). This approach can also be extended to sustainability studies to enhance one's grasping of one's life as being of the world, not "a part" or "apart" from it. Donna Haraway (2016) extends this idea of "being part" as "participating in" – an active and dynamic construction of "sympoiesis" that she defines as the process of "making with", like the

> critters which interpenetrate one another, loop around and through one another, eat each other, get indigestion, and partially digest and partially assimilate one another, and thereby establish sympoietic arrangements that are otherwise known as cells, organisms and ecological assemblages. (Haraway, 2016: 58)

In Haraway's account, knowledge, as well as knowing and thinking, are not separate components within self-contained "bodies". Rather, we come to live and think through assemblages in the flesh, emerging from the material and energetic assemblages of the Earth. Noting Haraway's critters is not to say that all actions and learning are reduced to mechanical instincts. Quite the contrary in fact. Recognising existence through the flesh makes it possible to transcend a view of "subjects" and "objects" into a view of ongoing "becoming", whereby "becoming" produces matter and it *matters*. Like the foetus in the female body (Grosz, 2011), it cannot be contained within a bounded object, but it *matters* as infant and mother contract and dilate in a field of ecological relations. "Becoming" thus provokes us to re-think the boundary between nature and culture as a process that never stops relating and/or mattering (Barad, 2011). Barad's theoretical work prompts/invites a speculative reading of time and space as uninterrupted flows of "nows" that matter in terms of the material-discursive constructions of STEAM. With the term "material-discursive" we point directly to the performative value of language as a means of positioning ourselves differently towards others. Linguistic forms invite different affective states and thus different modalities for attending to, listening to and paying attention. Such modalities sit at the core of the resulting discourses of inclusion/exclusion, participation/alienation from the process of co-production of futures. Hence, here we celebrate the conceptual elasticity that feminist new materialism offers in a quest not to find, nor seek, solutions but rather to generate new ways to think about STEAM as a practice of relational knowing.

close and integrated correspondence = drawing (really)

drawing & minibeasts as ECOLOGY

examining the divers ← drawing . inter-relationship

drawing as 'relational knowing'

minibeast + drawings
minibeast = drawings

'becoming'

drawing as a different modality

The interplay between the logic of the "designer" and the logics of the "maker" – as articulated by the anthropologist Tim Ingold (2013) – effectively captures the dimension of complementarity, as opposed to exclusion, that characterises this book. Drawing on the work of the sociologist Richard Sennett on the study of the work of craftspeople, Ingold introduces *foresight* as the ability to see forward, "*always being one step ahead of the material*" (Sennett, 2008: 175, emphasis added), not to preconceive a finished product. So, to anticipate is not simply a matter of predetermining, predicting or projecting a future state of affairs in the present, but "*of opening up a path and improvising a passage ... it is to look where you are going, not to fix an end point*" (Ingold, 2013: 68, emphasis added). In the same manner, as researchers and educators, we engage with future making as the central core of STEAM education: we seek to craft a landscape, drawing on practice as research, as opposed to trying to direct and prescribe. STEAM raises questions about what constitutes the "arts" and their role in STEM. We argue that these questions are productive sites of reflection to think more broadly about what it means to know the world: who asks the questions? How are the boundaries around problems drawn and defined? In what way is the dialogue across disciplines facilitated? What languages and tools are being used? And what is the nature of the relationship between knowers and the known which emerges as a result?

drawing as language & tool

4   Choreography of the Book

Through high quality research evidence, each chapter reflects on the implications that a reconfigured understanding of knowledge-making practices (STEAM) can have for educational research and practice. Each chapter involves "thinking with" theorists and theories but also, and at times, other authors and artists. Thinking with theory enables authors to make visible their use of various philosophical concepts in practices of inquiry, to situate the ways that theory is put to work through these pedagogical practices. The book is divided into four parts, thus enabling the reader to access a linear view which progresses from the broader articulation of posthumanist inquiry in Part 1, through to delineating specific questions and practices in the sciences and in the arts (Parts 2 and 3) to finally reconfiguring practice as research across the arts and sciences in Part 4. A horizontal and rhizomatic reading is also offered in the form of "traces on paper", enactments of thinking created by the editors in the process of writing and "becoming with" the research matter of each contributing chapter.

The book opens on the front cover with an illustration by the visual artist Diana Scherer (n.d.) titled "Interwoven/Plantroot Weaving", 2017. Her work engages with the troubled relationship between humans and nature, exploring the desire to control while opening to the variety of shapes and forms that comes as a result. The front cover image was chosen to identify the creative tension or entanglements, of limits and constraints, that are present in this book, as generative necessities.

While the book is organised in parts, each one considering a particular aspect of the STEAM proposition, the intention was to give life to the creative tension by *interweaving* different modes of reading, using words and images, academic discourses as well as more intuitive and poetic forms of understanding. In this vein, each section of the book opens with a short introduction followed by a hand-drawn picture by Laura Colucci-Gray, and a final one created by Pamela Burnard. We have called such pictures 'rhizomes' by taking the impetus from Deleuze and Guattari's conception (2004: 25): "A rhizome has no beginning or end; it is always in the middle, between things, interbeing, intermezzo". They were created by the editors in response to some of the *central lines* of discussion and exploration offered by contributors in each section. The four rhizomes increase in complexity, adopting higher-order forms of organisation moving from Part 1 to Part 4. The final rhizome, inserted in the Postlude, re-turns to the whole book, not seeking to organise and reconstruct but to allow for multiple, non-hierarchical entry points into the theoretical ideas and practices traced by the contributors across the book. Drawing on Ingold and Vergunst (2012), the act of "line making" as a "generative movement" is a term used here in contrast to make a "drawing" or a "diagram" (even if the desire to do so was felt strongly!), in order to refrain from reliving what had been read or experienced, summarising or even extracting suggestions for "best" practice for future planning and future teaching. So, the intention here is to invite readers to enter the rhizomes, while engaging in practice as research, exploring alleyways and openings to and from the chapters that follow. Following the lines is also an invitation to both authors of the book and readers to offer new readings and re-readings, going back and forth between the different sections, as generative of future entanglements.

5   Structure of the Book

5.1   Prologue: (Re-)Configuring STEAM in Future-Making Education

This chapter authored by the co-editors Laura Colucci-Gray and Pamela Burnard outlines the rationale for the book. It presents the current state of the debate on STEAM and it offers a renovated approach to theorising and practice, drawing on posthumanist accounts. The book does not seek to define or confine STEAM, viewing it instead as a flickering, dynamic experience that moves beyond the subjects. Is this a radical opportunity, we ask, for teachers, researchers and educators to make education a space that really *matters*?

5.2   *Part 1: Positioning STEAM in Future-Making Education*

Part 1 explores the possibilities arising from deconstructing the vexed relationship between "education" and "the future", questioning the linear model of outcomes-based education to recover the humanistic, democratic and ethical dimensions of future-making on a finite Planet. Authors explore underlying assumptions about knowledge and relationships in educational settings, and how such assumptions may be exacerbated in alternative readings of STEAM (see particularly Chapter 1, Anne Pirrie; Chapter 4, Ramsey Affifi).

Moving from linear, technocratic conceptions of education as "preparation for the future", chapter in this part sketch a set of views and possibilities of education as deeply connected to place, memory, experience and affective states over an extended "present" (see particularly Chapter 3, Karin Murris; Chapter 2, Margaret Somerville and co-authors).

Chapters in this part trouble the old-time separation between mind and body; thinking and doing; humans and non-humans. Authors enable us to see how learning, along with science and arts creativities, and the imagination, are deeply connected to actions and memory – and thus develop over time – in association with how we dwell and "make our path" in the world.

Chapters in this part offer both critical analyses of knowledge, and affirmative, productive accounts of educational modalities, drawing on the contributions of theorists and arts practitioners who have influenced cultural imaginaries of learning, creativity and education.

5.3   *Part 2: Why Does Science Matter?*

Drawing on the critical analysis of knowledge practices outlined in the previous part, Part 2 chapters problematise the acronym "STEAM" by drawing on the intersection of competing and complementary discourses in science education.

Seeking to refrain from advancing a particular conception of STEAM as an identifiable set of "creative pedagogies" for content delivery, this part "troubles" conceptions of science learning as the acquisition of abstract knowledge. The critique begins from illustrating how knowing in science is fundamentally embodied. Such recognition troubles the idea of language as "description" in science to uncover the performative and metaphorical dimensions which are at the core of the scientific imagination (see particularly Chapter 5, Laura Colucci-Gray). Looking through scientific practice from a socio-cultural and embodied perspective, each chapter offers an illustration of how the ways in

which we learn about the world are situated in a "relationship" of listening and attention (see particularly Chapter 6, Edvin Østergaard). Body apparatuses as well as instruments offer different modalities to attend to, affiliate with and tune in with the internal and the external world of human and non-human relations. Embodiment is also presented and discussed here as a way of re-visioning the unique relationship between humans and their tools (musical instruments as well as computers) as a potentially invigorating space for the development of greater sensitivity to the ways in which we perceive, make and inhabit a shared world. For example, a reflection will be offered on the insights achieved by children "rolling" with their bodies (see particularly Chapter 7, Sofie Areljung), or by the differing understandings which may come from different patterns of musical listening and notation.

Chapters in this part explore the potential of introducing a relational ontology in science education.

drawing as part of a relational ontology

5.4   Part 3: Why Do the Arts Matter?

This part does not advance a particular conception of arts or a particular theory about how art works as a subject. This part engages with troubling of different ways of (re)configuring STEAM as embodied learning and teaching, through the affective, agentic aspects and materiality of arts-based educational innovations. We do this by: (a) engendering corporeal cartographies of the body, bodies and bodily practices and relations (see particularly Chapter 8, Pamela Burnard et al.); (b) disrupting the outcomes-based models of schooling (see particularly Chapter 9, Anna Hickey-Moody, Christine Horn and Marissa Willcox); and (c) reflecting on the ways that arts creativities matter and manifest through STEAM (re-)configurings as sites of embodied relationships (see particularly Chapter 10, James MacAllister; Chapter 11, Jan van Boeckel).

Arts-based educational innovations are central to STEAM (re)configurings because they present productive and generative possibilities when questions inspired by new materialism are asked. In addition to asking *what arts making practices remake, reconfigure and re-present* (and what the making of art reveals), these innovations direct attention to material-discursive affordances, and they invite different sets of questions, such as: What kinds of work do arts do? What role do humans play in operating and producing arts-based educational innovations? What are the core aspects that manifest themselves at different moments in reconfiguring STEAM boundaries and relations that are neither defined nor bounded by subject disciplines? What sort of spacialities and temporalities do arts practices engender? How are specific practices of the arts mediated by STEAM practices? Do different arts in different spaces do different work and engender different bodies and bodily practices and relations?

drawing as a method for → trans-corporeality practices

Part 3 chapters ask where, how and when arts-based educational innovations come to matter. Authors invite curiosity into what gets produced in terms of material-discursive practices.

5.5   *Part 4: STEAM Reconfigurings in Practice*

This part offers accounts from research and pedagogical practice (practice as research), seeking to grapple with the opportunities offered by STEAM as a site of trans-corporeality. Each contribution provides examples of practices and "thinking with" particular theorists to surface ways of being, ways of learning and ways of thinking, that are stimulated and reinforced through inter- and transdisciplinary offerings of arts and sciences. The precise action of re-making subjects in and through research, and the iterative reconfiguring to which earlier chapters refer, are explored in ways that see teaching and learning in critically different ways: as sites of trans-corporeality for future-making education.

Chapters in this part span from illustrations of "practice as research" (see particularly Chapter 13, Kristof Fenyvesi et al.; Chapter 14, Nicola Walshe et al.; Chapter 16, Catherine Francis) to reflections and theorising on "research as practice" (see particularly Chapter 12, Lindsay Hetherington et al.; Chapter 15, Erik Fooladi; Chapter 17, Carolyn Cooke).

This part advances and stimulates thinking-through-practice and practice-as-research for enacting STEAM in everyday teaching and learning contexts.

5.6   *Postlude – Un-Conclusions: Disentangling the Assemblage of Science and Arts Creativities for Future-Making Education*

This section authored by Pamela Burnard and Laura Colucci-Gray offers a re-reading of all contributors from a posthumanist, new materialist perspective. It draws readers' attention to the mattering of discourses to uncover the expanding, participatory potential of STEAM as radical, dynamic and creative "reconfigurings" of the ecologies of learning and teaching.

5.7   *Epilogue*

This chapter authored by Tim Ingold looks back to earlier critiques of STEAM and the outcome-based discourse of education and it moves forward, anticipating lines of reconfigurings – lines of flight.

References

Barad, K. (2011). Nature's queer performativity. *Qui Parle: Critical Humanities and Social Sciences, 19*(2), 121–158.

research within STEAM education

Braund, M., & Reiss, M. J. (2019). The "great divide": How the arts contribute to science and science education. *Canadian Journal of Science, Mathematics and Technology Education, 19*(3), 219–236.

Calabrese Barton, A., Tan, E., & Greenberg, D. (2017). The makerspace movement: Sites of possibilities for equitable opportunities to engage underrepresented youth in STEM. *Teachers College Record, 119*(7), 1–44.

Carlson, D. (2015). Foreword. In N. Snaza & J. Weaver (Eds.), *Posthumanism and educational research* (pp. ix–xii). London: Routledge.

Colucci-Gray, L., Burnard, P., Cooke, C., Davis, R., Gray, D., & Trowsdale, J. (2017). *Reviewing the potential and challenges of developing STEAM education through creative pedagogies for 21st learning: How can school curricula be broadened towards a more responsive, dynamic, and inclusive form of education?* London: British Educational Research Association. doi:10.13140/RG.2.2.22452.76161

Colucci-Gray, L., Burnard, P., Gray, D., & Cooke, C. (2019). A critical review of STEAM (science, technology, engineering, arts and mathematics). In P. Thomson (Ed.), *Oxford research encyclopaedia of education.* Oxford: Oxford University Press. doi:10.1093/acrefore/9780190264093.013.398

Cultural Learning Alliance. (2016). *STEAM: Why STEM can only take us so far* (Briefing Paper No. 1). London: Cultural Learning Alliance. Retrieved August 26, 2019, from https://culturallearningalliance.org.uk/wp-content/uploads/2018/03/CLA-STEAM-Briefing-A4.pdf

Dahlin, B. (2001). The primacy of cognition – or of perception? A phenomenological critique of the theoretical bases of science education. *Science & Education, 10,* 453–475.

Deleuze, G., & Guattari, F. (2004 [1980]). *A thousand plateaus: Capitalism and schizophrenia* (B. Massumi, Trans.). New York, NY: Continuum.

Grosz, E. (2011). *Becoming undone: Darwinian reflections on life, politics, and art.* Durham, NC: Duke University Press.

Haraway, D. (2016). *Staying with the trouble: Making kin in the Chthulucene.* Durham, NC: Duke University Press.

Humes, W. (2013). Curriculum for excellence and interdisciplinary learning. *Scottish Educational Review, 45*(1), 82–93.

Illich, I. (1973). *Tools for conviviality.* New York, NY: Harper and Row.

Ingold, T. (2013). *Making: Anthropology, archaeology, art and architecture.* London: Routledge.

Ingold, T., & Vergunst, J. L. (Eds.). (2012). *Ways of walking: Ethnography and practice on foot.* Hampshire: Ashgate.

Isabelle, A., & Valle, Z. (2016). *Inspiring STEM minds: Biographies and activities for elementary classrooms.* New York, NY: Springer.

Kirchgasler, K. L. (2018). Moving the lab into the field: The making of pathologized (non)citizens in U.S. science education. *Curriculum Inquiry, 48*(1), 115–137.

Martinez, J. (2017). *The search for method in STEAM education.* London: Palgrave.

Maslyk, J. (2016). *STEAM makers: Fostering creativity and innovation in the elementary classroom.* Thousand Oaks, CA: Corwin.

Scherer, D. (n.d.). *About.* Retrieved August 26, 2019, from http://dianascherer.nl/about/

Segarra, V., Natalizio, B., Falkenberg, C. V., Pulford, S., & Holmes, R. (2018). STEAM: Using the arts to train well-rounded and creative scientists. *Journal of Microbiology and Biology Education, 19*(1). https://doi.org/10.1128/jmbe.v19i1.1360

Sennet, R. (2008). *The craftsman.* London: Penguin.

Shapira, M., & Priestley, M. (2018). Narrowing the curriculum? Contemporary trends in provision and attainment in the Scottish curriculum. *Scottish Educational Review, 50*(1), 75–107.

Sousa, D. A., & Pilecki, T. (2013). *From STEM to STEAM: Using brain-compatible strategies to integrate the arts.* Thousand Oaks, CA: Corwin.

Star, S., & Griesemer, J. (1989). Institutional ecology, "translations" and boundary objects: Amateurs and professionals in Berkeley's Museum of Vertebrate Zoology 1907–1939. *Social Studies of Science, 19*(3), 387–420.

Tytler, R., Prain, V., & Hobbs, L. (2019). Rethinking disciplinary links in interdisciplinary STEM learning: A temporal model. *Research in Science Education* [Preprint]. https://doi.org/10.1007/s11165-019-09872-2

PART 1

Positioning STEAM *in Future-Making Education*

∴

Introduction to Part 1

Pamela Burnard and Laura Colucci-Gray

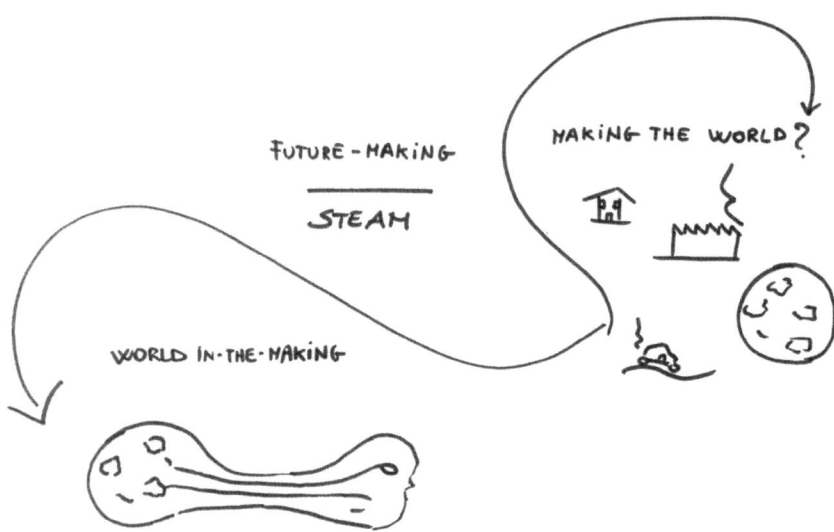

This image offers a visual interpretation of two forces in dialectical interplay: the narrow focus, focused on products and objects and the wide focus seeking to view products in relationship with processes and materials in relation to their transformations. The curved line moves sinuously between, around and through the page to bring the two dispositions in creative interchange.

Part 1 explores the possibilities arising from deconstructing the vexed relationship between "education" and "the future", questioning the linear model of outcomes-based education to recover the humanistic, democratic and ethical dimensions of future-making on a finite Planet. Authors explore underlying assumptions about knowledge and relationships in educational settings, and how such assumptions may be exacerbated in alternative readings of STEAM (see particularly Chapter 1, Anne Pirrie; Chapter 4, Ramsey Affifi).

Moving from linear, technocratic conceptions of education as "preparation for the future", chapter in this part sketch a set of views and possibilities of education as deeply connected to place, memory, experience and affective states over an extended "present" (see particularly Chapter 3, Karin Murris; Chapter 2, Margaret Somerville and co-authors).

Chapters in this part trouble the old-time separation between mind and body; thinking and doing; humans and non-humans. Authors enable us to see

© KONINKLIJKE BRILL NV, LEIDEN, 2020 | DOI: 10.1163/9789004421585_002

how learning, along with science and arts creativities, and the imagination, are deeply connected to actions and memory – and thus develop over time – in association with how we dwell and "make our path" in the world.

Chapters in this part offer both critical analyses of knowledge, and affirmative, productive accounts of educational modalities, drawing on the contributions of theorists and arts practitioners who have influenced cultural imaginaries of learning, creativity and education.

CHAPTER 1

Where Science Ends, Art Begins? Critical Perspectives on the Development of STEAM in the New Climatic Regime

Anne Pirrie

Abstract

This chapter explores the origins of the movement from STEM to STEAM, with a view to troubling the epistemological assumptions that underpin what at first appears to be a progressive project. STEAM appears to challenge traditional educational modalities (such as clear divisions between disciplines) in order to provide a broader canvas for human enquiry. It attempts to "value add" arts to STEM, yet this very concept of value adding epitomises the economic imperative that pervades contemporary educational discourse, and which has also been a key driver of the movement from STEM to STEAM. The main aim of this chapter is to develop a more nuanced understanding of the interrelationship between the arts and sciences, drawing on Bruno Latour among others. Reconceptualising the interrelationship between sciences and the arts has the potential to enrich our understanding of science, revitalise our teaching and make us open to new ways to respond to environmental challenges. What is required in the contemporary era is not mere addition in the sense of "value adding". Rather, what we need now is a more progressive project that entails the re-entanglement and re-enchantment of the ethical, political, moral, aesthetic and scientific dimensions of human enquiry across disciplines and fields of inquiry.

Keywords

arts – economic imperative – environment – Latour – Newton – Romanticism – science – two cultures

1   **Introduction: Critical Perspectives on the Movement from STEM
       to STEAM**

This chapter explores the origins of the movement from STEM to STEAM, with
a view to troubling the epistemological assumptions that underpin what at first
glance appears to be a progressive and ameliorative project. STEAM appears to
challenge traditional educational modalities (such as clear divisions between
disciplines) in order to provide a broader canvas for human enquiry. In contemporary terms, we might even say that the movement from STEM to STEAM –
that is to say adding "arts" to the study of science, technology, engineering and
mathematics (STEM) – is perceived to "add value" to a pre-existing initiative.
And yet the very notion of "value adding", namely the amount by which the
value of a commodity is increased by each stage in its production, encapsu-
lates the economic imperative that pervades contemporary educational discourse. It is perhaps not surprising, then, that this same economic imperative
also appears to have been a key driver of the movement from STEM to STEAM.
As we shall see, this has had some rather unfortunate consequences. I suggest
that these have ultimately been to the detriment of a broader understanding
of the interrelationship between apparently disparate areas of human enquiry,
such as the arts and sciences. I shall also attempt to demonstrate that the focus
on the economic imperative has also led to an impoverished understanding
of the nature of scientific and artistic practice *per se*. Even more importantly,
it has prejudiced our capacity to respond to environmental challenges. This
chapter puts forwards an alternative conception of knowledge in order to foreground new educational relationships and modalities.

My main aim here is to develop a more nuanced understanding of the
interrelationship between the arts and sciences. This will clear the ground for
a reassessment of the nature of teaching and learning in these areas. I shall
examine the role of the arts in enhancing human sensibility, with a view to
counterbalancing what I consider to be a constructive misreading of scientific
knowledge as being primarily about facts rather than values. As we shall see,
scientific inquiry is about more than a detailed understanding of empirical
processes: it also serves to cultivate a sense of wonder. I shall draw *inter alia*
upon the work of Bruno Latour (2016) in order to explore the interrelationship between sciences and the arts. He uses the term "new climactic regime"
to refer not just to climate change but also to "the whole range of climates
that have been modified". Latour refers to the ideal climate for producing wine,
that is, the particular combination of weather conditions, soil, temperature,
cultivation practices and so on. In the case under consideration here, the term
"new climatic regime" would include the modifications to the discourse of

education in recent years that have seen increasing emphasis on harnessing education to the ends of increased performativity and enhanced economic performance; and constructions of science and art that place them in different silos in an educational context. Reconceptualising the interrelationship between sciences and the arts has the potential to bring us back from a different planet, as it were. It is only by considering the arts and sciences *from the inside* rather than as reified categories that can be progressively realigned that we shall be better able to inhabit the Earth and to address the many challenges that we currently face. I shall suggest that what is required in the contemporary era is not mere addition in the sense of "value adding". Rather, what we need now is a more progressive project that entails the re-entanglement and re-enchantment of the ethical, political, moral, aesthetic and scientific dimensions of human enquiry across disciplines and fields of inquiry. This entails further endorsement of the need to theorise the relation between affect and cognition in science education (Alsop, 2005: 3). I attempt to argue that both of these developments are necessary if we are to recalibrate our relationship with human agency and develop a more nuanced understanding of the relation between science and the arts. This will entail a fundamental reassessment of the nature of teaching and learning in both science and in art and design, although there is not scope to do so here.

As we shall see below, brash expressions of the salient role of human agency and systematic neglect of the non-human pervade the discourse on the movement from STEM to STEAM. In order to re-balance our relationship with the world around us, we need to give voice to the non-human and the more-than-human, especially in these fragile times. This is vital if we are to ground ourselves more firmly *in* and *on* the Earth, and if we are to be *of* and *for* the Earth, rather than to float above it in a disembodied way, or metaphorically to shoulder the globe like the enfeebled descendants of Atlas. This rebalancing exercise will enable us to reframe our present engagement with the complex, fragile ecosystem to which we belong, and in due course to deepen our understanding of the nature of teaching and learning across the spectrum of human endeavour. Such an approach makes it possible for us to propose a far more radical agenda for change than that which is encapsulated by the current notion of STEAM.

It is worth bearing in mind the common-sense understanding of steam, which is nothing other than hot air. This is an element that appears to be in chronic oversupply in the increasingly fragile environment in which we have our being. Perhaps what is required now is that we let some cool drafts of fresh air run across the surface of a notion that has become rather overheated. Perhaps rebalancing our relationship with the Earth is simpler than we realise.

2   From STEM to STEAM: The Subordination of Art to *Techne*?

I shall begin by tracing the key moments in the movement from STEM to STEAM. The move to integrate the disciplines of science, technology, engineering and mathematics first became evident in the early 2000s. It gained fresh impetus following the publication of a report in the US entitled *Rising above the gathering storm* (National Academy of Science, National Academy of Engineering & Institute of Medicine, 2007). This report bears traces of the economic imperative as a key driver of educational change. It emphasised the links between economic prosperity, the "knowledge-intensive" jobs related to science and technology, and the level of (scientific and technological) innovation that were perceived to be necessary in order to address pressing societal problems.

I shall now briefly consider the origins of the kind of narrow instrumentalism that pervades *Rising above the gathering storm*. I think this is a necessary, if slightly unorthodox, move in light of the current debate on STEAM, especially as the hollow mantras of "economic competitiveness" and "global reach" simultaneously misrepresent the nature of intellectual enquiry and render us insensitive to the manifold challenges we face in the "new climactic regime".

One of the arguments advanced in this chapter is that contemporary rhetoric concerning the movement from STEM to STEAM places major obstacles in the way of thinking about the nature of intellectual enquiry, particularly when it comes to challenging the established orthodoxies inherent in giving STEM a fresh head of STEAM. As the attentive reader will already have discerned, I think this is unlikely to be achieved by subordinating art to narrow instrumentalist ends. Nor is it likely to be achieved by regarding science, engineering, technology and mathematics as unified, reified entities, without considering their multiplicity and foregrounding the production of interests that have led to the ascendancy of one field over another, or one sub-field within a field. By the same token, to adopt a narrow, instrumentalist view of art would be to run the risk of reducing it to the now obsolete sense of craft (*ars* in Latin, and τέχνη in Greek). It would also serve merely to reinforce existing hierarchical relations between science, technology, engineering and mathematics on the one hand and arts on the other. In the case of the movement from STEM to STEAM, there is a danger that art is regarded as a means of supplying what is required by science, technology, engineering and mathematics in order to generate "novel" and "creative" solutions to pressing social problems; and science, engineering, technology and mathematics, writ large, as it were, might be considered to draw upon what art (writ large) provides, for example, "igniting passion and interest in kids" (Rhode Island School of Design, n.d.). It appears that what all this boils down to is that that addition of the letter A to the acronym

STEM does not challenge the primacy of science, technology, engineering and mathematics over the arts in both the public imagination and in public policy. Moreover, it discursively positions science as the preserve of cognition, and affect as the preserve of the arts, thus reinforcing outmoded stereotypes. The philosopher and historian R.G. Collingwood's observations on aesthetics, first published eighty years ago, refer to the primacy of the economic imperative and thus continue to resonate today:

> We are apt nowadays to think about most problems, including those of art, in terms either of economics or of psychology; and both ways of thinking tend to subsume the philosophy of art under the philosophy of craft. To the economist, art presents the appearance of a specialized group of industries; the artist is a producer, his audience consumers who pay him [sic] for benefits ultimately definable in terms of the states of mind that his productivity enables them to enjoy. To the psychologist, the audience consists of persons reacting in certain ways to stimuli provided by the artist; and the artist's business is to know what reactions are desired or desirable, and to provide the stimuli that will elicit them. (Collingwood, 1958 [1938]: 19)

This reductionist vision of art as "handmaiden" to the sciences is evident in contemporary discourse around the notion of STEAM. For instance, in "Gathering STEAM on Rhode Island", a news item on the website of the Rhode Island School of Design (RISD), one of the world's leading design schools, claims made by the president of the school are set out as follows:

> Through tools such as data visualization and modelling, artists and designers are already working to make science understandable and real, and helping people to understand complex issues. By injecting art into the innovation dialogue, STEAM will help the country stay competitive in the 21st century. (RISD, n.d.)

In this section, I have drawn readers' attention to the limitations of traditional modalities of educational thinking. In sum, these place science on one side of a line that nobody drew and art on the other. I have also examined the implications of "injecting art into the innovation dialogue". An "injection" of art might enhance functionality, as it were, but it will not cure the patient lying spread eagled on the table of a fundamental malaise. We shall explore the development of STEAM further below, in relation to trends that were evident in the European education policy area around the same time.

3   Tracking the Gathering Storm

It is important to note that the policy developments relating to the movement
from STEM to STEAM in the US resonate with what was happening in education policy in Europe in the same period, especially in the "gathering storm"
that heralded the economic crash of 2008. The central aim of the Lisbon Strategy of 2000, the European Union's overarching program focusing on growth
and jobs, was to make the EU "the most dynamic and competitive knowledge-
based economy in the world, capable of sustained economic growth with more
and better jobs and greater social cohesion" (European Commission, n.d.). As
Pirrie and Thoutenhoofd (2013: 615) point out, the emphasis on competition
with a view to securing economic advantage that remains at the heart of the
European education policy agenda is "entirely consonant with the economic
foundations of the European Commission, founded in 1957 as the European
Economic Community (EEC)". In an increasingly fractured Europe marred by
the resurgence of identity politics, encapsulated and expressed in the vote for
Brexit, the ideal of greater social cohesion seems a more distant prospect than
ever – at both local and national levels. Latour (2016) suggests that the resurgence of identity politics, coupled with a desire to return to the land of old
("Make America great again") is a direct result of the gradual realisation that
the notion of the "globe" is utopian rather than 'topian' (i.e. relating to place,
from the Greek τόπος). Given the relevant coordinates, favourable weather
conditions and minimal infrastructure on the ground, a skilled pilot can land a
plane at a particular point on earth. He cannot, however, land it anywhere on
the *globe*.
    It is also worth noting that the extent to which narrow, functionalist under-
standings of "technological innovation" have served to promote the public good and address pressing societal problems. Indeed it is open to debate
whether or not the primary purpose of technological innovation is to contribute to the accumulation of capital and ever-wider social division rather than
to promote social good. It is, however, far from clear that (economic) "growth"
is an unquestionable good. Several commentators have pointed out that the
relentless focus on growth and making a contribution to the "knowledge economy" has had a pernicious effect on education at all levels. Nearly a decade ago
Gillies (2012: 240) drew attention to an unintended outcome of the emphasis
on human capital theory in EU policy discourse, namely, that "the only valued
aspects of education become those which have a direct, economic, wealth-
generating impact". The emphasis on economic growth may also explain the
focus on cognition rather than affect noted by Alsop (2005) in relation to science education, although there is not scope to explore that here.

Stefan Collini has roundly endorsed the view expressed by Gillies by mounting a rigorous defence of the humanities in higher education. As he has pointed out, the value of scholarship in the arts and humanities, and to some extent in the social sciences, cannot be viewed solely in terms of its contribution to economic prosperity (Collini, 2012: 100). He explains in the following terms:

> Even if it is allowed that there might be some non-material benefits from education for the *individual* – in terms, perhaps, of self-fulfilment or enhanced intellectual capacity – there is still a tendency to confine any possible *social* good to the usual litany about "productivity", "competitiveness", "innovation", and "growth". The discourse tends to be structured so that the non-economic is equated with the private, the economic with the public. (Collini, 2012: 99)

In terms of our current purposes, the following questions arise. Has the movement from STEM to STEAM challenged or merely endorsed these fundamental assumptions about the predominance of the market order? To what extent, if at all, has the shift from STEM to STEAM troubled conventional lines of demarcation between what are widely assumed to be radically different areas of intellectual enquiry? Are science, technology, engineering and mathematics still consigned to one side of the equation, as it were, and arts on the other? Do such divisions (which, incidentally, are to some extent reflected in the structure of this book) reflect the complexity of intellectual enquiry in fields as diverse as the applied parts of engineering, medicine or theoretical physics, or in digital media, fine art or textile design? Do such divisions between the arts and sciences writ large, as it were, merely reinforce what Stefan Collini (2012: 101) describes as the "hackneyed contrast" between the humanities and sciences? As we shall see, this latter distinction is encapsulated in the now largely discredited notion of "two cultures". This fails to take account of the manner in which the distinctive aesthetics of science, politics and the arts can be re-aligned and intertwined in order to advance our thinking in relation not only to the complexity of human enquiry, but also to the complexity of our environment and our understanding of our place within it.

At this point it is useful to be reminded of the definition of environment, namely, "the conditions or influences under which any person or thing lives or is developed" (*Shorter Oxford English dictionary*). The environment is not something "out there" upon which we can exercise our influence either as rational actors or agents of destruction, depending upon the discourse to which we subscribe. We *are* part of the environment, in much the same way that we are time. We are *enveloped* within the environment, just as we are enveloped within time. The fundamental shift in thinking required here is that phenomena such as the environment and time are not (simply) "resources" or "commodities" that we can waste or save. Rather, they are part and parcel of the very fabric of our lives.

This chapter marks an attempt to formulate some answers to some of the questions raised above. More specifically, it paves the way for an alternative conceptualisation of the interrelationship between science and the arts. This runs against the current of the pervasive discourse of the market and a higher-education environment dominated by the market order. This contribution will also serve as a place marker for *wonder, hesitancy* and *doubt*. As Alsop (2005: 4) points out, these are qualities that run through the sciences as well as the arts. My aim here is to attempt to reassert the value of "challenge, surprise, desire, joy, expectation and mystery" (Alsop, 2005: 4). It is also to stand up for the value of looking sideways rather than rushing headlong in pursuit of some predetermined end, as in the case of "from STEM to STEAM", or to track the gathering storm in the manner of a disinterested meteorologist. After all, we need to ask ourselves: What exactly is it that we are pursuing? Are we merely glancing like Narcissus into "a muddy pond of abstract nouns in which all distinctiveness gets lost" (Collini, 2012: ix)? The many variants on the theme of the globe ("global", "globalisation" and the associated terms "international" and the ugly neologism "internationalisation") that are evident in contemporary educational discourse are prime examples of the latter. Are we eagerly anticipating a future that will never come? Or are we invoking a vision of a future that we negate with our relentless focus on human agency, target setting and a cavalier disregard of the life of things in the here and now?

4   The "Two Cultures" Debate: Sciences versus Humanities?

Let us briefly return to the notion of "two cultures" referred to above. The English novelist and physical chemist C.P. Snow coined the term "two cultures" in 1959 at the Rede Lecture at the University of Cambridge. He invoked this expression to describe what he regarded as a fundamental division between the arts and sciences as distinctive modes of enquiry. This is an idea that continues to exercise considerable traction, despite the fact that, as Collini (2012: 101) points out, "there is no coherent intellectual basis for this conventional distinction – not in method or subject matter or purpose". In addition, the nature of scientific enquiry itself has become increasingly diverse in the intervening decades, as indeed has the range of what would be broadly classified as "arts". Collini goes on to suggest that "two cultures talk has its main current home, as it had its origins, among those who feel some kind of cultural inse-curity about their identities as scientists or among those who administer sci-ence rather than do it" (2012: 101). In his view, there is an inverse relationship between the level of scientific acumen displayed by particular individuals and the degree to which they espouse the notion of the two cultures:

> Indeed, as a rough rule of thumb we may say that the more distinguished the scientists are at their science, the more readily they acknowledge the shared character of intellectual enquiry and the more they are willing to make common cause with their colleagues in the humanities against various ways of talking (or measuring) that misrepresent this. (Collini, 2012: 101)

The writing of the theoretical physicist Carlo Rovelli bears the hallmarks of the best work in the humanities, offering us a unique glimpse into the inner life of physics. In his recent book *The order of time*, Rovelli (2018) brings together science, philosophy and art to unravel one of the greatest mysteries: the mean-ing of time. Paradoxically, the temporal order that underpins the relentlessly future-oriented movement from STEM to STEAM, which is characterised by an unwavering commitment to the principles of competition and the goal of eco-nomic advancement, invokes the Newtonian order of time. As Rovelli explains, this has largely been discredited, and not merely as the result of advances in theoretical physics. Rovelli draws upon sources as diverse as the ancient phi-losophers Aristotle and Anaximander, the poet Horace, the painter Matisse, and, in the extract below, The Beatles, to demonstrate that time is not abso-lute, true and mathematical as Newton suggested, but rather relative, apparent and common. In short, time does not flow uniformly outside us. Rather, time resides within us: we are time. And as Rovelli reminds us, our apprehension of the mystery of time is not entirely rooted in our rational selves, nor can it be entirely expressed in such terms. In the short passage below, cognition and affect are intertwined:

> We are glimpsing something about the mystery of time. We can see the world without time: we can perceive with the mind's eye the profound structure of the world where time as we know it no longer exists like the Fool on the Hill who sees the Earth turn when he sees the setting sun. And we begin to see that we are time. We are this space, this clearing opened by the traces of memory inside the connections between our neurons. We are memory. We are nostalgia. We are longing for a future that will not come. (Rovelli, 2018: 175)

While we are on the subject of dichotomies – a theme that pervades this book and to which we shall return in due course – it is important to note that the notion of "two cultures" did not suddenly come into existence in the 1950s. It was also very much apparent in the Romantic era, and most acutely during the first scientific revolution of the seventeenth century. This is a period that is generally associated with such luminaries as Isaac Newton (1642–1726), Robert Hooke (1635–1703), John Locke (1632–1704) and René Descartes (1596–1650). As Holmes (2008: xvi) points out, the first person to refer to a "second scientific revolution" was (ironically enough) "probably the poet Coleridge in his Philosophical Lectures of 1819". Holmes describes the evolution of "Romantic science" in the following terms:

> It was inspired primarily by a sudden series of breakthroughs in the fields of astronomy and chemistry. It was a movement that grew out of eighteenth-century Enlightenment rationalism, but largely transformed it, by bringing a new imaginative intensity and excitement to scientific work. It was driven by a common ideal of intense, even reckless, personal commitment to discovery ... This is the time I have called the *Age of Wonder*, and with any luck we have not yet quite outgrown it. (Holmes, 2008: xvi)

Excitement. Intensity. Imagination. Discovery. Recklessness. Wonder. Readers are invited to hold these words in their imagination, as a powerful antidote to the anodyne "biz-speak" that permeates contemporary education policy and the reductionist view of science and the arts as key drivers of "innovation" in a competitive, "knowledge-based" economy. The opening words of this paragraph disrupt the Cartesian tradition by foregrounding attitudes towards science as well as scientific attitudes (Alsop, 2005: 7). They also serve to remind us that there is also a "softer 'dynamic' science of invisible powers and mysterious energies, of fluidity and transformations, of growth and organic change" (Holmes, 2008: xviii). This is evident in the quotation from Rovelli above. Elsewhere in his recent book *The order of time* he speculates that "perhaps poetry is another of science's deepest roots: the capacity to see beyond the visible" (Rovelli, 2018: 21). Excitement, intensity, imagination, discovery and recklessness are necessary correctives to the modernist commitment to the more anodyne and colourless terms (productivity, innovation, competitiveness and growth) that have joined forces with a pre-existing emphasis on scientific rationality to signal a radical detachment from the material world. As Collini (2012: 101) has observed, it is often the case that distinguished scientists "are willing to make common cause with their colleagues in the humanities" and to resist the silo mentality that is often associated with research administration. Once again, Carlo Rovelli is a particularly eloquent case in point.

5   Voyages of Discovery

It is entirely fitting that Holmes (2008) locates "Romantic science" between two famous voyages of exploration: Captain James Cook's first round-the-world expedition on the aptly named *Endeavour* (a three-year voyage that began in 1768) and Charles Darwin's voyage to the Galapagos Islands aboard a ship named after a scent hound, the *Beagle* (begun in 1831). The idea of the exploratory voyage – lonely, perilous and without predetermined ends – is far removed from the narrow teleological focus that frames contemporary scientific endeavour, at least as it manifests itself within a policy discourse of competitiveness and sustained economic growth. The hallmark of Romanticism as a cultural force, irrespective of whether its exponents were scientists or artists, was a sense of awe, reverence and wonder, and embodied engagement with sea, sky and stars. "Wonder is the source of our desire for knowledge" (Aristotle, *Metaphysics* I, 2, 982). It is no small wonder, then, that this quotation appears in the opening pages of *The order of time* (Rovelli, 2018).

This gradual alignment between science and the arts was not all plain sailing, so to speak. Sometime between 1795 and 1895, William Blake (1757–1827), a seminal figure of Romanticism whose own artistic practice spanned poetry, painting and printmaking, completed a deeply satirical work entitled *Newton*, in the form of a watercolour-finished print. Alan Moore, an artist and writer who specialises in comic books, is perhaps particularly attuned to the qualities of caricature present in Blake's work. Moore (2014) describes Blake's portrayal of Newton as the "two-dimensional original of Eduardo Paolozzi's RA's titan British Library doorstop". The scale and durability of Paolozzi's bronze (1995), located on the threshold of a major seat of learning, only serves to remind us of the longevity of the "two cultures" dichotomy and the influence it continues to exert upon contemporary thought, including the movement from STEM to STEAM.

Blake's vividly satirical critique of what he considered a reductive scientific approach depicts a young Isaac Newton bending intently over a diagram that he is in the process of drawing with a compass. The taut and muscular figure seems entirely oblivious to the complexity of rock formation upon which he is seated. The rock is coated with algae, the intricate patterns and subtle colours of which are evident to the viewer. Newton appears to be submersed – literally – and yet he also appears to be "sit[ting] as if in judgement far above at least the intellectual cosmos" (Moore, 2014). Rapt in thought, Newton seems transfixed by what appears to be a simple line diagram on a parchment roll that emerges from a white drape. This gestures towards a celestial, other nature – the disembodied rationality and objectivity of scientific enquiry. Engrossed in "pure geometry without complications", Newton appears to be "immune to the more fractal charm" of the blue and orange lichens that are spattered across the rock formation. Blake could not forgive Newton for privileging rational thought above the spiritual dimension of human experience, and for directing his gaze away from the complexity, intricacy and subtlety of the world around him. In a poem contained in a letter addressed to his patron Thomas Butt, Blake (1980 [1802]) expressed his fervent desire for a broader vision of the world and humanity's place within it:

> May God us keep
> From single vision and Newton's sleep.

This bears repetition in the context of a discussion of STEAM. Indeed, we might wish that contemporary theists might implore God to keep us from a single, blinkered vision of economic growth. It distorts our sense of our place in the world as well as the nature of scientific and artistic endeavour.

William Wordsworth (1770–1850) offers a different perspective on the "single vision" of scientific objectivity that was the subject of Blake's critique. As a student at Cambridge, Wordsworth frequently encountered the full-size marble statue of Newton in the stone-flagged entrance to the chapel of Trinity College. Repeated engagement with this statue brought forth a rather different vision of Newton, one that challenged common understandings of the nature of scientific enquiry as a rational, value-neutral pursuit. Holmes (2008: xvii) describes how Wordsworth "animated this static figure, so monumentally fixed in his assured religious setting. Under Wordsworth's optic, Newton became a haunted and restless Romantic traveller amidst the stars". This is evident from this extract from *The prelude* (Wordsworth, 2001 [1850]: 34–35):

> And from my pillow, looking forth by light
> Of moon or favouring stars, I could behold
> The antechapel where the statue stood
> Of Newton, with his prism and his silent face,
> The marble index of a mind forever
> Voyaging through strange seas of Thought, alone.

Suffice it to say that in the contemporary world of hyper-connectivity, those who "voyage through strange seas of thought" are generally treated with a degree of circumspection, if not downright suspicion. But we shall let Newton rest for now. Alternatively, we might imagine him "voyaging through strange seas of thought" in a manner that is barely distinguishable from the *modus operandi* of a scientist of the Romantic era, or a poet or artist from the same period. Yet there is one important difference. In the former case, the vision is planetary, disconnected from the earth. In the latter, epitomised by Wordsworth, the loving gaze is cast upon a host of golden daffodils embedded in the earth. We shall return briefly to this theme in the concluding section of this chapter.

Now it is time to engage in the art of time travel, to vault across several centuries and to turn our attention to the origins of STEAM. Let us begin by considering developments at the prestigious Rhode Island School of Design, where the concept of STEAM originated.

6   Gathering a Head of STEAM

STEAM certainly has an august pedigree. It emerged from a renowned stable, namely the Rhode Island School of Design (RISD) in around 2011. Founded in 1877, the RISD was one of the first independent colleges of art and design in the US. It regularly features amongst the top design schools in the world (e.g. Design Schools Hub, 2015).

It is clear from the promotional material on the RISD website that part of the rationale for the development of STEAM was to maintain the school's leadership role in an increasingly competitive market. The economic imperative and the pressing need to "come up with novel and creative solutions to challenging problems" (RISD, n.d.) are evident in the language used on the website to describe the initiative. STEAM is regarded as a natural continuation of nineteenth-century advances in science and technology. The mission of STEAM is couched in a narrative of continuous progress: "Like the sweeping changes in the 19th century, RISD's STEAM initiative also aims to spur an innovation revolution, create jobs, and help Rhode Island and the nation maintain a leading edge in the global marketplace" (RISD, n.d.).

The objectives of the STEAM movement, as set out on the RSID website, are as follows:

> to transform research policy to place Art + Design at the center of STEM; encourage integration of Art + Design in K–20 education [i.e. schooling and participation in education by people of all ages]; and influence employers to hire artists and designers to drive innovation. (RISD, n.d.)

The rationale for the movement from STEM to STEAM is "to spur economic progress and breakthrough innovation", "to inspire a generation of creative problem-solvers" and to enhance "employability" amongst artists and designers.

The dissemination of STEAM across the world is rendered visible through an interactive map that portrays the initiative as a series of interconnected nodes spread across the globe. According to text that was available on the RSID website, the launch of the "global STEAM map" in 2014 enabled

> individuals and organizations involved in the movement ... [to] add information about themselves to the online tool as a means of sharing their ideas, activities and successes in this arena, connecting with others and showing the growing level of support for STEAM worldwide.

This reinforces the impression that the STEAM project is all about momentum and growth, and that this can be depicted in terms of nodes plotted across the surface of the globe. The movement from STEM to STEAM is about moving on, inexorably. It is about achieving coverage and leaving the past behind us. Yet paradoxically this also entails a vision of the future that is dictated by practices that are rooted in the past. It is about paying homage to the Newtonian order of time. This represents a missed opportunity fundamentally to reconsider the aesthetics of science, politics and art in the new climactic regime. It is only by engaging in the latter that we shall be able to trouble the traditional distinction between science and the arts and arrive at a more future-oriented philosophy of knowledge. Reconsidering the aesthetics of science, politics and the arts in these troubled and troubling times will also enable us to recalibrate our relationship with the Earth. This involves a fundamental re-evaluation of the lines of demarcation between humans and non-humans, just as it did of those between artists and scientists.

7   Conclusion: Facing GAIA

Bruno Latour characterises the three discrete forms of aesthetics referred to above as follows. The aesthetics of science refers to a lack of sensitivity to any change in climate without instrumentation and the "vast machine" of multiple scientific disciplines. We might refer to this as the further enmeshment of STEM. The aesthetics of politics is characterised by lack of representation of human and non-human entities without the "highly complex procedures of activists and politicians building common concerns" (Latour, 2016). The hallmark of the third term of reference, namely the aesthetics of the arts, is a lack of sensitivity to the contradictions, complexities, novelty and scale of the entanglement of humans and non-humans. In the case of the movement from STEM to STEAM, it falls to science, engineering, technology and mathematics to harness the power of art to drive a particular political and educational agenda. This is a political landscape that is devoid of people, let alone "activists and politicians building common concerns" (Latour, 2016). The non-human, and indeed the more-than-human (the transcendent), seem to have been driven out of the picture entirely. The movement from STEM to STEAM is a complex game that consists in pushing glossy and anodyne quantities (growth, economic competitiveness, globalisation, internationalisation) across a smooth surface, one that is entirely divorced from the deep rock, the soil and the upper atmosphere in which we have our being. Science has ceased to be topian in the sense depicted by Blake's study of Newton. We might almost say that STEM has branched out. Yet this playful organic metaphor belies the fact that it has become a vast machine, part of the military-industrial complex, and that it has been harnessed to the logic of sustained (yet unsustainable) economic growth. Science, like art, is seen from the outside, rather than from the inside (as I attempted to do in my brief exploration of Blake's Newton). Art has been added to provide edge, gloss and a simulacrum of soul to an essentially utopian project (i.e. one that is related to the globe) rather than a 'topian' project (i.e. one that is rooted in the earth and nourished by the atmosphere). Metaphorically at least, we have been "living on a different planet" for such a long time that we no longer recognise the Earth. She is now rising up to confront us with terrifying force.

Acknowledgements

I am greatly indebted to my colleagues Stephen Day, Senior Lecturer in Science Education, and Diarmuid McAuliffe, Lecturer in Art and Design, both at the University of the West of Scotland. Their continuing support has been invaluable to me in preparing this contribution, as has our shared commitment to bridging the divide between the arts and the sciences and to fostering dialogue across disciplinary boundaries.

References

Alsop, S. (2005). Bridging the Cartesian divide: Science education and affect. In S. Alsop (Ed.), *Beyond Cartesian dualism: Encountering affect in the teaching and learning of science* (pp. 3–16). Dordrecht: Springer.

Blake, W. (1980 [1802]). Blake, letter to Thomas Butt, 22 November 1802. In G. Keynes (Ed.), *The letters of William Blake with related documents* (3rd ed.). Oxford: Clarendon Press.

Collingwood, R. G. (1958 [1938]). *The principles of art*. Oxford: Oxford University Press.

Collini, S. (2012). *What are universities for?* London: Penguin.

Design Schools Hub. (2015). *Top 10 – Best industrial design schools in the world 2015*. Retrieved July 29, 2019, from http://www.designschoolshub.com/top-best-industrial-design-schools-world/

European Commission. (n.d.). *The Lisbon strategy in short*. Retrieved July 25, 2019, from https://portal.cor.europa.eu/europe2020/Profiles/Pages/TheLisbonStrategyinshort.aspx

Gillies, D. (2012). State education as high-yield investment: Human capital theory in European policy discourse. *Journal of Pedagogy, 2*(2), 224–245.

Holmes, R. (2008). *The age of wonder: How the romantic generation discovered the beauty and terror of science*. London: Harper Press.

Latour, B. (2016). *On sensitivity arts, science and politics in the new climactic regime*. Retrieved July 25, 2019, from http://www.bruno-latour.fr/node/692

Moore, A. (2014, December 5). Alan Moore on William Blake's contempt for Newton. *Royal Academy blog*. Retrieved July 25, 2019, from https://www.royalacademy.org.uk/article/william-blake-isaac-newton-ashmolean-oxford

National Academy of Science, National Academy of Engineering and Institute of Medicine. (2007). *Rising above the gathering storm: Energizing and employing America for a brighter economic future*. Washington, DC: National Academies Press. https://doi.org/10.17226/11463

Pirrie, A., & Thoutenhoofd, E. D. (2013). Learning to learn in the European Reference Framework for lifelong learning. *Oxford Review of Education, 39*(5), 609–626.

Rhode Island School of Design (RISD). (n.d.). *Rhode Island school of design*. Retrieved July 25, 2019, from https://www.risd.edu/

Rovelli, C. (2018). *The order of time*. London: Allen Lane.

Wordsworth, W. (2001 [1850]). *The prelude*. Retrieved July 25, 2019, from http://triggs.djvu.org/djvu-editions.com/WORDSWORTH/PRELUDE1850/Prelude1850.pdf

CHAPTER 2

Becoming Bird: Creative Pedagogies for Future-Making Education?

Margaret Somerville, Tessa McGavock and Keiren Stephenson

Abstract

This chapter explores the mattering of science and art creativities for future-making education through the transnational project *Naming the world: Enhancing early years literacy and sustainability learning.* Set in the context of the new geological age of the Anthropocene, the project was informed by posthuman and new materialist theorising, and the proliferation of ways these have been applied in early years learning. It is based on the belief that children of the Anthropocene will grow into a different future than the one we now know, so we need to learn with them and from them, in their everyday worlds. Through researching in collaboration with these children *Naming the world* seeks new ways of being, knowing and doing, and emergent creative pedagogies for future-making education. It troubles power politics and policy by transforming the power dynamics between university and practitioner researchers and through engaging with young children as a source of knowledge production and decision making.

The project was implemented in two phases: in the first phase university researchers collaborated with young children (0–5 years), through a process of deep hanging out. In the second phase children and educator researchers developed creative pedagogies in response. The chapter outlines the methodological and theoretical underpinnings of Phase 1, in "posthuman" and "new materialist approaches", and Despret's "curious practice". The difficult transition in between is explored as a liminal space of unknowing, a necessary space to enable transformative practices to emerge. The chapter also explores the emergent creative pedagogies that came into being through one of the projects from Phase 2: *What can we see outside?* (Becoming Bird Project). Through this project, new configurings emerged when Australian Indigenous eco-philosophies came into play, emphasising the necessity of emergence from unknowing for future-making education.

© KONINKLIJKE BRILL NV, LEIDEN, 2020 | DOI: 10.1163/9789004421585_004

Keywords

anthropocene – children as co-researchers – Despret – education for sustainability – Indigenous epistemologies – liminal spaces – new materialism – posthumanism

1   Introduction: Children of the Anthropocene

> However these debates will unfold, the Anthropocene represents a new phase in the history of both humankind and of the Earth, when natural forces and human forces became intertwined, so that the fate of one determines the fate of the other. Geologically, this is a remarkable episode in the history of this planet. (Zalasiewicz, Williams, Steffen, & Crutzen, 2010: 2231)

Much has been written about the age of Anthropocene since it was proposed as a new geological epoch by Crutzen and Stoermer (2000). A contested concept, formal recognition depends on establishing a date for which there is geological evidence of time's mattering. This might be visible in plutonium fallout from 1950s bomb tests in marine or lake sediments, ice layers or stalagmites and stalactites, in remnant plastics, or some kind of carbon signature marking a rapid rise in CO_2 emissions (Amos, 2016). This mattering is the not-yet of time, what will be visible in layers of Earth's geology some time into the future (Somerville, 2018).

Despite these geological debates, the concept of the new geological age of the Anthropocene has generated a proliferation of transdisciplinary scholarship in recognition of human entanglement in the fate of the planet (Zalasiewicz et al., 2010). It has been suggested, for example, that climate change, a signature phenomenon of the Anthropocene, is not only a change of the weather, but requires a fundamental change in how we understand the human, and new understandings of thought itself (Colebrook, 2010).

Children of the Anthropocene, born into the twenty-first century, growing up into a world we will never know, can help us to think about how to be human differently at the intersection of the present moment with the geological time of the not-yet. They return over and over again to Deleuze's

> indefinite time of the event, the floating line that knows only speeds and continually divides that which transpires into an already-there that is at the same time not-yet-here, a simultaneous too-late and too-early, a something that is both going to happen and has just happened. (Deleuze & Guattari, 1987: 262)

Perhaps because of this quality of future-making, early childhood education leads the field of educational research in the application of new posthuman approaches within Anthropocene scholarship (Somerville, 2019). These approaches can be loosely categorised as: common worlds, new materialism, and Indigenous–non-Indigenous intersections. Collectively these approaches enable the project to allow the emergence of new power dynamics which overturn the commonly accepted notion that (very) young children do not contribute to knowledge production, or to the formation of creative pedagogies for future-making education.

1.1   *Common Worlds*

Drawing on Latour (2004) and Haraway (2008), common worlds approaches enable a refocus on the diverse cultural and natural environments in which children are enmeshed. Children's lives are understood as situated within "the real, messy, imperfect and undivided natural and cultural worlds they (and we) inherit and inhabit with other species" (Taylor & Pacini-Ketchabaw, 2017: 133). Multispecies ethnographies are a characteristic of common worlds approaches (e.g. Taylor & Giugni, 2012; Taylor, 2013; Pacini-Ketchabaw, 2013; Taylor & Pacini-Ketchabaw, 2015).

1.2   *New Materialism*

Barad's concept of "intra-action" is theorised in *Meeting the universe halfway* through the central idea of entanglement: "To be entangled is not simply to be intertwined with another as in the joining of two separate entities, but to lack an independent self-contained existence" (Barad, 2007: ix). The individual subject emerges only through the mutual entanglements of different bodies of matter, each with their own force or agency. Barad calls this new ontology developed from quantum physics "agential realism", in which "the primary ontological unit is not independent objects with independently determinate boundaries and properties but rather phenomena that signify the ontological inseparability" of each (2007: 23).

1.3   *Curious Practice*

The concept of "deep hanging out" emerged once the project began, informed by Haraway's interpretation of Despret's curious practice in which the researcher "goes visiting" without any expectations of what might happen:

> Vinciane Despret thinks-with other beings, human and not. That is a rare and precious vocation. Vocation: calling, calling with, called by, calling as if the world mattered, calling out, going too far, going visiting. Despret listened to a singing blackbird one morning – a living blackbird outside

her particular window – and that way learned what importance sounds like. She thinks in attunement with those she thinks with – recursively, inventively, relentlessly – with joy and verve. She studies how beings render each other capable in actual encounters, and she theorizes – makes cogently available – that kind of theory and method. (Haraway, 2015: 5)

1.4   *Indigenous–Non-Indigenous Intersections*

The theme of Indigenous and western intersections addresses theoretical and methodological approaches that include both Indigenous and western ontologies and epistemologies. (Whitehouse, 2011; Taylor, 2013; Somerville, 2013; Duhn, 2015; Devine, Teisina, & Pau'uvale, 2012). The project proposal for *Naming the world* did not include Indigenous theorising, focusing instead on common worlds, new materialism and curious practice to inform 12 months of deep hanging out with young children. The incorporation of Indigenous cultural knowledges emerged as integral in the creative pedagogies developed in the Becoming Bird Project in the second phase of the study.

2   Transitions: From Young Children's Everyday Worlds to Creative Pedagogies

The transitional process from the infinite moments of deep hanging out in *Naming the world* to creative pedagogies for future-making education was made possible by the coding of the very large multimodal data set. The bringing together of literacy+sustainability learning was core to the project *Naming the world*. Educators typically understood sustainability learning as related to worm farms and veggie gardens, and literacy as about speaking, reading and writing. University researchers had to find words to explain how we had come to recognise sustainability learning in instances of vitality, aliveness and emergent engagement with children's worlds in their multisensorial becomings. Literacy learning, understood as embedded within those worlds, was understood as simultaneously emerging in movement, touch, embodied and sensory immersion, and their multiple modes of expression. The coding through reviewing and clustering infinitesimal moments captured in still photos, small videos, iPhone notes and fieldnotes allowed university researchers to crystallise their complex and challenging meanings for collaborating researcher practitioners. Seven discrete categories emerged from this coding:
– becoming animal
– bodily immersion elements (water, sand, mud)
– artefacts and imaginative play

- naming bodies, naming selves
- drumming, singing, dancing, rhythm
- movement, gesture, mime, performance
- becoming plant.

The multimodal representation of these categories opened different possibilities for educators about how literacy+sustainability might be understood differently from within young children's world-making practices. Still, nothing could have predicted the difficulty of the transition from the educator's obvious enjoyment of watching researcher presentations of their young learners, to its implementation in practice. The transition to Phase 2 required both university researchers and collaborating practitioner researchers to enter a liminal space of not knowing: the educators not knowing exactly how they might do this, and researchers not knowing how to support them. The university researchers needed to learn to step back, hold the space open, and remain in the anxious space of not knowing, in order to enable the new to emerge. Educator researchers needed to develop their own projects, taking control, ownership, and continuing on in their own unique ways of enmeshment in young children's worlds.

3   What Can We See Outside? Keiren's Project

From this liminal space of unknowing, several exceptional projects came to life, to reconfigure pedagogies through science and art creativities for future-making education. In this chapter we explore just one of these projects: *What can we see outside?* This project developed from one educator's observations that the very young children in her care (6 months to 3 years) were daily climbing onto chairs and furniture to look out of the window as their parents departed. There was nothing to see but the empty space of their vanishing parents. Through the integration of many diverse creative practices, children and educators constructed invitations for birds to visit the empty space, to gather nesting materials, food and water, and bathe themselves. Children came to know the birds that came as they created bird paintings and crafted birds with feathers. Through touching, feeling and talking to posters on the walls, they learned the birds' common and Darug names and modes of being.

3.1   *The Project Book*
The story of Becoming Bird is told in a beautiful project book, created by their educator, Keiren Stephensen, with words printed in different brightly coloured textas, alongside images of the children at each stage of the activity. The project book is an artefact of science and art creativities materialised in practice.

The following is a selection of verbatim extracts from the book of *What can we see outside?*

INTRODUCTION

The Empty Space: Of Parents' Departure

The big window in our room faces onto a grassed area and the car park is visible. Lots of the children wave goodbye to mum and dad as part of their settling-in routine each morning. As time went by, I realised there wasn't a great deal going on out there, and decided to think how the area outside could be enriched to provide stimulating, sustainable ongoing experiences for the children. We are hoping this can be an ongoing project that will involve the children in rich, complex activities, building a group dynamic of working together as we encourage respect and care for our world.

NESTING

We got everyone ready with shoes and jumpers – it was very windy. We told the children we were getting some sticks for the birdies, for the birdies to make a nest. I kept repeating these simple sentences as a foundation to build on over the coming weeks. As we do more and more things, the children will have deeper conceptual understandings. Everyone was excited. We sit on the grass and show the children the kinds of sticks and grass we could put in our bag for the birdies.

Tracy's Nest

After seeing our project, Tracy [Aboriginal/Gomaroi educator] brought in a bird's nest she had recently found. I showed the children. We carefully touched it, and looked at the sticks and soft feathers the bird had used to make a nest.

Chickens and Soft Feathers

The children have been watching the chickens grow and helping to take care of them. Zoe found a lovely soft feather. I reminded the children how the bird's nest had soft feathers in it, and we could look for more to give to the birdies. After finding some very soft feathers in the chicken coop, we brought a container in so we could collect them for our nest-ing material hangers. This became a scavenger hunt. It was tricky to find feathers under the leaves and grass, but with help from the older children we were able to collect enough to fill our container.

MAKING A BATH FOR THE BIRDIES

We looked around the centre to figure out what we could use to make a birdbath from found materials. Modelling this re-use builds knowl-edge in the children about sustainability being important, useful and practical. Participating in the whole process will help the children develop deeper appreciation and care for natural and constructed envi-ronments, as well as providing a rich, extended experience over time, which allows children to contribute, construct, explore and cooperate. We have lots of tyres in the yard, so we decided to use these to make the stand for the birdbath. We decided to use sand from some of the places it has been transported to around the outdoor environment.

We asked the children if they wanted to help make a bath for the birdies. We got the big wagon and brought it to the sand pile near the cubby house. We had shovels, and gave them out, telling the children we needed *lots and lots* of sand to build the bath. We told the children that we were going out the front to make the bath for the birdies, and directed them to roll the tyres out the gate of our room, through the foyer, and out the front door. The children were aware that this was turning into a crazy adventure! We rolled the tyres up the path and carefully round till they were out the front of our window.

Water in the Bird Bath

We went outside today to fill the birdbath, but as we first came outside, some of the children noticed a magpie walking around in the distance. Rachel, Aria, Kenna, Aiden and Charlotte stood quietly and watched. Charlotte pointed at the magpie as it walked around. Then we put the tub into the birdbath – now we wait and hope the birds will find it so we can watch them splashing outside our window ...

Bird Bath Visitors

We had so much excitement this afternoon when a noisy miner visited our unfinished birdbath. I called the children to the window, and they came running to see "the birdy having a bath". The noisy miner splashed and shook water from its feathers. Ellie pointed and said, "Birdy, bath" and laughed. The children were enthralled as the bird jumped around in a very playful way. Tracy, Jasmine and I were just as excited as the children. We are still constructing the birdbath. We need a bigger bath for it, and we are going to paint it white.

A great big magpie came splashing into our birdbath this afternoon. Max said, "Birdy! Bath!" The magpie stayed and had a big drink, hopping in and out of the water. Everyone stayed watching until the bird flew away.

BIRD CREATIVITIES

Jasmine found some wooden bird shapes and came up with a great idea to make a mobile. We got cotton buds and brightly coloured paint, and got the children to decorate them.

4–9 October "More bird making". We made some more gorgeous birds for our room, using glue and glitter and feathers.

Identifying Birds

Jasmine made some great posters about the birds we most commonly see around the centre. We plan to use them with the children to identify birds out of the window. Using texts in this way begins to lay foundations in literacy.

Dreamtime Story: How the Birds Got Their Colours

Today we read a dreamtime story from the Bardi people in Broome. This story tells how birds got their colours, and includes some birds we have seen outside, and have on our wall posters. This natural link between what we are doing and a story told to Aboriginal children allows us to show respect, and include First Australian ways of viewing the world in our regular activities. The children listened to this story. Kenna, Jacob and Zoe helped to name the colours of the birds. Jasmine showed us the crow poster, and the children could make the connection between the crow in the book and the crow on our wall. Kenna then pointed outside to where we had seen crows before.

Colourful Feather Masterpieces

We have been rereading our story about how the birds got their colours. The children now remember the black crow, and all the colours coming onto the birds. As a follow-on activity, Jasmine supplied lovely coloured paint, cardboard and feathers for the children to create colourful feathered masterpieces. We hung them all on the wall in our sleeping room.

Story and Feathers

Jasmine read our story again today; the children remain interested and pay close attention. When the story was finished, Jasmine gave everyone a feather. Rachel came up with her feather and held it against the black crow. Then all the children came up with their feathers to put them on the crow. After this we did another feather painting experience.

Totem

This Friday we will be celebrating kids' corroboree. Tracy helped us to make a totem pole, and for the top piece we made a rainbow lorikeet or *warin* (in local Darug language). There were so many coloured feathers to put on, and the children were able to work together to stick them on. I brought the rainbow lorikeet poster over to link the activity, and left it on the table. Zoe realised and brought it back to the wall where it belongs! We worked on this over a few days until it was absolutely gorgeous.

3.2 *Sustainability Learning for Young Children*

Interspersed within the handwritten pages of the project book is the creed university researchers developed from conversations in the liminal space of unknowing: words that stutter, words that fail to explain, but words that do their best:

– Our project is set in the context of human-induced changes to the Earth's climate and the recognition that humans are now entangled in the fate of planet Earth.
– We believe that this requires us to think differently about learning as including the rights of planet Earth and all living things and children's right to be part of the world.

– Children of today will grow into a different world than we knew and we
    need to learn with them and from them.
– In learning from the children through 12 months of deep hanging out we
    have come to understand sustainability learning as children's sustained
    engagement in activities that connect them to their bodies, to the matter of
    the planet (earth, air, water), and to its living creatures (becoming animal).
– The signs of this sustained engagement in sustainability learning are asso-
    ciated with excitement, intensity, vitality, where the senses and the child's
    body are fully immersed in what they are doing.
– In the process of this sustained engagement children are naming their
    worlds in many different ways including speaking and mark making as
    more conventional aspects of literacy, but also bodily movements, gestures,
    sounds and music/rhythm.
– We believe that further enhancing this sustained engagement in sustain-
    ability learning has the potential to change our worlds.

3.3   *Bright Words and Delicate Images*

The book of course is so much more than these words. Every page is overflow-
ing with vibrant printed text wrapped around photos of children in the different stages and activities of the project. There are hundreds of images, faces
poised in rapt attention, but especially hands, making hands, sensing hands,
touching hands, feeling hands, learning hands. Hands becoming other with
nesting sticks, paint, paper, feathers, spades, sand. Hands and faces joined
together in the affective intensity of each moment. A child with a feather held
out between thumb and index finger in one hand, nose and mouth poised in
an expression of surprise at the sensation, the other hand with fingers curled as
if they are feeling the surprise of the feather's sensation as well. These are the
images of future-making education becoming with science and art creativities.
They are Barad's intra-action where birds, feathers, nesting materials, paper,
glue, names, both English and Darug, are all entangled, producing each other
moment by moment. These are the transcorporeal common worlds where
children's lives are understood as situated within "the real, messy, imperfect
and undivided natural and cultural worlds they (and we) inherit and inhabit
with other species" (Taylor & Pacini-Ketchabaw, 2017: 133; see also Latour,
2004; Haraway, 2008). They become birds gathering sticks from the grass and
soft feathers for nesting materials, and feel the joy of birds as they splash in the
birdbath they made with the labour of their small bodies.

The project book as a material artefact stitches all of these things together. It
creates an assemblage of science, art creativities, matter, transcorporeality and
future-making education. It is only through the project book as artefact that

we can revisit the project. We revisit the project's beginning, with the empty space of departing parents, a symbolic loss, as an ideal place to start a project for the time of the sixth great extinction. It is a space for future-making education where the children return over and over again to the

> indefinite time of the event, the floating line that knows only speeds, and continually divides that which transpires into an already-there that is at the same time not-yet-here, a simultaneous too-late and too-early, a something that is both going to happen and has just happened. (Deleuze & Guattari, 1987: 262)

In this future-making education everything is entangled, but in the following we explore some of the possibilities as if they can be separated.

3.4   *Becoming Bird and Transcorporeality*

The process of the emergence of creative pedagogies for future-making education can be seen throughout the project book, as there is nothing that could have been determined beforehand. The beginning, for example, as a space of loss, the quintessential space of the sixth great extinction, is the place from which all of this originates. The processes of multispecies becoming through which children become birds evolves as they sit on the grass and learn the kinds of sticks and grass to collect for their nests. They learn through the touch of soft baby skin on feather down that the inside of a nest is made of soft feathers, so they gather soft feathers to provide nesting materials for the birds. They learn about baby birds as they watch a mother lapwing plover with her chicks, human babies becoming bird babies, in their intense fascination. They learn becoming bird by making birds with found feathers and colourful craft materials that create mobiles of birds flying/hanging in their learning space. They learn becoming bird by creating a birdbath where they observe birdies coming to splash, wash and bathe their feathers, just as they themselves are washed.

Their birdbath making is the work of tiny bodies, creating something from nothing, recycled tyres and sand that has been distributed out of the sandpit, bodily efforts moving a trolley of sand, filling the trolley, spading the sand from trolley into birdbath, over and over until all the tyres are filled. Images of babies in the book, hard at work, show that it is all the work of bodies moving, learning, doing with hands, feet, minds, bodies all integrated into the making.

3.5   *Science and Art Creativities*

Science becomes what they learn through these processes of intra-active becoming, where the matter of birds nesting, feathers, bathing and so on is mixed with paper, glue, glitter, words and names, all one. Language emerges simultaneously with their world making. "Birdy birdy", they say, as they watch the birds splashing in the birdbath they have made for them. They learn the common names of the birds they see, birds and posters becoming one as they learn and touch the posters that decorate the walls of their learning space: the masked lapwing plover, the raven crow, the galah, the magpies, the cockatoo, the rainbow lorikeet and the noisy miner. Through learning the Darug names of the birds they are connected to Indigenous meanings and understandings of the world, troubling the taken-for-granted power of the English naming practices and policies that valorise only standard English forms of language and ways of knowing the world.

4   Emergent Departure: Aboriginal Eco-Philosophies for Future-Making Education

The most significant departure from the original posthuman and new materialist theorising to emerge from the liminal space of unknowing was the incorporation of Australian Aboriginal ways of being, knowing and doing in *What can we see outside?*

There have been significant critiques of the Anthropocene literature for its focus on First World Western theories and approaches, and the most difficult thing to do is to integrate vastly different onto-epistemologies (ways of being, knowing and doing) in future-making education. How does this happen in a fundamentally racist culture where Aboriginal peoples have been massacred, dispossessed from their lands, and forbidden to speak language or practise culture? Because despite all this Aboriginal peoples continue to care for Country, to practise contemporary cultural forms of ancient ways of being, knowing and doing that evolved in the oldest continent by the longest continuing inhabitants on the planet. In this early learning centre, it is the vision of the director to embed Aboriginal cultural knowledge in early years learning. This aspiration required a long and committed learning journey on the part of the director.

Tessa's Story of Becoming with Aboriginal Knowledges

My personal journey has taken place over a number of years, supported, encouraged and made possible by a number of Aboriginal Elders, knowledge holders and families, who have shared in, observed and trusted my transformation over this period. To all of those amazingly generous people, I thank you. I would not be the educator I am today without you. At about the same time as I began my cultural learning, I requested assistance from the Bicultural Support Unit, as we had an Aboriginal child who presented some challenges to us, and we were sent the most amazing Gamaroi woman, Tracy Ryan.

Tracy quietly shared culture with educators, and she and I began having long conversations. She allowed and encouraged me to ask questions about culture, and her responses enlightened my under-standing of cultural practice and understanding. Over the following months, some of our Aboriginal families also began sharing aspects of cultural practice with me and, as my own cultural capacity grew, the sharing became more frequent and in-depth. I was somehow aware that snippets were being shared with me by a number of people, and then there was a waiting period to see what I would do with the new knowledge. This awareness was very deep, and I felt so privileged that various members of the local community were doing this. It was almost as if the families were taking responsibility for overseeing my learning journey!

Tracy has become not only a mentor to me. More than a close friend, she is my "sister from another mister", and continues to share culture with me, in many forms every day. We share families through yarn-ing, we laugh together and at each other, and we cry together and feel each other's joy, pain and struggles related to family births, deaths and illnesses.

Developing my own cultural capacity has strengthened me as an educator and as a person, and provides me with the skills to enrich our curriculum for the children through language, the arts and cul-tural knowledge. Families and children actively seek understanding of culture and protocols and, through collaboration, fully support our endeavours to strengthen the journey.

For me, as an educator, taking the concern of "doing it wrong" out of the equation and being able to ask open, honest questions about what *can* we do and why can't we do that, provided a safe space to learn and grow, without judgement. This allowed a close, trusting relationship to develop over time with Tracy.

I'm sure my endless curiosity nearly drove Tracy to distraction – once Aunty Jacinta's songs were embedded in my head, I wanted to learn Darug language. I used Aunty Jacinta's song lines to learn some words and taught these to the children, and they responded like little sponges, wanting more. This was a slow, gradual journey, and I was grateful I could allow it to be slow, so I could truly absorb all the new information, reflect on it, and look at how and if it could or should be used with the children, educators and myself. And the Aboriginal community allowed it to be slow, without expectations on me.

Families began to give feedback – Aboriginal families began to bring me things like emu eggs they had gathered on a hunt out west, and chatted to me about how this task is done. Others shared information about their own childhoods or that of their parents, where they came from and who they were. Many of their stories bought tears to my eyes, and a determination to collaborate with the community, in the hope the next generation of children would not experience the racism their own parents, grandparents and all who walked before them had suffered. If I could make some inroads into this, through the early childhood sector, that would influence how the next generation viewed Aboriginal people and culture.

In order to articulate the profound meanings of integrating Aboriginal culture with new Western posthuman and new materialist theorising for the Anthropocene, we explore the concept of "thinking through country" developed in collaboration with Immiboagurramilbun (Chrissiejoy Marshall).

It was through the director's long process of learning from and with Aboriginal people, and her close relationship with Aboriginal early years educator Tracy Ryan, that the children's learning was infused with Australian Aboriginal understandings of human entanglement in the world. This understanding is strongly based in Country, and evolves through many forms of creative engagement translated from ancient traditional practices that can be understood as "thinking through Country".

4.1   *Thinking through Country for Future-Making Education*

Thinking through Country is an onto-epistemological approach to research developed in collaboration with U'Alayi co-researcher Immiboagurramilbun/ Chrissiejoy Marshall (Somerville, 2013) through art, storytelling, language translation and multimodal (re)presentation. A painting called *Me, myself and I* is an ontological painting with multiple totemic images. The first image is of four swans. The swans are Mulgury (in a totemic relationship to the people), signalling their collective meaning as mythical creatures of the Niddeerie (the time of creation), as well as representing an individual's connection to a particular creature and its place. Chrissiejoy's mother is swan; Noongahburrah people collectively are swan. Swan belongs to the time and place of the creation of the land and people of Terewah, the home of the black swan, in the past, the present and the future. Those who carry that identity are both swan and place. Country, swan and person are together an ontological reality.

The painting becomes an onto-epistemology when connected to Niddeerie (the Dreamtime) in words translated into English from her grandmother's Erinbinjori language:

> At the beginning all was Mulgury. Only creative power and intent. Through the intent and power of our Creator, Mulgury reproduces into form to carve the beings and shapes of the world where the water meets the sky and earth sings the world to life. The pattern of life is Mulgury and Mulgury is traced in the Niddrie (the framework of the ancient laws within Niddeerie) of Mudri (person). Every tracing, every rock, tree, plant, landform, the water, fish, reptile, bird, animal, and Mudri is in the sacred relationship, through Niddeerie. The pattern, shape, and form of Mulgury is life, and all is a continuing tracing of Mulgury. (Ticalarnabrewillaring, 1961, translated by Immiboagurramilbun, quoted in Somerville, 2013: 53)

Australian Indigenous eco-philosophies are fundamentally about creation. They are a deep embodiment of science (how the world came into being) and art creativities ("Mulgury reproduces into form to carve the beings and shapes of the world ... the pattern, shape, and form of Mulgury is life"). They are intertwined in the Becoming Bird Project through the actions of Kamilaroi educator Tracy Ryan.

4.2   *The Bardi Dreaming Story of How the Birds Got Their Colours*

The reading and re-reading of this dreaming story was made meaningful through the integration of the whole assemblage of science and art creativities materialised as sites of transcorporeality for future-making education in the Becoming Bird Project. It was the gathering together of the empty space of loss, the becoming bird through nesting, bathing and creating mobile birds, it was the storytelling of the Dreamtime story, the creation story of the beginning of time. It was the time that is past, present and future, all becoming at once in the cyclical time of creation. Each time a child creates, learns, becomes, names bird, the world is created anew, sung into being for the time of the future that is already past in the making of the world. Becoming with Australian Indigenous ways of knowing and being in the world is fundamentally troubling of Western nature–culture binaries, recognising a future in which the human is fully entangled in the world's becoming and has always been. The common worlds of Latour and Haraway, and Barad's intra-active becoming with, inform new Western theoretical approaches of entanglement in the world's becoming.

Together they powerfully trouble power and policy in relation to learning, language, and ways of being and knowing the world.

4.3   *The Totem Pole: Creating Warin, the Rainbow Lorikeet*

In the making of the totem pole Tracy brought the story home, returning the story of creation to Darug Country. A totem is equivalent to Mulgury, the creature with which one identifies and is inextricably intertwined. For Chrissiejoy in her ontological painting it was the swan, the bird that gives its name to the Narran Lake, Terewah, the home of the black swan, Chrissiejoy's growing up place, her identity. For children in Darug Country, the warin, or rainbow lorikeet, with its glorious brightly coloured red, green and blue feathers, becomes their Mulgury, or totem. Through the making they become the rainbow lorikeet; warin and child are one, together an ontological reality. These actions sing the rainbow lorikeet into being over and over again where past, present and future are one.

Researching with young children opens us to the emergence of the new for future-making education. Western posthuman theories and methodologies of new materialism and common worlds multispecies methodologies informed the first phase of the project involving deep hanging out with young children in their everyday worlds. New insights emerged for university researchers and their educator collaborators as they searched for ways to explain the infinite moments of small videos, still images, iPhone notes and conversations that edged towards words they did not have. The transitional space from these new insights to the development of creative pedagogies for future-making education took place through a liminal space of unknowing.

This space was essential to allow the new to emerge in the form of the integration of the embedded Indigenous knowledges and cultural practices of the early learning centre. By bringing Indigenous and Western posthuman trajectories into conversation, each is potentially enriched to produce a more nuanced understanding of what it might mean in practice to teach, think and research relationally, ecologically and locally about global problems with children of the Anthropocene.

References

Amos, J. (2016, August 30). Geologists search for Anthropocene "golden spike". *BBC News*. Retrieved June 14, 2019, from http://www.bbc.com/news/science-environment-37200489

Barad, K. (2007). *Meeting the universe halfway: Quantum physics and the entanglement of matter and meaning.* Durham, NC: Duke University Press.

Colebrook, C. (Ed.) (2010). *Extinction: Framing the end of the species.* Ann Arbor, MI: Open Humanities Press.

Crutzen, P., & Stoermer, E. (2000). The "Anthropocene". *Global Change Newsletter, 41,* 17–18. Retrieved June 13, 2019, from http://www.igbp.net/download/ 18.316f18321323470177580001401/1376383088452/NL41.pdf

Deleuze, G., & Guattari, F. (1987). *A thousand plateaus.* Minneapolis, MN: University of Minnesota Press.

Devine, N., Teisina, J. P., & Pau'uvale, L. (2012). Tauhi vā, Spinoza, and Deleuze in education. *Pacific-Asian Education, 24*(2), 57–68.

Duhn, I. (2015). Making agency matter: Rethinking infant and toddler agency in educational discourse. *Discourse: Studies in the Cultural Politics of Education, 36*(6), 920–931. doi:10.1080/01596306.2014.918535

Haraway, D. (2008). *When species meet.* Minneapolis, MN: University of Minnesota Press.

Haraway, D. (2015). A curious practice. *Angelaki, 20*(2), 5–14.

Latour, B. (2004). *The politics of nature: How to bring science into democracy.* Cambridge, MA: Harvard University Press.

Pacini-Ketchabaw, V. (2013). Frictions in forest pedagogies: Common worlds in settler colonial spaces. *Global Studies of Childhood, 3*(4), 355–365.

Somerville, M. (2013). *Water in a dry land: Place-learning through art and story.* London: Routledge.

Somerville, M. (2018). Anthropocene's time. *Educational Philosophy and Theory, 50*(14), 1597–1598. https://doi.org/10.1080/00131857.2018.1461428

Somerville, M. (2019). Posthuman theory and practice in early years learning. In A. Cutter-Mackenzie, K. Malone, & E. Barrett Hacking (Eds.), *Research handbook on childhoodnature: Assemblages of childhood and nature research* (pp. 1–25). Cham: Springer. https://doi.org/10.1007/978-3-319-51949-4_6-1

Taylor, A. (2013). Caterpillar childhoods: Engaging the otherwise worlds of Central Australian Aboriginal children. *Global Studies of Childhood, 3*(4), 366–379.

Taylor, A., & Giugni, M. (2012). Common worlds: Reconceptualising inclusion in early childhood communities. *Contemporary Issues in Early Childhood, 13*(2), 108–119.

Taylor, A., & Pacini-Ketchabaw, V. (2015). Learning with children, ants, and worms in the Anthropocene: Towards a common world pedagogy of multispecies vulnerability. *Pedagogy, Culture, Society, 23*(4), 507–529.

Taylor, A., & Pacini-Ketchabaw, V. (2017). Kids, raccoons and roos: Awkward encounters and mixed affects. *Children's Geographies, 15*(2), 131–145.

Whitehouse, H. (2011). Talking up country: Language, natureculture and interculture in Australian environmental education research. *Australian Journal of Environmental Education, 27*(1), 56–67.

Zalasiewicz, J., Williams, M., Steffen, W., & Crutzen, P. (2010). The new world of the Anthropocene. *Environmental Science & Technology, 44*(7), 2228–2231. doi:10.1021/ es903118j

CHAPTER 3

Posthuman De/Colonising Teacher Education in South Africa: Animals, Anthropomorphism and Picture-Book Art

Karin Murris

Abstract

This chapter adopts Karen Barad's *agential realism* as a theory to de/colonise teacher education. For an agential realist knower, subject and object, mind and body, theory and practice are always in relation. One binary does not exist without the other independently – they are a *sympoietic* system ontologically. Hence, theorising involves *literally* being in *touch* with the world. Teaching and researching are not located in human agency separate from the world representing them through linguistic or other semiotic systems that are "substantialising" – we allow them to determine our understanding of the world.

An example of student teachers' engagement with picture-book art illuminates how the concept "animal" tends to be substantialised in (higher) education by working with definitions that "capture" the essence or meaning of concepts, including attempts to define what "animal" is by nature. Barad's concept of *intra-action* at the heart of her agential realism differs from "interaction" in that "nature" and "culture" are never "pure". Like the related concepts *diffraction* and *re-turning*, knowing, doing and being are always already entangled and affected by each other.

This chapter's rhizomatic experimentation with a Reggio Emilia-inspired philosophical curriculum gives learning and knowing a flavour of a *worlding* process. As part of a teacher education program, a field trip to an abandoned zoo on colonised land made the students think radically differently about anthropocentrism, anthropomorphism and human exceptionalism. Their diffractive artwork shows how the agential realist methodology of temporal diffraction can work to disrupt the colonising non-fiction–fiction, culture–nature and science–art binaries and calls us to think *from* animals, thereby becoming more sensitised to human exceptionalism and anthropocentrism.

Keywords

agential realism – temporal diffraction – animal studies – decolonising education – *sympoiesis* – Reggio Emilia – Barad – Despret

1   Rhizomatic Teacher Education at the University of Cape Town

The teacher education program at the University of Cape Town (UCT) is a
one-year Postgraduate Certificate in Education (PGCE). The program consists of three main parts: methods (practice), education studies (theories)
and school experience (practicum in schools). I am convener of the PGCE
Foundation phase[1] and conceptualised and co-designed its curriculum, and
I have taught one of its courses, Childhood Studies, since it started in 2014.
The latter's posthuman(e) orientation has proven to be a rich source for my
research writing (Murris, 2016a; Murris & Muller, 2018; Murris & Haynes, 2018;
Murris, Reynolds, & Peers, 2018; Murris & Borcherds, 2019a, 2019b) and has also
inspired others (see e.g., Kuby, Spector, & Thiel, 2019).

   This chapter draws on events from all three parts of the program, but mainly
from our experimentation with so-called "block teaching" for three courses
in methods (almost[2] every morning between 8 am and 11.30 am). Instead of
teaching Literacy, Life Skills, Childhood Studies and Special Studies (school
visits and field trips) every week, as lecturers we now take turns in teaching
one subject for a whole week during the methods slot. This chapter draws on
data created during one of my weeks teaching Childhood Studies. In close collaboration with another lecturer who teaches Life Skills and Special Studies,
our students' learning is made visible through pedagogical documentation in
a shared Google.doc folder (audio- and video-tapes, photos, field notes, lesson
preparation, our comments, etc.). This way of working is inspired by Philosophy for Children (P4C) and the Reggio Emilia approach to early childhood education (see in particular, Murris, Reynolds & Peers, 2018). This de/colonising[3]
pedagogical work involves wondering about the established meanings of concepts through philosophical questioning and provoking projects (*progettazione*[4]) by taking the concepts that emerge in philosophical enquiries further
through pedagogical documentation (Murris, 2016a, 2017b).

   Central to the forward movement of *progettazione* and the creation of new
understandings of concepts is the *transmodal* (Murris, 2018) switching of *one
hundred languages* (and a thousand more) to project forward as part of a process of intra-action in between human and non-human bodies (which is different from *self*-expression). 'Intra-action' is different from 'interaction' in that

it expresses the ontological idea that individuals emerge through their "entangled intra-relating" and does not assume that individuals exist before their interactions. The famous Reggio Emilia metaphor of "the hundred languages" comes from a poem written by Loris Malaguzzi (Edwards, 1995). A powerful critique of the privileging of the dominant two languages in (higher) education, reading and writing, the metaphor refers at one (practical) level to the introduction of material-discursive tools for meaning making in schools, such as visual arts, physical movement, video, digital cameras, augmented realities and computers. At a symbolic level, the hundred languages are, as Carlina Rinaldi (2006: 175) puts it, a "metaphor for crediting children and adults with a hundred, a thousand creative and communicative potentials".

A willingness to be open to surprises and the unexpected is key and the analysis below shows how I was affected by a radically different perspective on animals, severely troubling the long passion I have had for two of my favourite picture books. The concept "animals" took us for a walk to an abandoned zoo, provoked us to make sketches with charcoal on paper, activated our re-search on the internet, invited us to watch part of a Korean movie and a British documentary with a picture-book author, helped us ask and explore philosophical questions about a picture book, led us to knead playdough, helped us to fill and discuss two worksheets from *Storywise: Thinking through stories* (Murris & Haynes, 2002) (Figure 3.1) and much, much more, including a further search for academic articles on animals.

The Google.doc folder has made it possible for us to enact a *rhizomatic* curriculum that transverses the disciplines ("undisciplining" them). Connections between the carefully chosen "languages" by the educator (Murris, 2017b) help to move an enquiry forward *horizontally*, not *vertically*, like a *rhizome*. Gilles Deleuze and Felix Guattari (2014: 25) explain that "a rhizome has no beginning or end; it is always in the middle, between things, interbeing, *intermezzo* ... The tree imposes the verb 'to be', but the fabric of the rhizome is the conjunction, 'and ... and ... and'". Instead of starting from "the beginning", they "proceed from the middle, through the middle, coming and going rather than starting and finishing" (Deleuze & Guattari, 2014: 25).

Using a hundred languages in Reggio-inspired practices does away with foundations, nullifying endings and beginnings. It does not mean

> going from one thing to the other and back again, but a perpendicular direction, a transversal movement that sweeps one way *and* the other way, a stream without beginning or end that undermines its banks and picks up speed in the middle. (Deleuze & Guattari, 2014: 25)

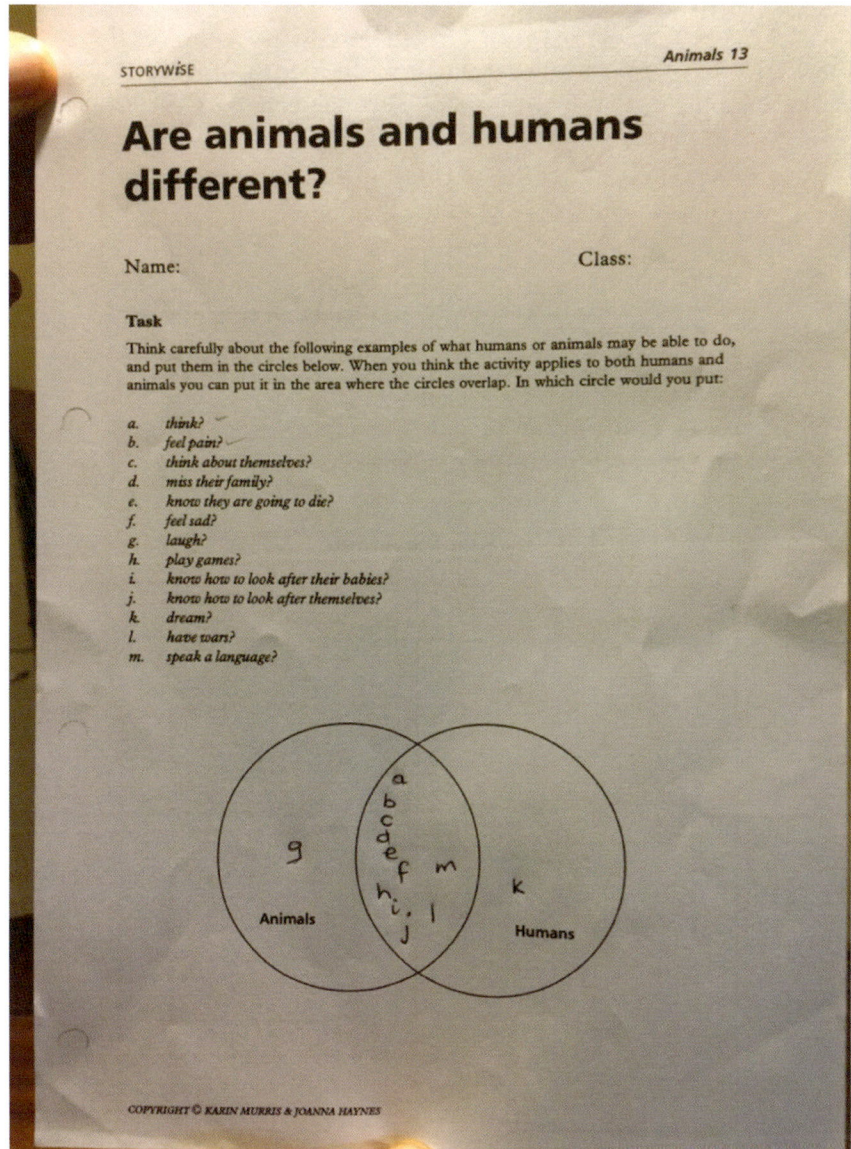

FIGURE 3.1   Are humans and animals different?

The principles of knowledge as rhizome are connection, heterogeneity, multiplicity (Deleuze & Guattari, 2014: 7–8), and "asignifying rupture", that is, "a rhizome may be broken, shattered at a given spot, but it will start up again on one of its old lines, or on new lines" (2014: 9) (like ginger root). The movement of a rhizome disrupts establishing the meaning of a concept such as "animal" through signifying a bounded individualised entity in the world. There are only lines, "no singular points or positions in a rhizome", such as those found in a structure, tree or root, and "any point of a rhizome can be connected to another" (2014: 7–9). A rhizome refers to a network of relations. Every rhizome contains stratification, territorialisation and signification, but also lines of deterritorialisation "down which it constantly flees" (Deleuze & Guattari, 2014: 9). Thought then becomes a matter of experimentation and problematisation (Dahlberg & Moss, 2005: 117), and these "lines of flight" are part of the rhizome, thereby escaping dualism and power-producing binaries – in this case between human–animal, real–fantasy, non-fiction–fiction and science–fiction.

In practice these principles mean constantly re-turning to or, put differently, diffracting through, or intra-acting with the documentation as recorded on Google.doc. In contrast to reflection, which assumes linear time, when diffracting through visual records of prior learning experiences (Murris, 2017b), I cannot enter a past that was never there for the "taking" (as in reflection). Re-membering is the "bodily activity of re-turning" (Barad, 2018: 239) which intensifies the affect that experiencing the experience has on human and non-human bodies. This diffractive em/bodied re-membering without assuming (self)identity is like an earthworm making compost: turning "the soil over and over – ingesting and excreting it, tunnelling through it, burrowing, all means of aerating the soil, allowing oxygen in, opening it up and breathing new life into it" (Barad, 2014: 168).

2   Humanising Animals and Animalising Humans

What "flashes up" (Barad, 2017) after re-turning to some of my "old" notes of students' learning are the questions of whether teachers should keep animals at school and, if so, what kind of animals, and who should look after them and how. The constant re-turning to these notes is a kind of *listening*. The annotated visualisation of selected events in class brings *energies* and *forces* to the *progettazione* that open up new possibilities (Olsson, 2009: 41). The conceptual focus is the key to a dynamic, evolving, rhizomatic curriculum and this week the concept "animals" kept e/merging, even though I had planned to teach children's rights.

Students' interest in animals was palpable and the questions above had been raised when visiting one of the university's partnership schools a few weeks before. This was picked up later by one of the students, Abbie Chetwin, in her visual essay (part of the formative assessment for Childhood Studies):

At Oakhurst School[5] animals are welcome and encouraged as integral participants in the children's education. The school has ducks, chickens, rabbits, guinea pigs, budgies, lovebirds, cats and dogs. The children have access to these animals not only for educational purposes (for example the Grade R class were observing some duck eggs, waiting for them to hatch) but also for personal enjoyment. The animals were also welcomed into the classroom on the condition that children treat the animal as "part of the class". When Bertie the budgie spent a lesson perched on a learner's shoulder he was receiving a lot of attention from the other learners who all wanted to have a turn stroking his beautiful green feathers. Seeing the commotion, my mentor teacher said to the class, "The same way you would feel anxious with people crowding around you, Bertie feels that too. If you cannot treat Bertie like one of your classmates and respect his space, Bertie will have to go back to Ms Parkinson". (Bertie was a teacher's personal pet that came with her to work every day.) The way the teacher humanised Bertie interested me at the time.

The idea of "humanising animals" keeps re-turning in our conversations. At the same time, the students really enjoy this school's unusually inclusive approach to animals. Having animals in school, let alone class, is unusual in South Africa. Experiences of live animals as part of education are rare. Teachers do teach the subject "animals" as part of the national curriculum requirements, but this tends to happen through non-fiction written resources and worksheets with representations of animals. In an effort to queer[6] these mainstream practices and guided by my very practical question *How should we teach the topic "animals" in the Foundation phase?*, I had been reading the picture book *Zoo* (Browne, 1993) to the students, as a way of showing that topics such as "animals" can also be taught through fiction and arts-based approaches, thereby disrupting the non-fiction–fiction and science–art binaries.

Elsewhere (Murris, 2016a: ch. 9), I explore in much detail Anthony Browne's complex decisions about censorship and child protection as author and illustrator, not only of *Zoo*, but also of another one of his picture books called *Little beauty* (2008a). I have always enjoyed how the artist plays provocatively with the discriminatory binaries culture–nature, science–art, human–animal, machine–life and reality–fantasy. In particular when working with *Little beauty* I focus on the latter and the adult–child binary. In fact, since the invention of childhood, child has been equated *conceptually* with an inferior animal that needs to be tamed. How the dichotomy[7] works in education is that supposedly children, as not fully human and ontological other, require culture (teachers) to cultivate them out of their so-called nature: their wild, immature, ignorant,

underdeveloped selves (Murris, 2016a). I have always embraced Browne's picture books (Murris, 1992, 1997, 2016a), because of their ethico-political nature
and their aesthetic power. As philosophical texts they are ideal provocations for
age-transgressive[8] philosophical enquiries with people of all ages. So, I shared
with the students my appreciation and admiration for this artist by watching
together an interview conducted by two children where he talks about his fascination for gorillas and how they remind him of his own dad – gentle and
strong at the same time (Browne, 2008b). The students were visibly moved and
excited by Browne's artwork.

   Zoo tells the story of a family of four visiting a zoo. The eldest of two sons is
the narrator. He tells about the traffic jam on the way up, the fights he had with
his brother, and how embarrassingly his dad behaved – the argument his dad
had with the man selling tickets at the zoo, his moodiness, and especially his
corny jokes. The traffic jam and the animals were all boring, he thought, but are
the animals bored too? His mum feels sorry for the animals – zoos are for people, not animals. His dad remarks that she would have second thoughts if the
animals chased her! For him the delight of the day was his lunch of a burger,
chips, beans and chocolate ice cream. His brother liked the monkey hats best,
while his dad liked going home best. That night the boy dreams of being in a
cage and the story ends with his question: "Do you think animals have dreams?"
The students developed open-ended questions (those Google cannot answer)
for enquiry in small groups. As I listened to their conversations, I noticed how
many of the students had picked up in Browne's illustrations how the humans
are increasingly pictured as "animalised" (e.g., with lots of body hair, a tail or a
cat's nose). Their questions they wrote down were as follows:

1.   Why are the children not interested?
2.   Can animals playfight in the way children do?
3.   [Question to the orangutan] How do you feel?
4.   [Question to the dad] Do you feel safe against the wall? Why do we have
     walls?
5.   *Are we animals too?*
6.   Who is more dangerous? As animals are you less predictable?
7.   Who is the animal really?
8.   Who did the wall feel?
9.   [Question to the orangutan] Are you depressed?
10. [Question to the orangutan] Why do you look so defeated?
11. [Question to the orangutan] Do you feel punished, like you are a crimi-
     nal?
12. *Are humans also in a cage?*[9]

It was striking how many questions were directly addressed to the orangutan –
a greying ape clearly on her own with her back to the viewer – the latter

positioned by the artist as looking into the cage. One small group of students freeze-framed and acted out this scene.

Instead of using their set of questions for a community of enquiry where they start answering the one question they have democratically voted for, as is usual in P4C (Murris & Haynes, 2002; Haynes & Murris, 2012; Murris, 2016a), I asked the students to pick up their chairs and to move into the open communal space in the middle of the building and sit facing one another other (Figure 3.2). Interestingly, the architecture resembles that of a prison. For this activity called "Mad Hatter's Tea Party",[10] I gave them two minutes to explore each question, which I read aloud, and after each turn I asked them to get up and move one place clockwise, so they would swap partners. The level of engagement was extraordinary and attracted a lot of attention from colleagues whose offices face this "quad" and who were either amused, curious or annoyed by the noise level.

FIGURE 3.2   "Mad Hatter's Tea Party" in the quad of the Neville Alexander Building, University of Cape Town

I had noticed that with some questions the two minutes were enough, but with others it was very difficult to stop the students talking when their two minutes were up, in particular when they were answering question 5: *Are we animals too?* It seemed a good moment to switch "languages" again and I invited them to think together with/in theory – a chapter by Helena Pedersen (2016: 21–33) entitled 'Conceptualizing animals' (one of the set readings for that week) – and to discuss key ideas in their diffractive journal groups.[11]

With an outing to a "zoo" planned for the next day, I saw the endless possibilities all contained in that point in time for the *progettazione*, diffracted through *Jetztzeit* or "thick now time". Inspired by Judith Butler's reading of Walter Benjamin and by reading these philosophers diffractively through one another, quantum theorist and critical posthumanist Karen Barad (2017: 33) explains that "*Jetztzeit* is a crystallisation of times, of multiple temporalities, blasted out of the continuum of history: a superposition of times – moments from the past – existing in the thick-now of the present". I will pick this idea up again below, like a *crystal*, and "will turn it around and around allowing the light to diffract through" it (Barad, 2017: 37).

For Barad, theorising involves literally being in *touch* with the world – teaching or researching is not something that is located in human agency. According to her (agential) realist position, "access" to the world does not require mediation, whether by consciousness, experience or language (Barad, 2007: 409 fn9). All knowledge is constructed (and this includes the students' visual essays as assessment) through "direct material engagement with the world" and not by "standing at a distance and representing" the world (Barad, 2007: 49). Barad (2012: n.p.,[12] emphasis added) writes provocatively:

> Doing theory requires being open to the world's aliveness, allowing oneself to be lured by curiosity, surprise and wonder. Theories are not mere metaphysical pronouncements on the world from some presumed position of exteriority. Theories are living and breathing reconfigurings of the world. *The world theorizes as well as experiments with itself.*

Barad's posthumanism invites researchers to sense the *real* force of imaginings and to be literally in *touch* with virtuality on the edge of being and no/thingness; it is an appeal to embrace the openness of the world's becoming in its materiality. Disrupting a metaphysics of presence, the temporality of progress and binary logic, I invited my students to be touched by the multiple temporalities diffracted through the empty space of the derelict "zoo" we were going to visit the next day. I invited them to abandon their reliance on what human eyes can see in order to decide what is real, and to imagine the "multiple different pasts in the present, some more distant than others", like when "we gaze up into the night sky and see specific spatial configurations of stars we call 'constellations', the stars are not all the same distance from us" (Barad, 2017: 34). However, my time with the students that day was not finished yet (perhaps it never will be) and their questions invited a further theorising of the concept "animals" – such a key concept for teaching and teacher education.

Are we animals too? Enquiring into "animal" involves the human–animal binary; hence it requires an investigation into what it means to be human.

3   Critical Posthumanism, Identity and De/Colonisation

Although not anti-human, the ontology posthumanists subscribe to invites researchers to resist putting the human at the centre of knowledge production, data creation and analysis, and challenges the idea that intelligence is in the human only. It also challenges individualism and the idea that identity is given, fixed, inherent and not produced or performed, thereby building on Derrida's notion of performativity and "after" him, Judith Butler's (Barad, 2007: 413 fn 39). This counts for individual humans as well as individual animals (for those who separate out the two concepts).

Are we animals too? For posthumanists, the production of bodily boundaries is not a matter of someone's individual, subjective experiences, or about how we know the world, but the way the world is put together ontologically. Barad's diffractive reading of queer theory and Niels Bohr's quantum physics provide experimental evidence that subject and object are inseparable non-dualistic wholes (Barad, 2011: 143). Posthumanism is about the implosion of nature and culture – a plea to rethink relationality without the nature–culture binary – as a Baradian phenomenon or what Haraway calls a *sympoietic* system. Sympoiesis, Haraway (2016: 58) explains, "is a simple word; it means 'making-with'", a "thinking-with", and implies that human and non-human bodies are always "on the move", dispersed and diffracted through time and space. Individuals are porous, unbounded entities and always already ontologically *a priori* in relation. This counts for all entities, whether human or non-human, at micro or macro level, as the latter distinction is after all "man-made" (Barad, 2007; Wynter, 2003). Critical posthumanism as a navigational tool offers a different *relational ontology* – more akin to African indigenous knowledges (Murris, 2019) and young children's form of life (Murris, 2000).

So what difference does this shift in subjectivity make for our relationships with our selves and "other" (non-human) bodies such as animals? *Are we animals too?* In order to enquire into these salient questions, especially in the period controversially called the Anthropocene (Haraway, 2016), I first explore the post-qualitative methodology of temporal diffraction to illustrate how it is possible to educate differently "about" animals in teacher education.

The diffractive methodology enacts a different non-linear temporality (Murris & Bozalek, 2019). For our field trip to the "zoo" on colonised land – remnants of what once was a fully functioning zoo as part of the estate on which the University of Cape Town was built – the students and I were accompanied by the lecturer of Special Studies and Brandan Reynolds, a local editorial cartoonist (see Reynolds, 2019). As a child he had frequently visited the zoo and he was going to guide the students in drawing the virtual animals that are there (and not there *at the very same time*) into existence. Brandan's stories from his childhood are not a returning to a past that ever was, because it was never simply present to begin with, as this would assume linear time.

Quantum field theory (Barad, 2007, 2018) troubles linear time: time as an arrow pointing forwards to the future, as a succession of discrete moments, with later moments replacing earlier ones and no possibility of re-turning. In linear time (*chronos*) the past is fixed and cannot be changed. This universal, objective time makes it possible to work towards a future-still-to-come, an endpoint where progress has been made and which children/students have to develop/grow towards. In this conceptualisation of time there is a single path for human development, where the intellectual development of the individual human "recapitulates" the development of the species – *independent of geo-political location* – from "savage" to "civilised". In this Western notion of temporality, each moment is split up from the other, but posthuman ontology disrupts *chronos*. Past, present and future are not like "beads on a string", but are always diffractively threaded through one another (Barad, 2007: 394). Temporal diffraction poses powerful questions for student teachers in South Africa to consider as they are encouraged to decolonise their curriculum and prepare their learners for a decolonised future. So how can this be done if time is not linear?

4   Philosophers, Animals and "Animots"

Helena Pedersen in her book *Animals in schools* (2016) explains how students are generally taught the "language of science" when it comes to animals; they are supposed to learn how to teach their children facts *about* animals using scientific taxonomies that identify, fix, separate and position animals in hierarchical abstractions far removed from their concrete, "messy" lives (Pedersen, 2016: 21–22). But as Pedersen comments, these classifications are not only "devices of learning"; they "also structure a specific way of thinking about them, of deducing knowledge about a certain animal from the characteristic of a generic animal of the same sort" (Pedersen, 2016: 23).

Deleuze and Guattari (2014) write that "aborescent" systems of thought and binary logic have dominated Western reality, with its images of knowledge such as "root", "foundation" and "ground". Although the brain is "much more a grass than a tree", they insist that many people "have a tree growing in their heads": thinking that is vertical and hierarchical with continuous binary cuts and nesting classifications (Deleuze & Guattari, 2014: 15). They argue that the brain is not one, rooted, like a tree, but an assemblage of multiplicities. And "thought and concepts can be seen as a consequence of the provocation of an encounter with difference" (Dahlberg & Moss, 2005: 8). We have seen this earlier with the asignifying rupture: the concept "animal" expresses a network of relations.

My student teachers (this year twenty-seven) had read a chapter in Pedersen's book ("Conceptualizing animals") and in their diffractive journal groups they explored, apart from scientific classifications, three other key concepts in her reading that generally speaking shape how we see, treat and teach about animals: zoomorphism, anthropomorphism and mechanomorphism. One student commented that "all these terms suggest inequality between humans and animals, and even between the animals themselves".

Mechanomorphism tends to be seen as a good way of teaching children about animals "as they are". The technical language and machine metaphors used to represent animals are seen as neutral and without any emotion, but as Pedersen points out the discourse is just as value-laden. It is a distinct way of othering animals and is human-centric as it creates an absolute distinction between humans and animals. A good example of this is when birds are referred to as "flying chemistry labs" (Pedersen, 2016: 27).

In zoomorphism animal qualities or characteristics are attributed to non-animals, often with negative connotations (the animalising of human behaviour). In the case of anthropomorphism, human characteristics are prescribed to animals, for example ascribing loneliness and sadness to the orangutan in *Zoo*. Other examples of anthropomorphism can be seen in the case above of Bertie the Budgie, or when biographies are attributed to animals. A good example of this, a student pointed out, is the gorilla in the picture book *Little beauty* (Browne, 2008a), eating a hamburger in a comfy chair while watching television as if he were a human. Importantly, both zoomorphism and anthropomorphism use the human species as a point of reference (Pedersen, 2016: 27). Helena Pedersen (2014) argues instead for doing justice to animals' own cultural interiority, biology and lifeworlds.

After exploring these different concepts, the students browsed through a wide range of picture books in their book club session at the end of the week and applied what they had learned, although as the students observed the majority of picture books they looked at are anthropomorphic (Figure 3.3). One student noted the zoomorphism in both Anthony Browne's *Piggybook* (1986) and *Zoo* (1993). In both stories, humans are likened to animals. In *Piggybook*, men are described as messy and untidy – as "pigs" – and the house they live in as a pigsty, but, as a student pointed out, pigs like rolling around in mess and mud, so it would be a perfect place for them.

FIGURE 3.3   Can I be seen by the animal? A range of picture books: zoomorphism, anthropomorphism or mechanomorphism? (Personal collection)

Vinciane Despret (2015: 91) notes that, for Haraway, scientists work on or *with* real animals, that is "face to face", as opposed to philosophers who tend to speak about animals only in their absence. Derrida calls these abstract, non-existent animals "animots" (in Despret, 2015: 92). However, even when scientists are "face to face" with animals they do not necessarily meet "their gaze" (Despret, 2015: 91). Inspired by Derrida, Despret's proposal is to break with the regime of representationalism and "cultivate a kind of becoming-sensitive to the world", not *starting from* philosophy, but *starting from* the animal and taking seriously the "act of being seen by the animal" (Despret, 2015: 91). To "think from", she explains, requires dignity and engagement that is entailed by the act of inheritance and a responsible responding to animals (Despret, 2015: 96). The act of inheritance could start with a story, but it cannot be representational. Despret (2015: 99) explains that representations are always "at once partial and totalizing", because they understand the complex network of relations "solely from the standpoint of the human". Despret's thinking *from* animals as a responsible responding to animals is what inspired my selection of images of our field trip to the zoo (my "agential cut": Barad, 2007), and Pedersen's concepts made me even more aware of the anthropomorphism and zoomorphism in my favourite picture books. Which story or image *starts* indeed from the animal (not the human) and how could I become more sensitive to the world, *so I can be seen by the animal*?

5   Groote Schuur Zoo Next to the University of Cape Town

An hour before the field trip to the abandoned zoo, the students had conducted independent research in the computer lab and browsed through hard copies of Sarah Ommanney's (2012) powerful Masters project at the School of Fine Art entitled *Lacuna: Groote Schuur Zoo*, an archive of sorts of what an internet site describes as "Cape Town's forgotten zoo".[13]

We discussed some of our findings about the zoo in small groups first. The zoo had been part of the estate of Cecil John Rhodes – a British imperialist infamous for inspiring the racism that according to some led to apartheid (see, e.g., Tobutt, 2016) and eventually gave rise to the Fallist movement (Murris, 2016b). He reportedly wrote: "I contend that we [the British] are the first race in the world, and that the more of the world we inhabit the better it is for the human race" (Rhodes, 1877). He had been given two lions and a leopard, after which he envisaged having a "spacious and beautiful building" constructed, but that never materialised, only a smaller cage building (Ommanney, 2012: 5). The conditions were so cramped that cubs had to be removed when a lioness had a new litter as they were at risk of being killed by their frustrated mother. Only when big enough to be safe they would be moved back after being bottle-fed by the zookeeper (Ommanney, 2012: 15). In 1930 the lion house was demolished, and the zoo finally closed down in 1975 (Figure 3.4). Even though the zoo might have been closed to the public, one of the students told us that according to her father (who was a student there decades later), the animals were still experimented upon at the University of Cape Town.

FIGURE 3.4   "Something strange happened here": The lions' den II in the Groote Schuur Zoo in
             Cape Town

The students were fascinated by reading about the zoo's design and layout then walking the "evolutionary story". Following a path straight through the middle, they walked up the mountain towards the more advanced and superior animals housed higher up than the animals less valued by Rhodes. It had been Rhodes' plan that all animals from the entire British empire would be present in the zoo (Ommanney, 2012: 15). In a recent interview, an academic at the University of Cape Town, Nick Shepherd, described how a plaque in front of the lion's den contained a map of the British empire and showed the "names of prominent cities with distances in miles and arrows". Moreover, "in conjunction with the sundial at the bottom of the zoo, it was meant to locate you, as an outsider, a settler, in space and time" (Ommanney, 2012: 15). The zoo was a place where the animals were studied, admired, but also teased by visitors and used for student pranks (Ommanney, 2012: 15).

Although the timing of our field trip had been planned, much of what happened around it had not been, in order to leave space for the unexpectedness of a rhizomatic curriculum. After telling the students about his childhood visits to the zoo and the lions' roars that could be heard across Cape Town when he was little, Brandan handed out charcoal and white paper. The choice and appropriateness of charcoal did not go by unnoticed by one of the students:

Our visit to the abandoned zoo moved me to think about animals' freedom. The zoo had an empty and eerie feeling. It felt like I was not supposed to be there and exploring the area made me feel like an imposter. I felt I was trespassing on the lions' space and I felt guilty for existing freely in a space in which other creatures had been caged and their freedom stolen from them. In [Figure 3.5], the artwork I created in response to this visit, [I] captured the eeriness with a ghostly silhouette of a lion lying at the foot of an immense wall of brick. Even the medium, charcoal, speaks of death and changing forms. I do not know whether lions or other animals died there, but I cannot deny feeling their presence, knowing that they were once alive but confined to the zoo.

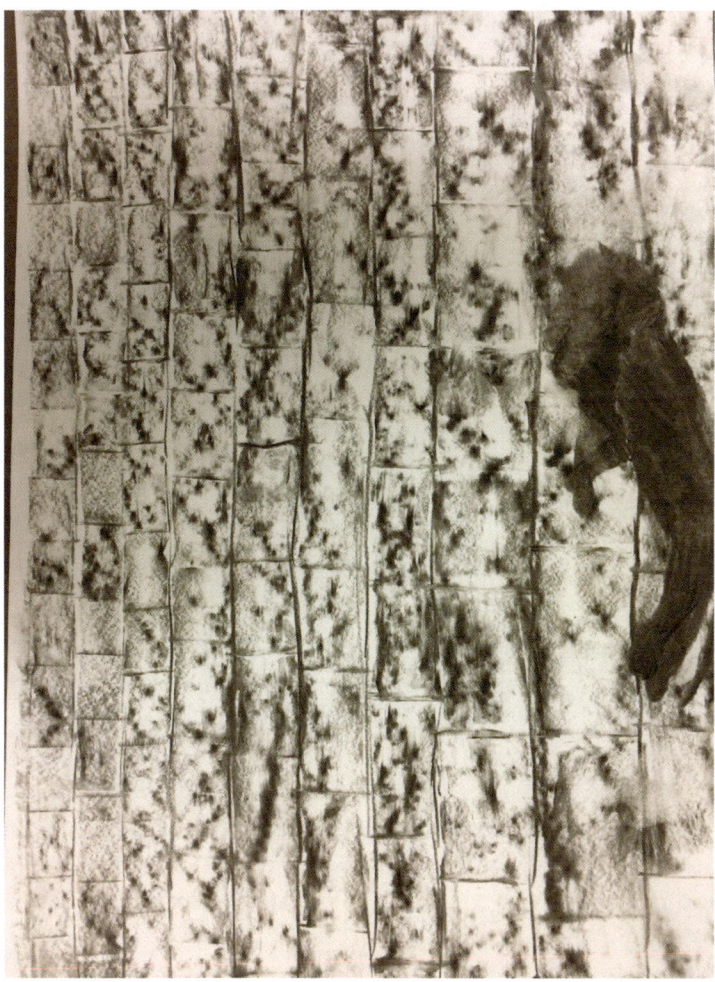

FIGURE 3.5   Abigail Mallows, The ghostly silhouette of a lion lying at the foot of a wall

The students wandered around, finding their own spaces and companions to work with. The students in Figure 3.6 chose their own cage, which re-minded me of their question 12, asked the day before in the context of the picture book *Zoo: Are humans also in a cage?*

<small>FIGURE 3.6   Are humans also in a cage?</small>

As I was walking around observing the students and sensing the heavy, solemn atmosphere, a couple of students drew my attention to graffiti sprayed across the wall in the lion enclosure saying, "Something strange happened here". When walking further away from the lions' den, the stripes of two students' T-shirts struck me as particularly poignant as their bodies were touching the land on which Cape zebras used to roam, with an eerie connection to (animal) prison bars (Figure 3.6). Diffracted through and entangled with my feelings were earlier readings about the lions and how they were fed with donkeys and horses. These were kept in the field behind the lions' den. Every Wednesday a shot could be heard (Ommanney, 2012: 31). Fed at 4.00 pm every day, the lions roared in anticipation before the meat was thrown through the top of the bars. Sarah Ommanney (2012: 31) describes how sometimes a leg got stuck, with the lions pulling and bending the bars, after which the zookeepers had to straighten the bars again with a "five-pound hammer". Donkeys and horses are like zebras, but clearly not enough like them to save their skin (see Figure 3.7).

FIGURE 3.7   "Thick now-time": Diffracting Cape human and non-human zebra stripes and bars
of the animal prisons (Hannah Sunpath and Megan Parker)

Diffracting Cape human and non-human zebra stripes is a performative
practice and *non-representational*. There is no human mediation between
human and the world ontologically, hence mapping or re-presenting is not
an option. The photo is not a *symbol* for something other than itself. Instead,
Barad's posthumanism invites researchers to sense the force of imaginings
and to be in touch with virtuality on the edge of being and no/thingness; it
is an appeal to embrace the openness of the world's becoming in its materiality. Disrupting a metaphysics of presence, the temporality of progress and

binary logic, the students were invited to be touched by the multiple temporalities in the zoo as constellation, the flashing up of images. In the crystallisation, "energy is released" offering "a revolutionary chance in the fight for the
oppressed past" (Barad, 2017: 37). Time is diffracted through the images created
by the students, which bear witness to "multiple different pasts in the present,
some more distant than others" (Barad, 2017: 34). See, for example, Figure 3.8.

FIGURE 3.8   Chantal Manton and her temporally diffracted lion in the Groote Schuur Zoo

Our co-researching on animals in schools had *touched* the students through
arts-based and a variety of other activities (using a hundred languages and
a thousand more) and they provoked the students to reconfigure colonising
relationships with other animals. For me, the temporally diffracted lion in
Figure 3.8 *starts* indeed from the animal. When I look at the drawing, I feel
seen by the animal as Despret would say, because it is not real in the sense of
actual existence as a live animal. It is the diffractive artwork that disrupts the
non-fiction–fiction, culture–nature and science–art binaries and calls me to
think and sense an increased awareness of my own human exceptionalism and
anthropocentrism. Surely temporal diffraction is the methodology we should
adopt when teaching children "about" animals in schools?

The key to adopting temporal diffraction is the idea that time is diffracted
through itself (as evidenced by quantum field theory). Material entanglements

include other times, "past moments that are alive in the present" (Barad, 2017: 46). The students' communal material acts through the rhizomatic curriculum enlivened through the *progettazione* made it im/possible to bring past moments alive in the thickness of the now-time of the present (Barad, 2017: 46), where past, present and future "bleed through one another". This student's drawing is *not* a representation, a product of an individual mind visualising *the* past, but the act of actualising, a bringing into existence, of the animals iteratively entangled with the violent and brutal colonised land of the Cecil Rhodes estate.

6   Are We Animals Too?

The way in which the picture book *Zoo* (1993) by Anthony Browne was used pedagogically raised many philosophical questions through the *concepts* (e.g., animal, human, cage) that escaped from the story as the project unfolded. The aim was clear: to work on a micro-political level (which is at the same time "macro" in posthumanism) to disrupt humanist identity and the power-producing binary nature–culture, which is also at the core of the human–animal binary. The unfolding was/is not unilinear, but multilinear, in/finite and un/predictable as I was listening to the students materially and discursively in thick now-time.

Not only on this occasion, but central in our PGCE Foundation phase program, is our curriculum focus on the changed relationality in between human, sub-human, and more-than-human. Moving beyond notions of individual flourishing to multi-species flourishing is *the heart* of our de/colonising teacher education program (see also, Murris, 2016a, 2019). For example, in our field trips we pay attention to discriminatory human–animal, human–plant, mind–matter and adult–child relations in segregated and enclosed spaces for humans and non-humans. These colonising spaces (zoos, schools, parks, etc.) assume non-egalitarian power relations and are regulated through various inside–outside binaries that include and exclude, keeping the "other" at a distance.

Although indicated above already, I now re-turn again to the question the students often ask and which I raised at the beginning of this chapter. *How should we teach the topic "animals" in the Foundation phase?* I have shown how posthumanism can inspire educators to teach the topics related to animals differently from scientific non-fiction books and worksheets. By using Reggio Emilia–inspired pedagogical documentation containing images, field notes of children's work, of them thinking together, working things out, often in pairs, small groups, and regularly as a whole class, science projects can be provoked focusing on key concepts that disrupt science–art, culture–nature and human–non-human binaries. Whether with student teachers or children a rhizomatic curriculum can be enacted inside and outside the classroom or the school building. Life is given to this experimental posthuman(e) way of teaching through philosophical enquiry and it can be provoked by carefully chosen picture books as philosophical texts (Haynes & Murris, 2012) or worksheets (see Figure 3.1).

Lesson planning (whatever the topic) involves a re-turning to material-discursive documentation, and learning becomes an ongoing reconfiguring of the world that leaves *material* traces that cannot be *erased* (Barad, 2018). The diffractive methodology of re-turning creates new openings, new provocations for rhizomatic teaching, new sedimentations of the world. This kind of learning as worlding (Haraway, 2016) includes, but also moves beyond, the factual, "scientific" mode of teaching about animals but without the science–art, culture–nature and human–non-human binaries. As humans, we are *of* the world, not *in* the world. This material-discursive ontological shift in subjectivity challenges educators to reimagine education as a more-than-human endeavour that dissolves the teacher–learner binary and instead proposes learning as a process of world making (worlding). Without absolute "insides" or "outsides", teacher and learners participate in the always ongoing re/configuring of the world. Barad (2007: 91) explains that learning is not

> about making facts but about making worlds, or rather, it is about making specific worldly configurations – not in the sense of making them up *ex nihilo*, or out of language, beliefs, or ideas, but in the sense of materially engaging as part of the world in giving it specific material form.

It involves playful experimentation by paying attention to how human and non-human bodies affect one's own being as part of the world. Living without bodily boundaries opens up spaces for imaginative, speculative, philosophical enquiries that rupture, unsettle, animate, reverberate, enliven and reimagine.

7   Re-Turning

Inspired by Karen Barad's writings on touching (2012) and *temporal diffraction* in particular (2007, 2018), I have adopted a post-qualitative methodology, thereby exemplifying what makes posthuman scholarship distinct in its affirmative forward movement, and showing the difference it makes ethically.

Reading with/in theory, I *re-turned to* (diffracted through) data created with my students as part of a teacher education program. This method is a kind of "slow" pedagogy *and* scholarship, re-turning and re-turning again (and again) to the same pedagogical documentation on Google.doc, creating "thicker" understandings (a "worlding" process: Haraway, 2016; Murris, 2017b). Through Reggio Emilia–inspired practices (*progettazione*), a rhizomatic curriculum in higher education unfolded.

The picture books I read and explored together with my students were Anthony Browne's *Zoo* (1993) and *Little beauty* (2008a). My chapter diffracts through various events as part of half a week's so-called "block teaching": student teachers' engagement with Browne's art (philosophical enquiries), a Korean movie,[14] interviews with Browne on DVD, browsing through picture books featuring animals, and our field trip to the remains of a zoo on the colonised land of the University of Cape Town's campus, guided by editorial cartoonist Brandan Reynolds. Our main question was: *How should we teach the topic "animals" in the Foundation phase?* The curriculum that e/merged affected students deeply as it made them aware of human-centredness and anthropomorphism in the way animals tend to be treated and how they are portrayed in children's literature. The key question that provoked much thinking and disturbance was their question: *Are we animals too?*

This question in turn inspired their visual essays and artwork – bringing the virtual animals that are there (and not there *at the very same time*) into existence. Our collaborative pedagogical work shows how picture-book art can do powerful de/colonising work when part of a rhizomatic posthuman project. This chapter gives a flavour of this still ongoing project with students who are be(come)ing Foundation-phase teachers. Our co-researching on animals in schools *touched* the students through arts-based activities and provoked them to reconfigure colonising relationships with other animals, which is desperately needed in the Anthropocene.

Acknowledgements

I would like to thank Brandan Reynolds for sharing his personal experiences of visiting the Groote Schuur Zoo when he was a child and for guiding the students with their charcoal drawings. Also, many thanks to my colleague Rose-Anne Reynolds and all the students of the PGCE Foundation phase 2019 at the University of Cape Town for our inspiring journeying and journaling together, and Hannah Sunpath and Megan Parker for giving me permission to use the photo in Figure 3.7. In particular I would like to thank Abbie Chetwin,

Abigail Mallows (Figure 3.5) and Chantal Manton (Figure 3.8) for their permission to publish parts of their visual essays – formative assessments for Childhood Studies. Finally, many thanks to Joanne Peers for the idea and inspiration to use Groote Schuur Zoo as a research site for our teaching and her guidance with some texts.

This writing is based on research that was supported by the National Research Foundation of South Africa (grant number 98992).

Notes

1 The Foundation phase in South Africa covers the 5–9 age range.
2 These are not the only method subjects, but the mathematics coordinator takes up a very different theoretical position in terms of the teaching of the subject. Hence the "almost", as the students have mathematics on Thursdays and Fridays 8.00–9.30.
3 As will become clearer below as the analysis unfolds, my work is de/colonising in the ontological sense by disrupting the nature–culture binary and including the non-human and more-than-human in the relational ontology that informs my pedagogy. Moreover, my teaching de/colonises in the epistemological sense in that it disrupts human exceptionalism, age discrimination (misopedy), misogyny and racism. Finally, I write 'de/colonising' because the slash expresses a changed relationality toward truth, as explored further in Murris (2018).
4 According to Carla Rinaldi (2006: xi, 206), *progettazione* cannot really be translated. It is a strategy, a daily practice of observation-interpretation-documentation – an emergent curriculum developed by the preschools in the city of Reggio Emilia, Northern Italy.
5 This is a pseudonym for the school. Pseudonyms have also been used for the teacher and the budgie.
6 Queering is an "undoing of identity".
7 The binary logic that was put in place by Western metaphysics (and reinforced by capitalism and Christian theology) renders nature (embodied experiences and the body) inferior to culture (the mind).
8 In collaboration with my friend and colleague Joanna Haynes, I have developed the idea that adopting picture books as philosophical texts for philosophy with children is an age-transgressive practice that calls into question many assumptions about age: it engages children (including very young ones) in kinds of thinking that have traditionally been reserved for adults and it proposes that adults who want to philosophise could benefit by becoming more childlike in their thinking (see e.g., Murris, 1997; Haynes, 2008; Haynes & Murris, 2012, 2017; Murris & Haynes, 2018).
9 The questions in italics kept re-turning in our learning together and re-turn below.

10 Students tend to be more familiar with the name "speed dating" for this activity, but I personally like the reference to Lewis Carrol's *Alice in Wonderland* and picturing the scene of these imaginary characters having tea together. I was introduced to this activity during a training by Roger Greenaway (2004).

11 At the beginning of the year, they are asked to silently line up according to their birthdays and when they all stand in a line I split them into groups of three. For the rest of the year, these groups diffractively engage with each other and with events in class, the readings, etc. online. Special time is allocated for their diffractive journaling at the end of each morning. The lecturer also diffracts through the students' writings and uploaded images online. See also Murris (2016a).

12 See https://www.diaphanes.de/titel/ontouching-the-inhumanthat-therefore-i-am-v1-1-3075

13 This internet site found by one of the students turned out to be incredibly informative and the visual images very helpful in orientating ourselves when we walked there later. See Brennan and Ernsten (n.d.).

14 The Korean film was *Spring, summer, autumn, winter ... and spring* (2003). We watched the first quarter ("Spring") and spent a morning exploring the ethics of letting a boy harm animals as part of educating him to be kind to and respect animals.

References

Barad, K. (2007). *Meeting the universe halfway: Quantum physics and the entanglement of matter and meaning*. Durham, NC: Duke University Press.

Barad, K. (2011). Nature's queer performativity. *Qui Parle, 19*(2), 121–158.

Barad, K. (2012). On touching – The inhuman that therefore I am. *Diaphenes, 1*(1), 153–164. Retrieved July 30, 2019, from https://diaphanes.de/titel/on-touching-the-inhuman-that-therefore-i-am--v1-1-3075

Barad, K. (2014). Diffracting diffraction: Cutting together-apart. *Parallax, 20*(3), 168–187.

Barad, K. (2017). What flashes up: Theological-political-scientific fragments. In C. Keller & M.-J. Rubenstein (Eds.), *Entangled worlds: Religion, science, and new materialisms* (pp. 21–89). New York, NY: Fordham University Press.

Barad, K. (2018). Troubling time/s and ecologies of nothingness: On the im/possibilities of living and dying in the void. In M. Fritsch, P. Lynes, & D. Wood (Eds.), *Eco-deconstruction. Derrida and environmental philosophy* (pp. 206–249). New York, NY: Fordham University Press.

Brennan, A., & Ernsten, C. (n.d.). Cape Town's forgotten zoo. *Partizan Publik*. Retrieved July 30, 2019, from https://www.partizanpublik.nl/54/cape-towns-forgotten-zoo/

Browne, A. (1986). *Piggybook*. London: Julia MacRae.

Browne, A. (1993). *Zoo*. London: Julia MacRae.

Browne, A. (2008a). *Little beauty*. London: Walker Books.

Browne, A. (2008b, August 20). Through a gorilla's eyes. *YouTube*. Retrieved July 29, 2019, from https://www.youtube.com/watch?v=xlqiFWoDqqI

Dahlberg, G., & Moss, P. (2005). *Ethics and politics in early childhood education*. London: Routledge.

Deleuze, G., & Guattari, F. (2014 [1980]). *A thousand plateaus* (B. Massumi, Trans.). Minneapolis, MN: University of Minnesota Press.

Despret, V. (2015). Why "I had not read Derrida": Often too close, always too far away (G. D'Amico & S. Posthumus, Trans.). In L. Mackenzie & S. Posthumus (Eds.), *French thinking about animals* (pp. 91–104). East Lansing, MI: Michigan State University Press.

Edwards, C. (1995, October 16–17). *Democratic participation in a community of learners: Loris Malaguzzi's philosophy of education as relationship*. Paper presented at an international seminar on Loris Malaguzzi, University of Milano. Retrieved July 26, 2019, from http://digitalcommons.unl.edu/cgi/viewcontent.cgi?article=1014&context=famconfacpub

Greenaway, R. (2004). Reviewing by numbers. *Reviewing skills training*. Retrieved July 29, 2019, from http://reviewing.co.uk/articles/reviewing-by-numbers.pdf

Haraway, D. (2016). *Staying with the trouble: Making kin in the Chthulucene*. Durham, NC: Duke University Press.

Haynes, J. (2008). *Children as philosophers: Learning through enquiry and dialogue in the primary school* (2nd ed.). London: RoutledgeFalmer.

Haynes, J., & Murris, K. (2012). *Picturebooks, pedagogy and philosophy*. New York, NY: Routledge.

Haynes, J., & Murris, K. (2017). Intra-generational education: Imagining a post-age pedagogy. *Educational Philosophy and Theory, 49*(10), 971–983. doi:10.1080/00131857.2016.1255171

Kuby, C. R., Spector, K., & Thiel, J. J. (Eds.). (2019). *Posthumanism and literacy education: Knowing/becoming/doing literacies*. New York, NY: Routledge.

Murris, K. (1992). *Teaching philosophy with picture books*. London: Infonet.

Murris, K. (1997). *Metaphors of the child's mind: Teaching philosophy to young children* (PhD thesis). University of Hull, Hull.

Murris, K. (2000). Can children do philosophy? *Journal of Philosophy of Education, 34*(2), 261–279.

Murris, K. (2016a). *The posthuman child: Educational transformation through philosophy with picturebooks*. London: Routledge.

Murris, K. (2016b). #Rhodes must fall: A posthumanist orientation to decolonising higher education institutions. *South African Journal of Higher Education, 30*(3), 274–294.

Murris, K. (2017a). Learning as "worlding": Decentring Gert Biesta's "non-egological" education. *Childhood & Philosophy, 13*(28), 453–469.

Murris, K. (2017b). Reading two rhizomatic pedagogies diffractively through one another: A Reggio-inspired philosophy with children for the postdevelopmental child. *Pedagogy, Culture & Society, 25*(4), 531–550. doi:10.1080/14681366.2017.1286681

Murris, K. (2018). Posthuman, de/colonising education and child(hoods) in South Africa. In K. Murris & J. Haynes (Eds.), *Literacies, literature and learning: Reading classrooms differently* (pp. 25–50). London: Routledge.

Murris, K. (2019). Posthuman child and the diffractive teacher: Decolonizing the nature/culture binary. In A. Cutter-Mackenzie, K. Malone, & E. Barratt Hacking (Eds.), *Research handbook on childhoodnature: Assemblages of childhood and nature research* (pp. 1–25). Dordrecht: Springer.

Murris, K., & Borcherds, C. (2019a). Body as transformer: "Teaching without teaching" in a teacher education course. In C. Taylor & A. Bayley (Eds.), *Posthumanism and higher education: Reimagining pedagogy, practice and research* (pp. 255–277). London: Palgrave MacMillan.

Murris, K., & Borcherds, C. (2019b). Childing: A different sense of time. In D. Hodgins (Ed.), *Feminist post-qualitative research for 21st childhoods* (pp. 197–209). London: Bloomsbury Academic.

Murris, K., & Bozalek, V. (2019). Diffracting diffractive readings of texts as methodology: Some propositions [Preprint]. *Educational Philosophy and Theory.* https://doi.org/10.1080/00131857.2019.1570843

Murris, K., & Haynes, J. (2002). *Storywise: Thinking through stories.* Newport: Dialogue Works.

Murris, K., & Haynes, J. (Eds.). (2018). *Literacies, literature and learning: Reading classrooms differently.* London: Routledge.

Murris, K., & Muller, K. (2018). Finding child beyond "child": A posthuman orientation to Foundation phase teacher education in South Africa. In V. Bozalek, R. Braidotti, M. Zembylas, & T. Shefer (Eds.), *Socially just pedagogies: Posthumanist, feminist and materialist perspectives in higher education* (pp. 151–171). London: Palgrave Macmillan.

Murris, K., Reynolds, R., & Peers, J. (2018). Reggio Emilia inspired philosophical teacher education in the Anthropocene: Posthuman child and the family (tree). *Journal of Childhood Studies, 43*(1), 15–29.

Olsson, L. M. (2009). *Movement and experimentation in young children's learning: Deleuze and Guattari in early childhood education.* London: Routledge.

Ommanney, S. (2012). *Lacuna: Grote Schuur Zoo.* Cape Town: Michaelis School of Fine Art, University of Cape Town.

Pedersen, H. (2014). Knowledge production in the "animal turn": Multiplying the image of thought, empathy and justice. In E. A. Cederholm, A. Bjorck, K. Jennbert, & A.-S. Lundgren (Eds.), *Exploring the animal turn: Human–animal relations in science, society and culture* (pp. 13–18). Lund: Pufendorf Institute for Advanced Studies.

Pedersen, H. (2016). *Animals in schools: Processes and strategies in human-animal education.* West Lafayette, IN: Purdue University Press.

Reynolds, B. (2019). *Editorial cartoons by Brandon Reynolds*. Retrieved July 29, 2019, from https://brandanreynolds.com/

Rhodes, C. (1877). *Confession of faith*. Retrieved July 30, 2019, from https://pages.uoregon.edu/kimball/Rhodes-Confession.htm

Rinaldi, C. (2006). *In dialogue with Reggio Emilia: Listening, researching, and learning*. London: Routledge.

Spring, summer, autumn, winter … and spring. (2003). Motion picture, LJ Film, South Korea. Directed by Kim Ki-duk. Retrieved July 30, 2019, from https://www.youtube.com/watch?v=H1GG6o-hPEA

Tobutt, R. (2016, November 15). Who was Cape Town's Cecil Rhodes? *Culture Trip*. Retrieved July 29, 2019, from https://theculturetrip.com/africa/south-africa/articles/who-was-cecil-rhodes/

Wynter, S. (2003). Unsettling the coloniality of being/power/truth/freedom: Towards the human, after man, its overrepresentation – An argument. *New Centennial Review, 3*(3), 257–337.

CHAPTER 4

Between Will and Wildness in STEAM Education

Ramsey Affifi

Abstract

The world is willed and wild, as are human contributions to it. Scientific and artistic practices are imbued with both dimensions in somewhat different ways. A dominant trend in the evolution of science has been to resist the wildness inherent in human and natural processes. But assuming things are or should be orderly is a hopeless and destructive premise. It often leads to increasingly forceful attempts to control, followed by ever wilder side effects. Science education is destined to serve destructive ends until its practitioners better understand and interrogate the relationship between these two very different, yet complementary, aspects of scientific knowledge and practice. On the other hand, some art forms invite a more integrated experience, appreciation and participation. As such, art holds important ontological, epistemological and ethical lessons for sustainable science education. This chapter explores how dialogue with art can help science educators uncover some of these lessons and foster more graceful complementarity between our will for order and our response to chaos.

Keywords

domestication – environmental philosophy – idiographic vs nomothetic inquiry – STEAM – sustainable science education – wild pedagogy

1 Introduction

Science blossoms wildness as it seeds domesticity. Unpacking this aphorism is the goal of this chapter and the educational activities it describes.

Domestication refers to the physical and conceptual ways we *will* order in our surroundings to keep a home. Conceptually, we "home in" on stable patterns and relationships in the world and these constancies give rise to a feeling that the world is orderly. Domestication is an *existential* project, extending the human home outward. This is warm welcome in a world of precarity. However, the patterns we pick out also become practical. Since at least the time of Francis Bacon (1900), science's explicit goal has been to harness regularities to regulate. If we understand how nature works, we will be able to control it for our own ends. We build and make things based on the regularities we identify, and restructure places, environments and lives. This impulse is often viewed with suspicion amongst science and technology studies theorists, and with good reason. On its own, the will to domesticate is self-destructive. Its asymptote is an earth monotonously understood without the thinnest residue of mystery, its plumbing and ventilations systems tidy and managed. Contemporary varieties of homelessness spill out as we accelerate towards this abyss, manifest in ecological disruption within and without.

However, scientific practices are also in the business of identifying, instigating and sometimes also appreciating the fact that phenomena invariably exceed our will to domesticate. I call this the experience of *wildness*, manifest every time things differ from our expectations. While sometimes uncomfortable, I consider it an equally vital existential requirement tied to our need to experience growth and development. Knowingly or unwittingly, scientific practices foster wildness in two interconnected ways. While scientists are guided by the hope or heuristic that the universe is orderly and rationally intelligible, new scientific discoveries do not make the world seem orderly for long. For all the harmony and comprehensible lawfulness a scientific theory may seem to convey, it invariably opens up new questions, mysteries and chaotic realms. A few examples illustrate this exciting point. Quantum theory suggested new particles (quarks and leptons), leading a model with its own oddities (does "dark matter" exist, and what is it?). Roald Hoffmann (1995) points out that, although chemists make predictions about the properties of a new chemical based on its structure, the new substance will expectedly also behave in unexpected ways. The discovery of inheritable biological material led to an increased appreciation of the functional contingency of genes (through alternative splicing, epigenetic modifications and so on (Noble, 2006). For the time being at least,[1] each fresh glimpse into the orderliness of phenomena comes with a new horizon. Science makes the world conceptually unstable even as it uncovers the rhythms and repetitions of the cosmos.

On the other hand, in this era of ecological disruption we are learning just how interconnected wildness and control really are. Our attempts to manage ecosystems lead to unexpected surprises each step of the way, and the term we have given this era, "the Anthropocene" (Steffen, Crutzen, & McNeill, 2007), is decidedly misleading given this epoch's chief insight is that humans are ironically *not* in control (Affifi, 2016). Latour describes this paradox aptly in his observation that "the Anthropocene" is a term "that scientists had to invent in their attempt to understand this Earth that seems to react to our actions" (2017: 3). For all our forming and fashioning and framing, we inadvertently prod the world to manifest attributes unseen within the limits of our conceptual schemes. Our will for order seems to be shaking wildness from its sleep.

In other words, by separating the will from the wild, science ends up rendering both aspects toxic. As the will to control destroys the wild and vital complexity of the world, it often exacerbates a second, destructive kind of wildness. Science is too often enlisted in a type of green-STEM thinking that maintains the need to domesticate and control[2] rather than reconciling science's tendency to order and chaos. Science education that does not work on reconnecting these two elements in scientific practice cannot be considered sustainable.

Art, for its part, engages will and wildness, though it understands and handles them somewhat more healthily. As we shall see, art is often explicitly engaged in attempting to integrate the human desire for purposive order with the fact that humans are always engaged in a more-than-human field of actors and processes that exceeds our grasp. As such, incorporating artistic practices into science education can sensitise students to important epistemological, ontological and ethical questions that arise through exploring the relationship between the will to domesticate and the wild. This turns out to be crucial for cultivating sustainable science curricula and pedagogy.

In this chapter, I trace a series of lessons dialoguing between artistic and scientific practice. A watercolour artist lays down a brush stroke but is at the whim of the water. If skilled, she does not attempt to deny or suppress the wildness of the water but to come to peace with it. I suggest that, when being active and being responsive work together, humans are capable of engaging *gracefully*. When will and wildness are integrated in our hearts, our existential need for both order and chaos are met in complementary relationship, and our inner ecologies can restore their balance. When integrated in action, the biosphere stands a chance to mend its wounds. I devote this chapter to exploring what a science education intent on such healing might look like. Sustainability is a complex and sometimes problematic term, but a sustainable concept of sustainability surely involves sustaining graceful relations.

One starting point for working this out involves recognising the role of understanding *unique* phenomena in science. Conventionally, we often think of science as a pursuit after nomothetic truths in the form of repeatable generalisations and patterns (seeking "laws" is seen as the cornerstone of deductive nomological scientific explanations: Hempel, 1965). The emphasis on nomothetic truths serves, but also exacerbates, our desire for control.

The technocratic dimension of science depends on this emphasis as part of its causal architecture. If x then y. So if we do x, we will get y. It is, however, a mistake to think that science is only, or is necessarily, technocratic. We need to actively resist this conflation in science education. Restoring balance in ecology means recognising and cultivating balance in inquiry. Science has always had an idiographic dimension to it as well. Evolutionary explanations for a particular species' adaptations, cosmology and geography all study the confluence of contingent factors that lead to the particular emergence of unique phenomena. When we study idiographically, we develop an appreciation for the complex interconnections involved in the creation and destruction of the world.

When we do not pay attention to the complexity behind unique events and we treat them solely as instances of a type or category, we simply treat them as an x, and expect a y. With this mindset, we deny the wildness of the world and invite it to come back and haunt us. However, the remedy is not simply to proclaim a science of the unique to set the twenty-first century right. As we shall see in the activities that follow, idiographic understanding also benefits from its counterpart. Kant (1934) is well known to have said that concepts without percepts are empty, but percepts without concepts are blind. I take this to mean that the unique and the general ultimately depend on one another, so science education needs to find ways of fostering integration between nomothetic and idiographic approaches to understanding the world.

I hope to present the notion that paying attention to wildness, and integrating it into science education, is a remedy to the current infatuation with order. The technocratic modus operandi underlying STEM is committed to seeking nature's order and redirecting it to create new order. But releasing science from the burden of this constrained *telos* has fitting relevance at this moment in the planet's saga. The events unfolding in the gracelessly branded "Anthropocene" bring into forceful awareness the fact that our attempt to transform the world into an orderly home only leads to homelessness. Within it is an important lesson that humanity needs to contend with, and in part surrender to.

But the Anthropocene is also a unique event, incompletely understood and to be responded to with a delicacy that defies our regular attempts to regulate. Science education that attempts to address the confluence of crises that characterise our time will need to explicitly equip learners with the ability to attend and respond to the particularities of this complex, evolving situation. This requires a more humble and dynamic integration between human ways of knowing and doing, and the world itself. Any approach to STEM that emphasises the power of nomothetic analysis at the expense of the sensitivity of its counterpart fails to provide students with the aptitudes needed to navigate the tumultuous challenges ahead. Any STEM without STEAM suffers from this excess and one-sidedness.

In the following subsections, I present a series of activities and discussions to foster a greater appreciation of the dialectics between will and wildness in science education. I have engaged students in some of the activities and discussions described, but never sequentially as presented here. I present what follows with the aim of opening discussion and experimentation. Pedagogy is itself a project that asks us to work between the two poles and to seek flourishing complementarities. As much as we can gain experience and techniques for our classrooms, teaching bereft of responsivity miscarries its opportunity to embrace the unique pedagogical relationships in the midst of evolving, to the detriment of students and teachers. Attempting an open-ended struggle between applying strategies and listening shows students how the dialectic works in action. By actively negotiating the role between the content taught and the context in which it is taught, by recognising that the medium is the message (McLuhan, 1964), science education teachers can reveal the artful science of pedagogy and provide vistas into the exciting wildness within it.

2 Revealing Similarity and Difference

It is important to introduce science students to the scientific power of art very quickly as many of them assume science and art are fundamentally different kinds of pursuits. This attitude reduces students' capacities to understand and engage with the dialectic between will and wildness in STEM studies.

For instance, I might introduce students to botanical illustrations, providing some context on why illustration has been used in botanical science, how it cultivates the power of observation, and how we cannot understand things clearly unless we have really looked at them. I may provide some quotations from scientists and artists who have converged on similar insights about the empirical potential of illustration. I provide enough evidence so that the blurring of the boundary is seen as at least feasible or intriguing. However, once students are open to it, arguments in defence of illustration are launched best by the eyes, pencils, papers and the object of study. So my focus is to quickly get my students drawing.

Perhaps I will gather two apples from the same tree on the same day, deliberately choosing two that look quite similar. I remind my students that the purpose of drawing today is not to produce beautiful art but to see the world more deeply and more clearly.[3] Students should attempt to draw each apple as carefully and with as much detail as possible, but should not be hung up on how realistic the fruits look on paper. At the end of the activity, I ask students about their experiences. How different and how similar do the two apples now appear to one another? In my experience, students see more differences and more similarities than they had previously been aware of. In becoming sensitised to similarity and difference, students witness the co-presence of order and wildness in nature. There is a lot to unpack from this deepened perception, and I develop the consequences in this and the next subsection.

2.1   *Differences between Things*

I then ask students if they have ever experienced the same thing twice. *Are there two of anything?* We see two apples and we treat them as identical. For many purposes this is appropriate. But they are not identical. Where did the idea $a = b$ (known as the "equality relation") come from? Are there *any* examples of this in the known universe? After discussing identical twins, fingerprints and snowflakes, students often propose that individual subatomic particles, or atoms of a given element, are identical to one another. The unstated assertion in science textbooks seems to be that equality relations occur at the atomic and subatomic level, so it is likely that at least some students will argue this. If they do not, I eventually ask students whether two hydrogen atoms are identical. Students may wonder if I am talking about isotopes, atomic variations of elements that differ by the number of neutrons. If so, I push back and ask what evidence we have that two atoms of the same isotope are identical? Students may appeal to the quantum indeterminacy of the location of electrons to account for the possible difference between two atoms. But what about the electrons themselves and what about the protons? Are they identical? This discussion can lead to a potentially profound ontological shake up. Why should we believe that the equality relation, which developed as a convenient way of treating phenomena in our direct meso-world experience of apples and trees, applies perfectly on some other scale of the universe? What does this mean for the world we think we live in?[4]

Drawing apples helps us get to the important idea that there is no obvious reason why the equality relation should hold anywhere. This unlocks epistemological, metaphysical and ethical questions. For instance, epistemologically, students can pursue the relationship between thinking and the world (and the sobering insight that our models of the world can never equal the world). However, this activity's greatest power lies in the metaphysical intrigue in store. A consequence of doubting the equality relation is the realisation that *the unpredictable perhaps pervades everything*. If two electrons are different from one another (however slightly), then maybe they sometimes behave differently too. What else could "being different" mean? Any description of a phenomenon ignores differences in its particular manifestations. But this implies *orderliness is an emergent property* rendered discernible by stalking generalities.[5] While emerged order has effects, its causal contribution is necessary but not foundational in the architecture of the world, in the same way that the evolution of species has in turn influenced evolution even though evolution does not require species to occur.[6] If students conceive the universe on a fundamental causal level as orderly, they are bound to conceive the wildness around them as "ultimately" merely an appearance, no different than a computer's random number generator dishing pseudo-wildness by algorithm. This is exactly what we see in the type of complex dynamics that occur in cellular automata simulation runs (e.g. Wolfram, 2002).[7] However, with wildness at its core, a world conceived fundamentally as repetition and mechanism is reconceived as developing themes and variations. This metaphysical point is itself full of ethical questions. People often make decisions based on the assumption that phenomena are well-behaved. We fail to see, or ignore entirely, the differences around us. When we see types, we treat instances as tokens and become as algorithmic as a computer. While knowledge of the world would not exist without categories, valuing the general over the specific is anti-democratic. Home-making run amok imposes a tyranny of the majority, with technocratic thinking its advanced manifestation.

2.2   *Self-Differences*

Until now, we have considered differences between things, but there are also *self-differences*. I define self-differences as the range of ways something is different from itself, in its parts or as a whole, across space and/or time. For example, on close inspection some apples reveal a grainy pattern on their skin. While the pattern may seem to cover a large portion of its surface, it is easy to see that the pattern itself varies. On the other hand, we might return to the apple a few days later and perceive visual transformations in the apple as a whole and in the various regions of its skin. Illustration is crucial in sensitising students to self-differences too.[8]

The difference between differences-between-things and self-differences is not always clear. The difference between two apples could be considered a self-difference when we consider the apples as part of one entity (say the variety "gala", or the species "apple"). Though as overquoted as it is misunderstood, this is what "the pattern that connects" meant for Bateson (1979), and this insight inspired Goethe (Bortoft, 2012). Bateson (1979: 11) explains that we can move up a relational hierarchy that exists in life and living processes (which he calls *Creatura*):

1. The parts of any member of *Creatura* are to be compared with other parts of the same individual to give first-order connections.
2. Crabs [the example he was using] are to be compared with lobsters or men with horses to find similar relations between parts (i.e. to give second-order connections).
3. The *comparison* between crabs and lobsters is to be compared with the comparison between man and horse to provide third-order connections.

The *epistemological turn* in step three is absolutely crucial because it indicates that human knowing and learning are living processes in relational continuity with biosphere. As we shall see in the discussion below, similarity hints of homology, which means a relationship of kinship and shared ancestry. On the other hand, we can look at an individual apple and consider the different regions of its surface as different entities. (They are, after all, made up of different cells that are in important respects autonomous!) Differences, whether within phenomena or within our own learning processes, indicate the young and tentative: variations within themes that emerged from prior variations.

FIGURE 4.1   "Pink Lady" and "Gala" apples painted by the author. Differences-between and self-difference are accentuated in perception through drawing

3 Thinking about the Causes of Difference

I then invite my students to consider reasons why two apples from the same tree are different. This introduces the idea that scientific thinking is not simply about producing generalisable claims but also about interpreting the genealogy of particulars. Illustration, as we have seen, can sensitise perception to difference underlying apparent similarity, and in so doing reveal phenomena available to genealogical inquiry. I ask them to keep this question in mind as they again take up their pencils and paper. In a later discussion, we muse: The particular location of the apple on the tree and its relative access to nutrients, the relatively different micro-ecology of each spot on the tree, differences in genetic and epigenetic process that have accumulated in each ... these are some of the many factors that might be involved.

We might follow up this activity with a discussion about the nature of "experimental error". Is it possible, if only in principle, to design away experimental error? Scientist and philosopher C.S. Peirce, in his defence of probabilistic reasoning (and of his non-deterministic ontology), long ago recognised that, the more we reduce influencing factors in an experimental design, the more the experiment becomes susceptible to contingent influence by the remaining factors. As he puts it, "[t]ry to verify any law of nature, and you will find that the more precise your observations, the more certain they will be to show irregular departures from the law" (Peirce, 1992: 304–305). A recent analysis of scientific explanation (Anjum & Mumford, 2018) asserts the continued evidence of the Peircean view that science studies *tendencies* instead of causes. The feral trajectories of subatomic particles in CERN detectors seems an example of this phenomenon. It may well be that every particle is contextually and historically situated. In principle, if not in practice, the context of an individual particle's emergence and development through time might be excavated, revealing the evolutionary nature of the universe.[9]

Does the difference between two apples emerge from the difference between particles? In other words, is it possible that real wildness occurs only at the fundamental level of the universe (whatever that is) with all higher order appearances owing its seeming spontaneity to that level? It is unlikely that students would agree with this assertion, but it is important to get them thinking about what is happening because the causal model they often apply to thinking about phenomena presupposes that "real" causality does not emerge at higher orders.

The roll of dice produces unexpected outcomes, but these are not based on the unexpectedness of individual particles within either them or the table they fall on. In this case, what individual particles are doing is irrelevant. New forms of randomness emerge wherever new forms of order emerge. Wildness is also an emergent property in dialectical complementarity with its counterpart. As in the case of particles, the spontaneous dimension of an apple can be thought of in several ways. One explanation can seek intrinsic differences within the specific apple. Another explanation can seek extrinsic differences in its environment. What is the difference between these types of explanation? And how might we think beyond the difference between "inside" and "outside"?[10]

Is a degree of relative regularity an emergent feature of interconnection, rather than the orderly base upon which the world is composed? Here blossom ontological questions that prime students for thinking about the relationship between order and chaos in natural processes. It also has obvious implications for learning for sustainability: with order only ever approximate, attempts to control on its basis seem set *a priori* to scatter side effects. How are design and technology to be reimagined from within an ontology that does presume that order is predominant? Considering such questions can help cultivate certain "sustainability virtues" such as *humility*, increasingly important as we develop technologies with ever more powerful intended and unintended effects on the world within which we live and depend.

3.1   *The Dialectic between Similarity and Difference*

We are now positioned to introduce, and then integrate, nomothetic and idiographic forms of understanding (Windelbrand & Oakes, 1980). While the former seeks the lawlike generality that binds together various instances of a phenomenon, the latter engages with the unique and contingent historical events that brought a specific thing into being. Students are likely to believe that nomothetic understanding is scientific while idiographic understanding is not. This is not, however, the case. Cosmology is an example of a broadly idiographic pursuit as it studies the evolution of a single entity (the cosmos) and tries to understand the various factors contributing to its development. Geology, ecology and psychiatry are also to different extents clearly idiographic.

I delve into the curious relationship between nomothetic and idiographic understanding through again taking lessons from our illustrated objects. It seems our capacity to engage well in one depends on our ability to engage with the other. We might say that idiographic and nomothetic thinking are dialectically interconnected (Affifi, 2019). We appreciate uniqueness best when we see it as variation of some general pattern. For example, particularities in a given apple are accentuated when we know it is a member of the variety "gala". Far from merely effacing difference, having this category can sensitise perception to subtler distinctions. In my view, this is a *hermeneutic* insight that flows from Gadamer's (1975) reconstruction of the concept of "prejudice". Given we enter all situations with a stock of meanings and understanding drawn from prior experiences, prejudices are for Gadamer inevitable in encountering phenomena. However, a prejudice is only problematic when it shields itself from revision. I "know" what apples are, and so I treat apples according to a template. When I do this, the individuality of each apple recedes from perception. But prejudices can also be invitational. Without prior understanding forestructuring the encounter, no specific apple could jut out and assert its individuality to perception. Careful drawing involves the continuous process of forming hypotheses about what one sees and examining whether or how one's subject violates those expectations. The immediacy of the loop between both modes of engagement means that the dialectic can be experienced viscerally. Art therefore can help us enter embodied modes of understanding that expose our conceptualisations to variance, and this variance can, in turn, furnish new conceptualisations. Here the mutual influence of our will to order and our perception of wildness is clearly felt.

Generalities give rise to exceptions, while exceptions give rise to generalities. This provides another potential clue into the interaction between order and chaos, showing how the development of knowledge often oscillates between each. Kuhn (1966) describes the clutch Newton's laws of mechanics held upon the scientific imagination. A period of "normal science" resulted, illustrating how prejudice impedes and informs progress in understanding the world. According to Kuhn (1966), relying on Newton's mechanical theory was initially fertile but eventually became irrational. Nevertheless, the ordering it provided was necessary for Le Verrier to then witness unexpected variance in Mercury's orbit that eventually led to relativity theory (Baum & Sheehan, 1997). Scientists can now explore the conditions under which general relativity does not make perfectly accurate predictions. For example, according to Moffat (2008), a modified form of Newtonian mechanics can more parsimoniously account for the spin of spiral galaxies, whereas the ad hoc supposition of "dark matter" is needed if we wish to explain these through general relativity. After exploring the transition from Newtonian mechanics to relativity theory, I ask students to think about it in relation to the act of drawing. The dialectic is similar to what happens with careful drawing, but the pace is orders of magnitude slower. It is difficult to see and harder still to feel. Art can therefore sharpen awareness of how idiographic and nomothetic thinking work together.

Until now, the examples given in both art and science concern understanding. Drawing exposes similarities and differences visually, just as scientific modelling exposes them conceptually. In noticing this similarity between art and science, we are able to draw closer interpenetration between them, and in particular to see how the nomothetic and idiographic are corresponding parts of the development of all scientific knowing. In what follows, I begin to interrogate the ways in which *knowing and practice* combine in light of the discussion and explorations above.

4   Practical Knowing of Will and Wildness

I now engage students with watercolour painting. This medium vividly exposes a more practical dimension of the interrelationship between will and wildness. Watercolour painting is a study of, engagement with and surrender to water.

I have students explore wet-on-dry, wet-on-wet, layering, and other techniques that reveal the dynamics and properties of water. Watercolour painting is an ongoing investigation into various hydrological processes, as water mediates between various interactants such as pigment, brush, surrounding air temperature and paper. Students will encounter, and at first resist, the fact that they cannot control the paint. Water flows, bleeds and dries up, while different pigments alter its viscosity in different ways. Like a canoeist in a river, they cannot fight the flow but must learn to work with it (see Figure 4.2 for an example).

FIGURE 4.2   Will and wildness in watercolour painting. Christine Chesterman created this beautiful piece in one of the author's environmental education Master's programme classes

Afterwards, I present paintings that gracefully interpenetrate the responsive contributions of the artist and the wildness of the water, and follow with a discussion connecting this activity to our earlier discussion about the relationship between order and chaos. Students are invited to interrogate the meaning of the word "graceful". It is an idea that turns out to have profound importance for how we think about developing sustainable societies.

After painting and discussing the experience of thwarted wills, I present cases where technologies generated through scientific theory produced unexpected side effects. For instance, we might consider genetic engineering (or editing), which routinely leads to unanticipated changes in an organism's physiology. Why does this happen? What is the difference between watercolour and these approaches? Here is an opportunity to consider what systems theorists call "time lags" (e.g. Meadows, 2008), a key problem aggravating humanity's capacity to will gracefully within a wild world. A gene is edited and inserted into an organism's genetic code. The developed organism may appear similar to its non-engineered counterparts with the exception of whatever properties were conferred on it by the edited gene. However, because DNA is complexly interconnected and its information is adaptively constituted by the cell negotiating contingent ongoing circumstances, the behaviour of the gene within the dynamic ecology of the genome is unpredictable. This wildness may not be immediately apparent and often depends on specific, non-routine tests (such as "omic" studies) (Affifi, 2017). The result of the time lag is that cause and effect are temporally separated, creating the illusion that unanticipated results are exceptional rather than ubiquitous and can be eliminated through a careful process.

The feedback loop between knowing, doing and consequence is tight and immediate with watercolour but drawn out and non-localised with these technologies. This difference leads to varied assumptions about the reliability of the knowledge. In watercolour, knowing about the relationship between oneself, one's paint, the paper and the water is an ongoing and literally *fluid* investigation. There never emerges a point where the artist can comfortably say that they know and can predict exactly what will happen, no matter how skilled. But in scientific exploration aimed at isolating well-behaved regularities and producing technologies from them, one easily forgets that the isolation was an artefact generated from how the regularity was identified, and only possible because the variation was very small, very slow or very non-localised. What might technology learn from art?

5   The Nomothetic in Painting

As painters develop proficiency, they develop shortcuts. For instance, instead of painting each individual crack and vein in a rock's face, the painter employs a certain kind of brush and brushstroke. The overall effect captures the pattern of the rock without replicating it exactly. In some way, the progressive development of artistic skill can be measured in the fewer steps required to produce a certain effect. In those who are skilled, this appears effortless and economical. While it is no doubt inspiring to watch such a landscape unfold before one's eyes, it is clear from the analysis above that the artist's skill eases passage over the specific and idiosyncratic. Specific details are unnecessary to observe, study and depict as long as the overall effect mimics the pattern constellated from the details. It does not matter that *this* particular rock is painted. What matters is that this kind of rock *could* look like this perched on the cliff edge. Watching a highly skilled painter on YouTube will quickly expose students to this idea.

In science, a theory provides a simplified operation that gathers together a number of different phenomena under some rule. It then enables the observer to make predictions with some degree of accuracy. A painter develops tricks, in some sense *embodied theories*, for how to depict their subjects. The operation is sensory and muscular, but the effect is analogous: tricks gather together a range of different phenomena that would require similar treatment and makes relatively accurate predictions about what effect a given intervention will have. In both cases, the actual complexity of diverse phenomena is reduced. Relevant aspects of the phenomena are identified as needing representation, the rest is treated as contingent. Another way of putting this is that embodied theory in artistic skill and scientific theory in empirical inquiry both commit to bifurcating pattern from noise. Variations within the pattern are seen as significant, whereas variations within the noise are tolerated and ignored.

With this observation, it becomes clear that studying appearances through art is no simple friend of the idiographic. Creating a painting has a nomothetic dimension to it. This is important because watching an artist (or developing an artistic skill) can reveal the dynamics of the relationship between the nomothetic and the idiographic. Because a painting is directly and sensorially experienced, it is easy to see the ways in which shortcuts depict and hide detail. In science, such differences are often lumped into a category called "experimental error". The term error reifies an ontological assumption that the variance is contingent upon the scientist's methods and not a necessary aspect of the relationship between the theory and the world itself.

6   Multispecies Will and Wildness

I now take students outdoors to learn that other organisms have their own wills and also seek order. Until this point, an implicit ontological dualism has pervaded between humans, as creatures who tend to control, and nature, as that which defies our attempts. In this section, I seek to destabilise this notion in several ways.

Population ecologists developed a concept called niche construction theory (Odling-Smee, Laland, & Feldman, 2003), which upholds that organisms modify their environments in ways that often benefit them. In doing so, they contribute actively to evolutionary processes by changing their selection pressures. What may seem wild to a human operating under Cartesian funnel-think may well be the ordering activity of a wren or a walnut tree. Conversely, the overlay of our engineering feats onto their homes will be experienced as a chaotic disruption despite its apparent elegance or symmetry to our eyes. Harking back to the last section's discussion: does a wren engage more like an artist or a technologist? This question proves immensely fruitful as I deepen my exploration with students. I leave it for you to consider with your students.

A great challenge in the ecological crisis is that we must urgently confront human devastation of the natural world, while also tempering the notion that humans are uniquely different from that world. If humans are seen as no different from other species, our destructive tendencies not different in kind and themselves "part of nature", a sense of urgency is lost. But any claim that we are different reifies a sense of exceptionalism (even if it is a demonic kind). We must resist dissolving the current situation into either pole, working to restore continuity in contexts that oppose it while highlighting differences in those who deny them to retain the status quo. We must resist overly domesticating or overly wilding our conceptions of the human too. We make our own homes, but we also contribute to the earth as a home both as a stabilising and as a disrupting force.

Just as we can recognise the domesticating motivations of the more-than-human world, so too can we acknowledge the wildness seeping from even the most controlled artefacts. Cities twitch and click with complex technologies, means of production spread like tentacles throughout fields, forests and neurons – here seems a good place to initiate this phenomenological excavation. What is the process underway if *not an ordering tendency out of control*, pulling the rest of the biosphere into its globalising dysecology?[11] A paradox: if we do not assert our wills against this colossal whirlwind, our own wildness will suffer. The broader globalising culture domesticates people (and other beings), providing one kind of freedom by denying others. Our task is to reject freedoms that feed the dysecology, but this requires discipline and control of the body, heart and mind. In short, while control unleashes wildness, rewilding requires control. This means that advocating "wild pedagogy" is one-sided (Crex Crex Collective, 2018). The name and impetus seem to veer away from recognising the ubiquitous co-existence of domesticity and wildness, rather than appreciating the more fundamental problem of asking what particular admixtures of each *do*. As such, the term risks redrawing familiar, albeit unhelpful, Cartesian distinctions. We must be clear about when, where and what wildness we nurture, and which we let go. Sustainable STEM education needs to work on such graceful reintegration.

7   Returning Home

Science's dominant operating ontology domesticates the universe in different ways. First, it assumes an underlying lawfulness. Even the quantum God that played dice with Einstein's brain was orderly, working through well-behaved entities whose probabilities can be mathematically described. Like all theologies, faith in a fundamentally orderly world has important existential dividends. There are times when humans need to experience the world as safe and stable. The will to see order is itself a form of terror management, a flight from the horror of impermanence, precarity and mortality.[12] Order allows us to live as though things are staying the same. Order is a hearth to which we can always return. A phenomenology of the human sense of "home" reveals the striving for, and occasional achieving, such an experience of eternity. In this sense, there is a considerable drive to use science to establish and re-establish the universe as our home.

Scientific explanations tend to focus on regularity rather than on dynamic contingency and change. The urge to use thought, observation and experimentation to identify pattern is existentially tied to a need for security and stability. The result is a skewed map of the world, with science foregrounding its order at the expense of its disorder. Inspired scientists may be romantically involved with mystery and confusion, but their products not their processes are handed down to society, in the form of new knowledge rather than new ignorance. School books focus on what we know and promote the idea that we know a lot of things.

This increasing sense of order is fed by and contributes to a second dimension of the ontology: the assumption that the world is similar enough to humans that our reasoning and perceptions can identify its order. Our order and the order of the world are similar. While many claim scientific knowledge is killing the anthropomorphic God, the universe increasingly has (human) reason built into its sinews and its skeleton. In an even deeper sense, successes in scientific theorising lead to the feeling that the human mind is, as Emerson put it, "a citizen of the universe" (1904: 221). Add to this the ways stable knowledge is translated via technology into remaking the world, and we really get a sense of the will to order being fundamental to scientific process.

And yet, *science invariably also ushers in new conceptions of disorder*. This is apparent in our measurements. It resides in how scientific understanding evolves, and in academics' search for ever new research projects to concoct and fund. Underlying the quest for uncertainty is an equally powerful existential driver. A world void of wildness is unbearable. A repetitive and predictable home becomes alienating. Within the hearth, the flames.

Certainty and uncertainty co-occur but in scientific practices they are often parcelled from one another and used differently. What is unified in a child's curiosity is severed by the march to fill students' brains with knowledge. This ensures that the enchanting side of science is reserved to the few who end up in research (and as research is increasingly directed to fiscal ends, too few among them). This is assured when science educators teach something closer to a "history of science" than facilitating scientific practice itself. When the products of Darwin's, Newton's or Boyle's investigations are presented, analysed and applied, engaging in scientific practice itself is relegated to infrequent and rather contrived lab work. This would be virtually unthinkable in art education, where experimenting, observing and hypothesising play a key role in exploration and discovery. The irony is that art education is truer to scientific method than science education. Art students are also therefore able to experience the combined joy of new insights, new capacities and new mysteries.

Finally, the relationship between order and chaos is not just about how our impositions of order are defied by a chaotic universe. The more-than-human world gets into its own rhymes and rhythms. Contending, as many postmodernists do, that all categories are "just" constructions conceals the fact that the world muffles its degrees of freedom under its own emerging regularities. The human capacity to categorise is not different in kind; it is just one manifestation of this dampening process. A sustainable science education needs to acknowledge the ubiquity of these complementary tendencies or it will continue to shepherd devastation. Denying intrinsic order tunes people out of the patterns of the world. Denying intrinsic wildness perpetuates rough and crude technocratic treatments that can stir an unheeded murmur or fluctuation into a tempest. Integrating art practice into science education can ensure that students feel this coherence viscerally and end up less likely to reify their distinction.

8   Conclusion

In contributing to a more sustainable world, science is often ascribed a technocratic role. This attitude is based on the premise that science is exclusively about discovering and harnessing order. However, order and chaos are co-present in all phenomena, including scientific knowledge, practices and applications. Sustainable science education needs to acknowledge and reconcile this misleading cultural split. When science is employed to impose order on the biosphere, the risk of side effects is underplayed while the ordering at work by its diverse species is ignored. This creates an ordered–disordered distinction along long-tired Cartesian grooves (humans and "nature"), rather than recognising each as complementary facets of everything. Drawing and watercolour painting are two ways of exposing new science educators to their co-presence, both in the world and in our engagements with it. Revealed is a dialectical relationship between nomothetic and idiographic elements, manifest as themes and variations in the things and processes around us, and in all human relationships. In an invitational spirit, I have tried to present philosophical discussion that might accompany the integration of art into science education. The authors contributing to integrating STEAM and STEM in the pages that follow are making important conceptual and practical headway. My hope is that this chapter raises more questions than it answers and that science educators take seriously the need to trouble the dichotomies explored here, not merely in topic, but in their pedagogical process.

Notes

1   It is currently an open-ended discussion whether there is an "end of science" (Horgan, 1996). However, even those who argue an end is near rarely insist this is because everything is knowable in principle. The claims of science ending are related to intrinsic epistemological, economic or political limitations. It could be that science progresses until permanent horizons appear. But this possibility would merely imply a permanent fissure between the known and the unknowable and retain some sense of wildness. Nor does such a position address the tendency for our interactions with phenomena to lead to unexpected results (even if these results are explainable in principle through existing scientific theory).

2   Through, for example, cutting-edge wind power, genetic engineering and ecological management.

3   The drive to produce beauty often, but not necessarily, leads to better observation. The aesthetic dimensions of inquiry are complex, and shall only be touched on briefly in the section "The nomothetic in painting").

4   In the end, it could be that subatomic particles behave in ways that perfectly match mathematical abstractions derived from our evolved way of categorising daily life. This would be a very *spooky* fact, well worth investigating but beyond this chapter's remit. According to Fermi-Dirac statistics, particles are treated as identical and defined by eigenvalues such as spin. Eigenvalues are "quantised", which means they are seen to take on discrete numerical values (integers and half integers). An open question is to what extent microvariations around these discrete values occur.
    Some questions to explore this idea: Could the regularity of chemical reactions be an aggregated effect of the fact that most hydrogen atoms behave in stereotypical ways? Could there be individual atoms that behave quite differently but have no

tangible effect on the properties of a sample? What does the fact that we can make generic statements about the properties of specific elements tell us about the possible distribution of variance within a sample? What might it say about the standard deviation of an element? Why would certain forms be vastly more probable than others?

Some examples. Scholars now question whether the species concept is appropriate for bacteria, given the ubiquity of horizontal gene transfer (Doolittle & Papke, 2006). Abiogenesis is thought to have occurred through the evolution of autocatalytic chemical networks (Kauffman, 1995). According to meme theory, information is also modelled to evolve without the need for species boundaries between the evolving ideas (Dawkins, 1976).

5 Some questions to explore this idea: Could the regularity of chemical reactions be an aggregated effect of the fact that most hydrogen atoms behave in stereotypical ways? Could there be individual atoms that behave quite differently but have no tangible effect on the properties of a sample? What does the fact that we can make generic statements about the properties of specific elements tell us about the possible distribution of variance within a sample? What might it say about the standard deviation of an element? Why would certain forms be vastly more probable than others?

6 Some examples. Scholars now question whether the species concept is appropriate for bacteria, given the ubiquity of horizontal gene transfer (Doolittle & Papke, 2006). Abiogenesis is thought to have occurred through the evolution of autocatalytic chemical networks (Kauffman, 1995). According to meme theory, information is also modelled to evolve without the need for species boundaries between the evolving ideas (Dawkins, 1976).

7 A cellular automaton is a grid of cells, with each taking on one of a set number of possible states (such as being either black or white). Rules are assigned for how the grid will behave as it is iterated. For example, the rule might be if a white cell has a black neighbour on its top left corner, it turns black; however, if a black cell has a white neighbour directly beside it, it turns white. After many iterations, some rules end up generating a lot of interesting behaviour, from oscillations to complex evolving structures, which has led people like Wolfram (2002) to assert the universe is essentially "computational". This idea has seized the imagination because it provides an intuitive way of seeing how vast scales of complexity can be generated by simple rules. It also metaphysically crowns the will to conceptually domesticate the universe because there is no wildness in the system: all cells are exactly the same size and shape, there are a discrete number of possible states, and all iterations of the rule are identical.

8 Some questions to explore: Does the chair you are sitting in stay the same? What about the individual particles that make it up? In what sense does it stay the same and in what sense does it change?

9 I do not imply that the universe is evolutionary in an exclusively Darwinian sense (such as advocated by Kelley, 2013), since Darwinian selection is insufficient in even biological explanations (Pigliucci & Müller, 2010; Walsh, 2015).

10 Getting beyond this dualism is a key motivation behind developmental systems theory (e.g. Oyama, Griffiths, & Gray, 2001).

11 I define a dysecology as a web of sustained and integrated feedback relations at the expense of the broader ecologies on which it depends.

12 According to Solomon, Greenberg and Pyszczynski (2015), humans seek to avoid awareness of mortality through falling back into the safety of their cultural world views or through engaging in activities that prop up their sense of self-esteem. While perhaps unavoidable, facing death is at least sometimes crucial for sustainability, given that these fallback evasions are often quite destructive (Affifi & Christie, 2018).

References

Affifi, R. (2016). More-than-humanizing the Anthropocene. *The Trumpeter, 32*(2), 155–175.

Affifi, R. (2017). Genetic engineering and human mental ecology: Interlocking effects and educational considerations. *Biosemiotics, 10*(1), 75–98.

Affifi, R. (2019). Light after eclipse: Themes and variations. *Environmental Education Research.*

Affifi, R., & Christie, B. (2018). Facing loss: Pedagogy of death. *Environmental Education Research* [Preprint]. doi:10.1080/13504622.2018.1446511

Anjum, R. L., & Mumford, S. (2018). *Causation in science and the methods of scientific discovery.* Oxford: Oxford University Press.

Bacon, F. (1900). *Advancement of learning.* Oxford: Clarendon Press.

Bateson, G. (1979). *Mind and nature.* New York, NY: E.P. Dutton.

Baum, R., & Sheehan, W. (1997). *In search of planet Vulcan: The ghost in Newton's clockwork machine.* New York, NY: Plenum Press.

Bortoft, H. (2012). *Taking appearances seriously: The dynamic way of seeing in Goethe and European thought.* Edinburgh: Floris Books.

Crex Crex Collective. (2018). *Wild pedagogies* (B. Jickling, S. Blenkinsop, M. D. Sitka-Sage, & N. Timmerman, Eds.). Basingstoke: Palgrave Macmillan.

Dawkins, R. (1976). *The selfish gene.* Oxford: Oxford University Press.

Doolittle, W. F., & Papke, R. T. (2006). Genomics and the bacterial species problem. *Genome Biology, 7*(116), 1–7.

Emerson, R. W. (1904). *The complete works of Ralph Waldo Emerson* (Vol. 8). Boston, MA: Houghton, Miflin.

Gadamer, H. G. (1975). *Truth and method.* New York, NY: Continuum.

Hempel, C. (1965). *Aspects of scientific explanation and other essays in the philosophy of science.* New York, NY: Free Press.

Hoffmann, R. (1995). *The same and not the same.* New York, NY: Columbia University Press.

Horgan, J. (2015). *The end of science.* New York, NY: Basic Books.

Kant, I. (1934 [1781]). *Critique of pure reason* (N. Kemp Smith, Trans.). Edinburgh: R. & R. Clark.

Kauffman, S. (1995). *At home in the universe: The search for the laws of self-organization and complexity.* Oxford: Oxford University Press.

Kelly, D. B. (2013). *The origin of everything via universal selection, or the preservation of favoured systems in contention for existence.* Newbury, OH: Woodhollow Press.

Kuhn, T. (1966). *The structure of scientific revolutions.* Chicago, IL: University of Chicago Press.

Latour, B. (2017). *Facing Gaia.* Cambridge: Polity.

Meadows, D. (2008). *Thinking in systems.* London: Earthscan.

McLuhan, M. (1964). *Understanding media.* New York, NY: McGraw-Hill.

Moffat, J. W. (2008). *Reinventing gravity.* New York, NY: HarperCollins.

Noble, D. (2006). *The music of life.* Oxford: Oxford University Press.

Odling-Smee, J., Laland, K., & Feldman, M. (2003). *Niche construction.* Princeton, NJ: Princeton University Press.

Oyama, S., Griffiths, P. E., & Gray, R. D. (Eds.). (2001). *Cycles of contingency: Developmental systems and evolution.* Cambridge, MA: MIT Press.

Peirce, C. S. (1992). *The essential Peirce: Volume 1* (N. Houser & C. Kloesel, Eds.). Bloomington, IN: University of Indiana Press.

Pigliucci, M., & Müller, G. (Eds.). (2010). *Evolution: The extended synthesis.* Cambridge, MA: MIT Press.

Solomon, S., Greenberg, J., & Pyszczynski, T. (2015). *The worm at the core: On the role of death in life.* New York, NY: Random House.

Steffen, W., Crutzen, P., & McNeill, J. R. (2007). The Anthropocene: Are humans now overwhelming the great forces of nature? *Ambio, 36*(8), 614–621.

Walsh, D. (2015). *Organisms, agency and evolution.* Cambridge: Cambridge University Press.

Windelband, W., & Oakes, G. (1980 [1894]). History and natural science. *History and Theory, 19*(2), 165–168.

Wolfram, S. (2002). *A new kind of science.* Champaign, IL: Wolfram Media.

PART 2

Why Does Science Matter?

∵

Introduction to Part 2

Pamela Burnard and Laura Colucci-Gray

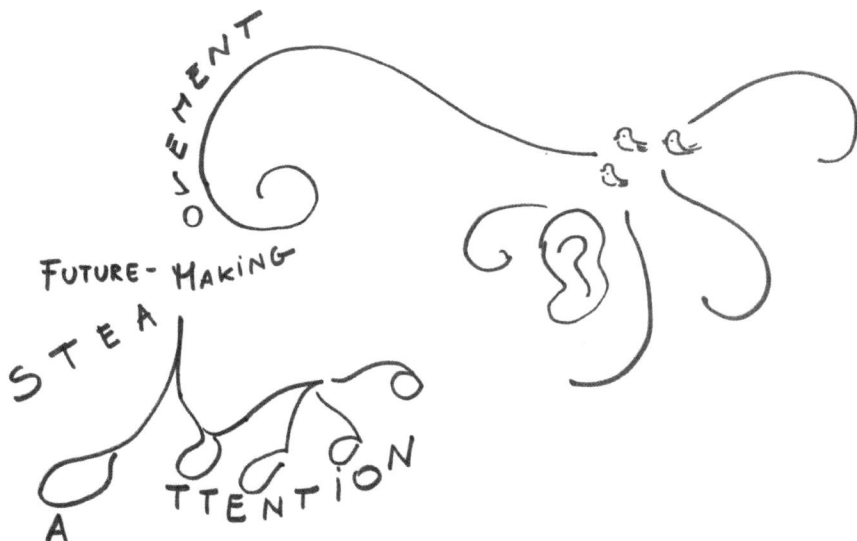

The line in this rhizome becomes more complex as it *moves* between recognisable forms
(i.e. the ear; the ducks) and letters forming words. This visual movement of the line is musical
in the sense that it *brings together* listener, listening and what is being listened to: there is no
separation between observer and observed: boundaries are sites of mutual co-construction and
intra-activity.

Drawing on the critical analysis of knowledge practices outlined in the previous part, Part 2 chapters problematise the acronym "STEAM" by drawing
on the intersection of competing and complementary discourses in science
education.

Seeking to refrain from advancing a particular conception of STEAM as an
identifiable set of "creative pedagogies" for content delivery, this part "troubles" conceptions of science learning as the acquisition of abstract knowledge.
The critique begins from illustrating how knowing in science is fundamentally
embodied. Such recognition troubles the idea of language as "description"
in science to uncover the performative and metaphorical dimensions which
are at the core of the scientific imagination (see particularly Chapter 5, Laura
Colucci-Gray). Looking through scientific practice from a socio-cultural and
embodied perspective, each chapter offers an illustration of how the ways in
which we learn about the world are situated in a "relationship" of listening and

© KONINKLIJKE BRILL NV, LEIDEN, 2020 | DOI: 10.1163/9789004421585_007

attention (see particularly Chapter 6, Edvin Østergaard). Body apparatuses as well as instruments offer different modalities to attend to, affiliate with and tune in with the internal and the external world of human and non-human relations. Embodiment is also presented and discussed here as a way of re-visioning the unique relationship between humans and their tools (musical instruments as well as computers) as a potentially invigorating space for the development of greater sensitivity to the ways in which we perceive, make and inhabit a shared world. For example, a reflection will be offered on the insights achieved by children "rolling" with their bodies (see particularly Chapter 7, Sofie Areljung), or by the differing understandings which may come from different patterns of musical listening and notation.

Chapters in this part explore the potential of introducing a relational ontology in science education.

CHAPTER 5

Developing an Ecological View through STEAM Pedagogies in Science Education

Laura Colucci-Gray

Abstract

Confronted with the multiplicity of environmental and social issues which are exploding around the globe, ideas and practices of scientific research have come under scrutiny. While the complexity of current problems is defying conventional, reductionist approaches, new readings of science and technology are emphasising the embodied and situated nature of knowledge, with greater attention to disciplinary integration, multi-modal communication and dialogue amongst different perspectives. This chapter positions STEAM at the intersection between competing and complementary discourses in science and technology, the descriptive and the performative, operating as part of an extended ecology of material, affective and cognitive relationships.

Adopting a relational and posthumanist ontology, the chapter will discuss scientific and artistic creativities as emerging *at the intersection between mind and nature*, and thus integral to the ways in which as individuals we "attend to" the world. This position foregrounds 'aesthetic perception' – the 'A' in STEAM – as a prime form of knowing, entangled with the lives of others, humans and non-humans, and recovers the ethical dimension in science and technology education. Drawing on the experience from a course in science education involving prospective primary teachers, the chapter will illustrate the pedagogical tenets of this approach and its implications for educating to act in a world in ongoing transformation.

Keywords

aesthetic perception – arts-based methodologies – attention – ecology of the mind – perspective taking – relational ontology

© KONINKLIJKE BRILL NV, LEIDEN, 2020 | DOI: 10.1163/9789004421585_008

1   Introduction: Global Issues and Global Metabolism

With the appearance of Ulrich Beck's *Risk society* – published in 1992 – for the first time open recognition was given to the growing sense of insecurity and danger characterising life in high-tech modern societies. A key factor in this analysis was the study of "unintended consequences" of the systematic modifications of the Earth's ecosystems caused by science and technological innovations.

In the definition given by Barnett (2012), problems of poverty, equality, wellbeing and sustainability are fundamentally "wicked problems", for which there are no ready-made solutions, and which arise on an ongoing basis from the actions that people take *in their environments.* Impacts and consequences are no longer contained at the local level, or within laboratories, in the same manner in which the relationship between science and technology is no longer contained within the dichotomy of theory and practice. Artificial intelligence, robotics and computing machines are entering the reality of everyday life without a firm theoretical basis upon which to predict the implications and consequences of such developments (Cerutti, 2018).

In this sense, the "wickedness" points to a sense of the formidability of effects which continuously exceed the heuristic powers of the knowledge systems from which they originated. More fundamentally, such changes are indicative of the fact that *nature* has entered the realm of human responsibility, profoundly challenging consolidated perceptions of humans and environment, and raising significant ethical questions for everyone involved. As Donna Haraway argues, the time of the Capitalocene with its focus on 'Species Man and its Tools' must give way to the Chtulucene, a time made of "ongoing multispecies stories and practices of becoming-with in times that remain at stake, in precarious times" (Haraway, 2016: 55). Of interest in Haraway's account is the critical stance towards human agency which is not positioned as external to "nature" and worldly phenomena. Rather, humans are viewed as "nexuses" of entangled material practices "in generative friction, or generative enfolding, rather than opposition" (Haraway, 2016: 61).

Such conditions call for a different stance towards the Earth, moving from a description of impacts to a dynamic, physiological approach, which in science has been described through the concept of global metabolism (Haberl, 2001). Drawing on the contributions of systems biology, a metabolic view focuses both on *products and transformations*, which enable living organisms to continuously build themselves and their own environment (Nicholson & Dupré, 2018). So "nothing makes itself", continues Haraway (2016: 58), as all beings are "collectively producing each other, as complex, dynamic, responsive, situated, historical systems" (Haraway, 2016: 68): what Haraway called Sympoiesis – or "making-with". Taking this view, this chapter argues for the necessity of acknowledging different and complementary approaches to knowing – drawing on both sciences and arts creativities – to understand how products and ideas, however defined, are both emerging and continuously re-made through the questioning of boundaries in material relationships. Such view entails a shift in thinking about science as a body of knowledge describing the world 'out there', to a process of 'making with' the research matter, whereby the process of 'doing' matters to the process of 'knowing', in dialectical relationship.

In delineating this line of argument, a range of authors are featured, from anthropology, to philosophy of science and education, with a particular focus on Gregory Bateson, whose ideas have preceded and informed current understandings of a relational, or ecological, view of the world. From this premise, first I discuss the limitations of a way of thinking focused on mental representations to advance the importance of a more sophisticated empiricism, which takes account of sensorial perception and aesthetic judgement in first person inquiry. In the second part of the chapter, I illustrate an instance from a course in science education in which students were introduced to arts-based approaches to observe and make sense of a flooded area which manifested itself with the emergence of a new "form". This is in itself a Batesonian approach: to use an instance from experience as a "metalogue" to revisit and illustrate habits of thinking which contribute to creating problems or obstacles to our perception, and to introducing a new perspective. Specifically, in the empirical section, I illustrate the dialectic between representation and perception, drawing on affective and aesthetic methods of inquiry.

The chapter concludes by configuring STEAM as a pedagogical stance with bearing significant implications for future-making education in general, and science education in particular; it demands teachers and educational researchers to find ways of teaching and undertaking research which encourage students to live through the performative space, to address diverse creativities of form, relationship and ways of communicating in a complex world.

2   Changing Conception of Science and Society: The Invitation
       to Dialogue

As outlined earlier, the recognition of wicked problems in science and society has given rise over the years to a reformulation of what was known as the contract between scientist and citizens. The publication of *Citizen science* by Alan Irwin in 1995 was a historical cornerstone in the field of social studies of science, giving way to new arguments about the roles and responsibilities of scientists vis-à-vis environmental questions. In the first instance, the nature of wicked problems was recognised, in the main, as a problem of data and information which could be best collected "at the site of action" and "at the point of need" by those who are directly affected by the issues at hand. On such a basis, citizens are expected to collect evidence of impacts and contribute such evidence to public debates. This line of thinking is recognisable in the current burgeoning number of citizen science initiatives, especially in the field of conservation biology: digital tools are deployed to gather large-scale information from lay people, mainly volunteers (Pagès et al., 2019), in order to fulfil policy expectations of socially relevant and socially responsible research.

Another line of thinking emerging around the same time as Irwin's book called for acknowledgment of the contested nature of what may be considered and construed as "evidence", by taking account of the expertise, but also the different cultural experiences and levels of involvement, of different stakeholders. In 1993, Funtowicz and Ravetz stated that under uncertain conditions – when the facts are contested and the stakes are high – there is a need to reformulate the contract between science and society, in order to grossly reframe Western science as one of the many, different legitimate perspectives on the world. In this view, the inquiry process would be open to a variety of disciplines – engaged in inter- and transdisciplinary exchanges – but also to the testimonies and understandings of the non-experts, included as part of an "extended peer community". The authors called this process "post-normal science" to radicalise the production of knowledge in society by "expertising democracy" and fundamentally, by "democratising expertise" (Liberatore & Funtowicz, 2003).

Faced with irreducible uncertainty, a new paradigm for knowledge production is thus being advanced based on some form of "connectivity" between different systems of knowledge, opening out towards dialogue between people, communities and cultures.

In philosophy, this approach has found illustration in the practice of dialogical dialogue (Hall, 2003), which begins from the assumption that the other is also an original source of human understanding, and that at some level the people who enter the dialogue have the capacity to communicate their unique experiences and understandings to each other: "dialogue seeks truth by trusting the other, just as dialectics pursues truth by trusting the order of things, the value of reason and weighty arguments" (Panikkar, as quoted in Hall, 2003).

Interpersonal dialogue focuses on the mutual testimonies of those involved in the process, keeping in mind that what the other brings is not a critique of personal ideas, but the witnessing of their experience, with their own values and systems of meanings. Entering dialogue as a "plurality of perspectives" is thus considered as enhancing both procedural legitimacy (through inclusiveness) and quality of knowledge (through extended peer review)" (Liberatore & Funtowicz, 2003: 149). Replacing the idea of a rigorous scientific "demonstration", this approach sought to expand the role of citizens from data collectors to "critics" and "creators", participating in a process of learning with epistemic and ethical sophistication, leading to "meaningful socio-ecological outcomes" (Dillon, Stevenson, & Wals, 2016).

3   Perspective-Taking

In this view, citizens and scientists alike are invited to take a much more significant role – and responsibility – in handling the res publica, for the assumption embedded in this form of dialogical and pluralist inquiry is that participation of all stakeholders would lead to a change of fundamental beliefs about what is deemed to be good and valuable for different people. Equally, if pluralism and dialogue permeates the public ethos, an important role is also played by education and the extent to which curricula and practices can prepare students to engage in meaningful dialogical exchanges.

In previous papers (Colucci-Gray et al., 2006; Colucci-Gray, 2009), I have explored with some colleagues the characteristics of the learning processes leading participants to acquire the communicative competences for dialogue. I deployed role plays as a methodology of choice to simulate the process of public participation, thus drawing on the performative power of drama to motivate students to act as part of a "high-stakes" decision-making process, and make sense of their ideas about the roles of science and technology in society (Colucci-Gray & Camino, 2016). Being a hybrid construct of cognitive and performative thinking, role playing is one of the most fundamental ways for humans to learn about how to act in social life, and to anticipate other people's actions, as children learn to pick up on the values and attitudes of their family members. Specifically, by taking on a role in the simulated scenario, students experienced the significance of coordinating different perspectives, not simply as a means to achieve a "more complete picture" of the issue, but as a way of understanding how different perspectives allow for radically different ways of thinking and being in the world.

Those earlier considerations contributed to an emerging agenda in science education concerned with the critical interface between science and democracy (see Bencze, 2017; Carlone et al., 2016, amongst others), arguing for a science education that enables students to be competent in the practice of democratic participation. However, what we did not sufficiently consider was that, in order for such an enlarged, civic perspective to take hold, a different and enlarged take on scientific knowledge would also be required; one which, following Wallace (2000), recognises the subjective realm of human perception, reasoning and language as an integral part of scientific inquiry, and situated at the roots of scientific creativity, rather than in opposition to it, as the old scientific materialism would have it.

Methodologically, this meant seeking to understand further the process of perspective taking in order to go beyond the idea of dialogue as a dyadic exchange of words between people, but more deeply, as a means to reformulate the ways in which we "draw the boundaries" that define ourselves, and the way we perceive ourselves in relation to other creatures. In practice, as Affifi highlighted, referring to the works of Gregory Bateson and John Dewey, "humans would have to continuously reconstruct their context so that they can work towards promoting democratic community aims" (Affifi, 2014: 580). To this purpose, I will now explore in greater detail the emergence of the "relational" view across the sciences, and how creativities in science and arts can be engaged to support greater integration across competing and complementary discourses in science and technology.

4   The Ambiguities and Challenges of "Seeing" Relationally in Science

Hutchins (2010) talks about cognitive ecology as the study of cognitive phenomena in context. In this view, cognition is not viewed simply as a logical process but as a biological phenomenon, subject as such by social and cultural factors. Drawing on the earlier work of Gregory Bateson (1972), with the concept of cognitive ecology, Hutchins refers to a metaphor for bringing together cognition with the broader social-environmental context, in a process of mutual co-production: "an understanding of cognitive phenomena must include a consideration of the environments in which cognitive processes develop and operate" (Hutchins, 2010: 706). Bateson showed the interconnections between the loops that define the mind and those which define the body, as cognitive processes are "extended" over the body-mind-environment complex. He famously illustrated this principle with a thought experiment, the case of the blind mind with a stick. Bateson wrote:

> Suppose I am a blind man, and I use a stick. I go tap, tap, tap. Where do *I* start? Is my mental system bounded at the handle of the stick? Is it bounded by my skin? Does it start halfway up the stick? ... If what you are

trying to explain is a given piece of behavior, such as the locomotion of the blind man, then, for this purpose, you will need the street, the stick, the man; the street, the stick, and so on, round and round. (Bateson, 1972: 459)

Bateson's work challenges the conventional, cognitivist perspective of psychology according to which cognition is bounded inside the brain, to advance an evolutionary view of cognitive processing as the dense web of "networks of pathways of messages" (1972: 251) across the long arch of the body. Some areas of the networks however will be denser or less dense than others. Key to such "density" is the act of boundary setting, which has been explored to a large extent across a range of disciplines, from philosophy and religion to cellular biology.

As Raimon Panikkar (1978) reported, the nature of scientific thinking is profoundly determined and influenced by the distinctive features of its method: the process involves actively extracting a section from a larger portion of reality, and this is usually and most notably the part which can be measured. All measures are then linked by means of deductive, logical operations and form the basis for the formulation of laws describing the behaviour of phenomena. This analysis cast light on one of the main characteristics of modern scientific inquiry in the Western world: the physical and conceptual ability to separate, circumscribe and define forms and phenomena and to bring them into relation (Woese, 2004), as exemplified by classifications based on differences and similarities to the ordering and groupings of various organisational levels.

However, a distinction exists between empirical reductionism, as a mode of analysis, and fundamentalist reductionism, rooted in the way of thinking of nineteenth-century classical physics, and which is in essence metaphysical: "It is ipso facto a statement about the nature of the world: living systems (like all else) can be completely understood in terms of the properties of their constituent parts" (Woese, 2004: 174). In his analysis of biology of the twentieth century, Woese (2004) cast light on how fundamentalist reductionism completely retooled the biologist's sense of what is important and what is fundamental, to the extent that those biological phenomena which were holistic, metaphysically challenging and not fundamentally understandable as collections of parts stopped being the concern of molecular biologists. Consequently, epistemological understandings of biology as a discipline influenced how biological knowledge was organised, the structure of academic curricula, the nature of biological disciplines and textbooks, and the priorities of funding agencies (Woese, 2004).

So, reductionism is not only a set of methods justified by the specific needs of the discipline, but it is also a social construct, which develops from the cultural and political constructions of "nature". As Wallace maintains, the act of separating the objective mind from nature (intended as that which can be scrutable and amenable to empirical investigation) has had the dramatic consequence of drawing scientists' attention away from the mind; similarly, consciousness, "being out of sight", naturally "dropped out of scientifically experienced reality altogether" (Wallace, 2000: 65).

The result is the well-known separation of knowledge from values and, most dramatically, the division between knowledge and human experience, including the possibility of understanding more fully our own human condition as sensing beings. For example, in an interesting account of the communication of the risks of earthquakes in the region of L'Aquila in Italy, Benessia and De Marchi (2017) point out the problem with entrusting scientific knowledge and its baggage of objectivity and uncertainty as the only route to policy making. Acutely, the authors signal the issues arising at the levels of the personal and ethical spheres of scientific practice: "the lack of a critical and reflexive attitude about the context, the aims and the values implied in that knowledge causes the emergence of contradictions, conflicts and most of all possible failures in terms of citizens' safety" (Benessia & De Marchi, 2017: 43). This recognition calls for a deeper and renovated understanding of the ways in which scientific thinking and scientific creativity develop, to overcome given assumptions about knowledge. In what follows I will bring together theoretical insights and perspectives from authors working at the intersection between sciences and the arts.

5   What Matters in Arts and Science Creativities?

Drawing on the insights of quantum mechanics and modern logic, Hillary Putnam (1988) argued that, as the circle of science expands – in terms of scale and magnitude of issues addressed – paradoxes indeed emerge, demonstrating that a God's eye view – or a view *from nowhere* – is impossible to achieve both in principle and in practice. For example, in quantum mechanics, the observer can consider any totality other than the one that includes the observer in the act of performing the experiment; the observer must always remain outside of the system. The implication is that human subjectivity will always exceed any closed system and cannot be completely objectified to validate one's knowledge. A similar set of reflections have also been advanced more recently in relation to big data in biology (see Leonelli, 2019): contrary to the belief of an empirical science which can finally describe "how the world is", no matter how complex, observations and measurements are always situated in a specific framework (Bogen, 2013), and the instruments used to generate those data are built to satisfy specific research agendas (Rheinberger, 2011).

Building on these insights, Leonelli (2019) has argued that data are "relational"; in other words, what is taken as "data" is subjected to change depending on the goals and methods used to generate and process such data as evidence, within a specific investigation. In addition, as the physicist John Bell showed, quantum mechanics is incompatible with the idea of an underlying reality resembling the world at the macroscopic level, which can be divided into parts linked by causal relationships. Rather, as Niels Bohr (1937) posited, it is not possible to identify an independent reality, either as a discrete phenomenon or as a product of a separate observer, because quantum particles are more appropriately measured as large-scale *aggregates* consisting entirely of interactions and relationships. In this view, data are relational not only on the basis of the cultural context affecting the researcher, but also ontologically, that is, they are part of a complex reality which cannot exist independently of the observer.

Such understandings have been revisited by contemporary feminist theorists such as Karen Barad (2007), pointing to the very act of the observation as a form of intra-action with the observed reality. In the manner of the diffraction of light waves through a surface, observing is a verb which cannot be disentangled from the organism as much as the organism cannot be extricated by the web of material and relational exchanges of which it is a part. Understanding the process of observation as "intra-action" posits the necessity to move towards a more sophisticated empiricism, one which takes human experience and human perception as the starting point for inquiry. It is at this important junction that the philosophy of science appears to pay increasing attention to the realm of the arts, as reported by Fritjof Capra (2008) and more recently Tom McLeish (2019), turning to the work of Leonardo Da Vinci. Specifically, he noted that Leonardo's quest to capture a complex reality through the notion of "perspective" was "nothing else than a thorough knowledge of the function of the eye" (Capra, 2008: 217). With this insight, he carefully investigated the pathways of sensory impressions generated by two moving eyes (as opposed to the fixed viewpoints of earlier studies), including the effects of atmosphere on visual perception.

Leonardo's newly elaborated theory of perspective went well beyond the linear perspective of his predecessors to develop those characteristic features of "dreaminess", "fuzziness" and poetic feel which characterise his painted works. According to McLeish (2019), what artistic and scientific imagination have in common is the commitment to imagine/give shape to what is not yet perceived. In the work of Leonardo, we note the perduring effort to bring together multiple observations of a phenomenon within a single drawing, giving the general impression of "a line in movement" as manifested in his celebrated drawing of "Water falling upon water", in which he is concerned with meticulous analysis of different types of water turbulence. Even when he was set to produce a realistic image of objects, "he blurred the outlines with his famous sfumato technique in order to represent them as they actually appear to the human eye" (Capra, 2008: 196).

In a way that is not dissimilar from Barad's (2007) notion of diffraction, the process of knowing which arises from a relational, ontological stance can be described as a form of co-creation between mind and material, a journey through which an initial idea becomes steadily neater, and progressively changes our initial assumptions about its form, contours or constituent parts. We can recognise some affinity with Leonardo's method here, in the attempt to render the detail of anatomical observation through the combination of different graphical techniques: individual parts separated from the whole, labelling of portions of the body and diagrams showing the functional relationships between anatomical forms. Yet, his concern was always to understand how different parts related to each other, in a way that reminds us of what McLeish refers to as the "boundary between representation and abstraction" (2019: 100). Such a boundary is continuously negotiated "as a battle" between what the artist conceives and the canvas, through a process of clearing of perception, attempting to "see" beyond the imperfections of our senses. Quoting Leonardo, "because by indistinct things the mind is stimulated to new inventions" (Da Vinci, as quoted in McLeish, 2019: 101).

Leonardo's illustrations are significant in showing why science matters in setting the foundations for a method in STEAM pedagogy. If, on the one hand, scientific and technological developments have led to the belief that creativity in science is largely aimed at remaking the Earth to suit human needs, on the other hand, current thinking in science is proposing a different view, which requires us to think, know and act *from within*, that is, as part of the web of sensorial, contextual and dynamic interrelations which connect us to others and to ourselves. This particular stance has been well explored in arts creativities, offering a set of methods and principles which are intended to correspond with new scientific insights. We now return to the work of Bateson to outline the implications for science education.

6   Aesthetic Perception and the Sensorium

Bateson's major insight was not that we must be nice to the environment, but that there is *a fundamental flaw in the way humans relate to the whole of which we are a part*: these are "pathologies of epistemology" (Bateson, 1972: 478). His critique was directed specifically at the linear and analytic ways of thinking that feed conscious purpose, for he saw them as inhibiting the unconscious and recursive processes upon which all creative art and science depend. In order to identify the quality of relational thinking he was seeking to describe; he used the word "grace" to indicate a way of recognising and re-accessing the sacred through aesthetic experience. Central to Bateson's quest was "truth" as metaphorically held in art and sacrament, and that which cannot be consciously accessed or told (Reason, 2007). Peter Reason provided this insightful summary:

> Bateson argued that artistic process, as both creative activity and active appreciation, is a tool for recovering the grace of embeddedness in the natural world. Art, because it is not subject to purposive, language-bound rationality, is capable of re-linking us with our context. (2007: 34)

Hence one of Bateson's most penetrating insights is that through aesthetic experience we are able to re-access much of the systemic wisdom that total reliance on conscious thought, purpose and intention – which typically drives technoscientific enterprise – has overlaid and largely sealed off from our perception. This insight opens the way to an appreciation of the phenomenological dimensions of scientific inquiry which have been obscured by the rationalist view. There are numerous contributions from scientists who sought to explore further the ways in which their work is rooted in their own sensorial experience of the world and how such embodied experience is at the heart of the ideas, imagery and conceptions formulating their thinking. For example, as Root-Bernstein argues, aesthetics is a form of cognition, for "scientists think not in equations or words or other logical abstractions, but emotionally and sensually" (2002: 61). It is important to emphasise visual and aural images, kinaesthetic sensibility but also proprioceptive feelings and the ability to perceive patterns, repetitions and analogies. Robert B. Woodward proposes:

> It is the *sensuous* elements which play so large a role in my attraction to chemistry. I love crystals, the beauty of their form – and their formation; liquids, dormant, distilling, sloshing(!); swirling, the fumes; the odors – good and bad; the rainbow of colors; the gleaming vessels of every size, shape, and purpose. Much as I might *think* about chemistry, it would not exist for me without these physical, visual, tangible, sensuous things. (1984: 237, emphasis in original)

According to Root-Bernstein (2002), "aesthetic cognition" is a kind of pre-logical and sensual thinking, led by emotions and intuition, which equates the fundamental basis of all scientific problem solving to modes of thinking and doing which are "similar if not identical" to those associated with the arts. The "experience of knowing what one feels" and "feeling what one knows" are very specific forms of understanding rooted in one's body that he calls "synosia". *Synosia* arises from the combination of sense and sensibility, and from an elision of the word *synaesthesia* (to combine senses) and *gnosis* (to know). An explicit translation process is required before ideas can be communicated and tested logically, and such a process of analysis often occurs "pictorially not verbally", and it is at the basis of creative scientific thinking. Many of the best scientists deliberately seek to acquire a complete "feel" for the systems they study (see Chapter 7 by Sofie Areljung, this volume), reporting that they are actually able to "become" part of the system, imagining what it is like to experience the world by "empathising" or "sympathising", taking the perspective of some component. As Martin Buber explained:

> Empathy means to glide with one's own feeling into the dynamic structure of an object, a pillar or a crystal or the branch of a tree, or even of an animal or a man, and as it were to trace it from within, understanding the formation and motoriality (*Bewegtheit*) of the object with perceptions of one's own muscles: it means to "transpose" oneself over there and in there. (Buber, 1920: 34)

While not uncommon in the history and philosophy of science, the "pictorial" in the form of metaphorical and analogical thinking has been recovered again in recent works on cognition, drawing on the earlier contributions of John Dewey and his understanding of the human organism as the "body-mind". Dewey's account foregrounds the sensorium, that is, the extended set of bodily operations which enable the ongoing tuning of oneself in space; the sensorium is at the heart of one's sense of "being", whereby perception in movement is at the heart of all action. Following Dewey (1896), the complexity of human thought, its reflective and linguistic abilities, and its analytical faculties cannot be disentangled from the physical limits deriving from its nature of "embodied cognition" (Gallese & Lakoff, 2005; Lakoff & Johnson, 1999).

Taking this insight further, both Barad (2007) and Haraway (2016) refer to the term "diffraction" to express the inherent entanglement of memories, affect and visual/sensorial material involved in any act of observation. Hence, the recognition of the sensorium challenges earlier constructs of empirical knowledge as derived uniquely from the use of instruments – and the body as subservient to their use. Epistemologically but also educationally, it becomes paramount to pay greater attention to our ability and modalities of perceiving, as our perception will affect the ways in which we "think" – and how we 'language' – the world and our place within it. As William James reported in *The principles of psychology* (1950: 424): "each of us literally chooses, by his way of attending to things, what sort of a universe he shall appear to himself to inhabit", and such "attending to" sits at the very root of judgement, character and will. According to James, an education which could offer practical directions for improving the faculty of attention would indeed be an education par excellence.

7   **Pedagogy Matters: Experiments of Knowing Relationally through STEAM**

Following the insights offered so far, and specifically thinking with the relational framing of Gregory Bateson, it is clear that "pedagogy matters", for we need to develop educational forms that are robustly congruent with the issues addressed. As Reason describes, the major purpose of educational practice is to fundamentally re-think the ways in which we teach, for "more of the same kind of education, even with different content, will not bring about the change of mind required" (Reason, 2007: 29). STEAM in this context is not offered as an improved set of teaching tools to transfer pre-established notions for explaining the order and functioning of things, but to welcome instead the education of attention by drawing on the power of 'aesthetic perception' – the "As" in STEAM – as the ability to learn from the world as it comes to us – in its variety and changeability.

In seeking to stimulate this form of perceptive and relational knowing in my teaching, I devised a series of activities integrating arts-based approaches to scientific inquiry, as part of an elective module in science education offered to first year university students enrolled in a degree program in primary education.[1] The activity reported here involved the observation of a body of water situated in a park nearby and the use of "drawings-as-text" (see Chapter 8 by Burnard et al., this volume), to support participatory and dialogical inquiry about the nature and formation of this new feature, which bore the circular resemblance of what is commonly referred to as a "pond".

As Barad explains, "knowledge-making practices, including the use and testing of scientific concepts, are material enactments that contribute to, and are a part of, the phenomena we describe" (2007: 32). In this vein, the use of drawings resonated with Gregory Bateson's (1972) "metalogues", which he described as a "conversation about a problematic subject", whereby "not only do the participants discuss the problem, but the structure of the conversation as a whole is also relevant to the same subject" (Bateson, 1972: 21). Bateson's metalogues typically involve the use of language to produce recursive iterations – or "patterns of thinking" – which are being explored during the conversation. Taking this idea further into my practice, the purpose of the drawings was indeed to give voice to students' embodied knowledge and experiences, but the drawings themselves were also 'experiments' in *knowing relationally*. I was interested in the ways students drew upon their experiential awareness to make sense of the multiple relational arrangements in place – "making-with" and enacting material entanglements – as Haraway (2016) indicated – becoming attentive to emerging forms in a changing world.

8   Is This a Pond?

It was February; the winter had been mild, and the ground was clogged up and wet. The task was "occasioned" by the events: a "watery form" appeared before us in the park. An area of depression in the ground had an uncanny resemblance to a pond, with the ripples in the water, its vegetation and fauna, including some ducks and swans (Figure 5.1). When I had moved to the city, around 13

FIGURE 5.1   A water body in a public park

years ago, I remembered well that this area was a large green space, covered in grass, with a bench in the corner. Bagpipers used to come here, to practise with their instruments out in the field. What had this area become? Its contours are clearly visible at the boundary between water and grass: a body of water inside a public park. But could this be a "pond"? What is being taken as a feature of a pond: its shape? Its flora, or its fauna?

According to Roth (2011), and resonating with the problem of epistemology advanced by Bateson, the reason why we act in the way we do is not linked to an ability to decode instructions from the brain in the manner of a computer following an original representation, but it is related instead to our immanent knowing: "there is no intermediary between some mind and the world. The gap is between this immanent knowing, which is the result of originary movements ... and explicit description" (Roth, 2011: 72). Roth advances the importance of taking the gap between descriptions and immanent knowing "as a matter to be investigated empirically", to be established after the action has occurred.

In the same way in which the question about the formation of the water body occurred to me – through immanent knowing and memory of the place – the exercise was designed to stimulate students' awareness of their own abilities to perceive, and how perception was mediated by the use of language. The word "pond" stimulates memories of round contours and physical boundaries which may be so familiar that they override other possibilities for thinking about how water gathers, especially in the urban context, where water is normally channelled and pumped. Sharing common features in the practice of ecological, appreciative inquiry articulated by Reason (2007), the task sought to engage aesthetic perception as generative of deep questioning of cultural and structural conditioning which may be preventing personal and collective change: "as human persons we participate in and articulate our world through experiential, presentational, propositional and practical ways of knowing" (Reason, 2007: 36).

Divided into small groups of 3–4, students were first asked to walk around the area by trying out a set of different "perspectives", given to them on a list, through which to observe and, in the manner of Buber (1920), to "get a feel for the system" in their own bodies. Examples included taking the perspective of an alien; of a bird; of a tree; of a child; of a fish, to stimulate thinking through value positions and cultural framings, as well as spatial and temporal understandings.

After the first observational phase, they were then asked to make a sketch of the area, leaving it entirely up to them to choose the scale of the drawing, what to include in their sketches as well as the choice of colours and techniques.

Specifically, attention here was given, recursively, to the pattern of drawing "boundaries" in order to make sense of the reality being observed. In the manner of Leonardo, and in line with the practice of understanding "drawings-as-texts", as described earlier, the object of the task was not to make an accurate representation, but to stimulate awareness of different vantage points, in order to clear one's perception of preconceived embodied memories and to stimulate new connections. They completed their drawings in class, and at the end, I asked them to decide as a group whether as a result of their observations they would agree to define the water body as a pond ... or not. They articulated their group decision verbally as part of a plenary discussion and contributed some individual reflections on the course's online discussion board.

9   Relational Knowing

The groups engaged with the task by producing very different sketches, which are reported below. Drawing on the phenomenological studies of van Manen, Stolz (2015) offers a detailed account of themes or "existentials": spatiality (lived space), corporeality (lived body), temporality (lived time) and relationality (lived other). Such themes are common to all human experiences, although importantly they are not all present or accessed in the same modality. This point has tremendous implications for learning, primarily that learning involves the exploration of the world from the perspective of the perceptive "I", thus from where one is – spatially, emotionally, psychologically or ecologically – and thus involves conscious or unconscious awareness of how things relate to each other and to ourselves in the world. Secondly, what appear to us as abstract objects are the result of our ability to define "their contours" by means of aesthetic experience, such as being tactile, kinaesthetic or visual. For example, we define a road as a stretch of ground bounded at the sides by means of the sensations we derive from touching the pattern of grass and gravel under our feet, although it is equally possible for other humans and non-humans to draw other paths – or "roads" – connecting point to point.

  Looking at the drawings through the lenses of such diversity of experiences, the first example (Figure 5.2) shows the observation of a group who decided to walk along the perimeter of the water body: they found that the water appeared to originate from a source, further up the hill, thus the contours of what they were observing did not appear at all round. They drew lines curving along a path, more akin to the shape of a river rather than a conventional pond as it may be found in a Victorian park.[2] When asked if what they drew was a pond, the students were clear that it was not, as what they were seeing that "it did not have defined boundaries": it was more like a "flooded area".

FIGURE 5.2   Flooded area

While the focus of the earlier group was largely on shape, depicting the area from a wide angle, the second group (see Figure 5.3) paid attention instead to the physical appearance of the water. Students drew the water in different and co-existing states, partly liquid and partly frozen, and the shimmering effects on the surface. Such observations go somewhat against conventional teaching of physics in school, whereby "states of matter" are often taught as if occurring in a linear sequence of transformations. In the drawing, the more diffused energy of the sun is depicted as an intra-action with the watery matter, affecting its density and fluidity as a scattering of effects, but also affecting the students' own perception of colour and texture in the watery space.

FIGURE 5.3   Disappearing "contours": Water in different physical states

The next three examples share some commonality in the way they emphasised the confines of the larger water body but also how they featured the presence of non-human inhabitants. By focusing on the "borders" of the pond, it is possible to view the swans (which are not visible in Figures 5.2 and 5.3), as sitting either within (Figure 5.4), or outside the boundaries (Figures 5.5 and 5.6). The drawing of a "boundary" between the water and the grassy area reveals the point of view of the student observers: standing as terrestrial organisms, on two feet on the ground, and clearly seeing themselves as "others" in relation to the swans. However, as was already shown in the two earlier examples, the line of separation may not be clearly defined. In Figure 5.4, this appears as a dotted line, a boundary which can be easily trespassed both by humans and non-humans.

FIGURE 5.4   Swans in the water

Recalling our experience at the park on that day, the students and I had to contend with the potential dangers of coming into contact with the swans. The activity required the students to make close observations, and in so doing they approached the waterline on several occasions, with the swans showing some distress at their presence, physically coming out of the water to make their presence "felt" on the border (Figure 5.5), the marker pen almost embossing the line on the paper.

Being responsible for the safety of the group, I warned the students to monitor the swans' reactions, while at the same time trying to teach them to "communicate" with them, stepping backwards and forwards until we could find a distance that was agreeable for all. The "drawing" of the line was thus both real and metaphorical and, in the words of Barad (2007), we were keeping the intra-actions dynamic and open, making with the materials, creating new relationships. In their visual renderings students adopted a humoristic and almost paradoxical stance – as shown in Figure 5.6 – as they grappled with an obvious

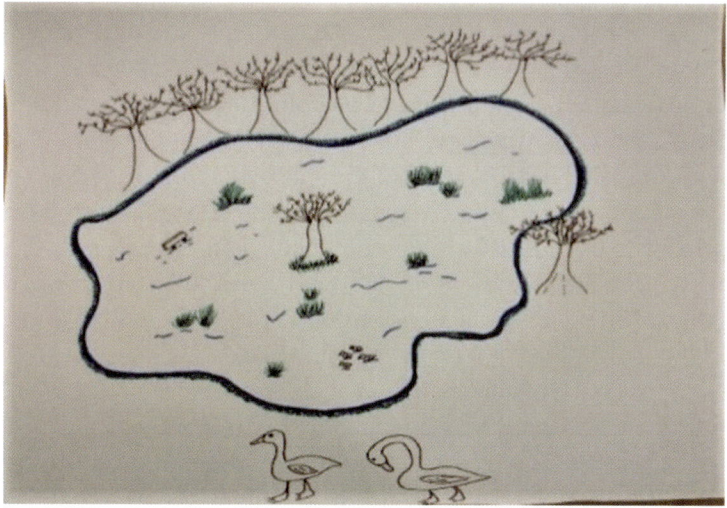

FIGURE 5.5   Swans outside the pond

ambiguity: What are the boundaries of this system? And who defines them? According to which criteria? At the surface level, the water appears to be "fenced off", gathering in a circular form to produce the appearance of a pond in a manicured park. In this view, the water formation "belongs" to the realm of human action. At the level of ecological relationships, however, the line is not so clear, as swans and other species – including a newly found type of plant – had taken the water that gathered in the public park as their home. The students referred to the bush-like grasses in the water (Figure 5.6) as "pond-grass", searching for a new term in the unknown and undefined water formation.

FIGURE 5.6   Negotiating boundaries and pond-grass

Looking at the drawings as a whole, it appeared quite clear to the students that the drawing of a boundary is a relational act, which depends on how we perceive the "other", and thus affects the "what and whom" we seek to include in our inquiries, and the nature of the questions being asked. While the original task was apparently concerned with the definition of an idea (i.e. the pond), the experience of drawing led students to find that this idea sits in vital relationship with other ideas, in a continuum that is difficult to interrupt. Remembering William James, the arts-based approach to the exercise allowed for different ways of attending *to* the world, beyond what might have been the specific and limited purposes of learning biological or ecological principles. The empirical investigation of perception was thus concerned with the nature of embodied experience, which, as van Manen (1997) went on to emphasise, has a temporal structure, one which can never be grasped introspectively, but retrospectively, with an interpretative element that relates the part to the whole, episode to totality. As Barone and Eisner report:

> the contribution of arts-based research is not that it leads to claims in propositional form about states of affairs, but that it addresses complex and often subtle interactions and that it provides an image of those interactions in ways that make them noticeable. In a sense, arts-based research is a heuristic through which we deepen and make more complex our understanding of some aspect of the world. (2011: 3)

In this particular case, we moved from seeking to define a pond, to understanding how different components link together to give rise to a complex ecosystem, and how the relationships between humans and "other non-humans" are negotiated through culture, ethics and politics.

10   Concluding Reflections

When asked to reflect on the experience they had on that day, students made a series of comments about their own experience of learning as well as pointing to important features of scientific thinking. For example, they considered problem solving: "We stood within the surroundings to create a map of the environment around us and solve the problem for ourselves". They also reflected on their ability to handle multiple, open questions: "The activity we had in Seaton Park gave us the opportunity to think a little more by ourselves, with help of questions that was open for many types of answers". They also reflected on inquiries in which different approaches and lines of thinking could be pursued:

> The mapping encouraged us to come up with our solution to the question of the stretch of water being a pond or not. I did not feel at any point I was influenced to pick one or the other and this allowed me to express my own ideas.
>
> By learning through a more student-led approach, children are likely to be more creative, meaning that all work produced will be somewhat different, and the children can then learn from each other's different perspectives and ideas. At Seaton Park we were given very few guidelines on the task meaning we could be creative in our approach.

The examples offered here invite an appreciation of the role of *aesthetic perception* – the "A" in STEAM – not only to acquire scientific skills, but to gain greater awareness of the ways in which we understand the community of Gaia, and develop greater responsibility for how we partake in our biotic relationships. As Affifi (2014) reports, *democratic dialogue* entails the ability to listen to and communicate with others that are different from ourselves. As we have seen over the course of the chapter, the modalities in which we enter into such communication are "framed" by language, cultural sensitivity and habits (Dewey, 1896). It takes an embodied experience to enable such habits of thinking and doing to emerge and become visible in the gestures of the hand, the choices of materials, the traces made on the ground as well as on paper. As Luigina Mortari states, the reconstruction of an idea, take for example the "pond" or the behaviour of the swans, means "to draw the web of cognitive relations in which this idea takes shape and changes" (2013: 195).

I argue that, as educators, we have an ethical responsibility to inquire into the nature of such "framings" and be open to assessing how they may be enhanced or significantly changed through science and technology education. For example, if economic drivers support less diverse forms of social and biological life (such as constructing roads cutting through communities or encouraging farming practices which destroy the soil and local knowledges), the resulting context will fundamentally disarm democratic dialogue. Such "disarming" is not simply ideological but physical, for boundaries are set relationally, and affect the ways in which materials and energy flow through complex systems, and how inequities are configured as a result: "it matters what relations relate relations" (Haraway, 2016: 35).

From this position, the development of *aesthetic judgements* is central to STEAM configurings as the capacity to go beyond the purely cognitive and be attentive to what counts, what matters, what is worthy of one's attention, what is beautiful, and what is grotesque. Through aesthetic sensibility it is thus possible to reconcile the hard, functional STEM subjects with a cognitive and affective ecology, in which we can learn to explore the unexpected and the unknown, and to sharpen our ability to "feel our presence" in the world. In this sense, I am reminded of Erin Manning's idea of being an 'intensive participant' by "coming-into-eventness of the field of relations" (Manning, 2013: 101). The relational capacity of being an intensive participant is always stretching the limits of predictability and form, with the implication that being a participant is not mandatory or prescriptive. Participation – and learning – is "making-with" within an ecology of relations.

I will conclude with a final entry from one of the students. One day at the end of the course, I asked students for their permission to access their drawings and comments on the discussion board. I had been invited to talk about the course at a conference and so I invited the students to share – if they wished – something they felt had been particularly significant for them. While all students consented to the use of their products, a girl responded to my invitation for additional contributions. She sent a photograph (Figure 5.7) that she took the day we went to the park, with some accompanying text:

FIGURE 5.7
"To paint a water lily" by
Ted Hughes

I took the picture on the 4th of February 2016. The reason I took the picture was because I liked how the sun beamed through the tree and found the reflection on the pond interesting. To me, the picture shows the two contrasts of above the water and below, how the sun is out, blue sky and clouds causing quite a calm scene compared to the water being quite dark suggesting the fear of the unknown.

The way I interpreted the picture was that below the water was so different to above the water and it was trying to hide something by showing a reflection instead. It reminded me of the poem "To Paint A Waterlily" by Ted Hughes.

Taking photographs was not a requirement of the task, and as a lecturer who partook in the activity with the students, I was both pleased and surprised to see that more had been happening on that day than what I had anticipated. This picture was shared by the students to convey not simply what was 'significant' from what Bateson's referred to as purposeful learning perspective (e.g. learning the science of the pond) but what *mattered* to her on that day, at the start of the course. While the sun was beaming through the trees, she saw the limits of reflection, which hides and conceals what may be lying – only apparently still and untroubled – beneath what we think we already know. Like the "long-necked lily flower" – in Ted Hughes' poem – "which deep in both worlds, can be still as a painting, trembling hardly at all". And so, as educators we need to continue asking how we can support the creative exploration of the limits of our perception; and how we can learn with humility, side by side with the unknown.

Notes

1   The experience reported here was offered in the second session of a 10-week elective course involving 30 students enrolled in the first year of the Degree in Primary Education. Three students on the course chose the module as an elective part of their degrees in Geography and Biological Sciences. The course was offered in the academic year 2016–2017. As the course was open to all students in the University, emphasis was not given to the professional aspects of primary teaching. Instead, the focus was on offering students an opportunity to gain a broader understanding of the nature of scientific inquiry and to embed educational principles and practices in the choice of interactive, dialogical and participatory teaching strategies used on the course.

2   Due to insufficient printing quality, the original image which had been scanned from a photograph of the original work made by the students, was re-drawn by the

author. In re-drawing the image, I have taken care of using a fine line marker – the students had used a lead pencil – to retain the impression of their own original mark. While the drawing is inevitably different from the original, this copy enables the reader to appreciate the shape and contours of the students' perception of 'the pond' not as something 'bold and round' but emerging from long and sinuous lines on the paper.

References

Affifi, R. (2014). Deweyan education and democratic ecologies. *Educational Studies, 50*(6), 573–597.

Barad, K. (2007). *Meeting the universe halfway: Quantum physics and the entanglement of matter and meaning*. Durham, NC: Duke University Press.

Barnett, R. (2012). Learning for an unknown future. *Higher Education Research & Development, 31*, 65–77.

Barone, T., & Eisner, E. (2011). *Arts-based research*. London: Sage.

Bateson, G. (1972). *Steps to an ecology of mind*. Chicago, IL: Chicago University Press.

Beck, U. (1992). *Risk society: Towards a new modernity*. London: Sage.

Bencze, J. L. (Ed.). (2017). *Science & technology education promoting wellbeing for individuals, societies & environments*. Dordrecht: Springer.

Benessia, A., & De Marchi, B. (2017). When the earth shakes … and science with it: The management and communication of uncertainty in the L'Aquila earthquake. *Futures, 91*, 35–45.

Bogen, J. (2013). Theory and observation in science. In E. N. Zalta (Ed.), *The Stanford encyclopedia of philosophy*. Retrieved from http://plato.stanford.edu/archives/spr2013/entries/science-theory-observation/

Bohr, N. (1937). Causality and complementarity. *Philosophy of Science, 4*(3), 289–298.

Buber, M. (1920). *Die Rede, die Lehre, und das Lied*. Leipzig: Inselverlag.

Capra, F. (2008). *The science of Leonardo*. New York, NY: Anchor Books.

Carlone, H. B., Benavides, A., Huffling, L. D., Matthews, C. E., Journell, W., & Tomasek, T. (2016). Field ecology: A modest, but imaginable, contestation of neoliberal science education. *Mind, Culture, and Activity, 23*(3), 199–211.

Cerutti, M. (2018). *Il tempo della complessita*. Turin, Italy: Raffaello Cortina Editore.

Colucci-Gray, L. (2009). Role-play as a tool for learning and participation in a post-normal science framework. In: D. Gray, L. Colucci-Gray, & E. Camino (Eds.), *Science, society and sustainability* (pp. 188–210). New York, NY: Routledge.

Colucci-Gray, L., Barbiero, G., Camino, E., & Gray, D. S. (2006). From scientific literacy to sustainability literacy: An ecological framework for education. *Science Education, 90*(2), 227–252. doi:10.1002/sce.20109

Colucci-Gray, L., & Camino, E. (2016). Looking back and moving sideways: Following the Gandhian approach as the underlying thread for a sustainable science and education. *Visions for Sustainability, 6*, 23–44. doi:10.13135/2384-8677/1869

Dewey, J. (1896). The reflex-arc concept in psychology. *Psychological Review, 3*, 357–370.

Dillon, J., Stevenson, R. B., & Wals, A. (2016). Introduction to the special section: Moving from citizen to civic science to address wicked conservation problems. *Conservation Biology, 30*(3), 450–455.

Funtowicz, S. O., & Ravetz, J. (1993). Science for the post-normal age. *Futures, 25*(7), 739–755.

Gallese, V., & Lakoff, G. (2005). The brain's concepts: The role of the sensory-motor system in conceptual knowledge. *Cognitive Neuropsychology, 22*(3), 455–479.

Haberl, H. (2001). The energetic metabolism of societies, Part I: Accounting concepts. *Journal of Industrial Ecology, 5*(1), 11–33.

Hall, G. (2003, July 4–6). *Multi-faith dialogue in conversation with Raimon Panikkar*. Paper presented at the Australian Association for the Study of Religions Annual Conference, Brisbane. Retrieved August 9, 2019, from https://resource.acu.edu.au/gehall/Hall_Panikkar.htm

Haraway, D. (2016). *Staying with the trouble: Making kin in the Chthulucene*. Durham, NC: Duke University Press.

Hughes, T. (1998). *To paint a water lily, in Lupercal*. London: Faber and Faber.

Hutchins, E. (2010). Cognitive ecology. *Topics in Cognitive Science, 2*, 705–715.

Irwin, A. (1995). *Citizen science: A study of people, expertise and sustainable development*. London: Routledge.

James, W. (1950 [1890]). *The principles of psychology*. New York, NY: Dover.

Lakoff, G., & Johnson, M. (1999). *Philosophy in the flesh: The embodied mind and its challenge to Western thought*. London: Basic Books.

Lenton, T., & Latour, B. (2016). Gaia 2.0. *Science, 361*(6407), 1066–1068.

Leonelli, S. (2019). The challenges of big data biology. *eLife, 8*, e47381. https://doi.org/10.7554/eLife.47381

Liberatore, A., & Funtowicz, S. (2003). "Democratising" expertise, "expertising" democracy: What does this mean, and why bother? *Science and Public Policy, 30*(3), 146–150.

Manning, E. (2013). *Always more than one: individuation's dance*. Durham, NC: Duke University Press.

McLeish, T. (2019). *The poetry and music of science: Comparing creativity in science and art*. Oxford: Oxford University Press.

Mortari, L. (2013). *Aver cura della vita della mente*. Florence, Italy: Carocci Editore.

Nicholson, D. J., & Dupré, J. (2018). *Everything flows: Towards a processual philosophy of biology*. Oxford: Oxford University Press.

Pagès, M., Fischer, A., van der Wal, R., & Lambin, X. (2019). Empowered communities or "cheap labour"? Engaging volunteers in the rationalised management of invasive alien species in Great Britain. *Journal of Environmental Management, 229*, 102–111.

Panikkar, R. (1978). *The intra-religious dialogue*. New York, NY: Paulist Press.

Putnam, H. (1988). *Representation and reality*. Cambridge, MA: MIT University Press.

Reason, P. (2007). Education for ecology: Science, aesthetics, spirit and ceremony. *Management Learning, 38*(1), 27–44.

Rheinberger, H.-J. (2011). Infra-experimentality: From traces to data, from data to patterning facts. *History of Science, 49*, 337–348.

Root-Bernstein, R. (2002). Aesthetic cognition. *International Studies in the Philosophy of Science, 16*(1), 61–77.

Roth, W.-M. (2011). *Passibility: At the limits of the constructivist metaphor*. London: Springer.

Stengers, I. (2015, December 29). The intrusion of Gaia. *An Inquiry into Modes of Existence Blog*. Retrieved August 2, 2019, from http://modesofexistence.org/isabelle-stengers-the-intrusion-of-gaia/

Stolz, S. A. (2015). Embodied learning. *Educational Philosophy and Theory, 47*(5), 474–487.

van Manen, M. (1997). *Researching lived experience: Human science for an action-sensitive pedagogy* (2nd ed.). London: Althouse Press.

Wallace, B. A. (2000). *The taboo of subjectivity: Toward a new science of consciousness*. Oxford: Oxford University Press.

Woese, C. (2004). A new biology for a new century. *Microbiology and Molecular Biology Reviews, 68*(2), 173–186.

Woodward, C. E. (1984). Art and elegance in the synthesis of organic compounds: Robert Burns Woodward. In D. B. Wallace & H. E. Gruber (Eds.), *Creative people at work: Twelve cognitive case studies* (pp. 227–253). New York, NY: Oxford University Press.

CHAPTER 6

Listening in Science Education: Fostering Students' Lifeworld Experiences

Edvin Østergaard

Abstract

STEAM education usually aims to use art and music as tools to enhance learning in the STEM subjects. However, a true merging of the visual arts and music with the STEM subjects presupposes an appreciation of the genuine character and contribution of all the STEAM subjects. This chapter discusses the contribution of musical listening skills to phenomenon-based science education, where the careful investigation of phenomena forms the basis for conceptualisations and theory. Science teacher students are accustomed to using pre-presented concepts to demonstrate or explain phenomena, rather than beginning from lifeworld experiences. Fostering attentive listening, such as through music education, is one way to develop students' sensitivity to how they perceive, understand and inhabit our everyday world. This chapter draws on Husserl's critique of modern science, Harvey's notion of the "ontological reversal", Heidegger's ontology of listening, Ingold's anthropology of the senses and John Cage's notion of more-than-musical listening to explore how attentive listening can give learners a deepened understanding of sensed phenomena. The chapter also discusses possibilities and constraints when it comes to integrating the arts and music into STEM subjects. It proposes that teachers should develop students' understanding of the relations between lifeworld phenomena and their scientific representations, fostering the art of paying attention and connecting to their lifeworlds, as well as expanding their scientific knowledge.

Keywords

acoustics – Cage – Heidegger – Husserl – listening – phenomenology – science education – STEAM

1   Introduction

In the science teacher education program at our university, I conduct an annual session called "Sound and Sensibility" about acoustics phenomena. Here, I ask my students about the significance of training the skill of listening in science teaching. One of my 2019 students answered that listening is part of observation and that it is "an important part of a science school subject because it is through observation that we experience [the world]; we bring with us these experiences into the subject". The student further expanded on the importance of being able to listen:

> Listening is important in many contexts. We can for example hear when we shift gear, we hear when the water is boiling, we hear when the lid of a bottle of lemonade is not screwed on properly – it is important to bring this [experience] into the science lab and into fieldwork.[1]

Here, the student connected the personal experience of everyday listening to school science. By drawing on examples from everyday experiences, the student situates the skill of listening in a context where listening makes sense. As our ears are always engaged in listening, all the time, it is not difficult to find examples. We listen, whether it is a focused listening or a more diffuse form of listening, embracing "the whole of the space/time continuum of sound" (Oliveros, 2005: 13). Our ears bring to us the events in the world; our ears connect us with the time and space of our surroundings. The science education questions are: How can the skill of attentive listening be appreciated and trained in science class? How can science teachers maintain and develop students' relationships to their lifeworlds?

In this chapter, I elaborate on the art of listening and audial awareness within science education. The hub for my discussion is a three-year empirical study in my science teacher education class on acoustics and listening. The purpose of "Sound and Sensibility" is, first, to ground concepts (such as frequency) in experience (such as the sounds of ringing crystal glasses) and, second, to refine students' listening skills. "Sound and Sensibility" is part of the project "The Phenomenology of Audial Experience", where I explore music-science efforts to foster attentive listening in education. My research takes place within the broader discourse of the kinship of aesthetics and science education (e.g., Bellocchi, Quigley, & Otrel-Cass, 2017). In a STEAM education context, it seems fruitful to explore the visual arts' and music's rich tradition of aesthetic practices as well as their potential to open up new understandings and rationalities (Østergaard, 2019b).

The concept of STEAM education is fairly new and lacks a clear-cut defini-tion (Colucci-Gray, Burnard, Cooke, Davis, Gray, & Trowsdale, 2017). It intends to promote and develop the integration of the arts into the subjects science, technology, engineering and mathematics. When we add an A to the acronym STEM, it raises questions concerning: (i) how the arts could be integrated into the STEM subjects, (ii) disciplinary, interdisciplinary and/or transdisciplinary considerations (that is, the level of integration), and (iii) what we mean when we talk about "the arts". When art is included in STEM subjects, the focus seems to be primarily on visual arts and media, not on the performing arts and music (Gershon & Ben-Horin, 2014). Conventionally, music and the visual arts are regarded as different school subjects, even though they have much in com-mon, especially when mirrored against science, technology and mathemat-ics. Following Colucci-Gray et al.'s recommendation to be more explicit about what STEAM is (2017: 8–9), I will here discuss it as an interdisciplinary educa-tional initiative that seeks to strengthen the learning of *all* of the five subjects. I am critical of attempts to use the arts and music as a means to improve sci-ence learning alone. The mutual collaboration between the STEAM subjects should embrace all the subjects – both (in my case) science and music.

My discussion is guided by the following questions: How can we facili-tate our science students' learning the art of paying attention? And how can we – science teacher educators – make our teacher students trust their life-world experiences? My focus is primarily on the skill of listening itself and its potential for bridging students' rich lifeworld experiences and school science.

I start by broadening the background of the discussion. I explore, first, the phenomenology of Husserl and his critique of modern science, leading to what Harvey (1989) coined *the ontological reversal*; second, Heidegger and his ontol-ogy of listening; and third, Ingold's anthropology of the senses and John Cage's notion of more-than-musical listening. After this, I present and discuss some findings from the teaching unit "Sound and Sensibility". In the final section, I will discuss some challenges of teaching listening and acoustics in parallel as well as possibilities and constraints when it comes to integrating the arts and music into STEM subjects.

2   Experiencing the World

With a starting point in phenomenological philosophy, I will now develop the foundation of sensing and attentive listening as active engagement in/with the world.

2.1   *The Lifeworld as Science's "Forgotten Meaning-Fundament"*

In his posthumous work, *The crises of the European sciences*, Edmund Husserl discusses the bases of natural sciences. He uses his grasp of the lifeworld as the source and basis of all knowledge of reality to ground his critique of what he refers to as "Galilean science", a scientific process by which sensible qualities (qualities perceived by the senses) are turned into measurable units. Husserl regards Galilean science as the starting point for a cultural and historical process of a *mathematisation of nature*; the process by which "*nature itself* is idealized under the guidance of the new mathematics", and as a result, "nature itself becomes – to express it a modern way – a mathematical manifold" (Husserl, 1970: 23, emphasis in original). To understand the laws of nature, it is made measurable by idealisation and (mathematical) quantification. The mathematically described and idealised world, Husserl claims, is mistaken for the everyday world. There has been

> [a] substitution of the mathematically substructed world of idealities for the only real world, the one that is actually given through perception, that is ever experienced and experienceable – our everyday life-world. This substitution was promptly passed on to his successors, the physicists of all the succeeding centuries. (1970: 48–49)

By processes of idealisation and abstraction, science has taken a position above the fluctuating appearances of everyday life, claiming to provide sound knowledge about it. For Husserl, however, science as meaningful human activity presupposes, "both historically and for each new student", a grounding in the lifeworld, "the intuitive surrounding world of life, pre-given for all in common" (121). The lifeworld for a physicist, he explains, "is the world in which he sees his measuring instruments, hears the time-beats, estimates visible magnitudes, etc. – the world in which, furthermore, he knows himself to be included with all his activity and all his theoretical ideas" (121). The lifeworld is neither an object nor a conceptual framework. It is the world in which we live our lives. Husserl was himself not critical of natural science or mathematics, being a mathematician who delighted in theory, especially in axiomatics (Heelan, 1987). What Husserl criticised about natural sciences was not the use of mathematical models *per se*, "but that, (generally) led by a false metaphysics, it (generally) mistook them for reality" (1970: 370). Husserl's critique implies a re-turning toward human lifeworld experience as it appears prior to conceptualisations; a return to the lifeworld as experiential ground.

Following Husserl's notion of the lifeworld as "the forgotten meaning-fundament of natural science" (1970: 48), Harvey (1989) defines *the ontological reversal* as an ontological position where abstract models from science are considered more real than everyday reality itself. "And it is implicitly believed, though rarely professed, that after the world is [mathematically] determined in this fashion, nothing is left over" (1989: 65). Here, models for a "hidden" reality behind experienced phenomena take on a higher ontological status than the experienced phenomena themselves (Dahlin, 2001). This ontological position also seems to form an implicit assumption among science teachers, when teachers use lifeworld objects in class to illustrate abstract models and theories. When teaching about acoustics in physics class, a sine tone[2] is often played to illustrate the wave model.

From a science education perspective, the ontological reversal has consequences for both the value of fostering sense experiences in science class and the value of using the students' personal experiences in the learning process. As long as theoretical, scientific knowledge is taken as the real cause behind everyday experiences, teachers tend to put less emphasis on students' own perceptions and experiences (Dahlin, Østergaard, & Hugo, 2009).

Just as the ontological reversal has some severe consequences for teaching, so does the ontological *re*-reversal; proposing that the ontological primacy of the perceptual lifeworld must replace that of abstract scientific models. Such models are recognised as reductive abstractions that do not explain *everything* about a phenomenon. An explicit emphasis on sense experience in science class, a central claim of phenomenon-based education, aims to balance the major focus on scientific conceptualisation in today's science class.[3] To appreciate sense experience in science class is in line with the intention of restoring the value of students' lifeworld experience (Dahlin, Østergaard & Hugo, 2009). I will return to the challenge of teaching acoustics and training the skills of attentive listening later.

2.2   The Ontology of Listening

Heelan (1987) notes that Husserl's later philosophical works may have been heavily influenced by Martin Heidegger's *Being and time*, particularly when it comes to Husserl's new approach to a philosophy of the natural sciences. In *Being and time*, Heidegger develops the idea of listening as an embodied activity of engagement in the world. Just as we take for granted our being-in-the-world as a primordial foundation, that we *are* and that the world *is*, so the ability to listen is seldom questioned. Heidegger shows that our mostly un-reflected sense experiences form the foundation upon which our meaningful acquaintance with the world rests. Heidegger's term *Dasein* (literally "Being-there") refers to human existence *in* the world, not as one thing related to another thing, "but rather in the sense of being *engaged* with things"

(Gorner, 2007: 4, emphasis in original). For Heidegger, all human experience is embedded in a context, and human experience becomes understandable only in this specific context (Espinet, 2016).

In *Being and time*, Heidegger (1962) differentiates between listening to speech (*Rede*) and hearing other sounds. Acoustically speaking, human speech is, of course, also sounds, but it is different from other sounds because of its immediate claim to intelligibility; speech claims of the human (grown-up) listener that what is spoken is understood. Listening as expectation of meaningful content becomes clearer, Heidegger argues, in those cases "where the speech is indistinct or in a foreign language", because here, "what we proximally hear is *unintelligible* words, and not a multiplicity of tone-data" (207, emphasis in original). Further, Heidegger discusses our audial experience of being-in-the-world by contrasting hearing with our capacity to hearken (*Horchen*). Harkening is "phenomenally still more primordial than what is defined 'in the first instance' as 'hearing' in psychology – the sensing of tones and the perception of sounds" (207). Heidegger does not explicitly refer to music at this point, even with his hint at "sensing of tones". Rather, he opposes noise to the sounds of familiar, everyday objects. The sound of water boiling is familiar to us because it is embedded in our lifeworld activity.

The phenomenon of attentive listening shows our ability to dwell alongside and not opposite to the world's goings on. Hearing and perception of noise are more superficial, Heidegger argues, than hearkening and listening to speech. According to Heidegger's phenomenological space analysis in *Being and time* (1962: 135–148), sounds and listening appear differently in geometrical and existential space, the first being describable by laws of physics, the latter by the pre-scientific, pre-conscious and self-evident space of existence. In existential space, listening is not mere monitoring of wave compressions that reach the ear from an acoustic source. Here, listening is not a sequential process, that is, first, the sound is produced, then transmitted from its source to the ear, and subsequently transformed into meaning. Such a chronology makes sense in geometrical space. In existential space, however, we *already* "hear" the events that we are alongside as meaningful. In existential space, there is no first or afterward; there is only simultaneity. When we say that we hear water boiling, we simultaneously refer to our being-one-with the world's events.

Heidegger's ideas of the meaning of listening in our *Dasein* has proven fruitful in various settings. I will now turn to anthropology and music, and the notion of heightened acoustic awareness of the world's sounds.

2.3   *The Anthropology of the Senses*

Listening is not something we choose to do. Phenomenologically speaking, our ears are constantly at work. The world comes to us as sound as it "stimulates directly to immediate change because it reports a change" (Dewey, 2005: 246). Listening means being part of the changes because sound brings to us "the very movement of the world's coming-into-being" (Ingold, 2000: 245). However, we can choose to pay attention to some sounding events rather than to others. We can also choose to purify the sense of listening just as a violinist can refine the skill of mastering the instrument. By doing so, we need to restore "hearing to its proper place in the sensorium" (246) in a culture marked by visual-spatial language.

A major contribution to restoring the skill of listening comes from the composer John Cage. By directing attention away from conventional settings, the musical performance, or the performing musicians, Cage introduces a new way of listening. He aims to liberate sound from an inherent musical meaning by opening up our ears to the diversity of the world's sounds. Musical listening is thus brought out of the concert hall and into everyday life. The critical task of today, Cage argues, is to teach people how to listen unbiasedly. To open ourselves up to the world,

> we must consider the *ecology* even more than the individual. It is not simply by observing the individuals, but by reintegrating individuals into nature, by opening the world to the individual, that we will get ourselves out of this mess. (Cage, 1981: 56, emphasis in original)

Somewhat unexpectedly, coming from a composer, Cage rejects the possibility of using music to reinforce listening to the surroundings. Music, as it is usually heard, tends to *get in the way* of listening (Cage, 1961). Regarding musical modernism's emancipatory dimensions, "Cage's work is a freedom-from musical listening coupled with a freedom to truly hear what is there to be heard" (Peters, 2018: 3). When discussing the possibility of transfering skills between music and science education, as I have in relation to sustainability education (Østergaard, 2019a), I am sure always to have Cage's warning in the back of my head.

Cage's notion of more-than-musical listening is echoed in environmental artists' idea of a soundscape and disciplines like soundscape ecology and bioacoustics (Østergaard, 2019a). Just as a landscape signifies the environment's visual character, a soundscape is an environment as we hear it. In his critique of the concept of soundscape, the anthropologist Tim Ingold (2011) introduces "taskscape", an array of related activities. For Ingold, the skill of listening is the capability of acting in and in relation to the world, the possibility of "genuine intersubjectivity" and of "a participatory communication of self and other through shared immersion in the stream of sounds" (Ingold, 2000: 247). Embeddedness comprises all senses, a synaesthetic experience rather than the listening sense standing alone. If our hearing is a mode of participatory engagement with/in the environment, Ingold argues, "it is not because it is opposed in this regard to vision, but because we 'hear' with the eyes as well as the ears" (277). When regarding listening and grounding in the world from an embodied perspective, "the environment that we experience, know and move around in is not sliced up along the lines of the sensory pathway by which we enter it" (136). This point is vital to bear in mind to avoid the skill of listening being valued as superior to the other sensorial skills.

Listening is related to the sensation of being rooted and embedded in firm ground (Østergaard, 2017). It would be wrong, however, to suppose that sensory experience is inevitably tied to place. In practice we may be anchored to the ground,

> but it is not light, sound or feeling that holds us down. On the contrary, they contrive to sweep us off our feet. Light floods, sound drowns out … and feeling carries us away. Light, sound and feeling tear at our moorings, just like the wind tears at the limbs of trees rooted to the earth. (Ingold, 2011: 134–135)

Being embedded in the flow of the world's events is to experience "the very movement of the world's coming-into-being" (Ingold, 2000: 245). What are the educational consequences of such a perspective? How does attentive listening support the ways in which science teacher students learn about the world and how they are embedded in the world?

3   Learning about Sound – Learning to Listen

Since 2004, I have taught a phenomenon-based teaching unit on sound and acoustics in the teacher education program at the Norwegian University of Life Sciences. In this section, I will discuss an empirical study where students express their views on and knowledge about sound and the act of listening. Against this background, I discuss approaches to a phenomenological science *Didaktik* as well as efforts to promote listening.

3.1   *Conducting a Lesson on Sound for Science Teacher Students*
"Sound and Sensibility" is an optional course for our science teacher students that lasts for 3 hours and involves four steps. First, the students are asked to close their eyes and carefully listen to their surroundings. They note down

what they hear, and we discuss the relationship between personal sound experiences (e.g., the clear sound of a flute being played) and scientific sound concepts (e.g., frequency). Second, I conduct a guided sound exploration of crystal glasses and bottles with various amounts of water, in addition to other sound objects. Third, the students explore sound-producing objects that I have brought with me (small music boxes, tuning forks, etc.) or what they find in the room. Fourth, we discuss the basic sound concepts (frequency, noise, amplitude, timbre, decibel scale) related to the audial experiences, as well as the relationship between listening experiences and understanding sound using both scientific and everyday concepts. After the teaching session, the students answer a written questionnaire with the following questions: (i) If asked by a person you know is not skilled in science, "What is sound?" what would you answer? (ii) If asked to describe the importance of practising the skill of listening in science education, what would you answer? (iii) If asked to describe your ability to listen, what would you answer?

Typical answers to the first step, where students describe what they hear in the nearby surrounding, are: "people breathing", "the cracking of a light tube", "high-frequency sound of the air ventilator", "sounds from children outside", "moving feet on the floor", "gurgling noise from my own body" and "a door being shut". The answers are descriptions of either the sound itself ("a cracking sound") or the object producing the sound ("people breathing").

I will now present and discuss the students' responses to the three questions from 2016, 2018 and 2019 (responses from 22 students in all). The numbers of statements from the students are put in parentheses (each student made several statements). Under each question, I have grouped the answers into categories.

(i)   Categories concerning answers to the question "what is sound?":
      –   *Sound as waves*: responses like "air as vibrations", "sound waves", "pressure waves", "air compressions", etc. (24)
      –   *Sound as sensation*: responses like "it is what you hear", "sound is a sense experience", "all the different things you experience through hearing", etc. (6).

(ii) Categories concerning the purpose of practising the skill of listening in science education:
      –   *Describe and understand sound*: responses like "listening is an important part of understanding sound", "to understand/capture the sound phenomena", etc. (14)

– *Practice scientific method*: responses like "sense experiences are essential in science education", "sensing is often neglected ... as part of scientific method", etc. (7)
– *Miscellaneous*: responses like "listening ... helps us to concentrate better", "important in discussions and interpersonal relations", etc. (5).

(iii) Categories concerning the students' views on their own ability to listen:
– *High self-assessment*: responses like "yes, I can listen!", "I can hear every single sound and react to it swiftly", etc. (9)
– *Low self-assessment*: responses like "low hearing ability", "I am not a skilled listener", etc. (7)
– *Improve the skill of listening*: responses like "that [the listening ability] I have to practise!", "It is difficult to be attentive, but I will practise it", etc. (6)
– *Miscellaneous*: responses like "[I am] sometimes absent", "when I hear 'pure' sounds, I try to place them on a scare according to which tone the sound resembles the most", etc. (3).

The responses from the students to question (i) show that a majority of them employ the wave model to describe sound. However, when asked to describe what they hear around them, none of the students actually *hears* waves, vibrations or air compressions. What they hear is "sounds from the air ventilator", "a car passing outside" or "a door being shut" – expressions that refer to life-world experiences. In a few statements, the experience of listening is directly connected to the sensation of sound, for example, "all the different things you experience through hearing". In response to question (ii), a majority of the students connect the purpose of listening to understanding and describing the sound. None of the answers indicates listening with a grounding purpose, and only one answer connects listening to interpersonal relations. In only seven statements, the students express a relationship between the skill of listening and scientific methods. The results indicate that the students indeed see the relevance of strengthening audial observation as part of scientific inquiry. However, they seem to be more familiar with sight and visual representations of sound than with employing their listening ability when exploring sound scientifically. The students show a somewhat reluctant attitude toward accepting listening as a useful start to explain sound phenomena. Only a few of them bring in their rich audial experience when conceptualising acoustics. Finally, as a response to question (iii), less than half of the students have a high self-assessment when it comes to personal listening skills. In only six statements, the students express an interest in improving their personal listening skills.

3.2   *Approaches to a Phenomenon-Based Science Didaktik*

This study shows science teacher students' explorative processes and their verbalised lifeworld experiences of being listeners. There seems, however, to be a contradiction between the students' personal audial experiences and the hegemony of visual representations when reflecting on sound. In an earlier study based on "Sound and Sensibility", we concluded that there is a need for science teacher students to develop the courage to use their immediate perceptual lifeworld experiences as raw material when teaching about acoustics (Østergaard & Dahlin, 2009). Ten years later, this conclusion still seems to be valid. Moreover, the recent results emphasise our responsibility as teacher educators to encourage students to trust their listening ability in sound explorations, as well as to support their efforts to bridge audial experience and scientific concepts.

Now, if we consider the students' responses related to the ontological reversal, the assumption that scientific knowledge and abstract models are superior to lifeworld phenomena (Harvey, 1989), the wave model seems to override the students' personal experiences of listening. Also when asked about the purpose of training listening in science subjects, very few of the students express their personal expertise. There are, thus, arguments for an ontological *re*-reversal, an ontological position where lifeworld phenomena have regained their primary position, which has pedagogical implications (Dahlin, Østergaard, & Hugo, 2009). The essential idea of phenomenon-based science education, a phenomenology applied to science teaching and learning, is to practice careful phenomena inquiry (Østergaard, Dahlin, & Hugo, 2008). Here, the careful investigation of phenomena forms the basis for conceptualisations and theory. When aesthetic experience is at the core of phenomenon-based education, it is because aesthetics is equal to sense perception and sensory entanglement with the world rather than to art or beauty (Østergaard, 2019b). "Sound and Sensibility" starts with an exercise of attentive listening. The results presented above raise the question of whether listening is a once and for all given skill or, on the contrary, whether the skill of listening should and could be refined and improved.

For my science teacher students, putting words to what they hear is unusual, probably due to their background as trained scientists (most of them have a master's degree in science before they enter the teacher education program). They seem to have little experience in both accurate sound descriptions and careful listening. After years of science education in school and university, they are accustomed to an *illustrative-deductive* approach to learning science, characterised by using already presented concepts to demonstrate or explain phenomena (Østergaard & Dahlin, 2009). Now, what they meet in "Sound and

Sensibility" is a *genetic-inductive* approach to learning. Here, the students' lifeworld experiences of sound phenomena are not mere illustrations of the (introduced) concepts; rather, both the sound phenomena and the students' former listening experiences form central events to which the student can return to deepen their experience. Here, scientific concepts (i.e., frequency) can give the learner a deepened understanding of the sensed phenomenon. The science teacher could take as a starting point an experience of sound as "all the different things you experience through hearing" and thus incorporate students' experiential knowledge when teaching about sound and listening. To promote listening in science class, first, the students should be encouraged to trust their listening ability and the fact that their ears are extremely exact instruments, and, second, the teacher should intentionally train students' listening skills to facilitate deeper learning.

Thiel (1990) describes an example of a phenomenon-based teaching experience in a teaching lesson for fourth grade science students' exploration of sound. When hitting a tambourine, the students discuss how the sound is produced and how it is possible for them to hear it. The teacher takes on the role of facilitating the children's own intuitive exploration of the phenomenon. The teacher does not judge the students' somewhat unscientific wondering and reasoning. At all times, the teacher acknowledges their listening skills and their eagerness to explore the phenomena; however not without guiding the process. This is an inductive learning process because the students are always in contact with the experience. It is also a genetic process, as the sound concepts are "generated" on the basis of common experiences and furthering discussions.

4   The Potential of Music–Science Cooperation in STEAM Education

After several years of teaching about sound and acoustics, my focus has gradually shifted from: What is sound and how do we understand sound? to: How do we listen, and how does the experience of listening contribute to an understanding of what sound is? Also, I have become more conscious of the way I formulate the questions to which the students respond. A question like "What is sound?" invites them to answer in a fact-oriented manner, especially when posed to sciences-schooled students. This might be a reason why students tend to answer "waves" when asked about sound. However, a question like "Have you heard a sound today? Describe it!" encourages the students to describe sounds more freely as they hear and experience them. If science education is also about educating students' experiences and personal engagement, then such a question is highly relevant (Østergaard, 2017).

How can students be encouraged to refine their attentive listening? As I have discussed elsewhere, there are several possibilities (other than acoustics) for combining science and music in education (Østergaard, 2019b). In biology class, for example, the students can learn to distinguish between bird species according to their different voices. Is this ability akin to music students' learning to distinguish between various instruments in a complex orchestral setting? As Kagan and Kirchberg (2016) claim, persons who stimulate their musical ear have an "aesthetic training in the experience of complexity" (1495). Cooke and Colucci-Gray (2019) report a similar observation. In a project on science and music students, they note that listening to the surroundings is "a means of recognising one's responses and one's role as part of a context" (181). Also in sustainability education, an acoustic sensuousness as heightened awareness of the world's sounds seems to be fundamentally relevant (Østergaard, 2019a).

There are both possibilities and constraints concerning integrating the arts and music into STEM education. First, real integration has the potential to improve learning in all five subjects. Such integration requires, however, a mutual understanding concerning the genuineness of each subject and which aspects and skills from each subject can be shared with other subjects. It further requires skills of interdisciplinary collaboration, skills that most teachers have to learn explicitly. Second, any interdisciplinary educational work will be confronted with constraints concerning current school cultures and the customary division of school subjects. Both teachers and students probably experience the gap between music and science as larger than that between mathematics and science, a fact that requires special attention towards integrating art subjects into the STEM subjects. A true merging of the visual arts and music with the STEM subjects presupposes an acceptance of the genuine character of art and music rather than using them as tools to achieve better results in the science-technology subjects. Finally, perhaps the most significant potential in STEAM education lays in fostering students' sensitivity to how they perceive, make sense of, and relate to the living world. Fostering such sensitivity might counteract the tendency in the current school system to train students to "slice up" the world according to particular school subjects.

It is tempting to anticipate a transfer of trained skills from science class to music class and vice versa. There are, however, very few empirical studies dealing with this question (Østergaard, 2019b). Listening as an observational skill is rarely taught systematically in science class. This is in contrast to the schooling of observation skills in art education and listening skills in music education. Perhaps the interdisciplinary measures implicit in STEAM education provide the proper conditions to train listening skills, connected either to collaboration between two subjects (e.g., music and physics) or to an overall STEAM intention of developing students' sensitivity to the surrounding world. It would be wrong to conclude that there is a lack of positive correlation between music and science education. It does indicate, however, that achieved abilities in distinct subjects are not necessarily readily transferable from one subject to another. Cage (1961) rejects the possibility of using music to reinforce listening to the environment, as musicians and composers are too occupied with the sounds of their own music. For my part, I argue that the fact that musicians and music students are trained in listening implies both an educational tradition and personal experience that can be shared with other subjects and other teachers, especially in STEAM education.

5   The Act of Attentive Listening

When my science teacher students take hold of the wave model when describing what sound is, it is as if one can hear science speaking. It is, with Husserl's notion of the mathematisation of nature, the sound of sense qualities – "moving feet on the floor" – being turned into measurable units – "pressure waves with various speeds and amplitudes". The wave model is, of course, not wrong; the problem occurs when it replaces audial lifeworld experiences as it is regarded as ontologically more valuable. There are thus several problems with the tendency to let models override experience in science class. First, whereas the models are suited to explaining certain aspects of the phenomenon, *all other* aspects of the experienced phenomenon seems to appear as irrelevant. These dimensions tend to be overheard and thus students miss a broad spectrum of rich lifeworld experience that could have been exhibited in class. Second, the very act of aesthetic sensing is degraded to a kind of second-order activity, regarded as neither relevant nor useful in science class. Because wave pressures cannot be heard, students are implicitly taught that hearing is unusable for (theoretically) understanding sound. Here, the teacher lets go of the opportunity to train students' skill of careful listening.

In "Sound and Sensibility", sense explorations form starting points for learning about both scientific and everyday sound concepts (Østergaard & Dahlin, 2009). Here, an underlying teacher attitude is that *phenomena are worth listening to*. Even though we are always bound to relate to representations of an explored phenomenon, the phenomenon will still always be more than the sum of its representations. To avoid confusing an *experienced* phenomenon with the *represented* phenomenon, the teacher should explicitly point to the relation between students' lifeworld phenomena and their derived aspects that are suitable for science class.

Science teachers face some challenges when applying phenomenology to the learning process. Perhaps the most profound one is the challenge of *suspended judgement*. To avoid jumping to conclusions, the teacher should let the phenomenon first sound in its manifold expressions. A plea for a more open, non-judgemental way of observation is echoed in Cage's request for an unbiased form of listening. Whereas Cage refers to musicians' and composers' narrow way of listening (to music), the science teacher might employ an *aesthetic* kind of listening that contrasts with an *explanatory* type of listening. Refining openness toward the manifold aspects of the sensed phenomenon is perhaps the most valuable contribution of music, art, and artistic practice to science education.

Within the context of STEAM education, a genuine fostering of the art of paying attention presupposes an interest in "the Other", be it lifeworld phenomena or the learning student. An ontological re-reversal in science education might for us educators simply start by paying closer attention to what our teacher students experience and how they express these experiences. When a student, as a response to my question on the significance of training listening in science teaching, describes the sound when "the lid of a bottle of lemonade is not screwed on properly", I hear a student connecting to the lifeworld. Training the skills of lifeworld bonding seems to be of vital importance in STEAM education. Fostering attentive listening is connected to the overall goal of developing students' sensitivity to how we perceive, understand and inhabit our everyday world.

Notes

1   Science teacher student with a background in biology, 16 January 2019.
2   A sine tone is an overtone-free tone with a sinusoidal waveform. With very few exceptions (for instance a tuning fork) a sine tone is generated artificially.
3   In Østergaard (2017), I equate sense experience with *aesthetic* experience, a comparison that enables us to discuss the potential kinship of scientific and artistic work in education.

References

Bellocchi, A., Quigley, C., & Otrel-Cass, K. (2017). *Exploring emotions, aesthetics and ellbeing in science education research*. Basel: Springer.
Cage, J. (1961). *Silence*. Middletown, CT: Wesleyan University Press.

Cage, J. (1981). *For the birds*. Boston, MA: Marion Boyars.

Colucci-Gray, L., Burnard, P., Cooke, C., Davis, R., Gray, D., & Trowsdale, J. (2017). *BERA research commission. Reviewing the potential and challenges of developing STEAM education through creative pedagogies for 21st learning: How can school curricula be broadened towards a more responsive, dynamic, and inclusive form of education?* London: British Educational Research Association. doi:10.13140/RG.2.2.22452.76161

Cooke, C., & Colucci-Gray, L. (2019). Complex knowing: Promoting response-ability within music and science teaching education. In C. A. Taylor & A. Bayley (Eds.), *Posthumanism and higher education* (pp. 165–185). London: Palgrave Macmillan. doi:10.1007/978-3-030-14672-6_10

Dahlin, B. (2001). The primacy of cognition – or of perception? A phenomenological critique of the theoretical bases of science education. *Science & Education, 10,* 453–475.

Dahlin, B., Østergaard, E., & Hugo, A. (2009). An argument for reversing the bases of science education – A phenomenological alternative to cognitionism. *NorDiNa, 5*(2), 201–215.

Dewey, J. (2005). *Art as experience*. London: Penguin Books.

Espinet, D. (2016). *Die Phänomenologie des Hörens* [The Phenomenology of Hearing]. Tübingen, Germany: Mohr Siebeck.

Gershon, W. S., & Ben-Horin, O. (2014). Deepening inquiry: What processes of making music can teach us about creativity and ontology for inquiry-based science education. *International Journal of Education & the Arts, 15*(19). Retrieved June 30, 2019, from https://www.scribd.com/document/248216225/International-Journal-of-Education-the-Arts

Gorner, P. (2007). *Heidegger's Being and time: An introduction*. Cambridge: Cambridge University Press.

Harvey, C. W. (1989). *Husserl's phenomenology and the foundations of natural science*. Athens, OH: Ohio University Press.

Heelan, P. A. (1987). Husserl's later philosophy of natural science. *Philosophy of Science, 54*(3), 368–390.

Heidegger, M. (1962). *Being and time* (J. Macquarrie & E. Robinson, Trans.). Oxford: Basil Blackwell.

Husserl, E. (1970). *The crisis of European sciences and transcendental phenomenology* (D. Carr, Trans.). Evanston, IL: Northwestern University Press.

Ingold, T. (2000). *The perception of the environment: Essays on livelihood, dwelling and skill*. London: Routledge.

Ingold, T. (2011). *Being alive: Essays on movement, knowledge and description*. London: Routledge.

Kagan, S., & Kirchberg, V. (2016). Music and sustainability: Organizational cultures towards creative resilience – A review. *Journal of Cleaner Production, 135,* 1487–1502.

Oliveros, P. (2005). *Deep listening: A composer's sound practice*. New York, NY: iUniverse.

Østergaard, E. (2017). Earth at rest: Aesthetic experience and students' grounding in science education. *Science & Education, 26*, 557–581.

Østergaard, E. (2019a). Music and sustainability education – A contradiction? *Acta Didactica.* doi:10.5617/adno.6452

Østergaard, E. (2019b). The attentive ear. *Journal of Aesthetic Education 53*(4), 49–70.

Østergaard, E., & Dahlin, B. (2009, April 17–21). Sound and sensibility. Pre-service science teacher students bridging phenomena and concepts. In *Proceedings from 2009 NARST Annual International Conference* (p. 328). Reston, VA: NARST.

Østergaard, E., Dahlin, B., & Hugo, A. (2008). Doing phenomenology in science education: A research review. *Studies in Science Education, 44*(2), 93–121.

Peters, G. (2018). John Cage and the "freshening" of education. *Journal of Aesthetic Education, 52*(4), 1–20.

Thiel, S. (1990). Grundschulkinder zwischen Umgangserfahrung und Naturwissenschaft [Primary school children between personal experience and science]. In M. Wagenschein (Ed.), *Kinder auf dem Wege zur Physik* [Children on their way towards physics] (pp. 90–180). Weinheim, Germany: Beltz Verlag.

CHAPTER 7

Science-Arts as Verbs: New Figurations in Early Childhood

Sofie Areljung

Abstract

This chapter examines how STEAM education may transform education in the STEM subjects towards education for a sustainable future. Particularly, it examines the potential of combining science and arts in preschool practice (children aged 1–5 years) for the sake of fostering sustainable knowing and being in the world. Here, it pursues the idea that everyday science verbs (e.g., rolling, bouncing and sticking) may be referents for children–matter relations in which science learning and creativity emerge. The chapter includes two stories from a collaboration with preschool teachers who have implemented verb-based science-arts education in practice. In one story, the verbs "sprout and grow" were combined with painting and drama, and in the other story, the verb "shade" (to cast a shadow) was combined with music, dancing and painting. Grounded in Edvin Østergaard's plea to make more room for aesthetic experience in science education, in Barbara McClintock's scientific creativity and "feeling for the organism", and in Karen Barad's agential realism, the chapter portrays examples of science-arts education that allow children to be intensely involved in the world. It concludes that the arts may help children not only to communicate and explore science phenomena, but also to sympathise with nature's goings on *from within*; from their own multifaceted experiences of what it is like to cast a shadow, sprout and grow.

Keywords

agential realism – arts – Barad – early childhood education – entanglement – feminist science studies – Østergaard – McClintock – science education – sustainability

1   **Science Education for Sustainable Being and Knowing with/in
       the World**

In a recent IPCC[1] report, Allen and colleagues (2018: 54) write that "human influence has become a principal agent of change on the planet, shifting the world out of the relatively stable Holocene period into a new geological era, often termed the Anthropocene". The name Anthropocene has been suggested because humankind has caused and causes such an immense impact on the basic ecological functioning of the planet (Crutzen & Stoermer, 2000). As such, the name Anthropocene sheds light on the unsustainable pattern that humans, perceiving themselves as the superior species on the planet, pursue at the expense of all other species.

   In order to live sustainably, we need to shift our thinking and acting from the anthropocentric view towards realising that we too are parts of the intricate ecosystems of our planet and that we depend on the animals, plants and materialities around us. What role does science education play in bringing about such a shift? Pursuing that question, I turn to Edvin Østergaard (2015, 2017), who has criticised science education for making science foreign to students' lives. He points out the fundamental problem that in science education reduced models of the world are considered to be more true than the world itself, and more true than the students' own experiences of being in the world. Drawing on the work of the philosophers Martin Heidegger, John Dewey and Bo Dahlin, Østergaard suggests that science education should bring students' first-hand experiences of the world into the classroom. If students are given opportunities for aesthetic experiences of the world, they may (again) experience being rooted in the world – in contrast to considering nature as background scenery that has little to do with their own lives (Østergaard, 2015).

   I read Østergaard's critique of science education through a feminist critique of science. Feminist science studies have, since the 1980s, exposed that power hierarchies matter in whose questions are considered worthy of investigation, what methods of knowledge production are considered valid, and whose interpretations and conclusions count (see Crasnow, Wylie, Bauchspies, & Potter, 2018). Correspondingly, Østergaard (2015) points out that (unfortunately) reductionist models, and not students' own experiences of the world, are what counts as valid forms of knowledge in science education. Furthermore, feminist science studies have challenged many of the binaries, such as objective–subjective and masculinity–femininity, that often regulate our thinking about the world (e.g. Harding, 1986; Keller, 1992). These binaries are problematic since they imply mutual exclusiveness, where one part is perceived as superior to the other. Studying the history of science, Schiebinger (1989) has shown that Western science has defended the boundaries between itself and non-science by using binaries such as reason–emotion, fact–value and masculinity–femininity, associating the first words with science and the second words with non-science. This is used to imply that emotions, values and femininity do not belong within the science community. Although Østergaard does not engage explicitly with gender issues, I read that he too is concerned about the narrow frames that science and science education have created for themselves, since they push subjectivity and emotions out from the arena of science knowledge production.

Another powerful binary in the history of science is human–nature. Ecofeminists have highlighted that the human–nature binary creates thought figures that position humans as the superior species in the world, somehow unattached to nature, while nature is positioned as passive and inferior; an economical resource to be exploited by humans (e.g. Mellor, 1997). In recent decades, posthumanist feminist scholars have sought to disrupt the human–nature binary by depicting humans as entangled with other species and materialities, hence drawing humans down from their pedestal to the level of nature (e.g. Barad, 2007). Posthumanist theorist Karen Barad (2003: 829) states that "[w]e do not obtain knowledge by standing outside the world; we know because 'we' are of the world", thereby providing a contrast to the science ideal of an independent, unbiased human being, who learns about nature at a safe distance from nature. In that sense, posthumanist perspectives correspond with the urgent calls for humans to think and act sustainably from a position entangled with nature – not detached from nature.

Drawing on the work of Dewey and Dahlin, Østergaard (2017) proposes that aesthetic experiences unify person and phenomenon, an idea which in my view aligns with the posthuman tenet of humans being entangled with nature. For example, he writes that, in the aesthetic experience of listening, "the listener and the listened are one" (Østergaard, 2017: 569). Tying aesthetic experience to sustainability, Østergaard asserts that humans who have created personal relations with the environment are more inclined to live sustainably, since "[w]hat you care for, you tend to protect" (2017: 579). For sustainability education, he proposes that science education should be involved in cross-curricular cooperation with the arts subjects because this can enable students to cultivate their creativity, and practise their attentiveness towards the world, for example by listening (as in music) and seeing (as in visual arts). Furthermore, Østergaard (2017) suggests that science education should provide spaces where students can encounter lifeworld phenomena in all their richness and all their languages, and make it possible for students to become more intensely involved in the world and refine their sensibility towards the world's on-goings. This chapter is my attempt to portray how such science education may take form in practice. Hence, I use this chapter to illustrate the transformative potential of STEAM education, that is, the potential to fundamentally question and rework education in the STEM subjects towards fostering students' creativity as well as their connectedness with and sustainable being in the world.

2   The Sciencemaking Project

A year ago, I initiated the project ScienceMaking (NaturvetenSkapande) in collaboration with a pedagogical development centre and eight preschools. Three of the preschools were for children aged 1–3 years, two for children aged 3–4 years, and two for children aged 4–5 years. Aiming to explore the pedagogical potentialities of science-arts integration, I asked the preschool teachers to combine sciences (biology, chemistry or physics) and arts (drama, dance, music or visual arts) in ways that they found to suit their respective practices. I also asked them to draw upon science verbs when planning their projects. I explain below why I stated these particular restrictions/openings.

2.1   *Why Science and Arts?*
One reason I wanted to explore the interface of science and arts was simply that arts activities seem to be a common way to handle science teaching in preschools in Sweden, where I live and work (see, e.g., Westman & Bergmark, 2014; Areljung & Sundberg, 2018). In my previous research collaborations with preschool teachers, I had encountered several examples of science-arts activities that stimulated my thinking (particularly children painting "the sensation of their best rolling": Areljung, 2019) but whose pedagogical potential I could not fully grasp. There was something intriguing in children's multifaceted, to a large extent non-verbal, way of exploring and communicating about science phenomena that forced me to challenge my preconceptions about what science education can be. I should mention that I have a background as a school teacher in mathematics and science. Ever since I came into the field of research on science in preschools in 2012, I have sought to, and been forced to, expand my thinking about science education because I have experienced many times that my school-teaching-based ideas were too narrow to allow true and constructive collaboration with preschool teachers. Consequently, I entered the ScienceMaking project with the assumption that science-arts integration harbours the potential to disrupt the human–nature and objective–subjective binaries that often constrain what counts as valid knowledge production in STEM education. I was aiming for a comprehensive story of knowledge production that allows for children's subjective contributions and entangled being in the world (see Areljung, Ottander, & Due, 2017).

2.2   *Why Creativity?*

Lev Vygotsky (2004: 9) has defined creativity as a matter of reworking elements of one's past experience and using them to generate propositions and behaviour that are new to oneself, not necessarily to all. I adhere to that definition and, rather than seeing creativity as something quick and flexible, look for a creativity that grows from deep involvement with the world. I do not set a distinction between arts creativity and scientific creativity, but what I have in mind is the work of cytogeneticist and Nobel laureate Barbara McClintock. As reported in Evelyn Fox Keller's (1983) biography, McClintock studied corn plants and she was sensitive towards the plants' characteristics and changes, as well as their patterns and inconsistencies:

> Over the years, a special kind of sympathetic understanding grew in McClintock, heightening her powers of discernment, until finally, the objects of her study (the plants) become subjects in their own right; they claim from her a kind of attention that most of us experience only in relation to other persons. (Keller, 1983: 200)

What Keller labels as McClintock's "sympathetic understanding" and heightened "powers of discernment" resonates with Østergaard's (2017) plea for students to be intensely involved with the world and to practise their sensibility towards the world. According to Keller's biography, McClintock's groundbreaking discoveries emerged from within her close relationships with the corn plants she studied, from her "feeling for the organism". Remarkably enough, it turned out that several of the preschools in the ScienceMaking project were planting corn as a part of their respective science-arts practices. How did creativity emerge in these practices?

2.3   *Why Science Verbs?*

Preschool science themes are often framed by nouns, such as the forest, water or fungi. While nouns direct us towards objects, the approach advocated in this chapter is to focus on verbs. Basing science teaching on verbs that address physical phenomena (e.g. rolling, bouncing, flying), chemical processes (e.g. melting, sticking, mixing) and biological processes (e.g. breathing, growing, decomposing), I argue that one may identify several of the intangible, yet experienceable, science phenomena that permeate everyday preschool practice (Areljung, 2018a). My previous work (Areljung, 2018b) indicates that science verbs help teachers to envision science education beyond the early childhood traditions of favouring the tangible (cf. Cannella, 1997), such as science themes water and fungi, and beyond the occasional, decontextualised experiments that are a common way for Swedish preschools to deal with the chemistry and physics parts of the curriculum (Swedish Schools Inspectorate, 2017).

In this chapter, I attempt to think with Barad's (2003, 2007) *agential realism*, which assumes that entanglements are the primary ontological entities, not bodies or objects. Everything is always entangled with something else, Barad claims, and the perceived boundaries of an object emerge within those entanglements. Correspondingly, knowing occurs as a part of the world makes itself intelligible to another part. I posit that verbs mark the events in which intelligibility is made. The idea can be illustrated by an example of children treading and jumping on a wooden board placed over a ditch in the forest (see Areljung, 2019). The wooden board makes itself intelligible to the children as the treading and jumping reveal that the wooden board is slippery and flexible. At the same time, the children make themselves intelligible to the board as the jumping and treading reveals their weight, varying body posture and the friction of the sole of their shoes. Without the treading and jumping (verbs), the slipperiness, flexibility or body weight of the board and children (nouns) would not have emerged.

3   Producing Children-Science-Arts Stories

During the ScienceMaking project, the eight teachers and their colleagues implemented, documented and reflected on verb-based science-arts activities in their local preschools and in meetings with me and the other project participants. Meanwhile, material data was produced in the form of photos, videos, writings and audio-recorded meetings. The analytical process was inspired by what Barad (2007) refers to as *agential cuts* and *diffractive reading*. In accordance with her idea that knowing emerges from within human–matter entanglements, Barad proposes that researchers make agential cuts whenever they attempt to focus on only a part of the world's complexity. As a contrast to traditional views of researchers as actors producing knowledge about the world from a place somewhere outside the world, the idea of research through agential cuts implies that researchers' memories, wishes and perceptive abilities all contribute to producing the agential cuts and hence to producing new knowledge. In this project, the teachers and I have cut out different parts of practice, depending on what we have been able to perceive, what we found relevant or remarkable, what resonated with our previous experiences, and what we wanted to convey to others (teacher colleagues, parents and academics). Yet, the individual is not the sole producer of an agential cut. Barad (2007) means that cuts are co-produced by humans, technologies and discourses. As I see it, the teachers and I were involved in an ongoing conversation (see Barad, 2014), sometimes synchronous, when we met physically, but most often asynchronous, through material/cuts such as writings and photos. These conversations happened across three cycles, with each bringing about several cuts:

- *First cut (the task):* I decided that teachers should use science verbs and combine science and arts in their local projects. For each cycle, I also specified a challenge, for example, to use two different art forms to examine the same phenomenon/verb.
- *Second cut (implementation and documentation):* The teachers decided how to implement the project in their daily practice (including what science verbs and what arts) and how to document what happened.
- *Third cut (reflection documents):* The teachers selected and interpreted pieces of practice in writings and photos, some of which they shared with me [data: teachers' documents].
- *Fourth cut (local meetings):* The teachers chose what parts of practice and documentation to highlight in meetings with their colleagues. I took part in one meeting per preschool, discussing their video- and photo-based stories from practice [data: my notes].
- *Fifth cut (project meetings):* The teachers selected examples to discuss with all participants in the project group (nine preschool teachers, three teachers in a pedagogical development centre, and me – divided into groups of three to five persons) [data: audio recordings].

After the three cycles (cuts 1–5), I re-read the data and made additional cuts as I selected what children–science relations to create the stories around. In this chapter, I present one story about sprouting/growing and one about shading. I constructed the stories guided by the following questions:

- How do the arts contribute to reinforcing the children–science relations?
- What is the noun-verb dimension at play in the children–science relations?
- How does creativity emerge in the children–science relations?

The teachers' and my agential cuts were combined in diffractive readings, rendering patterns of differences and emphases as the cuts were layered on, and read through, each other (Barad, 2007). A recurring difference was that I was oriented towards children's relations to the science phenomenon and arts expression particularly, while the teachers tended to perceive situations in a more holistic manner, knowing the children well and being attentive to their relations to others as well as to several areas of preschool pedagogy. Initially, I was only able to make agential cuts regarding how arts could help teachers to help children to produce distinct conclusions about scientific phenomena, such as "a plant needs water and light to grow" or "the size of the shadow depends on where I stand in relation to the lamp". However, reading the teachers' agential cuts and conclusions through my own, and thinking with Barbara McClintock, Karen Barad and Edvin Østergaard, I have been able to grasp that the preschool projects did not primarily produce those types of distinct outcomes. Instead, the science-arts projects made way for a much more holistic type of learning, one where children could develop a feeling for the science phenomena "growing" and "shading" as they danced, painted and dramatised them.

In terms of emphases, the teachers primarily shared situations that they found fascinating because the children acted in ways that the teachers had not seen before. Since I was unaware of the children's history, parts of what happened in these situations stood outside of my science education research horizon. I believe that the events and interpretations that were pertinent and thought provoking for both the preschool teachers and me were particularly relevant to build on in research about, with and for preschools.

4   Story 1: Sprouting and Growing

The first preschool is for children aged 1–2 years. Here we find three teachers, including Nina, who was the preschool's representative in the project. During the project, I had access to the teachers' reflection document (more than 100 slides in a PowerPoint format where each slide provided text and/or photographs), in which they continuously described and commented on their project activities. Their overarching project theme was "sprouting, growing and withering" and in the first pages of the reflection document the teachers state:

> By using different plants as tools, children will be given the possibility to explore different techniques and modes of expression in the atelier as well as how the body moves when we explore the verbs grow, sprout and wither. We want the children to encounter, experience and explore plants to show them an ecological and caring approach towards nature and each other, together with aesthetic learning processes.

According to the teachers' reflection document, the children encountered many different organisms (potatoes, carrots and different seeds), and arts activities (drama, painting and dancing) during the project period. For this story, I have cut out the parts that I found relating to children–sprouting and children–growing relationships. Therein, I identified several intertwined dimensions, of which the two most significant were:

– The story of *Lilla frö* (*Little seed*) – the book was read, referred to in daily conversations, dramatised and danced (while playing classical music).

– Planting and taking care of seeds – the children investigated seeds, plants
  and soil with many senses and tried to make sure that the plants got enough
  sun and water to grow and survive.

Central to the preschool's work was the picture book *Lilla frö* (*Little seed*) by
Sara Gimbergsson (2014). The book starts as "a little seed fell to the ground"
and next, there is a picture showing that the seed just laid there, as it could "not
crawl, not walk". Then came an earthworm who asked the little seed what it
would become when it got old. The seed did not know. In the rest of the book,
there are pictures and text illustrating that the sun shone, wind blew, snow
fell, and the seed fell asleep. When the snow melted, the seed woke up with a
"wiggle" in its legs ("sprattel i benen") and felt small threads (roots) growing out
from the legs into the soil. Then a sprout came out of the little seed's head, with
small leaves unfolding. In the pictures, the seed is anthropomorphised with
eyes, nose, mouth, arms, legs and hair. On the last page we cannot see the seed,
only a fully grown flower without human attributes above the ground, greeted
by the earthworm's "How big and beautiful you have become!"

The teachers read the story many times and put copies of the 13 pictures on
the preschool's wall. The reflection document shows that Nina led the children
in dramatising the story of *Little seed*, accompanied by classical music. Just as
in the story, the children/seeds were still on the floor, not able to move, and
then covered by a layer of snow (pieces of fabric placed on children by the
teachers or other children). Then there was "wiggle in the legs" (Figure 7.1) and
a sprout growing out of the head. Finally, the children/seeds were waving in

FIGURE 7.1   Dramatising *Little seed*: "Wriggling" legs. The original photo was taken by the
              preschool teachers and is here reproduced in an edited format, with the teachers'
              permission

the wind. The teachers wrote in their reflection document that "wiggle in the legs" was a good metaphor for the process of roots emerging from the seed, and that the wiggling movement as such ignited joy. Overall, they noted that children did not show any "limitations in terms of moving or empathy" during the growing/sprouting drama activity.

During the project period, teachers and children planted different seeds and eventually sprouts emerged from the soil and grew into plants. The children watered the plants and tried to make sure that they had enough sunlight. On one occasion, when the teachers had removed some corn plants from the soil for children to examine, the teachers noted the following utterances (keep in mind that the children are very young):

Child:	*Look, little seed!*
Teacher:	Yes look, this is the corn seed we planted before, but what is this? (Teacher points at the roots.)
Child:	Do not know.
Teacher:	They are roots. They are the ones that drink the water that we give to the plants.
Child:	*Roots!*
Child:	*Dance.*
Teacher:	Should the roots dance?
Child:	Yes!
Child:	Music!
Teacher:	Should we put on music so the roots can dance?
Child:	Yeees!

I have marked the comment "Look, little seed!" in italics because it indicates that the child associates the corn plants in front of her/him with the story of the little seed. Second, I noted that when teacher pointed at the roots, saying that they drink water, the child responded "Roots!" and then immediately "Dance!" My interpretation is that the roots evoked an association with moving, with dancing, possibly from the child's previous experiences of dramatising the sprouting and growing of the little seed. As I read the children's utterances, the *noun* "roots" seemed to be a stepping stone towards the desired *verb* "dance". A similar shift, from noun to verb, happened in another activity, where teachers had projected a video of sunflowers on a wall (Figure 7.2). The wall was covered with a large piece of paper and the teachers provided children with paint and paintbrushes, planning that children would paint on the sunflower projections. While the video was running on the wall, some of the children painted long green lines on the sunflower image and the teachers noted the following utterances:

Child:	Grows and grows and grows …
Child:	Grow long! Ha ha, look!
Child:	Little seed!
Teacher:	Can little seed grow?
Child:	Yes, look. Grows long.
Teacher:	Does little seed get a wiggle in its legs?
Child:	Yes, ha ha! (Lays down on the floor, wiggling the legs)
Teacher:	What happens then?
Child:	Grows a sprout!

FIGURE 7.2   Painting on a video projection of sunflowers. The original photo was taken by
the preschool teachers and is here reproduced in an edited format, with the
teachers' permission

In their reflection document, the teachers wrote: "It is obvious that children
make connections to the book *Lilla frö* (*Little seed*) during activities where
something grows. The children remember the process from a little seed, until
it grows up." Guided by the teachers' conclusion, I notice that one of the children commented that the sunflowers on the video "grows and grows", and then
a child said, "Little seed!" The teachers – and I – suggest that the children connect the word and event "grow" with different representations of plants. For
example, when the teacher asked if the little seed can grow, the child pointed
at the projection/painting, saying "Yes, look. Grows long." What is also striking
is that the teacher's question about whether the little seed gets a "wiggle" in its
legs seemed to encourage the child not only to answer "yes!" and laugh but also

to lay down on the floor to wiggle her/his own legs. Here, I posit that creativity is working in a Vygotskyan (2004) sense as children make new connections between different parts of their worlds. As the project unfolds, the children appear to express that the tangible seed in the soil is connected to the seed in the picture book *Little Seed* and to the sunflowers on the video. With their body language, the children indicate that it is the rooting (wiggling the legs), sprouting (from the head) and growing (from small and crouching to tall) that connect these different versions of living plants.

Barbara McClintock said that plants "can do almost anything you can think of. But just because they sit there, anybody walking down the road considers them just a plastic area to look at, [as if] they're not really alive" (quoted in Keller, 1983: 200). Yet, it seems that, in the children's eyes, touch and bodies, the seeds or plants did not "just sit there". I claim that children did not perceive the seeds as capsules, with distinct outer boundaries hiding and confining the core. Rather, the seeds (nouns) seemed to harbour a promise of pending processes (verbs) – of rooting, sprouting and growing – that the children had experienced before and wanted to experience again, for example by dancing and wiggling their legs. I claim that a traditional science education approach to a plant/growing project would be to assume that children gain knowledge about plants by touching, smelling and observing seeds and plants. In such a view, seeds, plants and children have distinct borders and children may learn *about* what seeds and plants look like. They may also learn that plants need water and light to grow and survive, all at a distance. In contrast, I suggest that the verb-arts figurations employed in this project enabled children to experience how some of nature's important processes feel in the body – to know, feel and empathise with the sprouting, rooting, growing parts in the world.

5   Story 2: Shading (Casting a Shadow)

The second preschool is for children 2–3 years old. Four teachers work here and Vera was the preschool's representative in the project. The teachers did not employ the same reflection technique as the preschool mentioned above, but they have shared two 2-page reflection documents as well as photos from activities with me. Their overarching theme was "shining and shading" and in one of their reflection documents they state that their project aim was to let children experience the relationship between their own bodies and their shadow, as well as the shadows related to their friends and other objects. The teachers told me that in the beginning of the project, many of the children did not seem to be aware that they had a shadow or that there was a relationship between how they moved and how their shadow moved.

Most of the project activities took place in a room with white walls and a round carpet on the floor. The main light source was an overhead projector, directed towards one of the walls. On the wall to the left, there was a large mirror, and to the right a curtain. Initially, children mostly ran back and forth in the room, noticing that their shadows got smaller as they approached the wall and grew larger as they moved away from the wall. They also jumped up and laid down, noticing that their shadow disappeared when they were lying on the floor. The teachers told me that in some cases, when the shadow would not show on the wall because the children had (unintentionally) moved to a certain angle in relation to the overhead projector, children would go looking for the shadow, for example behind the curtain. The teachers interpreted these situations as children not yet having discovered the relationship between their own body and their shadow (see Figure 7.3).

FIGURE 7.3   One child following the shadow's movement on the wall and one child spinning
(wondering if the shadow will still be there after the full turn?). The original
photo was taken by a preschool teacher and is here reproduced in an edited
format, with the teacher's permission

After a number of occasions where children, the overhead light and the room had been the main components, the teachers introduced music into the equation. Their idea was to encourage dancing and to draw attention to how one's shadow moves. In a project meeting, with representatives from all pre-schools present, Vera presented video sequences from these music-shading activities. One of the videos showed a child moving her arms and hands in repetitive patterns, carefully following the shadow on the wall. Another video showed a child who spun around. Vera commented:

> When we introduced music, there were much smaller movements com-pared to when we did not have music. When we did not have music, the children ran from one wall to the other, or walked to the front and then to the back. Now they remain at the same distance (from the wall and shadow), focusing on something else.

During this project meeting, Vera's group discussed whether and how the arts mattered to children exploring the delicate and specific aspects of their rela-tionship with their shadow, in contrast to their previous large movements back and forth, and up and down. Vera suggested that adding music to the shading activity had encouraged the children to conduct repetitive movements and thereby the children had, for example, noticed that when they move their hands and fingers in a certain way, the shadows move in that way too, every time. Fur-thermore, music and dancing seemed to encourage some of the children to spin around on the spot. One video showed a child who, after each full turn, immediately looked at the shadow on the wall. Vera said: "I think the child is curious about 'When I spin, is the shadow still there when I come back?'" One of the other teachers in the discussion group suggested that the children seemed occupied with investigating "Who am I?" and "Who or what is the shadow?"

Similar questions – about children exploring the distinctions and similari-ties in their relationship with their shadow – surfaced when the teachers and I discussed a shading/painting activity that they had conducted. For that activ-ity, the teachers had directed an overhead projector towards a large sheet of paper, taped onto the wall, and provided children with paint and brushes. The teachers told me about a child who had painted on the shadow's head and then pointed to her own head. Then she painted on the shadow's stomach and this time she looked down at her shirt. According to the teachers, it seemed as if she expected to find paint on her stomach, as if what happened to the shadow should happen to her body too.

I claim that the verb "shade" marks the relationship between children and the ephemeral phenomenon shadow. Following the teachers' emphases on what occurred in the videos of shading-dancing activities, my interpretation is that many of the children in this preschool were intensely involved in the shading, continuously examining and reinforcing their entanglement with their shadow. First, it was a matter of big movements, seeming to establish that there is some connection between the children's and the shadow's moving. Then the music seemed to encourage children to do something other than their practical examination of the binaries back–forward (corresponding to the shadow's big–small) and up–down (corresponding to the shadow's here–gone). Some children started to perform repetitive movements and, seemingly systematically, examine the finetuned nuances in their relationships with their shadows. Yet, the relationship was not completely reliable for some of the children, who went looking for their missing shadow behind the curtain, or did not seem to be sure that the shadow would still be there after they had spun around. I suggest that creativity emerged as children found out new ways to test the nuances and boundaries of their relationships to their shadows while dancing. Their repeated spinning and increasingly finetuned movements can be seen as acts of both science and arts creativity since they produced shadow figurations and dance figurations that they, according to the teachers, had never produced before (cf. Vygotsky, 2004). The same goes for the activity where a child painted on the shadow's stomach.

At the same time as children became more intensely involved with their shadows, I suggest that the children and shadows made themselves intelligible to each other, emerging as bodies within the shading (Barad, 2007). For some children, their repetitive examinations through dancing appeared to establish the link that "when I move, the shadow will move too". Yet, the direction of the link was not necessarily established. The child painting on the shadow on the wall indicated with painting and gestures that she perceived a connection between the shadow's head on the wall and her own head. It appears that she expected a two-way causality, where painting on the shadow's stomach should render a stain of paint on her stomach too. In my interpretation, the shading phenomenon was a playmate (cf. de Freitas & Palmer, 2016) and, while playing, children explored the boundaries of their relationship with that playmate, asking: *Will the shadow still be there when I stand up again or after I have made a full turn? Will my stomach be painted when I paint on the shadow? Who am I and who is the shadow? Where do I end and where does it begin?*

6   Conclusion

I wanted to use this chapter to illustrate the transformative potential of STEAM education. My idea was that arts could contribute to disrupting the objective–subjective and human–nature binaries that often constrain what counts as valid knowledge production in STEM education. Correspondingly, I wanted to explore how science-arts education could foster students' creativity as well as their connected and sustainable being in the world. In my view, the preschools who took part in the project have provided examples of science-arts figurations that enable children to develop an intense involvement with nature (Østergaard, 2017). Within the children's involvement with science phenomena, scientific creativity emerged. As they invented new ways to test and reinforce their relationships to plants/growing and shadows/shading, they developed a "feeling for the phenomenon" (cf. McClintock's "feeling for the organism": Keller, 1983). Meanwhile, arts creativities emerged as the children invented new ways to express and investigate phenomena in dance, paint and drama.

To summarise, I suggest that, while traditional science education presumes an active noun (the child) learning about a passive noun (nature), verb-based education makes a space for children to learn science from within child–nature entanglements, as they and the science phenomenon make themselves intelligible to each other (Barad, 2007). In my view, the preschools who took part in the project have provided examples of science-arts figurations that enable children not only to use the arts to examine and communicate about shadows, light, plants and seeds, but also to experience what it is like to *be* a shading, sprouting, rooting and growing part in the world.

Note

1 The Intergovernmental Panel on Climate Change (IPCC) is a United Nations body. To date, the IPCC has 195 member nations and thousands of scientists who assess scientific papers to summarise reasons, impacts and risk mitigation in relation to climate change: https://www.ipcc.ch/about/ (accessed 12 June 2019).

References

Allen, M. R., Dube, O. P., Solecki, W., Aragón-Durand, F., Cramer, W., Humphreys, S., … Zickfeld, K. (Eds.). (2018). *Global warming of 1.5°C: An IPCC special report on the impacts of global warming of 1.5°C above pre-industrial levels and related global greenhouse gas emission pathways, in the context of strengthening the global response to the threat of climate change, sustainable development, and efforts to eradicate poverty.* Geneva: Intergovernmental Panel on Climate Change.

Areljung, S. (2018a). Capturing the world with verbs: Preschool science education beyond nouns and objects. *Contemporary Issues in Early Childhood* [Preprint]. https://doi.org/10.1177/1463949118805438

Areljung, S. (2018b). Why do teachers adopt or resist a pedagogical idea for teaching science in preschool? *International Journal of Early Years Education* [Preprint]. https://doi.org/10.1080/09669760.2018.1481733

Areljung, S. (2019). How does matter matter in preschool science? In C. Milne & K. Scantlebury (Eds.), *Material practice and materiality: Too long ignored in science education* (pp. 101–114). New York, NY: Springer.

Areljung, S., Ottander, C., & Due, K. (2017). "Drawing the leaves anyway": Teachers embracing children's different ways of knowing in preschool science practice. *Research in Science Education, 47*(6), 1173–1192.

Areljung, S., & Sundberg, B. (2018). Potential for multi-dimensional teaching for "emergent scientific literacy" in pre-school practice. *Journal of Emergent Science, 15*, 20–27.

Barad, K. (2003). Posthumanist performativity: Toward an understanding of how matter comes to matter. *Signs, 28*(3), 801–831.

Barad, K. (2007). *Meeting the universe halfway: Quantum physics and the entanglement of matter and meaning.* Durham, NC: Duke University Press.

Barad, K. (2014). Diffracting diffraction: Cutting together-apart. *Parallax, 20*(3), 168–187.

Cannella, G. S. (1997). *Deconstructing early childhood education: Social justice and revolution.* New York, NY: Peter Lang.

Crasnow, S., Wylie, A., Bauchspies, W. K., & Potter, E. (2018). Feminist perspectives on science. In E. N. Zalta (Ed.), *The Stanford encyclopedia of philosophy* (Spring 2018 ed.). Retrieved May 22, 2019, from https://plato.stanford.edu/archives/spr2018/entries/feminist-science

Crutzen, P. J., & Stoermer, E. F. (2000). The "Anthropocene". *Global Change Newsletter, 41*, 17–18.

de Freitas, E., & Palmer, A. (2016). How scientific concepts come to matter in early childhood curriculum: Rethinking the concept of force. *Cultural Studies of Science Education, 11*(4), 1201–1222.

Gimbergsson, S. (2014). *Lilla frö.* Bromma, Sweden: Opal.

Harding, S. G. (1986). *The science question in feminism.* Ithaca, NY: Cornell University Press.

Keller, E. F. (1983). *A feeling for the organism: The life and work of Barbara McClintock.* New York, NY: Freeman.

Keller, E. F. (1985). *Reflections on gender and science.* New Haven, CT: Yale University Press.

Mellor, M. (1997). Women, nature and the social construction of "economic man". *Ecological Economics, 20*(2), 129–140.

Østergaard, E. (2015). How can science education foster students' rooting? *Cultural Studies of Science Education, 10*(2), 515–525.

Østergaard, E. (2017). Earth at rest: Aesthetic experience and students' grounding in science education. *Science & Education, 26*(5), 557–582.

Schiebinger, L. (1989). *The mind has no sex?* Cambridge, MA: Harvard University Press.

Swedish Schools Inspectorate. (2017). *Förskolans arbete med matematik, naturvetenskap och teknik.* Retrieved May 136, 2019, from https://www.skolinspektionen.se/sv/Beslut-och-rapporter/Publikationer/Granskningsrapport/Kvalitetsgranskning/forskolans-arbete-med-matematik-teknik-och-naturvetenskap/

Vygotsky, L. S. (2004 [1930]). Imagination and creativity in childhood. *Journal of Russian and East European Psychology, 42*(1), 7–97.

Westman, S., & Bergmark, U. (2014). A strengthened teaching mission in preschool: Teachers' experiences, beliefs and strategies. *International Journal of Early Years Education, 22*(1), 73–88.

PART 3

Why Do the Arts Matter?

∴

Introduction to Part 3

Pamela Burnard and Laura Colucci-Gray

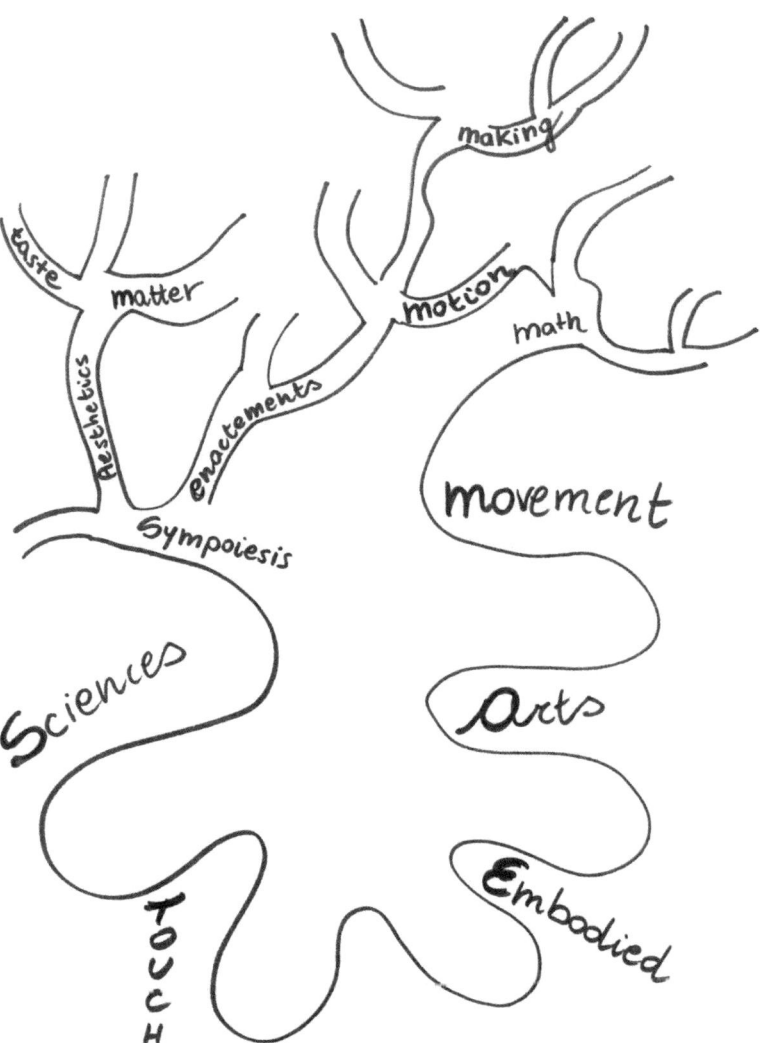

Based on what Deleuze calls rhizome as an "image of thought", this visual rendering recalls the botanical rhizome fanning and branching into the soil as well as into the air. This image can be viewed up-side-down as well as the right way up. The line of the rhizome is both splitting and connecting as the generative intra-activity produces and co-produces new forms and new arrangements in symbiotic and sympoietic relations. *"Rolling inward enables rolling outward; the shape of life's motion traces a hyperbolic space, swooping and fluting like the folds of a frilled lettuce, coral reef, or bit of crocheting"* (Haraway, 2016: 68, emphasis added).

© KONINKLIJKE BRILL NV, LEIDEN, 2020 | DOI: 10.1163/9789004421585_011

This part does not advance a particular conception of arts or a particular theory about how art works as a subject. This part engages with troubling of different ways of (re-)configuring STEAM as embodied learning and teaching, through the affective, agentic aspects and materiality of arts-based educational innovations. We do this by: (a) engendering corporeal cartographies of the body, bodies and bodily practices and relations (see particularly Chapter 8, Pamela Burnard et al.); (b) disrupting the outcomes-based models of schooling (see particularly Chapter 9, Anna Hickey-Moody, Christine Horn and Marissa Willcox); and (c) reflecting on the ways that arts creativities matter and manifest through STEAM (re-)configurings as sites of embodied relationships (see particularly Chapter 10, James MacAllister; Chapter 11, Jan van Boeckel).

Arts-based educational innovations are central to STEAM (re)configurings because they present productive and generative possibilities when questions inspired by new materialism are asked. In addition to asking *what arts making practices remake, reconfigure and re-present* (and what the making of art reveals), these innovations direct attention to material-discursive affordances, and they invite different sets of questions, such as: What kinds of work do arts do? What role do humans play in operating and producing arts-based educational innovations? What are the core aspects that manifest themselves at different moments in reconfiguring STEAM boundaries and relations that are neither defined nor bounded by subject disciplines? What sort of spacialities and temporalities do arts practices engender? How are specific practices of the arts mediated by STEAM practices? Do different arts in different spaces do different work and engender different bodies and bodily practices and relations?

Part 3 chapters ask where, how and when arts-based educational innovations come to matter. Authors invite curiosity into what gets produced in terms of material-discursive practices.

Reference

Haraway, D. (2016). *Staying with the trouble. Making kin in the Chtulucene*. Durham, NC: Duke University Press.

CHAPTER 8

Reconfiguring STEAM through Material Enactments of Mathematics and Arts: A Diffractive Reading of Young People's Intradisciplinary Math-Artworks

Pamela Burnard, Pallawi Sinha, Carine Steyn, Kristóf Fenyvesi,
Christopher Brownell, Olivier Werner and Zsolt Lavicza

Abstract

The current movement to integrate arts within STEAM education is relevant not only for responding to complex societal and economic problems of the twenty-first century, but in that it carries its own sets of processes, questions and paradigmatic shifts that decentre dominant discourses in education. This chapter argues onto-epistemologically that arts uniquely engender *a "mutuality" of disciplines* constituted in the intra-actively entangled production of new knowledges through knowing and doing enactments within STEAM (re)configurings. It argues this is a form of critical intradisciplinarity. This chapter, which draws on an exceptionally significant data set, reports a novel analysis of a sample of drawings called "math-artworks". These were created by South African young people in Grades 8–12 following a series of mathematics-art-experiential workshops. Theoretically framed by posthuman feminist new materialism, the chapter diffractively reads three of these drawings. It asks what matters in mathematical-art drawings by using Karen Barad's concept of diffraction as a methodological practice for reading these drawings as data. The chapter uses diffractive reading to evaluate what it is that "math-artworks" advance, as encountered in the material enactments of South African young people. It also asks whether these configurings of intradisciplinary knowledge making generate new pedagogic repertoires. It argues accordingly that STEAM is a form of critical intradisciplinarity that is capable of activating future-making education.

Keywords

Barad – diffractive analysis – future-making education – intradisciplinarity – new materialism – new pedagogic repertoires – posthuman – (re)configuring STEAM – relational knowing

© KONINKLIJKE BRILL NV, LEIDEN, 2020 | DOI: 10.1163/9789004421585_012

1   **Introduction**

The concept of STEAM education is fairly new and lacks a clear-cut definition (Colucci-Gray et al., 2017). STEAM education intends to promote and develop the integration of the arts into the subjects science, technology, engineering and mathematics. In this chapter we argue that the arts do *not* need to be integrated within STEM subjects. On the contrary, the disciplinary formations or (re)configurings offered by the arts in STEAM education create enabling spaces for a *mutuality of disciplines* which have the potential to introduce students to future-making education.

   In this chapter, we rethink the concepts of interdisciplinarity and multidisciplinarity in the context of the territorialisation of knowledge (Ingold, 2018: 75). *Multidisciplinarity* becomes reduced to friction, as disciplines are either used side by side (multidisciplinary) or adopted in parallel or sequentially from one domain to another. *Interdisciplinarity* denotes building a bridge *between* disciplines, where disciplinary identities remain preserved (Collin, 2009). Interdisciplinarity is perceived as a process whereby learning occurs from a disciplinary-specific basis for the purpose of solving a common problem. *Transdisciplinarity*, on the other hand, seeks to preserve various disciplinary perspectives and confront them with each other. Transdisciplinarity does however acknowledge the "different realities" and ways of thinking in different disciplines, but at the same time it challenges the differing parties or disciplines to readjust their perspectives. Transdisciplinary learning differs from interdisciplinary practices in that it occurs when participants share a conceptual framework to draw together disciplinary-specific theories or concepts. Research tells us that interdisciplinary and transdisciplinary learning moves learners beyond knowledge acquisition to knowledge collaboration and knowledge production (Beane, 2011). The separate, subject-based organisation of curriculum as it currently exists in many schools is a longstanding legacy of theories of psychology and mental discipline which, although discredited by the turn of the twentieth century, still influence curriculum theories.

   The configurings of mathematics and art encounters in STEAM are never simply "mirroring", "interfering" or "meeting" from their disciplinary distances. In fact, within the individual and mutual *spacetimematterings* (Barad, 2003) of mathematics and art there is an *entanglement*, signifying the ontological inseparability of "agentially intra-acting components" (2003: 815). We draw heavily on Karen Barad, a Professor of Feminist Studies, Philosophy, and History of Consciousness at the University of California, Santa Cruz. Why? Barad reinterprets theoretical thinking from both the social and natural sciences to define a new theory of knowing, which rejects both positivist and purely discursive

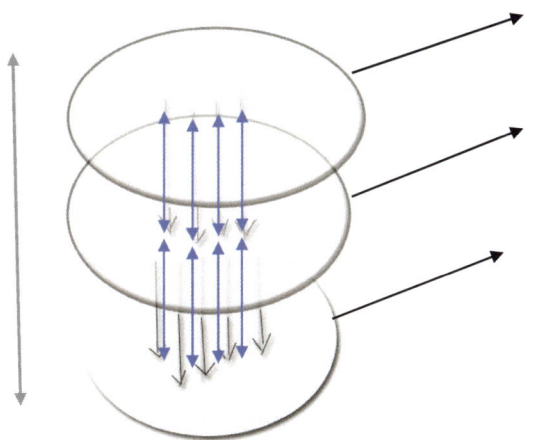

The circles represent the different disciplines, their contexts, formations, systems and framings.

The blue arrows indicate the permeability of the disciplinary layers holding all related information on the fields.

FIGURE 8.1   Reconfiguring disciplines

theories of knowledge. In connecting discursive and material aspects of reality, Barad's (2007) "onto-epistemology" also resonates deeply with STEAM (re)configuring because of how made material objects (in this case the mathematical-art drawings-as-text task) invoke a new set of pedagogic strategies for future-making education. Barad explains that "[t]o be entangled is not simply to be intertwined with another, as in the joining of separate entities, but to lack an independent, self-contained existence ... individuals emerge through and as part of their entangled *intra-relating*" (2007: ix, emphasis added). For Barad, *intra-activity* is that which builds an understanding of the inseparability of the "observed object" and the "agencies of observation", the observer and the observed, and our intra-action with other bodies (both human and non-human) produces subjectivities and performative *enactments*. Emerging anew from the *agentially intra-acting* formations, phenomena and components (human and non-human) – in this case, of the two disciplines, mathematics and art – we are able to (re)formulate and re-turn the math-art materiality into a dialogic "appreciation of the intertwining of ethics, knowing, and being" (Barad, 2007: 185). This is a math-art connection making and doing, or what Barad refers to as ethico-onto-epistemology. Such cutting together-apart of *agentially intra-acting binaries* – as with math–art, mind–body, social–science, material–discursive, discourse–affect, textual–visual, theory–practice, historical–political and geographical–socioeconomic – reveals how 'boundaries are there but never determinate or permanent, always changing and becoming' (Murris, 2018, p. 20). This allows us to see differences relationally, to diffract and differentiate, and re-turn our "gaze" on math-art. In response, intradisciplinarity *neither begets dominance of any one discipline* (as observed in interdisciplinarity) *nor does it maintain the distance between individual disciplines* (reflective of multidisciplinarity), or demand readjustments (as with transdisciplinarity). Instead, through our study we observe that intradisciplinarity (as shown in Figure 8.1) is constituted of permeable layers of differing disciplines, including their conceptual frameworks, practices or norms. It relies on the relational and dynamic entanglements, intersections and differences offered by the disciplines, allowing for emerging assemblages and plateaus that generate common ground – or disagreements. Their material-discursive agencies (re)new formations and phenomena, shaping a new space for (re)connected thinking and practice. Intradisciplinarity actualises and uncovers the un/foldings between subject disciplines.

In this chapter we ask how art(s) come to matter in the relational knowing enabled by reconfiguring of STEAM. How does art(s) in STEAM set up relational knowing, that is, putting knowledge(s) and the mutuality of disciplines to work intra-actively?

What follows is a methodological rationale for our analysis of drawings-as-text. Our concept of "drawings-as-text" necessitates a rethinking of drawings as a material enactment of mathematics and art. The drawing is seen as a text for interrogating, which is different from how drawings are "voiced" and viewed in secondary school art classes. We are asking what young people can tell us – as explored in justifications for the use of visual methods (Thomson, 2008; Murris & Thompson, 2016) – and also what they add as an onto-epistemic reconfiguration of voice, through material enactments with mathematics and art drawings-as-text. For Barad, it is impossible to separate or isolate practices of knowing, doing and being because "they are mutually implicated" (2007: 185). The physical world is not at a distance, on the other side of a line, but all "knowledge-making practices, including the use and testing of scientific concepts, are *material enactments* that contribute to, and are a part of the phenomenon we describe" (Barad, 2007: 32, emphasis added). From Barad we are alerted to how the use of images opens up powerful ways of knowing, being and doing that do more than merely represent but rather emphasise the new that is produced through the "drawings-as-text".

2   Analysing Material Enactments: Materialising Diffractive Methods

This chapter draws on an earlier international project which focused on making math–art connections (Fenyvesi et al., 2019). The aim was to improve student outcomes in mathematics, particularly in rural areas of South Africa. Growing out of the experiential workshops generated by Kristof Fenyvesi, one of the authors of the study,[1] and organised by Nelson Mandela University's Govan Mbeki Mathematics Development Centre (GMMDC) in 2018, as part of their STEAM education development program, a math-art drawing competition was launched. It was free and open to all secondary school learners from Eastern Cape Province.[2] The original study, initially reported at a conference in 2018 by Fenyvesi et al. generated over five hundred math-artworks accompanied by individualised statements of expression.[3] These were contributed by children, youth and teachers from 37 schools of varying socioeconomic status across the Eastern Cape Province, the poorest of South Africa's nine provinces. The math-art competition was designed in response to South African learners' low mathematics performance, as demonstrated in national and international studies (Spaull, 2019). Arts was introduced to stimulate thinking about and expressing mathematics creatively, particularly as creativity has risen from tenth to third place in the ranking of top skills listed by the World Economic Forum (2016). Learners from Grades 8 to 12 were encouraged to participate, with the objective to understand learners' "inward" and "outward" performance (between the mathematics and arts, for future making).

What is particular to the South African context? There appears to be a sustained divide between historically "white" and "black" schools based on socioeconomic disparities, language differences and the impact of former educational policies. While historically "white" public education includes more affluent schools with better teacher training and a focus on motivating learners, the historically "black" schools are economically disadvantaged, suffering from diminished efficacy, low teacher expectations and motivation, a resistance to change, and lack of appropriate infrastructure (see Wolhuter, 2014; Spaull, 2019). Further, mathematics education in South Africa continues to rely on rigid, traditional pedagogies concerned only with lower cognitive levels, despite researchers arguing for more learner-centred and creative approaches to teaching mathematics (Wolhuter, 2014). In contrast, Tsanwani et al. (2014) found that a positive perception (of oneself, mathematics and their teachers) appears to influence disadvantaged learners to persist in mathematics. Fenyvesi et al. (2019) argue that studies of embodied mathematics (wherein maths is performed, whether through visual art, dance or music) have shown positive results, particularly for children with disabilities and learning difficulties. Out of the total of 500 drawing submissions, 113 were selected by the competition organisers to be studied by this chapter's authors, who then created their own criteria for analysis of 87 submissions, then narrowed them down to 20 final math-artworks to be re-read and (re)configured.

The study drew on the concept of diffraction (see Haraway, 1997; Barad, 2007) as a methodological practice of reading "insights through one another" and making diffractive or different, entangled understandings that led to "new cuts".[4] Doing so made it important also to examine the contemporary formal education system in South Africa which, having emerged from post-Apartheid politics only two decades ago, remains highly unequal. For the purposes of this chapter, the authors have not re-visited older readings but rather diffractively read anew a sample of three of the twenty artworks.

Our research team included seven mathematics and art experts with a particular interest in education, who have contributed to STEM, STEAM, mathematics, and the study of arts and creativities education and research. Hailing from diverse countries (Finland, USA, South Africa, India and the UK), they have extensive experience both in the practice of and researching STEAM education.

Our first task involved coding for mathematical and art knowledge, skills, practices, and meanings from the initial selection of 200 drawings and statements of intent offered from the total of 500 drawn by the South African youth and children.[5] Of these, 20 math-artworks and their accompanying statements that were most frequently selected by the team formed the basis of our study. This prompted the team to develop an entangled, intra-acting, disciplinary criteria for selecting these pieces of work. We decided upon math-artworks that offered: a "deep" and differentiated understanding of mathematics and art; greater abstraction and creativity in "doing" math-art literacies, concepts and knowledges; a richer, more embodied and relational understanding of math–art connections; and an investment beyond the realms of the curriculum. It led us to investigate and emphasise the social, cognitive and psychological aspects of mathematics and arts.[6]

Finally, this dataset of math-artworks was then narrowed down to three drawings that enabled us to make multiple-level and ongoing connections between the conceptual and the experiential, the cultural and the historical, the concrete and the abstract, the visual–textual, and the rhythmic and the unstructured, facilitating a "deep" diffraction of the matter of matter. It opened up a transitional space, a field of emergence where terms that make up binaries (self–other, subject–object, math–art, inside–outside, ontologies–realities) intersect, cross over and participate in a shared realm of relational knowing.

3 Doing Diffractive Analysis

Building on Barad's notion of "entanglement", which expresses the idea that reality and language, nature and culture, matter and meaning are inextricably entwined (Barad, 2007: 3), we engaged in an extensive and diffractive reading of the individual artists' "knowing" and "doing" (performativity, affect and disciplinary differentiations). In particular, our reading elaborated how specific nuances generated by the students', as well as researchers', intra-actions and embodiment of mathematics and arts access differing knowledge formations and build understanding of the materiality of the two disciplines within their specific *spacetimemattering*. While multiple, enmeshed and shared insights drew this qualitative analysis away from habitual, normative readings, diffraction also enabled an understanding of unpredictable patterns producing different knowledges generated by differing disciplines. In time, these became active sites for: excavating the connections emerging from math-artwork inquiries located across differences (geographical, economic, political, sociocultural); understanding how inequalities influence learner perceptions and experiences of mathematics; and garnering transdisciplinary insights to develop a discursive math-art method. Emerging from team discussions and the "new cuts" offered by the two disciplines, the following sections acknowledge that diffractive analyses produce more questions than answers (often revealing knowledges only in analysis, after the coding of qualitative inquiry).

The practice of diffraction has made us ask further questions in our re-reading of the math-artworks accompanied by their statements of intent, which were generative and iterative. What is the painting comprised of? What elements, symbols or artefacts complete it? Who is the artist/youth/learner? What does their art say? How far does it entangle with their written statement? What is interesting to the artist in making the math–art connections? What are the specific indications of the iterative (re)configurations (of the material, discursive, social, political, geographical, temporal or conditional) and elements (line, colour, symbols, formulae, metaphor, layout, concept) within the provided materials? We then started to brainstorm "What else is going on here?" and explored the artworks collaboratively. This urged us to move away from a humanist analysis or an anthropocentric gaze (that is, to not only focus on humans, their knowledges, emotions or intentions) to entangle with the matter (content, idea) and its materiality (making, materials used). We asked: What material or matter is interesting to the artist? Do the materials help construct particular emotions, concepts, ideas or knowledges? Does it matter that certain colours, shapes or figures are featured? What do the materials or matter permit or prevent? What do they invite, exclude or regulate? What about the matter and materiality of mathematics and arts as disciplines? What do their materialities and discourses include, emphasise or neglect? Do we assume that the mathematics and the arts knowledges are separate entities, and what difference would it make for our analysis if considered one? What did this math-art activity of drawing, making connection and reflecting do? How did the act of drawing open up "new" spaces or cuts that provoked young people's imagination, to think differently, to test ideas, make affected connections or create intra-active spaces?

In terms of the social or political conditions of these young people's everyday lives, of maths and art, spaces and time, we asked: What does it mean to engage with the discursive materiality of the mathematics and art, particularly for South African youth? Are there emerging binaries in their entanglement with math-art? If so, which of these are assumed, neglected or open to entanglement? Where, when and how is the young people's agency expressed? What is the role of knowledge and who decides upon it? And whose knowledge matters?

In this following section, we show how reading diffractively presents spaces for building a relational, entangled yet differentiated understanding of the math-artwork phenomenon, and argue for intradisciplinarity, a new cut emerging from the study.

4   Diffractively Reading Math-Artworks (Drawings-as-Text)

What follows is our own enactment of diffractive analysis. To do so, we chose three of the most frequently selected artworks for diffractive analysis (see Table 8.1 for an introduction to the three students). In engaging with the material, social, political and geographical conditions of math-artworks, we have read and (re)read the images, re-turning their gaze from individual disciplinary perspectives to the *dynamism of forces* (Barad, 2007: 141) in which all constitutive "things" work mutually and inseparably. We are drawn away from habitual, normative readings. These drawings-as-texts become active sites for *excavating* the connections emerging from math-art inquiries located across differences (geographical, economic, political and sociocultural).

4.1   *Doing Diffractive Readings of Drawing-as-Text 1:* The Stressed Vitruvian Man *by Euclid*

> Artist's statement: This artwork implies how Mathematics is involved in our daily lives. It gives the impression of *how intact Maths is* and [how] *effective Maths is.* Upon the decision of choosing this specific image, I made it clear that Mathematics could have a *positive or negative impacts.* A few examples of *how we experience Math daily* are measurements of our clothing; which is why in my artwork you will see the right side has measurements that is in centimetres which is used to measure clothes. *Clothes* require accurate calculations together with the fact that

TABLE 8.1   Additional details concerning student, school, and competition

Artwork title & student name	Student details (Grade, age, gender, subjects taken, SES)	School type (size, gendered, location – city/rural) & math and art teachers	Competition entry details
'Mechanism' by Jabulani	Grade 12, 17 years, male Race: coloured SES: lower average income group Learner was in grade 12 last year which is the final year of school. School attendance: good Learner stays close to the school: ~1.5 km Jabulani chose Mathematics and Physical Science for FET (grade 10–12). Jabulani's results for maths and science for grade 11 and 12 were low.	Quintile 3 (non-fee-paying), public secondary school, co-ed, urban Public state school in city residential suburb. The residential suburb was allocated to the coloured community during apartheid but is now a multicultural residential area. The school is a secondary school for grade 8–12 learners. There are ~1043 learners. Maths teachers are qualified to teach Maths. Art is not taught as a subject for grade 10–12. There is no Art Club at the school. Thus, learners with an interest in art do this on their own at home.	This drawing was Jabulani's first and only entry to the competition. The drawing shows his very keen interest in engineering, geometry and design.

(cont.)

TABLE 8.1   Additional details concerning student, school, and competition (*cont.*)

Artwork title & student name	Student details (Grade, age, gender, subjects taken, SES)	School type (size, gendered, location – city/rural) & math and art teachers	Competition entry details
'Soul Number' by Annika	Learner was in grade 10 last year and currently in grade 11. She is part of a Maths and Science project on Saturdays. Her attendance there is excellent and her marks in the project classes are higher than the marks that she gets at school. Annika chose Mathematics and Physical Science for FET (grade 10–12). Her school results for maths and science for grade 10 and 11 were average but tends to fluctuate a lot	Quintile 4 (not full fee paying), public school secondary school, only girls, urban The school is on catholic church property. The school is in a residential area in the city of Port Elizabeth. The residential suburb was allocated to the coloured community during apartheid but is now a multicultural residential area. The school is the last Catholic Secondary School for multi-racial pupils in the Northern Areas of Port Elizabeth. All these areas are economically deprived, and unemployment is very high. The school is a secondary school for grade 8–12 learners.	This drawing was Annika's second attempt on entering the competition. Her first attempt was only a drawing of a girl but when questioned by a teacher on the link to maths she changed the drawing to include the number lines.

(*cont.*)

TABLE 8.1 Additional details concerning student, school, and competition (cont.)

Artwork title & student name	Student details (Grade, age, gender, subjects taken, SES)	School type (size, gendered, location – city/rural) & math and art teachers	Competition entry details
		There are ~563 girls enrolled.	
		Maths teachers are qualified to teach Maths.	
		Art is not taught as a subject for grade 10–12. There is no Art Club at the school. Thus, learners with an interest in art do this on their own at home.	
'The Vitruvian Man' by Euclid	Grade 11, 16 years, male Race: Black SES: Low income group (single parent)	Private school, co-ed, urban. The school is a private school that was established in 2012 as a result of the need for a caring educational facility that could provide education in an urban environment.	This drawing is a self-portrait. Euclid entered the competition because he wanted to get recognition for his artwork and not due to an interest in mathematics.

(cont.)

TABLE 8.1   Additional details concerning student, school, and competition (*cont.*)

Artwork title & student name	Student details (Grade, age, gender, subjects taken, SES)	School type (size, gendered, location – city/rural) & math and art teachers	Competition entry details
	Learner was in grade 11 last year and currently in grade 12. Distance of the learner's home to school is ~7 km and popular mode of travel is by mini-bus taxi. Euclid results in maths were not good enough to continue to grade 12 with maths and he was moved to the mathematical literacy class. However, his other subjects results are good to average. One of Jabulani's other artworks was selected to put on the front page of the school newspaper. He sells his artworks for an income.	A partnership with churches and the community resulted in an educational model where everyone could be accommodated. The school is situated in the business district of the city in a building that originally housed shops and offices. The school has learners from grade R–12 (thus combined junior and secondary school). There are ~900 learners in the school. Maths teachers are qualified to teach Maths. Art is not taught as a subject for gr 10–12. There is an Art Club at the school and learners are encouraged to take part.	When asked about his inspiration, he replied: "I was inspired from Leonardo's drawings, his old notebook. I entered the competition because I was fascinated with art and tried to excel more in my art. I tried to get exposure for my art".

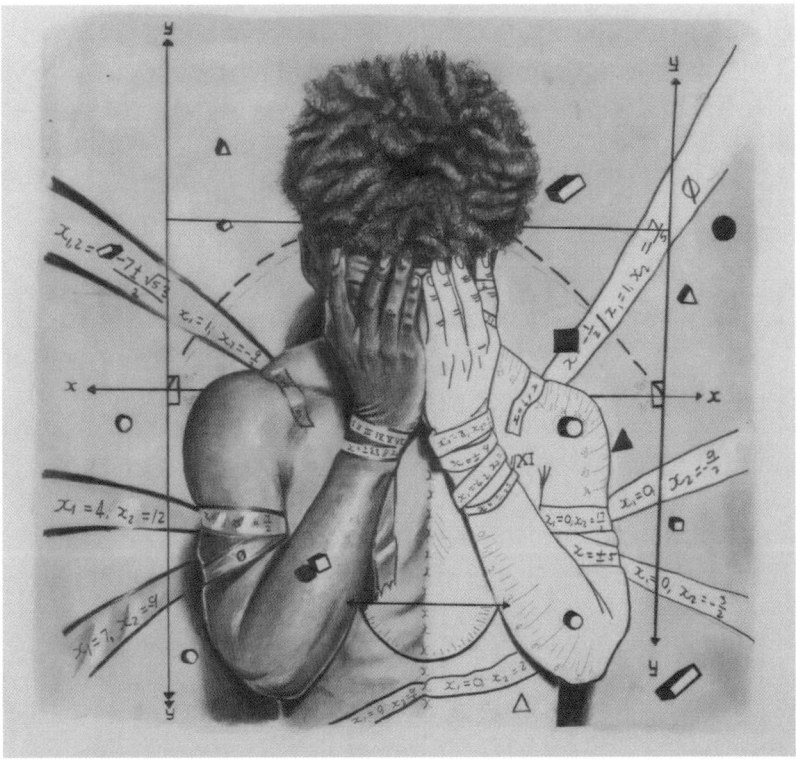

FIGURE 8.2   *The stressed Vitruvian man* by Euclid,[7] a male, aged 16 years, in grade 11 at a private
school that facilitates learners from less privileged backgrounds and thus has a
socioeconomically varied environment

our *bodies* are asymmetrical; which you see the left side does not look
like the right side. We need our measurements to make sure we get the
right fittings. My artwork illustrates the simplicity which is how the effect
of maths has been ignored and neglected. My illustration also *shows the
reality of Mathematics*, that even though it is interesting and effective,
Mathematics could prove to be stressing especially for teenagers who
have other interests. *The artwork has the main figure who is stressed.* I've
indicated that his head is slightly bowed to show the negative impact.
The *hands* which cover the *face* are an indication of frustration. This has
brought about the reality which I didn't intend to hide. The answers to
the equations represent that there is always a solution. This is a form of
encouragement to the mathematical society. I placed the equations on
different places to show that there are different ways to get the answer.
On the same note, I've shown that if done frequently Math could cause
a *negative toil* inside every part of the brain. The two sides have different

shading as indication to the *positive* (simple art, no shading) and *negative* (complicated side with shading) influence of the subject on a person. I call it "The Stressed Vitruvian Man"; would be the modern version of Da Vinci's artwork. I admire the artist a lot and I feel we might have the *same ideals* on art. The lines on the background are from the Vitruvian Man with his *arms* open and *legs* spread out.

This young man's drawing focuses on himself, his hair, his hands and his body, and shares how he thinks of and experiences the consequences of mathematics education. He has drawn a self-portrait in which he cannot separate the learner from what is learned as a way of being (and continuous becoming) in the world. This seems dependent, in this time and space, on giving expression to a form of knowing and his experience of the subject. For this young man, it seems that learning is understood in response to an essentialist view on development and learning where he is judged (and seen here to be judging himself) in relation to his own mathematical development and progression, and status (or lack of) as a mathematician. The monotonality reflects different shades of black with strong cultural references. The bi-tonal hands are productive of difference that comes to matter in the cultural and historical elements and cultural associations of anxiety, emotions and bodily reactions which connect and take action with/in his body. He communicates stress, solemnness and seriousness. Does this produce a view that normalises young people in accordance with dominant views on mathematical development? As researchers and observers of this drawing, we are invited into the world of the mathematician and artist, as part of his world.

The artist seems not to separate the mathematics from the art. The patterns show evidence of superimpositions – the new patterns created are the effect of difference and mark where learning has occurred. The learner is not separated from *what* is learned. He seems to be thinking with and through the relational nature of mathematical concepts, expression and form. While the mathematical concepts featured here include algebraic expressions of solutions to equations, the ideas of analytic geometry and its reliance upon an origin point at the intersection of orthogonal axes, and the mutuality in methods of solving systems of equations intra-acts with two-dimensional space projected from a three-dimensional space, evoking visually stunning and mathematical complexity. We also see that the human body is the seat of mathematical knowledge and through Euclid's art we see him as a knowledge producer. The intra-action between mathematics and arts is mutual and relational: things "are" because they are in relation to and influencing each other. We connect with a young man and his experience of mathematics, which is inscribed on his body.

What else is going on here? Our next thought is that the learning of mathematics is practices of knowing *in* being mathematical, which is something experienced through the body. Karen Barad argues that you cannot isolate knowing from being, since they are mutually implicated. We see this clearly in this drawing, which is putting to work a mediated image of Leonardo DaVinci's *Vitruvian man*. We see a close material-discursive relationship drawn and displaying what appears to be more than a subject–object divide. As Karen Barad states, "knowing is a matter of *part of the world making itself intelligible to another part*" (2007: 185, emphasis added). We connect with a young man. We connect with the maths equations inscribed on his body, from his body, through his body. We see the maths doing something to him, stressing him out, closing him down. All of these are overlapping forces. They are entangled with/in his body, clothes, gestures and emotions in the production of his realities as he becomes *The stressed Vitruvian man*. With his head positioned/held/balanced/almost hidden between his hands, with just a tiny peephole small enough to see through, his divided body and divided encounter with mathematics materialises, in the careful pencil shading. We see how learning is produced through participation in the "math-artwork" operating on the learner and the learner operating on the maths through complex intra-actions of multiple *material-discursive* (bodily, material and discursive) productions (Barad, 2003: 8).

An epistemological device is attributed to the artist; it is assumed that he cannot separate mathematics from its embodied meaning. The maths is experienced. The maths is performed. The maths is inscribed on his body, which is divided by shadings and by ruler markings that measure his left/white arm. All within this space is given agency because of the intra-action between what is left out and put in through the plight of knowing the limits of his mathematical knowing, as a normalising, self-managing discursive practice of knowledge acquisition. Is this a result of the structure and struggle of the rational mind, the lived experience of mathematics? Why has he drawn himself? How can a self-portrait express mathematical knowings? What if he is genetically preprogrammed to unfold in predetermined directions? What if he is not a blank slate, though, but rather is reflecting an educational space and place which is seen to be "filled" with knowledge. He seems to be asking: Why is learning mathematics so hard? Barad (2007: 91) states very clearly that the point is not that knowing has material consequences, but "practices of knowing are specific material engagements that participate in (re)configuring the world".

The experience of *doing* mathematics, learning (*knowing*) mathematics and expressing mathematics seems to involve differences; with different effects conveyed by nuanced shades of grey, black, slate, charcoal. At best, it would seem that doing mathematics involves interacting realities and ruptures. Or is there a continuum drawn across a maths–art binary? The association with mathematics, inscribed and unfolding across the artist's body, intra-acts with creative lateral connections that are drawn to show an association between the art and the human exceptionalism of polymath Leonardo da Vinci and his *Vitruvian man*, which shows the proportions of the human body. He is making clear that *The Vitruvian man* is based on *de Architectura*, a building guide written by Roman architect and engineer Vitruvius. It matters to him that, as a master of the arts, sciences and everything in between, Leonardo da Vinci is a "Renaissance man". Intended to explore the idea of proportion, the piece is part work of art and part mathematical diagram, conveying the old master's belief that everything connects to everything else. There is a great deal of detail concerning and connecting the proportions of the body and the regulation of the body through the spatial-material organisation of the body. There is a great deal of matter mattering as floating mathematical shapes, floating in space and still intra-acting with the body, in front, beside and behind, returning as reminders or cues to ask: "What is mathematics?" "When is mathematics?" "Why does mathematics matter?" The shadings matter a lot. The shadings shed light on the relational nature of difference; thinking with and through difference as a matter of "mathness" and "artness" in the world.

The drawing seems to be working with barriers to enjoying mathematics while making new patterns of thinking and doing. There is a demonstration of a lot of skill and technique. There is also a binary shading which attends to the relational nature of mathematics and art. Here Euclid seems to speak of the asymmetry of our bodies. Maybe this is deconstructive, working with barriers, rather than a reductive view of teaching and learning. A polarising of learners' emotional wellbeing and the troubling of intellectual needs are the effect of mathematics. Is this inconsequential? What do we hear, in the commentary, about the learner questioning and experiencing feelings, ideas, shifts in consciousness and an imagining of different realities? Could he be trying to suspend disbelief and work in fictional contexts using a range of mathematics devices, dilemmas and demands? Could this be an expression of deep understandings about the need to enact and embody mathematics learning and about his making the familiar strange inside the art "work"?

How is art offering a power-producing intra-action between mathematics and being a young man growing up in South Africa? What matters? This does not look like a comfort zone. He appears not to be inviting or sustaining a desire to engage with (dis)comfort. What else counts then? Is there a challenge here to traditional conceptions of why education matters? In order to see the world through another's eyes (could it be Leonardo di Vinci's?) we must enter into their world and understand how it looks. Perhaps this is what it is to be "wide awake" to activate our mathematical imaginations, to really see "the abandoned ones, the homeless ones, the broken windows, the redesigned museum, what is absent, what is realized" (Greene, 1978, p. 45)? Is he trying to re-imagine mathematics as an alternative reality? Is he envisaging what might be possible (social imagination) and hopefully bringing about a change in himself as he becomes aware of how the mathematics and art work, connect, overlap, interfere and change in themselves in intra-action and together create an interference; what we call "learning"? Can he see that embedding the arts in learning experiences can play a pivotal role in enhancing students' imaginative and creative capacities while improving and fostering such understanding? Are these multiple intra-acting agents that are connections to spacetime mattering? What else matters and becomes possible future realities because of this? The critical issues here are that there are no inherent and clear borders between matter and discourse and no clear borders between being and knowing, being and doing. This makes knowing just as much a matter of the body and material as it is a matter of understanding and thinking through these subjects of mathematics and art, which cannot be separated but merge intra-actively. Euclid is thinking with and through mathematics and art and making new patterns of thought (superimpositions), deconstructing power-producing binaries (mind–body, mathematics–art) and showing how these disciplines overlap and change in themselves in intra-action, being concerned with what they *do* and how they are connected and co-constituted.

4.2   *Doing Diffractive Readings of Drawing-as-Text 2:* Soul number *by Annika*

Artist's statement: In my drawing I have chosen to use numberlines as numbers can go on till *infinity* and our *hair* grows continuously, *non-stop*, this is a comparison between the two. The numberlines as *hair* is representing the *roots of our lives* as we cannot go one day without counting or using numbers to represent or solve anything. I have drawn a *little demonic girl* and as you can see the numbers close to her *head* are small numbers, but as they go on, the numbers increase continuously and there is *no end*. This represents the *knowledge we obtain in our everyday lives*, subjects and Maths. I've used *black and white because those colours are drab* and my interest in Maths before was *boring*. The little bit of red shows my *slow interest* in Maths. To me Maths is like a *demon slowly stealing my soul*, like I'm *becoming addicted* to it and *starting to enjoy* it.

FIGURE 8.3   *Soul number* by Annika, a female, aged 15 years, in Grade 10 at a fee-paying public
school where the school community is from low to average socioeconomic
background

In "cutting together-apart"[8] (Barad, 2014; Chappell et al., 2019; Murris &
Bozalek, 2019) Annika's math-artwork, the immediate question to arise is: Is
this articulated as a self-portrait? Is she taking what she finds inventive and trying to work carefully with the details of patterns of thinking in their materiality
of mathematics and art as predicated on her own view of herself? Even if not,
working reiteratively with the math-artwork and the statement offered, the
image appears to be internalised, giving us access to an inner world. Consider
the "othering" of the demonic girl before the math-artist's growing self-rela-
tion to maths, as it multiplies and is embodied ("like a demon slowly stealing
my soul", "becoming addicted"). Making connections (between the material,
descriptive, conditional and conceptual dimensions) in this young woman's
math-art realities involves "re-working the spacetimemattering of thought patterns and not turning away from or leaving behind" (Murris & Bozalek, 2019:
1512).

Annika offers insights into her worldly spaces of school–home, everyday–
extraordinary, material–conceptual, production and performative understandings of practices of knowing. Most markedly, the image appears to have been
excavated from the wider materiality of Japanese manga or anime, at once
crossing over boundaries of spacetime, culture, physical location and economics. This is what Barad refers to as the move toward "performative alternatives",

enabling a *"performative* understanding of discursive practices" beyond representationalism (2003: 802, emphasis in original).[9] The artist communicates the complex and sophisticated mathematical concept of infinity and number sequencing with dexterity, revealing a remarkable metaphoric quality and abstraction of ideas and of self (pre- and post-math-art self, manga self, South African self, student self, math-artist self). The number-lines in the form of the flowing hair create visual texture, rhythm and nuanced compositional definitions. Does this intimate that knowledge is "unending", hinted also by hair drawn so that it seems to continue past the page? There is an abundance of symbolism (monotone image with focus on one eye, hair related to "roots of our lives" and the concept of infinity) and visual codes (unending number-lines, stitched lips, the red eye) in the image. We begin by asking why red? Is it indicative of a growing passion, a self-demonisation or evocative of both these imageries? The featured use of grey related to the drab, contrasting with one red eye, introduces a dramatic and embodied affect. Is this a symbolic self-reference to the ongoing nature of the young woman's developing relationship with mathematics, previously considered "boring"? Annika's monotone shading, and use of black and white spaces, further transform the math-artwork into a visually and emotionally meaningful entanglement embodied by the artist.

The young woman offers differing sites for reading the descriptive matter diffractively. To start with, the title itself, *Soul number*, has multiple connotations (soul music emerging from black subcultures, maths in music, internalisation of maths) for the "new" math-artist's "being-becoming". The head itself and the encompassing hair is framed by numbers. Does this relate to the artist's reconfiguration of maths as inescapable, to maths as the "roots of our lives"? Within the descriptive material-discursive matter of the statement, we see the unfolding of the young woman's mind regarding the nature of mathematics and her personal encounter (and thereon entanglement) with it. Reflecting on the ubiquitous quality of mathematics, she considers how our lives "cannot go one day without … using numbers to represent or solve anything". But she acknowledges that she has employed monotones as a metaphor for the "drab" in mathematics, with the red eye wide awake in this artful expression. At first, such description and depiction of mathematics seems sinister, as she indicates the reason for the colouring of the eye is to signify her slowly growing interest, possibly to the point of addiction. Her embodiment of knowing offers insights into her pathways of intradisciplinary formations.

Locating the conditional or mutual co-existence of material-discursive matter within this math-artwork led to the young woman's declaration that our lives "cannot go one day without" maths. Is this observation conditional, founded on the hierarchies of STEM subjects adapted by nation-states for their own devices? Mathematics is further related to "knowledge we obtain in our everyday lives"; why is art not? Does the South African formal education system or families relegate art to a secondary status? Or is it in fact a more personal reflection, emerging from the enactments of math-art pathways? The (re)readings of her thought patterns, as offered by the image, always drew our adult or gendered "gaze" to the sewn lips, quietened out of the image and the text. Does this imply the debilitating effect of mathematics teaching and learning on her, silencing her voice, cognitive abilities or personal attributes? Is it symbolic of her plight as a young woman in South Africa or as a fan of manga, anime or gaming? Further, the young woman's emotive self-critique (via the demonic subject) begs the question: Is the self-demonisation a reflection of her incapacity for mathematics or others' expectation of being maths capable? It guides acknowledgement also of the material realities of "'being-of-the-world', not 'being-in-the-world'" (Barad, 2007: 160), reducible neither to one or the multiple. As Barad writes:

> [W]hat is at issue and at stake is a matter of the nature of reality, not merely a matter of human experience or human understandings of the world. Beyond the issue of how the body is positioned and situated in the world is the matter of how bodies are constituted along with the world, or rather as "part" of the world (i.e., "being-of-the-world", not "being-in-the-world"). (Barad, 2007: 160)

This math-artwork is abundant in (re)configurations of conceptual matter emerging from the encounters with and meetings of the two disciplines. This is seen in Annika's characterisation of numbers as hair roots and hair as infinity, a smiling mouth but with the lips sewn together, and the red eye with what appears to be ink/tears flowing down the face. These create spaces for "evocative dissonance" as they appear to suggest an overall happy, curious and creative demeanour inflicted by repressed anxieties or suppressed anger felt by the social and intellectual distances created by maths. Reflecting on her affective responses to mathematics, this "math-artful" expression seems highly charged. Annika's embodiment of math-art and its materialisation in everyday life is visible in the mathematical concepts employed, primarily hinting at infinity via the "non-stop" number sequencing. Metaphorically represented, infinity is seen in Annika's usage of sequences embedded in the hair of the figure. The realism of transforming complex mathematical concepts into an aesthetically expressive and intrinsically evocative "math-art" drawing-as-text reveals perspicuity and strong conceptual/technical knowledge. The image foregrounds such "ongoing being-becoming" (Barad, 2014: 181–182). We see this in the subtle distinctions between the colours red and grey that have differing and similar connotations in different countries, systems and social traditions; the symbolic use of mathematical symbols and techniques; and the cross-cultural travel of Japanese materials such as manga and anime books or films, which have found appreciation in the Eastern Cape region of South Africa.

4.3   Doing Diffractive Readings of Drawing-as-Text 3: Mechanis by Jabulani

> Artist's statement: This drawing shows us the relation between *engineering and geometry* and how they are related to engineers and designers. Cars are not only *built* and *sold*. They are carefully thought through and *designed* machines which come in all shapes and sizes. During the period of *designing a car*, everything must be *measured* and *shaped* precisely. If one part is not measured or shaped to specifications, one of the major components which is *aerodynamics* will be *negatively affected*. This then influences the fuel consumption/*economy*, due to drag and air friction. Geometry and EGD are subjects which prepare learners to pursue a *career* in this field. At my school *we do not have the opportunity* to nurture our *skill* in the *arts, design or mechanics/engineering*. A *lack of resources and interest* shown by *our government deprives learners* like myself an opportunity to get a head start to get the necessary foundation that would prepare one for such a *career*.

Jabulani's composition of his math-artwork directs attention to the forward placement of the car in relation to the mathematical expressions set in the background, as they fade out in perspective. Both are articulated with and through the other. Both are affected by and affect each other. Both are entangled. What is striking about the image are its clean lines, the conceptualisation and precision of the drawing, the artist's technical aptitude in realising his vision. It brings together "discipline-specific cognition"[10] and materiality translated via implicit binaries – a mutual co-existence of a whole (maths–arts, concept–practice, economics–education, local–global, dominant–disadvantaged). Hence, the car, as a subject of the math-artwork itself, seems to have been decisively divided into two parts. We notice the colour (blue-grey on the left, and red and yellow on the right) and form (realistic versus graphic). Is this an expression of the mutual co-existence of mathematics and arts? Or is this devised to contrast the technical with the artistic, which cannot be separated in processes of knowing and doing (Barad, 2007)?

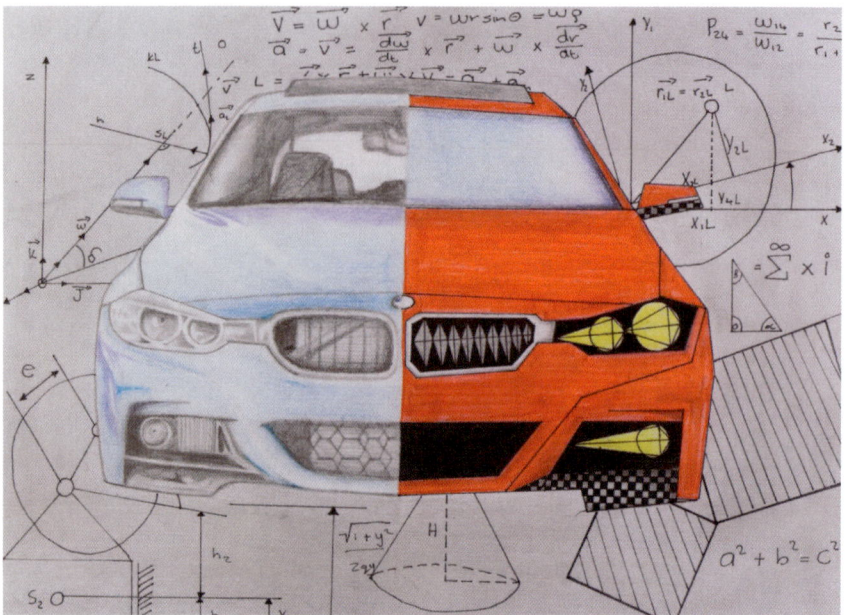

FIGURE 8.4   *Mechanis* by Jabulani, a male, age 17 years, in Grade 12 at a non-fee-paying public
school, from a low socioeconomic background

Analysing the artwork diffractively at once urges "going deep" and considering "what else?" Why did the young man choose automobile design to express
his mathematical-artful concepts in the first place? Where does this young
man's proclivity for the automobile industry emerge from, even as he reflects
that his school does not provide "the opportunity to nurture our skill in the arts,
design or mechanics/engineering"? Does it have any references to the popular
subculture related to motor car or dirt racing and design? In asking what else
is going on, the car's framing by mathematical formulae and symbols raises the
question of their function. How do they relate to the car, if at all? Have they
been employed creatively, allowing the observer's imagination to take over?
Or are these in fact accurate mathematical formulae and calculations used
in car making, employed here to heighten the idea of precision? Is the young
man being allegorical in making available the view of the car interiors seen
through the left side of the windscreen, and not the right, or is it merely the
prying and controlling adult "gaze" interpreting a play of math-art identities?
If metaphoric, in this instance does it signify the young man's embodiment or
the specific enactments of the two distinct disciplines?

   In *excavating* the young man's relationship with the *matter that matters*, the
artist's *materiality* of math-art and agency of math-art matter shows no boundaries between aesthetic skills (for example, use of symbols and metaphor or

layout and design) and technical knowledge (say, drawing three-dimensionally, application of perspective). These intra-active forces mutually perform the specificities of the two disciplines but also the learner's specific personal experience ("we do not have the opportunity") and economic conditions (lack of resources and interest). Jabulani's math-artwork makes explicit connections to the conditional dimensions of the young man's lived math-art experience. This is set up in relation to his analysis of the *political conditions* of education (government depriving learners) and socioeconomic status (of the school or home) and future employability as he reflects on the lack of "necessary foundations". He says: "A lack of resources and interest shown by our government deprives learners like myself an opportunity to get a head start ... that would prepare one for such a career". Such self-expression/reference/interest offered by Jabulani's artwork, and statement, provides discursive material for dialectic entanglements. This is demonstrated in his understanding of the interrelationship between mathematics, art and economics as significant to designing vehicles but also in reflections about how these may shape his future career path. So, does his intention to show "the relation between engineering and geometry and ... engineers and designers" reveal an instinctive humanising of the discipline?

Aesthetically, the *conditional dimensions* invite questions with regard to the cultural connotations of using the colours blue (left side of the car) and red (right parts). Red could be symbolic of excitement at completion, or indicative of passion for one's dream. Blue is positively associated with cool temperatures, soothing to the eye, but also depression (thus "having the blues"). Were such references considered? If so, were these intentional or innate? The colours may also reflect the learner's (dis)agency with reference to mathematics as a human practice or the warmth and cold of the disciplines as lived experience, whilst also making the embodiment of math-art explicit. Studying what matter matters here, through a material-discursive dialectic lens, necessitated moving beyond traditional textual literacy to include colours, symbols and implicit codes. Consider why the young man chose to include symbols such as sigma and infinity (not directly related to car making) alongside what appear to be formulae for aerodynamics, acceleration, pressure and light reflection). Why are the mathematical symbols dispersed in the background, foregrounded only by the finished product, the car? Does it seek to build understanding of the dispersed nature of knowledge and information to be garnered or is it in fact emphasising them as building blocks for necessary outcomes, finished or unfinished? His understanding of the wider conditions (say, his school's or his own economic status or politics that limit disciplinary conditions) suggests an agentic self or, in Barad's terms, an "agentic realism" on Jabulani's part, through which he makes new "cuts" that add to the existing math-art assemblages.

These new "agential cuts" allow for the *conceptual* and the non-representational, expressed beyond the boundaries of the two disciplines, and economics and geopolitical conditions. The conceptual connections made available by Jabulani's math-artwork present evident intersections of the artist's *knowingdoingbeing*. He opines, "Cars are not only built and sold. They are carefully thought through", thus attending to the relational nature of math-art values and economics. We see this also in multiple voicings of the word "mechanism", which references: (a) the "mechanics" of making, whether a math-artwork or a physical car, (b) the political "mechanisms" (governance, hierarchies of disciplines and knowledge itself) that reproduce social inequities, and (c) the "machinations" of connecting and implementing the conceptual with the conditional, actions to ideas, and self within its wider contexts. Artistically, inquiry about the distinct differences presented between the left of the car (realistic but appearing to be a blueprint, outlined in blue-grey tones), and the right (graphic and seemingly completed illustration, in red), draws attention to the artist's abstraction, metaphoric quality and interest in representation.

This math-artwork offers multilevel connections. This young man has made a carving of the material realities of his intradisciplinary pathways to experiencing mathematics as art and art as mathematics. He seems to be seeking out the relational aspects of math–art intra-actions, relating them to economy, governance, careers and lack of resources.

5   Resisting Easy Answers: Troubling the Practice of Knowing

At the beginning of this chapter we argued that there is a critical need to deepen understanding of how arts knowing in STEAM configurings comes to matter. We have introduced new evidence on how the materials used to make art and to think discursively with mathematics offer new understandings of how mathematics and art can intra-act. We have seen in these three cases different (re)configurations of STEAM; where being, knowing and doing enactments of mathematics and art not only engender a "mutuality" of disciplines but also produce new knowledge that is capable of activating a future-making education.

In this chapter, we featured research that reports a novel analysis of a sample of drawings-as-text which we have called "math-artworks" that were created by Grade 8–12 South African students following a series of mathematics-art-experiential workshops. We conducted diffractive readings using feminist new materialism, where a sample of three drawings-as-text generated insights and new questions, opening up other possible meanings/matterings concerning the connectivity between mathematics and art and what possibilities become available when young people experiment and explore the material and discursive dimensions of mathematics and art simultaneously.

In trying to make visible the intra-active play between mathematics and art, the practices of knowing enact what we know (knowing), who we are (being) and how we action this (doing). In secondary school, teachers recognise that they are asking young people to make huge leaps to conceive of themselves as "doing" and "acting" but also "being" mathematicians and artists. This practice of knowing invokes/provokes/invites paying close, responsive and response-able (enabling response) attention to a new set of pedagogic strategies for future-making education. Troubling the hegemonic notions of what constitutes mathematics education/learning and art education/learning, framed by feminist new materialist perspectives, opens up the possibilities that subject disciplines can be more engaging, relevant and less alienating. STEAM ca (re) configure and activate a future-making education by attending to differences in all their detail, creatively repatterning STEAM as specific material engagements and practices of knowing. Tracing these entanglements is key.

We ask what does such a math-artwork drawing-as-text task and the diffractive analysis of these math-artworks invoke in terms of configuring pedagogic strategies for future-making education? We experimented with Karen Barad's (2007) concept of diffraction as a methodological practice of reading, which offered much more than simply an alternative form of analysis or an alternative to teacher reflection. Rather, we found that diffractive analysis became a metaphor which depicts "insights through one another", which expresses the idea that reality and language, nature and culture, matter and meaning, are inextricably intra-actively entwined (Barad, 2007: 3). We engaged in a complex reading of individual young people's practices of knowing and doing as evidenced in the material enactments that contributed to, and were a part of, intradisciplinary practices of relational knowing. This itself offers a pedagogic strategy, inviting new ways of teaching based on questions and dialogue, and different ways of perceiving the subjects and the learners.

As STEAM practitioner educators and researchers, we need to look closely at what intradisciplinary practice is and why it matters for future-making education. The "entanglement" of the material has agency of its own. This lies at the heart of Barad's philosophical position of agential realism where we need *to pay attention to matter as well as meaning* as practitioner educators and researcher communities. We need to continually disrupt and uproot the presumptions upon which siloed subject knowledge is based and rethink how STEAM practices can create novel worlds without imposed constraints on what is possible when we venture into the intradisciplinary knowing between mathematics and the arts. We invite readers to ask what this enables teachers to develop. Our view is that teachers should shift emphasis to rethinking how the material artefacts of learning embody and shape practices and perceptions of knowing things differently. Pedagogic strategies for future-making education also need to recognise the agency of STEAM practice as a way to advance understanding and insights into how young people – the makers of the future – understand themselves in the enactment of and meaning making between mathematics and art. At the mutually constitutive centre of intradisciplinarity and future-making education, the pedagogies pertinent to the arguments presented in this chapter, we end with Ellsworth (2005: 55), who explores a relation among different possibilities:

> In excessive moments of learning in the making, when bodies and pedagogies reach over and into each other, the pedagogical address and the learning self interfuse to become "more" than either intended or anticipated. The instability and fluidity of pedagogy hold the potential for an unknowable and unforeseeable "more", and the actualisation of that potential is what springs the experience of the learning self.

Acknowledgements

We would like to sincerely thank all of the schools and students, but particularly the three South African young people, who participated in this study.

Notes

1 The GMMDC offers annual regional two-day GeoGebra conferences for in-service mathematics educators, which in 2017 emphasised a STEAM education focus, particularly for participants from disadvantaged regions. Dr Kristof Fenyvesi established connections with GMMDC through his experiential math-art workshops. In 2018, to create further awareness about STEAM and math-art connections, together they developed the Math-Art Competition, initially launched across Eastern Cape Province, to encourage pupils and educators from high schools to create art from maths. It is intended that the competition will be conducted on a larger scale in the following years.

2   The Math-Art Competition was advertised through local media and emails to schools, and ran for two months. Flyers and entry forms were handed out at learner programs held after school hours. Currently the math-artworks are in the Bridges Children and Youth Math-Art Collection, and were on show in July 2018 in the Swedish National Museum of Science and Technology during the Bridges Stockholm Conference (www.bridgesmathart.org/bridges-2018).

3   The study is reported in a book chapter by Fenyvesi et al. (2019).

4   Any act of observation makes a "cut" between what is included in and excluded from what is being considered – memories, belongings and attachments to material and visual cultures – in a process that rebuilds, folds and expresses constellations of significance in their lives (see also Barad, 2003; Hickey-Moody, 2018).

5   Some of these math-artworks were incomplete, barely attempted or without a statement of intent, thus not included.

6   These included the aesthetic, cognate, critical, creative, affective, embodied, attitudinal, conditional, material, discursive, emotional and temporal dimensions of mathematics and arts literacies and learning.

7   We use pseudonyms throughout.

8   In her article "Diffracting diffraction", Barad (2014: 177) reflects on the "material conditions of *exteriority-within-phenomena*" (emphasis in original), explaining how entanglements are not *unities* and do not erase differences since they exist not only between two entities or systems (say, insider-outsider) but also within the outsider and insider of oneself, at once bending, converging and interrupting the object of examination in co-constitutive and multiple ways (see also Chappell et al., 2019; Murris & Bozalek, 2019).

9   Barad, in moving away from representationalist beliefs, contests the "excessive power granted to language to determine what is real" (2003: 802) and the representation of pre-existing things, and offers a performative understanding of discursive practices. She adds that performativity, if properly construed, is "actually a contestation of the unexamined habits of mind that grant language and other forms of representation more power in determining our ontologies than they deserve" (802). She suggests that a move toward "performative alternatives to representationalism" shifts the focus from "descriptions and reality (e.g., do they mirror nature or culture?) to matters of practices/doings/actions", thus foregrounding critical questions around ontology, materiality and agency (802).

10 By "discipline-specific cognition" we mean theories, concepts, processes, skills, literacies, knowledges and material and discursive resources made available by individual disciplines. Materiality is related to the physical material and matter, and audiovisual cultures. It may include aesthetic material, cultural artefacts, derived and indicative symbols, place, apparatuses, skills, policy documents or self-reflection notes amongst others.

References

Barad, K. (2003). Posthumanist performativity: Toward an understanding of how matter comes to matter. *Signs: Journal of Women in Culture and Society, 28*(3), 801–831.

Barad, K. (2007). *Meeting the universe halfway: Quantum physics and the entanglement of matter and meaning.* Durham, NC: Duke University Press.

Barad, K. (2014). Diffracting diffraction: Cutting together-apart. *Parallax, 20*(3), 168–187.

Beane, J. A. (2011). Curriculum integration and the disciplines of knowledge. In J. Sefton-Green, P. Thomson, K. Jones, & L. Bresler (Eds.), *The Routledge international handbook of creative learning* (pp. 193–199). Abingdon: Routledge.

Chappell, K., Hetherington, L., Ruck Keene, H., Wren, H., Alexopoulos, A., Ben-Horin, O., ... Bogner, F. X. (2019). Dialogue and materiality/embodiment in science|arts creative pedagogy: Their role and manifestation. *Thinking Skills and Creativity, 31,* 296–322.

Collin, A. (2009). Multidisciplinary, interdisciplinary and transdisciplinary collaboration: Implications for vocational psychology. *International Journal for Educational and Vocational Guidance, 9*(2), 101–110.

Colucci-Gray, L., Burnard, P., Trowsdale, J., Cooke, C. F., Davies, R., & Gray, D. S. (2017). *Reviewing the potential and challenges of developing STEAM education through creative pedagogies for 21st learning.* London: British Educational Research Association.

Ellsworth, E. (2005). *Places of learning: Media, architecture, pedagogy.* New York, NY: Routledge.

Fenyvesi, I., Brownell, C., Burnard, P., Sinha, P., Olivier, W., Steyn, C., & Lavicza, Z. (2019). Mathematics and art connections expressed in artworks by South African students. In L. Bresler (Ed.), *On art and science.* Dordrecht: Springer.

Greene, M. (1978). Wide-awakeness and the moral life. *Landscapes of learning* (pp. 42–52). New York, NY: Teachers College Press.

Haraway, D. (1997). *Modest_Witness@Second_Millenium. FemaleMan_Meets_oncoMouse: Feminism and Technoscience.* London: Routledge.

Hickey-Moody, A. (2018). New materialism, ethnography, and socially engaged practice: Space-time folds and the agency of matter. *Qualitative Inquiry* [Preprint]. https://doi.org/10.1177/1077800418810728

Ingold, T. (2018). *Anthropology and/as education.* Abingdon: Routledge.

Murris, K., & Bozalek, V. (2019). Diffracting diffractive readings of texts as methodology: Some propositions. *Educational Philosophy and Theory, 51*(14), 1504–1517. doi:10.1080/00131857.2019.1570843

Murris, K. (2018). Posthuman child and the diffractive teacher: Decolonizing the nature/culture Binary. In Am. Cutter-Mackenzie-Knowledges, K. Malone, & E. Barratt Hacking (Eds.), *Research handbook on childhoodnature: Assemblages of childhood and nature research* (pp. 1–25). Dordrecht: Springer.

Murris, K., & Thompson, R. (2016). Drawings as imaginative expressions of philosophical ideas in a Grade 2 South African literacy classroom. *Reading & Writing – Journal of the Reading Association of South Africa, 7*(2). https://doi.org/10.4102/rw.v7i2.127

Spaull, N. (2019). *Priorities for education reform in South Africa.* Stellenbosch: Stellenbosch University. Retrieved August 13, 2019, from https://nicspaull.files.wordpress.com/2019/01/spaull-priorities-for-educ-reform-treasury-19-jan-2019.pdf

Thomson, P. (2008). Children and young people: Voices in visual research. In P. Thomson (Ed.), Doing visual research with children and young people (pp. 1–21). London: Routledge.

Tsanwani, A., Harding, A., Egelbrecht, J., & Maree, K. (2014). Perceptions of teachers and learners about factors that facilitate learners' performance in mathematics in South Africa. *African Journal of Research in Mathematics, Science and Technology in Education, 18*(1), 50–51.

Wolhuter, C. C. (2014). Weaknesses of South African education in the mirror image of international educational development. *South African Journal of Education, 34*(2), 1–25.

World Economic Forum. (2016). *The future of jobs: Employment, skills and workforce strategy for the fourth industrial revolution.* Geneva: World Economic Forum. Retrieved August 13, 2019, from http://www3.weforum.org/docs/WEF_Future_of_Jobs.pdf

CHAPTER 9

STEAM Education, Art/Science and Quiet Activism

Anna Hickey-Moody, Christine Horn and Marissa Willcox

Abstract

This chapter takes up the feminist new materialist concepts of "diffraction" and "intra-action" as ways of thinking about children's embodied and imaginative knowledge through, and in relation to, aspects of the world that can be classified as the non-human. It employs these new materialist frames of "diffraction" and "intra-action" to show how art/science intra-act through "quiet activism" in children's art. It argues that this work can be considered a vernacular form of STEAM education that radically re-situates, and indeed deconstructs, forms of science education proposed through outcomes-based curriculum, and extends children's sense of themselves as entangled in their environment. The data theorised in this chapter is drawn from findings from a multi-sited ethnographic project that runs in 13 sites in 6 cities. This ongoing empirical project utilises art as a research method in primary school classrooms and informal educational settings, ostensibly to explore issues of social value and community belonging. However, across the last three years working in the UK and Australia, children, unprompted, have returned repeatedly to concerns about the environment, climate change and pollution. The children are so enmeshed in their broader environment that some draw self-portraits of themselves as landscapes. The arts-making practices reported here have led children to create speculative and imaginative scientific inventions that were designed to respond to the now inevitable effects of climate change and that merge art and science in unexpected ways. In developing the concept of quiet activism as an inherently interdisciplinary art/science (STEAM) method of environmental and art education, this chapter argues for an intra-active and diffractive, interdisciplinary and speculative model of embodied pedagogy. Children's creative, quiet activism teaches us interdisciplinarity in dynamic and applied ways.

Keywords

art/science – Barad – climate change – diffraction – embodiment – imagination – intra-action – speculation

1   **Introduction**

> Diffraction as a way of thinking draws attention to the agency of the
> non-human, the ways that the materials used to make art can change
> thinking and can change relationships between people ... building
> more than human relationships. Arts-based practices offer an ideal way
> not only of accessing but also of reorganizing emotional investments.
> (Hickey-Moody, 2018: 8)

This chapter is authored by a team of researchers working on the Interfaith
Childhoods project. We show some ways in which arts practices and creative
experimentation can be seen as invaluable methods for imagining new scientific solutions to climate change and, as such, might be taken as an example of
a new form of STEAM education. We bring this strong empirical base together
with recent work arising from feminist new materialism (Revelles-Benavente &
González Ramos, 2017) and posthuman research practices in education (Jones &
Hoskins, 2016). We contend that these bodies of literature show the significance of making and, specifically, they illustrate the utility of the materiality
of making as a core component of pedagogies of change. Making materialises
the imagination and gives form to speculative possibilities, speculative new
futures that might offer alternatives to current endemic practices of environmental degradation: practices in which the environment is unrealistically
imagined as an endless stream of replenishing resources. In contrast to such
popular imaginings of natural resources as being "endless", and cost free, the
speculative and imaginative work of the children with whom we work across
different countries and cities returns repeatedly to explore new ways in which
environmental resources might be protected and used more wisely. Through
giving this creative, imaginative and material work a theoretical grounding
in feminist new materialist and posthuman theories of education, we suggest
that children's materialisations of "other worlds" and "other ways" need to be
considered as initial inroads into new, environmentally sustainable futures
and taken as a model for STEAM education.

2   **Contextualising Our Empirical Data**

The theoretical work undertaken in this chapter is very much a response to
the empirical findings of our research. The data that inspired this chapter, and
which we theorise below, is drawn from the Interfaith Childhoods research
project. Anna Hickey-Moody began this project in 2016 with a faculty research

grant from the Faculty of Arts and Social Sciences at the University of Sydney. The earliest data theorised in this chapter (the invention of "sustainability city") was generated as part of this pilot study. The project then received funding from the Australian Research Council and RMIT University. From 2016 on, fieldwork has run with the same groups of children and adults in Manchester, London, Sydney, Melbourne, Adelaide and Canberra. There are multiple sites in many of these cities, and at the time of writing fieldwork is ongoing and the project has over 360 participants. These are comprised of children who take part in the arts workshops and their parents, family members and/ or carers who take part in focus group discussions and follow-up interviews. This methodology offers us children's and parents' perspectives on belonging, community, values and "what really matters" to them. These lines of inquiry were developed to mobilise faith networks as needed, but not impose them on others. The child is positioned as the authority on what matters to them, and through art making children are given the opportunity to invite other children into their world views. Similarly, parents' values and perspectives are valued as "folk knowledges" of culture, and these knowledges are held alongside other often quite different views in community focus groups. As the facilitator of the focus group discussions with adults, Anna Hickey-Moody tries to both understand and recognise diverse perspectives and also mediate conflict if it arises. Twenty-five arts-based research workshops have been run to date in Australia and the UK, 21 in-depth interviews have been undertaken with parents or carers and 21 adult focus groups undertaken. During this process, the ways in which children were invited to make art collaboratively, and the kinds of materials made available to them, were kept as similar as possible.

To facilitate this process of encouraged collaboration and to ensure that the workshops are as similar in format as possible, Anna Hickey-Moody has developed a set of nine lesson plans to encourage collaboration through art making that scaffold and build children's skills and are implemented in a sequential order with groups. The first three of these lesson plans are included in this chapter as a resource for readers to draw on in their own pedagogical practices. The lessons have been designed to support debate and imaginative responses, and to encourage collaboration and the exploration of values. They have proven effective and enjoyable for young people aged 5–12 but can be modified or developed in order to be used with different age groups. The three lesson plans included in this chapter are critically important parts of our methodology. It was during these workshops that themes of concern over climate change and climate distress and inventive solutions for environmentally sustainable futures began to emerge.

The emergence of themes of concern over climate change, climate distress and inventive solutions for environmentally sustainable futures were not only striking because these themes were so pronounced, but also because the children were not being asked to explore climate change or environmental sustainability. Children were being asked to explore values, "what really matters" to them, and what values they want to bring into the future. These broad themes for engagement were developed as a way of bringing religious and non-religious children together in conversation and to scaffold collaboration. The specific prompts issued by adults, as detailed in the lesson plans included below, did not address climate change. Enduringly, children presented their concerns about climate change and used their creative time and art resources to imagine more sustainable cities for the future. Some of the innovations imagined by children that you will read about as this chapter continues include cars and buildings that have feathered wings so they can fly without harming the environment by creating emissions, turning streets into rivers so that marine life can live on in safety and humans can travel by boat rather than by car to save the planet, and mobile community facilities such as flying recycling plants, mosques and football (soccer) pitches, which can be shared by people from different places to reduce the burden on one community.

Across countries, and indeed across cities within the same country, these themes recur. The invention of the flying mosque in Manchester is echoed in the invention of a flying car in Sydney, which resonates with flying recycling centres and soccer fields that were created by children in Melbourne. The link to STEAM education here is "organic", in the respect that it is a result of the children using arts-based methods as a form of radical, speculative scientific practice. Children across the globe are collectively imagining and *imaging* environmentally sustainable futures. As has been made clear by the contextualisation of the project above, this is made all the more striking by the fact that the adults involved in the project were not asking the children about climate change. The research team were asking the children about what really matters for the future, and what a future city composed of everything that really matters might look like. In theorising this work as youth voice, we take our cue from the children, and take their work as a folk, or popular, example of what STEAM education could look like.

3   Intra-Action and Diffraction as Useful Ways of Understanding the Materiality of Learning

In the last five years, posthuman research in education has increasingly mobilised ideas of diffraction and intra-action as useful ways of understanding the material aspects of learning. Much of this work draws on the theories of Karen Barad (2007). In our approach, we too mobilise the ideas of diffraction and intra-action. Diffraction, as it is explained by Barad, is an "overarching trope" (2007:71) for her book *Meeting the universe halfway*, and is "marked by patterns of difference" (2007:71). Barad explains that "diffractions are attuned to differences – differences that our knowledge-making practices make and the effects they have on the world" (Barad, 2007: 72). To put this another way, the radical differences imagined by children, such as feathered wing-limbs being attached to cars, or mosques that fly across cities, are different ways of *making* the world that need to be understood as having effects. For example, imagining something *makes it possible* and diffracts a "newer, winged version" of the unwinged car back onto all contemporary un-winged cars. Citing Haraway, Barad explains that "a diffraction pattern does not map where differences appear, but rather maps where the *effects* of differences appear" (Haraway, 1999: 300, as cited in Barad, 2007: 72). Diffraction then becomes an analytic tool, a "tool of analysis when attending to and responding to the effects of difference" (Barad, 2007: 72).

The idea of a diffraction pattern brings with it the knowledge that context is completely and materially formative, a discovery that was made by Niels Bohr in what is known as the "two-slit experiment" (Barad, 2007: 102–105). In this experiment, Bohr, and many others after him, discovered that water creates a diffraction pattern when it passes through two slits. Marbles do not. If marbles, or matter, are fired through two slits, the resulting patterns form two lines that mirror the slits. If water, or waves, pass through two slits, each slit creates a semi-circle of ripples, which "break" into each other as the centre of the circle expands and crashes into the neighbouring circle. This results in diffraction patterns that repeatedly mark the wall onto which the slits face in many different ways. A similar messy or distributed diffraction pattern occurs across the back wall when the experiment is conducted with quantum particles. However, when *observing* the movement of quantum particles during the experiment, the behaviour of the particles changes, and the experiment results in two lines of quantum particles along the back wall. When left unobserved, the particles behave like waves, and when observed they behave like matter. This is taken to prove that the act of observation, or the context in which something takes place, is a crucial agent in how things "work" or behave. This observation is crucial to our work here. The children are responding to their daily experiences of climate change through their artwork and, while they are not usually given the imaginary power to reinvent the world in their school curriculum, they create this opportunity as soon as there is space made for such a venture. As Barad reminds us: "space, time and matter do not exist prior to the intra-actions that constitute entanglements" (2007: 74). Waves – of sound, light and liquid – are always diffracting. The word used to characterise the moment when two waves overlap or intra-act is *interference*. There is now "direct empirical evidence that *matter* – not just light – manifests *wave* behaviour under the right experimental circumstances" (Barad, 2007: 83, emphasis in original). The world changes when it is given space to, and children change the world to what they want in the future when they are given space for such inventions.

Intra-action is embedded in this double-slit experiment, namely, the concept that matter has agency is proven by it and the enmeshment of particles with one another is foreshadowed by wave behaviour. Barad explains entanglement through explaining that: *"Entanglements, like superpositions, are uniquely quantum mechanical – they specify a feature of particle behaviour for which there is no classical physics equivalent"* (Barad, 2007: 270, emphasis in original). Here "agency is cut loose from its traditional humanist orbit. Agency is not aligned with human intentionality or subjectivity. Nor does it merely entail resignification or other specific kinds of moves within a social geometry of antihumanism" (Barad 2007: 177). Barad goes on to explain that agency "is a *matter of ... enactment ... It is the enactment of iterative changes to particular practices*" (Barad, 2007: 178, emphasis in original). As we demonstrate, the children's speculative scientific inventions through art can be seen as their own ways of diffracting the fear of climate change with which they live on a daily basis and also as an enactment of their agency, a global environmental enmeshment in which they show ways they see change should be possible. As such, these ideas of diffraction, intra-action and enmeshment are fundamental to the way we understand the politics of the children's artworks as an intervention in the Anthropocene, or contemporary global climate.

We build on the work of feminist scholars in education, specifically Ringrose and Renold (2016), Ivinson and Renold (2016), de Frietas and Sinclair (2018), Jones and Hoskins (2016) and others. These theorists have enlivened Barad's work with situated, social and political dimensions she often fails to recognise. Intra-action and enmeshment understand *agency* as a dynamism of forces (Barad, 2007: 141). Separate bodies in proximity to one another impact on each other in ways that can be understood or seen as co-constitutive. Schools, their pupils and teachers are co-constitutive in ways we can only begin to understand. An enmeshed understanding of curriculum, space, time and imagination shows us they are indeed co-constitutive.

4   Creative Learning in STEAM Education

Fostering student's creativity is an important aspect of contemporary pedagogy in subjects such as music and arts, but also in the sciences, maths, physics and chemistry. Teachers and theorists in the field increasingly acknowledge the importance of creativity over rote learning to prepare students for contemporary workplaces that require flexibility, innovation and collaboration. The ability to think creatively enables students to find ingenious approaches to classroom problems, even though these may not always lead to realistic solutions. Such "out of the box" thinking can open new avenues of thought that lead to a variety of solutions to a variety of issues, including the inception of winged cars to address climate change. Pam Burnard and other contributors to this book refer to this as "possibility thinking", based on a concept developed by Anna Craft (2015). "Possibility thinking" (Cremin, Burnard, & Craft, 2006) is conceptualised as the ability to envision possibilities that may seem unrealistic at first glance but may hold the potential for innovative solutions. The importance of creativity in STEM subjects is not always as well acknowledged, and sometimes creative approaches clash with other aspects of the educational model. Burnard and White call this the "'counterpoint' of freedom and control" (2008: 667). Possibility thinking and its creative (and at times tentative) outcomes are not always compatible with an educational system that foregrounds results over processes, and that applies across-the-board standards to measure performance and quality of outcomes. In addition, it is increasingly difficult for teachers to comply with quality benchmarks while at the same time fostering creativity and self-confidence in students. The key term here is "rebalancing pedagogy" (Burnard & White, 2008), or balancing the sometimes opposing requirements that dictate the implementation of strict benchmarks alongside more creative and innovative practices.

An increasing emphasis on creativity in the teaching of subjects previously considered "hard science", such as maths and engineering, indicates that there is room for creative practice in STEM subjects. Practitioners and theorists acknowledge the need to prioritise meaningful learning and creative reasoning over rote learning and imitative reasoning (Lithner, 2015). Creativity, while hard to define, can be learned and taught, like other skills, and some practices lend themselves to the teaching and learning of creative approaches. Activities such as art, drawing, painting or collage encourage students' imaginations, and enable them to visualise their ideas and think through, share and discuss them with others. The examples in this chapter will illustrate some of these processes.

The expansion of the STEM acronym (science, technology, engineering, mathematics) to include the arts, resulting in in STE(a)M or STEAM, suggests that subjects such as fine arts, music and language have an important role to play in fostering creative thinking (Burnard & White, 2008; Craft et al., 2014; Burnard et al., 2018). Choosing to focus on creativity in science subjects necessitates a move away from the right-wrong dichotomy, as well as a re-thinking of the roles of teachers and learners. As Burnard, Craft and their collaborators have pointed out, ownership, agency and control are key elements that enable creative approaches (Burnard & White, 2008; Craft et al., 2014). Teachers must learn to appreciate a variety of contributions as valid ways forward in the problem-solving process, and to adopt a co-creative or participatory approach, in which students and teachers work out potential solutions together. This requires a more collaborative learning environment with room for risk taking, student agency, additional time to try out innovative ideas, and spaces that are specifically designed to foster creativity, which Burnard and colleagues (2018) refer to as "possibility spaces". Reconceptualising education in this way acknowledges students' ability to work out complex problems as well as each student's previous experience and ability to share knowledge and become a teacher in their own right. These collaborative and creative approaches reinforce creative thinking and affirm students' confidence in the contributions they are able to make to solving complex problems.

Such collaborative and innovative approaches are important because children play a crucial role in addressing societal problems, in particular those by which they will be primarily affected, such as environmental and climate change. Children are increasingly becoming active as advocates and agents of change, through initiatives such as school strikes, by leveraging social and other media, and through their role as "silent" or "everyday activists" in their family and school environment (Walker, 2017a, 2017b). Children are aware of and concerned about current environmental changes and the problems they will inherit. Around the world, they are increasingly making their voices heard, and they are becoming active at local and even global levels (Turns, 2019; Tchinda, 2018). Many children are highly motivated, and they are able to use their enthusiasm and motivation to effect change by motivating the adults in their lives to make positive changes. Research has shown that children can leverage considerable influence in this respect (Hiramatsu et al., 2014; Istead & Shapiro, 2014; Kuczynski et al., 2016; Stafford & Brain, 2017; O'Neill & Buckley, 2019; Lawson et al., 2018).

While some research suggests that identifying as an environmental activist has more to do with perceived identity rather than the wish to work towards a more sustainable future for some young people (Collins, 2019; Satchwell, 2013), this at least indicates that living a sustainable lifestyle and being politically active with regards to the environment is seen as attractive and desirable. Environmentally conscious children grow up to be environmentally conscious adults, which means that environmental education and fostering environmental literacy is an important step in working towards more sustainable societies (von Braun, 2017).

Children learn about their environment from a variety of sources, among them their parents and families, friends, and in the school or childcare environment (Hedefalk, Almqvist, & Östman, 2015; Nche, Achunike, & Okoli, 2019). Here, environmental education is increasingly becoming part of the mainstream school, preschool and childcare curriculum (Satchwell, 2013; Öllerer, 2015; Riede, Keller, & Greissing, 2016; O'Neill & Buckley, 2019). Educating the next generation about environmental issues is seen as a valuable strategy in working towards a sustainable future (Walker, 2017b; Ramanathan et al., 2017; Lawson et al., 2018). In order to implement environmental education successfully in the curriculum, educators need to take a holistic approach, so that the theme of environmental sustainability is included in the whole range of subjects. Teachers must also continue to keep their knowledge about environmental issues and potential solutions up to date (Öllerer, 2015). Teaching children about the kinds of behaviours that are environmentally damaging is not always enough to change behaviours (Satchwell, 2013, 2016). Spending time outdoors can help children develop a greater sense of connection with the environment, and so this is often seen as an important part of environmental education (Hedefalk et al., 2015). In addition, environmental education is moving away from teaching students about facts and figures and towards enabling students to act for change (Hedefalk et al., 2015). Strategies that focus on creativity and possibility thinking are useful in this respect, because they can enable children to identify potential solutions and approaches to mitigate climate and environmental change, and give them the confidence to act on them even if they seem unusual or fanciful at first.

While some approaches to environmental conservation are tried and tested, such as a reduction in car journeys, using the bike instead of the car, or in the case of environmental pollution picking up rubbish, recycling or reducing the use of single-use plastic, other potential solutions require more imagination. These include, for example, the creation of enzymes that break down plastics, or the use of geoengineering to reduce the increase in global temperatures (Low & Schäfer, 2019). Approaches include strategies for carbon capture or sequestration, for instance turning carbon into fertiliser or rocks, distributing sulphur in the atmosphere to reduce the amount of light that reaches the surface of the earth and seeding oceans with iron to promote algal blooms. While these ideas require rigorous modelling, research and trials in order to assess and evaluate their risk against their potential benefit, it is important not to dismiss them out of hand. Even if these ideas are never implemented, they may lead researchers towards practical solutions that turn out to have real benefits. In this, they are examples of the kind of "possibility thinking" we have discussed above.

Along with scientific efforts led by universities and think tanks, some young people are already developing creative solutions to address pollution in the environment. In 2011, a Dutch teenager saw so much rubbish in the ocean during a holiday in Greece that he decided to invent a device to capture floating debris (Venema, 2014). He is now the CEO of his own charitable organisation with more than 80 staff, has won various design and leadership awards, and has launched the first and second full-scale prototypes of his device. In 2019, an Irish teenager developed a way of removing microplastics from water with the use of magnetic fluids – and won a Google Science Fair prize for his effort (Ebrahimji, 2019).

From this track record, or mobilising this history of invention leading to innovation, we propose that we need to position the child as pedagogue and their creative, speculative knowledge as the curriculum for STEAM education, with a view to developing an environmentally sustainable future.

5   Climate Change Identities

Posthuman art education projects prompt children to create meaning through making, and this meaning-making process, in turn, re-informs educational research, theory and practice (Hickey-Moody, 2016; Ringrose, Warfield, & Zarabadi, 2018; Renold & Ringrose, 2019). Using a feminist new materialist frame, our positioning of the Interfaith Childhoods collaborative art education workshops as an intervention in STEM demonstrates that knowledge creation leading to innovation is an iterative process which can evolve through creative and embodied art making. Barad urges us to remember that "the body reacts to the forces, manifest as shifting material alignments and changes in potential, and becomes not simply the receiver but also the transmitter or local source of the signal or sign that operates through it" (2007: 189). As she suggests, the body when it receives a force, a powerful application of something external, internalises this power, and then transmits it. Bodies here are not simply the receivers of knowledge, they transmit and (in effect) become a symbol or signal for the things that they have already internalised. In posthuman art education, this takes on a variety of forms. We see children who embody issues of climate change, exclusion and inequality, and transmit these feelings and forces through their art. As seen in the images and lesson plans included below, the children we do artwork with are prompted to speak about and create art around identity, community and belonging. In this art-making process, we are increasingly seeing more drawings that represent identity and "what really matters", in the form of climate issues. Drawings of landscapes with lightning bolts, flooded oceans, plastic-littered streets and rubbish-filled seas (see Figures 9.1 and 9.2) come to be. There are self-portraits of children picking up trash and recycling (see Figure 9.3) and images of bugs, soil and wild animals. These symbols of identity have admittedly come to us as a surprise. The embodied passion for climate action is one we never perceived would emerge so early in our arts workshops without any prior discussion. Our preliminary conversations with the children around "what really matters" to them, to different cultures, religions, families and communities are sometimes cast aside to make way for climate change.

A young boy from one of our sites in Melbourne, a refugee from Papua New Guinea, drew himself as an ocean filled with plastic. Figures 9.1 and 9.2 are examples of his identity pictures. Gary was asked to draw his identity by way of what truly represented him. Many children draw their friends, family, religious symbols, favourite foods, sports and increasingly climate change. Through the pedagogic practice of expressing "what really matters" by creative material processes, Gary's identity in these pictures developed through a materialisation of the effects of climate change. He portrayed his identity through angry lightning bolts and a plastic-filled ocean. An embodied identity of a plastic-filled ocean for a 7-year-old boy speaks to the inherent enmeshment of climate action education in schools, homes and community space. Through the act of making, what stood out specifically from this art-making process for Gary was his description of some of the types of plastic that he filled the ocean with. They included knives and pistols.

FIGURE 9.1
Gary's identity picture, day 1,
Melbourne, 2019

Gary described his identity picture to us:

Marissa: Do you want to tell me about your picture? We like to learn
            about the story behind your pictures.
Gary: This is about the climate changing. This is a whirlpool, this is
            heaps of beer bottles, this is three knives and one pistol and a
            double-barrelled shotgun. And this is plastic bags with bottles
            in them, and this is a bird getting stuck in the rubbish.
Marissa: Oh, wow! So the pistols are with the birds getting stuck in the
            rubbish?
Gary: Yes.
Marissa: And how come you drew climate change? Is that really impor-
            tant to you?
Gary: Yes, yes. (Melbourne, May 2019)

FIGURE 9.2   Gary's identity picture, day 2, Melbourne, 2019

Marissa: So, Gary, you drew climate change. What is this? [Points to
            blue tissue]
Gary: That's coal and fossil fuels.
Marissa: And do you want to tell me about why that's important for
            your picture?
Gary: Cause coals and fossil fuels are destroying the ozone layer, and
            now there's a big hole in it.
Marissa: Yeah, that's very important!
Gary: So, that's a big impact to the world. (Melbourne, May 2019)

Gary's embodied experience of "climate change identity" is constitutive of how material and creative processes of learning pre-empt scientific understandings and quiet activism. Identifying as a climate activist has largely to do with a perceived identity for many of the children we work with. As mentioned earlier in this chapter, part of this creative process undertaken in our fieldwork highlights the restructuring of learning environments where "learners" are encouraged to be the "teachers" and, in doing so, feel empowered to have their voices heard as young activists and change makers (Craft, 2015) Similarly, Mohammed, a young Muslim boy from Melbourne, drew his identity as himself recycling. Figure 9.3 shows an example of climate change action, which he exemplified as an integral part of his own principles and family values. He described his picture to us:

Mohammed:	That's me grabbing a plastic bottle and putting it in the recycling bin.
Marissa	So you're grabbing a plastic bottle and putting it in the recycling bin?
Mohammed:	Yes.
Marissa:	Why are you doing that?
Mohammed:	Because normally people would just throw it out and it would end up in the ocean. And there are just giant places of plastic in the ocean.

FIGURE 9.3
Mohammed's identity picture,
Melbourne, 2019

Marissa: Yeah?
Mohammed: And the animals mistake it for food, so then they eat it
                     and then die. (Melbourne, May 2019)

Mohammed's representation of the act of recycling is supported by his in-depth understanding of the detriment of single-use plastic consumption to the environment and the ocean. When Mohammed was asked where he learned about the importance of recycling and the effects of plastic on the ocean, he said "my family". Climate action education is evidently being taught in more settings than the classroom. The possibilities that arise from artistic interventions in STEM education are seen here through the creative expressions of community, belonging and identity. Young climate activists co-create solutions to climate change in the "future cities" artwork below. While imagining components of what makes an *ideal* "future city", the young participants often come up with solutions to climate change. We therefore enable and prompt "possibility thinking" (Cremin et al., 2006) in material pedagogies (Hickey-Moody, 2018; Page, 2018) through creations that resemble eco-oriented scientific inventions. Masterpieces of geo-engineering often come to be through winged cars, rivers that act as streets and flying recycling plants. Ryan, an 8-year-old, white, British boy from Manchester, drew bugs and soil as representations of "what really matters" to him and his identity (see Figure 9.4). His recognition of the importance of bugs and soil for biodiversity at such a young age materialises in his passionate drawing of bees with glitter, and rocks and soil. Even more striking, in the third image zombies are presented alongside the earthly drawings of rocks and grass. Ryan's imagined world of zombies that live alongside bugs represents an apocalyptic future, one where climate change may result in a devastating effect on human life. When asked "what really matters" in the world, Ryan replied enthusiastically: "dirt!", "insects!" Drawing pictures of dirt, grass, rocks and detailed insects, he then moved on to draw the zombies that would take over the world if all the insects died out. The symbols of climate change and the environmental activist identities shown in this section emerged from the "Identity Images" lesson plan included below. The images in Figure 9.4, when juxtaposed, can ultimately be seen as interventions in identity making and positioned as intra-active agents in creating new imagined realities. The political aspect of the children's artworks being situated within the Anthropocene is discussed later in our understanding of the children's STEAM inventions in relation to the possibilities of "geo engineering". The climate change identities expressed here go hand in hand with the collaborative "possibility thinking" that emerges from the material pedagogical practices of creating sustainable cities through shared values. See Lesson Plan 1 "Identity Images" and Lesson Plan 2 "Future Cities Canvasses" below.

FIGURES 9.4   Ryan's identity pictures, Manchester, 2018

Lesson Plan 1
Title: Identity Images

Grade level: 5/6
Duration: 2–3 hours

Overview: To create a self-representation in any style, realistic, abstract
                   or otherwise, adding collage materials for expressive tex-
                   ture, then eliciting a story through dialogue surrounding
                   the image.

Objective: To support the children to reflect on, name and/or repre-
                   sent aspects of their identity; identify images, symbols or

styles that encapsulate who they are; and how that self is connected within their social groups, i.e. who/what is important to them.

Materials: A4 cartridge paper 120 gsm, lead pencils, erasers, colour pencils, oil and chalk pastels, crayons, collage materials, glue, scissors.

Procedures:
– Lead a discussion on identity.
– Support the children to draw their images, looking up things on devices should they require a template.
– Offer collage materials for depth, texture and dimension.
– Record children telling stories about their images, asking open-ended questions and guiding away from purely describing the setting.

6 Imagined Solutions

In our art session which follows the identity-drawing workshop, we draw "future cities". These future cities work with community values and the necessary compromises and communication practices that come with the act of sharing space. As seen in Lesson Plan 2 below, this workshop is about collaboration as much as creation. Around 3–4 children share a large canvas and discuss how their city will look and what they need to do/draw for it to take shape. They incorporate the needs of all of the students who are taking part in the activity. This could mean having a mosque, church and temple side by side. It can sometimes materialise as parks filled with pandas and streets that are rivers. The beauty of this collaborative practice partly comes from the discussions that pre-empt the drawing practice. Sometimes, heated debates arise when trying to incorporate all the various needs and desires into the imaginative futures. In the two figures (Figures 9.5 and 9.6) from our workshops in Sydney, the children made a large canvas that featured four different cities in one shared world. They incorporated Joy Palace, Equality City, Friendship City and Sustainability City.

This shared world features a string of "friends" holding hands, wind turbines, penguins, green spaces and pomegranate trees. The children in this workshop were some of our younger participants, aged 3–8. They drew a corner of the world as a pink palace that was colourful and full of hearts, love and joy. The

FIGURE 9.5   Joy Palace, Equality City, Friendship City and Sustainability City in the making,
            Sydney, 2016

FIGURE 9.6   "Sustainability City", Sydney, 2016

intersections of equality, friendship, joy and sustainability diffract common
notions of how adults might perceive the world. The children's reconceptualisation of a future that was sustainable and therefore filled with acceptance and
love is one which speaks to the "possibility thinking" we encourage throughout
this process.

FIGURE 9.7   "All the streets are rivers", Manchester, 2017

Another piece that shows the effects of fostering creative contemporary pedagogical practices is the future city in Figure 9.7, which showcases a sun-filled living space, with rivers that act as streets. The rivers are filled with happy octopi and sea creatures, and a UFO flying mosque. This imagined world, made in Manchester, is intended to show a post-climate change era where the streets are rivers, either because of mass flooding or as a means to travel with minimal emissions. It is unclear whether the streets are filled with water because of climate change-induced natural disasters, or if this is a way to mitigate car travel. This diffracted view of the flooded world, as being filled with flying buildings and happy octopi, provides a feeling of hope for the future. It shows the emotional intelligence of the children in their understanding that, although climate change is a hugely depressing issue, with humans at the centre of this detriment, the imaginative solutions they initiate can diffract the way we live and breathe in the anthropogenic world. What would happen if all the streets were rivers?

The imagined city in Figure 9.8 is noticeably green. The relationship between the natural environment and community space is central to what that the children have imagined here. These children are from Adelaide, a city that is surrounded by parklands, so this geographical feature of their home city may have influenced their imagination, and so too the fact that these children are from a higher socioeconomic category than all of the other children and families in the study. Yet, this city (Figure 9.8) shows the significance given to communal "outdoor space" such as parks, pools, playgrounds, forests, trees

FIGURE 9.8   Adelaide church youth group "Green City", 2018

and zoos in the children's imagined worlds. These outdoor spaces, which are (to some extent) featured in *all* of the collaborative children's works across the UK and Australia, vary depending on their actual lived geographic locations and access to green space. In Figure 9.8, the green space is very much a symbol of what brings communities together. As seen in the "Future Cities Canvasses" lesson plan below, we work on sharing not only things, but places. What does it mean to share space and how do we make sure everyone is happy? For the Adelaide child participants, this shared space featured a variety of animals. Children can often become animals in their performance pieces. In the "Green City" (Figure 9.8), the buildings border the painting, while the focus is on a big central park. All the roads lead to a communal green space. Through this material pedagogical practice, we learnt from the children's collaborative co-creation that, by diffracting common notions of "owning land" and "privatisation of space", the coming together of people and animals alike in green open spaces makes way for a future that is sustainable, shared and green.

Lesson Plan 2
Title: Future Cities Canvasses

Grade level: 5/6
Duration: 3 hours

Overview:	To work on community values. To collaboratively create a city of the future, working in groups of 3–4 children on a large canvas, incorporating aspects of previous "identity" and "what really matters" images of urban spaces, then eliciting a story about community values that is embedded in the picture.
Objective:	To facilitate the creation of group works building on previous reflective exercises, culminating in a collaboratively planned future city on a large canvas.
Materials:	Large canvas (30 x 40 inches), lead pencils, erasers, colour pencils, oil and chalk pastels, crayons, paint pens.

Procedures:
- Lead a discussion on what is necessary for sharing space (communication, listening, planning, taking turns, compromise, team work), and on the spaces/ people/things a future city requires – it can be realistic or futuristically imagined – e.g. floating buildings, imagined farming systems, communal spaces.
- Support the children to draw their images, looking up things on devices should they require a template. It is important that the children work collaboratively, not sectioning off the canvas.
- Record children telling stories about their images, asking open-ended questions and guiding them away from purely describing the setting.

7   STEAM Inventions

Arts-based education processes allow creative encounters to unfold (Hickey-Moody, 2013). In thinking about climate change solutions and inventions, children create imaginative, mobile versions of the things that we use every day, often with the idea of producing low or no emissions. Unprompted, when drawing imagined cities, children represent buildings that fly with bird-like wings, and recycling centres on clouds. Mosques and churches are often mobile or floating so that, when anyone needs to pray, they can call their religious place of worship to their location. There are endless possibilities that arise from the art/science inventions children imagine on canvas and paper, through texture and colours. We use the noun art/science because we believe these knowledge systems are inherently enmeshed and co-constitutive. The flying soccer pitch inside an ice-cream cone was thought up by a young Australian-Eritrean girl in Melbourne who loves to play sports with her friends. The interest in flying cars, buildings and soccer pitches speaks to more than just mobile ease: the young people in our workshops understand the significance of emissions, coal and fossil fuels and present a simpler way for people to get around. What if cars flew with bird-like wings?

FIGURE 9.9   Cars that fly with bird-like wings, Sydney, 2016

The intervention of arts education into STE(A)M research and engagement brings more than just a visual lens to scientific learning; it promotes creative creations and innovative inventions through material pedagogies (Page, 2018) and arts-based knowledge making. Taking cues from the natural world is an established scientific method called "biomimetics" or "biomimicry". Well-known examples include the invention of Velcro by an engineer, George de Mestral, who was inspired by burrs stuck to the fur of his dog; less well-known examples include adhesives that mimic the way geckos are able to climb walls, self-cleaning surfaces inspired by the leaves of the lotus flower, and many more. Barad (2008) demonstrates this looking to nature in her theorisation of the diffracting arms of the brittle star. She notes that humans look to nature to create new things that ultimately already exist in our environments. Barad applies the theoretical frame of "diffraction" to the scientific discovery of the many light-changing lenses of the brittle star and its survival method of breaking off and losing some of its arms to distract predators. Ophiuroids are also positioned as a part of this world, as a part of the environment. She asks:

> When is a broken-off limb only a piece of the environment and when is it an offspring? At what point does the "disconnected" limb belong to the "environment" rather than the "brittlestar"? Is contiguity of body parts required in the specification of a single organism? Can we trust visual delineations to define bodily boundaries? (Barad, 2008: 327)

In Figure 9.9, we see a reconfigured body of a car that jumps across spacetime in contextually specific ways. It is both human, animal and machine, bringing a new reality to the concepts of human transportation and the limits of technology, flight and hybridisation. The boundaries and binary divides imposed on the systems and structures which define us, such as cars versus animals, are broken down and diffracted by the children's imaginative ways of creating new things. By looking to nature in their STEAM inventions, children address issues of sustainability and climate change through art making. "Possibility thinking" arises in these intra-actions and ties in with current developments in technology, such as the invention of drones to deliver anything from vaccines, medication and blood reserves to pizza. This also implies that solutions are already available if one knows where to look for them. Our findings indicate that it is also important to guide children's thinking towards carrying out more imaginative research and innovation: inventions which reject ideas that are either not feasible, unethical or damaging. Our ethnographic observations suggest that most of the participating children included "biomimicry" into their artistic inventions in ways that would benefit the whole of the community including themselves. This is nicely demonstrated in the case of the flying ice-cream factory/soccer pitch (Figure 9.10).

The examples of "possibility thinking" discussed previously give way to the notion that geo-engineered solutions can often come from creative young minds, minds that grew up in a world constantly reminding them of the sometimes-bitter reality of living in a never-ending state of climate crisis (Low & Schäfer, 2019; Venema, 2014). As we see in the images of the flying recycling centre (Figure 9.11) and flying mosque (Figure 9.12), these are examples of creative

FIGURE 9.10   Flying ice-cream factory with an internal soccer pitch, Melbourne, 2019

material pedagogies that result in imagined solutions to real-world problems. The proximity of prayer centres and places of worship are a continuing issue for people of faith (Winfred White, 2018) and access to such centres needs to be considered a key part of any successful environment. In workplaces, many people who practise the Muslim faith are asked to leave the building and pray at prayer centres offsite. This creates a workflow issue and is not an ideal working situation for most. Hence, the mobility of the mosque and recycling centre speaks to more than just transportation and emission mitigation; it is an embedded expression which presents a solution to a longstanding social problem, unconsciously addressing the need to provide everyone equal access and rights to believe in their associated values and faith systems.

FIGURE 9.11   Flying recycling centre, Melbourne, 2019

FIGURE 9.12   UFO mosque, Manchester, 2017

It seems significant that an enduring feature of the data is that children position themselves as inventors. Indeed, they choose their art/science practice as
a method of invention, which they apply to the problem of climate change.
This is very much aligned to the practice of invention explained by Lury and
Wakeford through their suggestion that "An inventive method addresses a specific problem and is adapted in use in relation to that specificity; its use may
be repeated, but the method is always oriented to making a difference" (2012:
11). The enmeshment of young bodies in earth's increasing global warming
produces this child-inventor and speculative practitioner of art-science. Prag-
matism lies at the heart of inventive methods: "inventive methods are neither
totally inclusive nor exclusive, neither completely open nor completely closed,
but instead are linguistic, perceptual, and material manoeuvers that are able
to give themselves over to the problem at hand" (Lury & Wakeford, 2012: 13).

As seen in the final lesson plan, or diffractive device, below titled "Values
Images", encouraged collaboration is a key strategy we mobilise in creating
space for children's inventive methods and creative practices. Encouraged collaboration enables possibility thinking and intra-active engagements that have
the ability to create new agential realities where the children's imagined worlds
come to life in material ways. The values, traditions, practices and beliefs that
families, religions, systems and cultures hold dear evolve into art/science innovations that express and embody values and beliefs, while operating ethically
and sustainably in this world. Through diffracting elements of material change,
we see shared value and belief systems evolve into creative interventions in
STEAM education and research. This type of co-creation and collaboration has
the capability to create new agential realities and demonstrates the significance of curriculum that allows for the imaginative moving of time, space and
place, creating sustainable, happy cities that are green and filled with cars. It is
through these intra-acting inventions and inventor identities that emerge from
children's enmeshment in climate change that we learn how the intersections
of science and posthuman art education come to be more than human.

Lesson Plan 3
Title: Values Images

Grade level: 5/6
Duration: 2–3 hours

Overview: In pairs children discuss and work on a collaborative image incorporating "what really matters".

Objective: To support the children to reflect on, name and/or represent aspects of "what really matters" to them – nationality, family, sport, religion – working in collaboration with another person who may have different ideas/views.

Materials: A4 cartridge paper 120 gsm, lead pencils, erasers, colour pencils, oil and chalk pastels, crayons, collage materials, glue, scissors.

Procedures:
- Lead a discussion on what we need to share (listening, kindness, compromise), and on "what really matters".
- Support the children to discuss, plan and draw their images, looking up things on devices should they require a template.
- If time allows, an additional step of collage can be incorporated.
- Record children telling stories about their images, asking open-ended questions and guiding them away from purely describing the setting.

8   Conclusion

Being enmeshed in climate change has clearly had a profound influence on the ways in which the children in our study see themselves. Responding to this enmeshment with immanent disaster, children imagine themselves as inventors: art/science is the means by which they can create solutions to issues they think are the most pressing. Contemporary STEAM education needs to be conceived specifically in relation to the climate change context, as it is their enmeshment in this context that leads young people to position themselves as inventors (for further examination of enmeshment as a fundamental re-definition of relationality, see de Frietas, 2017). As a way of responding to "the problem at hand" (Lury & Wakeford, 2012: 13), STEAM education can foreground children's imagination and allow them to learn about relationships between art and science. More than this, STEAM education allows children to bring these two areas together in speculatively visioning a world yet to come. Educators need to remember that climate change is constitutive of the "*conditions which define possible types of predictions regarding the future behavior of a system*" (Bohr, 1935, emphasis in original, as quoted in Barad, 2007: 274). Educational contexts and curriculum are systems, and influences on these produce curriculum development and student subjectivity. As our data shows so clearly, children's behaviour is already defined by the Anthropocene. Adopting a reflexive approach to this in the development of STEAM curriculum will work with, rather than against, children's ecological enmeshments and value their work of quiet activism. We very much hope the strategies for implementing this approach we share in this chapter are of use, and we welcome feedback and further discussion.

References

Barad, K. (2007). *Meeting the universe halfway: Quantum physics and the entanglement of matter and meaning.* Durham, NC: Duke University Press.

Barad, K. (2008). Queer causation and the ethics of mattering. In N. Giffney & M. J. Hird (Eds.), *Queering the non/human* (pp. 311–338). Aldershot: Ashgate Publishing.

Burnard, P., Dragovic, T., Jasilek, S., Biddulph, J., Rolls, L., Durning, A., & Fenyvesi, K. (2018). The art of co-creating arts-based possibility spaces for fostering STE(A)M practices in primary education. In T. Chemi & X. Du (Eds.), *Arts-based methods in education around the world* (pp. 247–282). Gistrup: River Publishers. https://doi.org/10.17863/CAM.21144

Burnard, P., & White, J. (2008). Creativity and performativity: Counterpoints in British and Australian education. *British Educational Research Journal, 34*(5), 667–682. https://doi.org/10.1080/01411920802224238

Craft, A. (2015). *Creativity, education and society: Writings of Anna Craft* (Selected by Kerry Chappell, Teresa Cremin & Bob Jeffrey). London: IOE Press.

Craft, A., Cremin, T., Hay, P., & Clack, J. (2014). Creative primary schools: Developing and maintaining pedagogy for creativity. *Ethnography and Education, 9*(1), 16–34. https://doi.org/10.1080/17457823.2013.828474

Cremin, T., Burnard, P., & Craft, A. (2006). Pedagogy and possibility thinking in the early years. *Thinking Skills and Creativity, 1*(2), 108–119. https://doi.org/10.1016/j.tsc.2006.07.001

de Freitas, E. (2017). Karen Barad's quantum ontology and posthuman ethics: Rethinking the concept of relationality. *Qualitative Inquiry, 23*(9), 741–748. https://doi.org/10.1177/1077800417725359

de Freitas, E., & Sinclair, N. (2018). The quantum mind: Alternative ways of reasoning with uncertainty. *Canadian Journal of Science, Mathematics and Technology Education, 18*(3), 271–283. https://doi.org/10.1007/s42330-018-0024-1

Ebrahiimji, A. (2019, August 2). This Irish teenager may have a solution for a plastic-free ocean—CNN. *CNN.* Retrieved from https://edition.cnn.com/2019/08/01/us/irish-teen-wins-google-science-fair-trnd/index.html

Hedefalk, M., Almqvist, J., & Östman, L. (2015). Education for sustainable development in early childhood education: A review of the research literature. *Environmental Education Research, 21*(7), 975–990. https://doi.org/10.1080/13504622.2014.971716

Hickey-Moody, A. (2013). Affect as method: Feelings, aesthetics and affective pedagogy. In R. Coleman & J. Ringrose (Eds.), *Deleuze and research methodologies* (pp. 79–95). Edinburgh: Edinburgh University Press.

Hickey-Moody, A. (2016). A femifesta for posthuman art education: Visions and becomings. In C. A. Taylor & C. Hughes (Eds.), *Posthuman research practices in education* (pp. 258–266). New York, NY: Palgrave MacMillan. https://doi.org/10.1057/9781137453082_16

Hickey-Moody, A. C. (2018). New materialism, ethnography, and socially engaged practice: Space-time folds and the agency of matter. *Qualitative Inquiry* [Preprint]. https://doi.org/10.1177/1077800418810728

Hiramatsu, A., Kurisu, K., Nakamura, H., Teraki, S., & Hanaki, K. (2014). Spillover effect on families derived from environmental education for children. *Low Carbon Economy, 5*(2), 40–50. https://doi.org/10.4236/lce.2014.52005

Istead, L., & Shapiro, B. (2014). Recognizing the child as knowledgeable other: Intergenerational learning research to consider child-to-adult influence on parent and family eco-knowledge. *Journal of Research in Childhood Education, 28*(1), 115–127. https://doi.org/10.1080/02568543.2013.851751

Ivinson, G., & Renold, E. (2016). Girls, camera, (intra)action: Mapping posthuman possibilities in a diffractive analysis of camera-girl assemblages in research on gender, corporeality and place. In C. A. Taylor & C. Hughes (Eds.), *Posthuman research practices in education* (pp. 168–186). New York, NY: Palgrave MacMillan.

Jones, A., & Hoskins, T. K. (2016). A mark on paper: The matter of Indigenous–settler history. In C. A. Taylor & C. Hughes (Eds.), *Posthuman research practices in education* (pp. 75–93). New York, NY: Palgrave MacMillan.

Kuczynski, L., Pitman, R., Ta-Young, L., & Harach, L. (2016). Children's influence on their parent's adult development: Mothers' and fathers' receptivity to children's requests for change. *Journal of Adult Development, 23*(4), 193–203. https://doi.org/10.1007/s10804-016-9235-8

Lawson, D. F., Stevenson, K. T., Peterson, M. N., Carrier, S. J., Strnad, R., & Seekamp, E. (2018). Intergenerational learning: Are children key in spurring climate action? *Global Environmental Change, 53*, 204–208. https://doi.org/10.1016/j.gloenvcha.2018.10.002

Lithner, J. (2015). Learning mathematics by creative or imitative reasoning. In S. J. Cho (Ed.), *Selected regular lectures from the 12th International Congress on Mathematical Education* (pp. 487–506). https://doi.org/10.1007/978-3-319-17187-628

Low, S., & Schäfer, S. (2019). Tools of the trade: Practices and politics of researching the future in climate engineering. *Sustainability Science, 14*(4), 953–962. https://doi.org/10.1007/s11625-019-00692-x

Lury, C., & Wakeford, N. (2012). Introduction: A perpetual inventory. In C. Lury & N. Wakeford (Eds.), *Inventive methods: The happening of the social* (pp. 1–24). Abingdon: Routledge. https://doi.org/10.4324/9780203854921

Nche, G. C., Achunike, H. C., & Okoli, A. B. (2019). From climate change victims to climate change actors: The role of eco-parenting in building mitigation and adaptation capacities in children. *Journal of Environmental Education, 50*(2), 131–144. https://doi.org/10.1080/00958964.2018.1553839

Öllerer, K. (2015). Environmental education – The bumpy road from childhood foraging to literacy and active responsibility. *Journal of Integrative Environmental Sciences, 12*(3), 205–216. https://doi.org/10.1080/1943815X.2015.1081952

O'Neill, C., & Buckley, J. (2019). "Mum, did you just leave that tap running?!" The role of positive pester power in prompting sustainable consumption. *International Journal of Consumer Studies, 43*(3), 253–262. https://doi.org/10.1111/ijcs.12505

Page, T. (2018). Teaching and learning with matter. *Arts, 7*(4), 82. https://doi.org/10.3390/arts7040082

Ramanathan, R., He, Q., Black, A., Ghobadian, A., & Gallear, D. (2017). Environmental regulations, innovation and firm performance: A revisit of the Porter hypothesis. *Journal of Cleaner Production, 155*, 79–92. https://doi.org/10.1016/j.jclepro.2016.08.116

Renold, E., & Ringrose, J. (2019). JARring: Making phEmaterialist research practices matter. *MAI: Feminism and Visual Culture, 4*. Retrieved August 2, 2019, from https://maifeminism.com/introducing-phematerialism-feminist-posthuman-and-new-materialist-research-methodologies-in-education/

Revelles-Benavente, B., & González Ramos, A. M. (Eds.). (2017). *Teaching gender: Feminist pedagogy and responsibility in times of political crisis.* London: Routledge.

Riede, M., Keller, L., & Greissing, A. (2016). The importance of positive messages and solution-oriented framing of climate change: A case-study in the context of secondary school education. In R. Hinger (Ed.), *Zweite "Tagung Der Fachdidaktik" 2015: Sprachsensibler Sach-Fach-Unterricht – Sprachen Im Sprachunterricht* (pp. 97–128). Innsbruck, Austria: Innsbruck University Press. https://doi.org/10.15203/3122-51-2-06

Ringrose, J., & Renold, E. (2016). Cows, cabins and tweets: Posthuman intra-active affect and feminist fire in secondary school. In C. A. Taylor & C. Hughes (Eds.), *Posthuman research practices in education* (pp. 220–241). New York, NY: Palgrave MacMillan. https://doi.org/10.1057/9781137453082_14

Ringrose, J., Warfield, K., & Zarabardi, S. (Eds.). (2018). *Feminist posthumanisms, new materialisms and education.* New York, NY: Routledge.

Satchwell, C. (2013). "Carbon literacy practices": Textual footprints between school and home in children's construction of knowledge about climate change. *Local Environment, 18*(3), 289–304. https://doi.org/10.1080/13549839.2012.688735

Satchwell, C. (2016). Creating meaningful opportunities for children to engage with climate education. In K. Winograd (Ed.), *Education in times of environmental crises: Teaching children to be agents of change* (pp. 91–101). New York, NY: Routledge.

Stafford, E. R., & Brain, R. G. H. (2017). The inconvenient youth: Exploring how high school teens voluntarily influence (pester?) others on confronting air pollution via a clean air poster contest. *Sustainability: The Journal of Record, 10*(6), 340–351. https://doi.org/10.1089/sus.2017.0016

Tchinda, L. (2018, June 27). *5 Young environmental activists making a difference in climate change* [Medium]. Retrieved August 27, 2019, from UN CC: Learn website https://medium.com/uncclearn/5-young-environmental-activists-making-a-difference-in-climate-change-f211e070ab53

Turns, A. (2019, June 28). Meet generation Greta: Young climate activists around the world. *The Guardian.* Retrieved from https://www.theguardian.com/environment/2019/jun/28/generation-greta-young-climate-activists-around-world

Venema, V. (2014, October 17). Mopping up a sea of plastic. *BBC News.* Retrieved from https://www.bbc.com/news/magazine-29631332

von Braun, J. (2017). Children as agents of change for sustainable development. In A. Battro M., L. Pierre, S. S. Marcelo, & von B. Joachim (Eds.), *Children and sustainable development* (pp. 17–31). New York, NY: Springer.

Walker, C. (2017a). Embodying "the next generation": Children's everyday environmental activism in India and England. *Contemporary Social Science, 12*(1–2), 13–26. https://doi.org/10.1080/21582041.2017.1325922

Walker, C. (2017b). Tomorrow's leaders and today's agents of change? Children, sustainability education and environmental governance. *Children & Society, 31*(1), 72–83. https://doi.org/10.1111/chso.12192

Winfred White, D. (2018). *The issues and perceptions of Muslim employees concerning religious accommodation in the workplace* (PhD dissertation). Walden University, Minneapolis, MN. Retrieved August 16, 2019, from https://scholarworks.waldenu.edu/dissertations/5809/

CHAPTER 10

Embracing the Serpent: Education for Ecosophy and Aesthetic Appreciation

James MacAllister

Abstract

This chapter draws upon Arne Naess and Ronald Hepburn to think through some limitations of approaching environment and sustainability education via knowledge from science and technology alone. Naess thought that ecologists instinctively understood what many others struggle to – that the equal right to live and blossom is a normative value that should be granted to all living things and not just humans. Nonetheless, Naess held that ecology is a limited science. It is limited because scientific methods can generate descriptive facts about the world but not values to guide action in the world. For the formation of personal ecological values that guide action, or what Naess calls an "ecosophy", systematic philosophical thinking about self-realisation and nature is needed. Those who develop their own "ecosophies" recognise that human and non-human life are intrinsically interconnected and that, as such, all of life suffers when humans think and act as if they are not interconnected. Hepburn also saw serious limits to scientific knowledge. For Hepburn, scientific method requires the stripping away of all the embodied experiences that make people human. This chapter argues that from Hepburn and Naess we can learn that a balanced education is not confined to inculcating scientific knowledge or skills. Instead it also involves the exploration of ecological values as well as serious aesthetic appreciation. The chapter concludes by discussing how Ciro Guerra's film *Embrace of the Serpent* might be educational. It is claimed that the film offers viewers an opportunity to think about human–environment relations in alternative and more ecophilosophically fruitful and aesthetically serious ways. *Embrace of the Serpent* illustrates how and why arts and especially film-based educational interventions can come to matter.

Keywords

aesthetic appreciation – art – ecosophy – *Embrace of the Serpent* – film education – Hepburn – Naess – nature

1   The Environmental Crisis and Deep Ecology

There was recently a piece on the BBC news website about a team of scientists who are setting up a research centre in Cambridge that will consider radical technological solutions to "fix" climate change on Earth (Ghosh, 2019). This initiative is being coordinated by Professor David King, former chief scientific advisor to the UK government. The "geo-engineering" solutions under consideration by staff in the new Centre for Climate Repair include "refreezing the poles" and "greening" the oceans. In the former proposal, seawater would be pumped high into the air above the polar regions via vast masts in remotely controlled boats. The idea here is that the greater quantity of salt particles in the air would make the clouds in the area more reflective and, in turn, cool the poles below them. In the latter proposal iron salts would be dropped in the oceans to fertilise them and stimulate the growth of masses of algae that would absorb carbon dioxide in the air and render it less harmful for the environment. Looking to science now is understandable. However, the notion that science and technology can in themselves "fix" climate change is not without critics. Arne Naess (1990) for one argues that the belief that scientific and technical solutions can solve the environmental crisis is one of the pillars of the shallow ecological movement. Naess is deeply critical of this movement as it rests on shallow ideological assumptions about the nature of the good life. Shallow ecological thinking sustains the idea that the good life is one of high production and consumption and material affluence.

Naess argues that humans should not respond to the environmental crisis by focusing on developing technical solutions that allow high-consumption lifestyles in the West to be maintained. Instead the crisis can prompt reflection about alternative sources of meaning in life; it can help human beings "choose a new path, with new criteria for progress, efficiency and rational action" (Naess, 1990: 26). For Naess it is not primarily new technological solutions that are needed. Instead people in the developed world, who contribute most to climate change, need to fundamentally rethink what they value and how they live. In an influential paper Naess (1973) outlined his concerns about shallow ecological thinking and his preference for deep ecological thinking. According to Naess the shallow ecological movement does fight against pollution and resource depletion, but it has the central objective of ensuring the continued health and affluence of people in the developed world. The deep ecological movement in contrast is characterised by seven very different norms. It firstly rejects the shallow "man-in-environment" image in favour of the "relational, total-field image". Following Spinoza, Naess (1990) maintains that living things are intrinsically interconnected such that if living beings A and B are related

intrinsic value
deep ecology

the very nature of both is changed by being in that relation. Deep ecology secondly embraces "bio-spherical egalitarianism". Naess argues that the right to
live and blossom should be expanded to all living things and not just humans.
He says it is "intuitively clear" to the ecologist in the field that the restriction of
the "equal right to live and blossom" to humans alone "is an anthropocentrism
with detrimental effects" upon both human life and other life forms (Naess,
1973: 96). The idea that non-human life is intrinsically valuable is a key facet
of the deep ecology movement, where "the value of non-human life forms is
independent of the usefulness these may have for narrow human purposes"
(Naess, 1990: 29).

The movement thirdly favours ecosystems and human lifestyles that are
"diverse and symbiotic". Naess remarks that "ecologically inspired attitudes
therefore favour diversity of human ways of life, of cultures, of occupations, of
economies ... and they are opposed to the annihilation of seals and whales as
much as to that of human tribes or cultures" (1973: 96). Naess fourthly explains
how an "anti-class posture" means that future plans are only worthy of endorsement from the deep ecology movement when they expand classless diversity
of human ways of life. Naess fifthly acknowledges that deep ecology fights
against "resource depletion and pollution". While this is the only or core objective of shallow ecology, for followers of deep ecology all seven principles need
to be prioritised. The movement sixthly endorses "complexity not complica-
tion". This means not ignoring the need to develop new technologies and environmental policies but only doing so in responsible and sustainable ways and
with due recognition of human ignorance of the complexity of ecosystems.
The deep ecology movement lastly calls for "local autonomy and decentrali-
zation" so as to, amongst other things, reduce energy consumption. In sum-
ming up his argument Naess stresses that the seven norms of the deep ecology
movement are not derived from the practice of ecology but from philosophy.
Ecology he says is "a limited science which makes use of scientific method"
(1973: 99) to generate descriptive hypotheses about the world. Philosophy on
the other hand is prescriptive and descriptive, containing "*both* norms ... value
priority announcements *and* hypotheses concerning the state of affairs in our
universe" (1973: 99, emphasis in original).

Naess's concepts of shallow and deep ecology open up some vital questions
for educators, perhaps especially those in the sciences, arts and humanities.
How should educators and education policy makers respond to the environmental crisis? Should the focus be placed on teaching the next generation spe-
cialised scientific and technological skills to help them "fix" climate change, or
should students be encouraged to think about choosing a new path informed
by the values and norms of deep ecology? In what follows I argue that

environmental and sustainability education ought to involve much more than the teaching of climate-fixing skills. Environment and sustainability education can be enriched, I will claim, via student engagement with deep ecological values as well as serious aesthetic reflection upon art and nature. There are three main steps to my argument. I first outline Naess's concept of Self-realisation, in the process explaining why his deep ecology can survive Watson's objection of anti-anthropocentric biocentrism. I secondly draw upon both Naess and Hepburn to question the idea that scientific, objective knowledge is more valuable than knowledge from subjective human experience. I thirdly argue that from Hepburn and Naess it can be learned that a balanced education is not confined to inculcating scientific knowledge or skills. Instead it also involves the exploration of ecological values as well as serious aesthetic appreciation. I pull the chapter together by explaining why I think *Embrace of the Serpent* is an ideal stimulus for reflection on the environment and sustainability. I argue the film has rich educational possibilities as it invites viewers to think about human–environment relations in ecophilosophically fruitful and aesthetically serious ways. I conclude that *Embrace of the Serpent* illustrates how and why arts and especially film-based interventions can come to matter in education generally and STEAM programs specifically. Here I note that, though film can be manipulative, it can also be an educative art medium when it broadens the ethical horizons of spectators.

2   Overcoming Anthropocentrism through Self-Realisation

Naess's deep ecology has proven controversial. Watson (1983) suggests Naess adopts a position of "anti-anthropocentric biocentrism" – a position that hinges on the idea that human desires, goals and interests should not be privileged over those of other species. Watson is not in favour of this position. He thinks it requires humans to unfairly curb their natural evolutionary instinct for flourishing and survival. Watson does agree with Naess that human action should promote ecological diversity. However, what justifies Watson's belief here is not the principle that all species have an equal right to live and blossom. Instead, Watson believes ecological diversity is desirable, as "human survival depends on it" (1983: 256). Watson maintains that Naess and other "ecosophers" do not approach the *egalitarian* aspect of bio-spherical egalitarianism as seriously as he does. He picks up on Naess's (1980) assertion that non-human animals should be cared for, for their own good, by humans. Watson thinks this indicates that "ecosophers" like Naess want to set humans apart from other species in ways that are not egalitarian. He argues it is not egalitarian to conclude that human behaviour is so destructive of the environment that humans, unlike other species, ought not be allowed to live out their evolutionary potential. Watson (1983) suggests that in any genuine bio-egalitarianism, human beings would be allowed to live out their evolutionary potential, like all other species, even if the results prove self-destructive. In the final sections of this chapter I will show how the arts, and specifically film, might encourage *film* students to develop new and deep ecological sensitivities rather than the shallow human-in-the-environment values Watson seems to prefer. However, I will first consider whether Watson's depiction of Naess's work is fair.

It is true that Naess thinks human beings should care and accept responsibility for the flourishing of other living beings. Naess after all states that a "specific feature of human make-up is that human beings consciously perceive the urge that other living beings have for self-realisation and that we must therefore assume *a kind of responsibility for our conduct towards others*" (Naess, 1990: 170, emphasis in original). However, I do not think Watson's objection that bio-egalitarianism is "anti-anthropocentric" is ultimately persuasive. Naess (1973, 1990) after all grants that some killing, suppression and exploitation of non-human life forms will be a necessary part of any human life lived in step with bio-egalitarianism. He says the principle "has sometimes been misunderstood as meaning that human needs should never have priority over non-human needs ... this is never intended. In practice, we have ... greater obligation to that which is nearer us" (Naess, 1990: 170). Naess (1984) responded to Watson, rejecting the idea that he or any other philosopher he knew had adopted an ecosophy of anti-anthropocentric biocentrism. Naess (1984) maintained that, while non-vital interests of humans should yield to the vital interests of non-humans, the vital interests of humans can take precedence over the interests of non-humans. The killing of a wolf is not always morally justified for the ecosopher but it would be to save a human life.

Naess (1990) actually insists that humans, like other animals and plants, have a right to self-realisation, to the unfolding of their potentialities to the fullest. Naess comments that his ecosophy "says yes to the fullest realisation of man" (1984: 270). However, for Naess the fullest Self-realisation (with a capital S) of humans involves not the narrow pursuit of egoistic goals but "deep identification ... with all life forms" (1990: 85). For Naess, Self-realisation includes personal as well as community realisation. Importantly, Naess (1990) believes humans, other animals and plants all have a right to Self-realisation. Naess does not then, as Watson has it, deny that humans should be able to realise their evolutionary potential. He rather thinks they have evolved to the point that it is now part of their nature to be able to understand and care for other living things and have an *ecological consciousness*. Naess remarks that "the emergence of human ecological consciousness is a philosophically important idea: a life form has developed on Earth which is capable of understanding and appreciating its relations with all other life forms and to the Earth as a whole" (1990: 166). In sum, Naess's deep ecology can survive the objection of anti-anthropocentric biocentrism. This is important from an educational as well as philosophical perspective. In light of this, educators who want to explore the merits of sustainable living with students need not rely upon reasoning from human self-interest and the anthropocentric argument that ecological diversity is desirable because human survival depends upon it. Instead an eco-logically richer account of human personhood and Self-realisation can be discussed as worth striving for.[1]

3   Science and Values, Ecology and Ecosophy

> A detailed investigation of the evaluations in a given ecological or other scientific investigation will never uncover the values at the end of this process. At the end of the scientific process lie ultimate assumptions of a philosophical kind. (Naess, 1990: 40)

So far, we have seen that in his early defence of the deep ecology movement Naess (1973) suggested that ecologists instinctively understood what many oth-ers struggle to understand – that the equal right to live and blossom is a nor-mative value that should be granted to all living things and not just humans. Nonetheless, Naess also held that ecology is still only a limited science – limited as scientific method can generate descriptive facts about the world but not val-ues to guide action in the world. In later work he elaborates on this theme. In *Ecology, community and lifestyle* (1990) Naess says that when scientists make value judgements and develop prescriptions to guide action and policy they do not do so as scientists, but as generalists and philosophers. He reasons that it is simply not logically possible to derive values from scientific hypotheses *alone*. Naess does acknowledge that norms about what ought to be done are often at least in part informed by hypotheses about how the world is structured. None-theless, Naess draws a rather Humean distinction between two types of state-ment, *norms* and *hypotheses*. Norms are "prescriptions or inducements to think or act in certain ways" (1990: 42) while hypotheses are revisable and are staples of scientific method. Naess indicates that normative statements ought to be revisable like hypothetical ones. However, at base a hypothetical statement aims to describe what the world is like. A normative statement, in contrast, prescribes general guidelines for thought and action. Naess remarks that while

norms / hypotheses [handwritten marginal note]

ecosophy
world view

ecology "may comprise a great deal ... it should never be considered a universal science" (1990: 39) as it cannot by itself generate norms to guide action. Nor can ecology by itself represent the sort of total philosophical world view that Naess thinks needs to underpin well-thought-through ecological values.

For the formation of a personal code of ecological values that guide action, or what Naess calls an ecosophy, systematic philosophical thinking about self-realisation and nature is needed, not scientific experiment alone. Naess maintains that philosophy can mean two things. It can be "(1) a field of study, an approach to knowledge; (2) one's own personal code of values and a view of the world which guides one's own decisions" (1990: 36). Naess adds that "ecosophy" is the name for the second meaning of philosophy that asks questions about ourselves and nature. Naess explains that an ecosophy is a "philosophical worldview" borne out of "conditions of life in the ecosphere" (1990: 38). Naess stresses that having a world view about life on Earth is different from careful and systematic philosophical expression of that world view. A philosophical world view is not just an approach to knowledge formation as in the case of the scientific method. Instead it involves many components including but not limited to epistemology, ethics, ontology, philosophy of science and aesthetics (Naess, 1990). Naess wrote *Ecology, community and lifestyle* in the hope that it would encourage readers to try to give more systematic expression to their own ecosophies. In this respect Naess believed that individual supporters of the deep ecology movement should develop their own personal ecosophies. These do not need to be founded on any particular philosophy or religion but will nonetheless generally be consistent with all the principles of the deep ecology movement. Those who develop their own ecosophies would certainly recognise that human and non-human life are intrinsically interconnected and that, as such, all of life suffers when humans think and act as if they are not interconnected. Attending thoughtfully to the deliverances of subjective human experience is a vital part of this relational-field aspect of Naess's ecosophy.

4   Objectivity and Subjectivity in Ecosophy and the Sciences and Arts

Naess maintained that all attempts by scientists and philosophers to provide descriptions of things in themselves, independent of any sensory and subjective experience of them, had failed. Naess (1990) followed Whitehead in rejecting the idea that nature is a "dull affair" without sound, scent or colour. In particular Naess disputed the validity of the seventeenth-century distinction between primary and secondary qualities.[2] Primary qualities were said to be *objective* in the sense that they were *in the objects themselves*, independent of any human subject beholding the object. Primary qualities include geometric properties like shape, weight and size. Secondary qualities like colour or taste in contrast were said to be *subjective*. They are not in the object itself but are rather projected into it by a human subject. Naess suggests that, from this perspective, human subjectivity is severed of value, with prestige belonging to the "core of reality, which is real, measurable and scientific" (1990: 53). Naess argues that ontologically this gets things the wrong way around. For Naess it is primary properties that lack real-world content. He remarks that "the geometry of the world is not *in* the world" (1990: 57, emphasis in original). Naess argues that in his ecosophy³ secondary qualities are genuinely deemed to be real qualities in the natural world. However here the qualities are not to be found just in objects in themselves. Instead reality is relational.

To illustrate this point Naess asks his readers to imagine they have put one of their hands in their pocket and the other in the cold outside air. If they then put both hands in a bucket of water, he says one hand will experience the water as warm and the other as cold. For Naess these divergent experiences of the same phenomenon do not mean that human subjectivity is inherently unreliable or that sensory experiences of objects are mere projections. Naess believed it is possible to account for different perceptual experiences of the same thing, not by discounting the evidence from subjectivity but by developing an alternative "relational-field" (1990: 55) ontology. Such an ontology takes into account the totality of interrelated experiences that go into any sensory engagement with objects. Naess maintains there is no contradiction in saying something like water A is warm in relation to hand A, but cold in relation to hand B. He stresses that the content of reality here is not just the senses and consciousness of the subject but also the objects and properties in the world: the water, cold, hands and warmth. Naess suggests such relational statements are precise and true representations of reality and not mere subjective impressions of it. Naess was not the only twentieth-century philosopher interested in how human subjectivity could enrich understanding of the environment.

In a manner reminiscent of Naess, Ronald Hepburn (1990) argues that there are two different "thought models" for understanding reality. One model is the "objectifying way", the other, the "subjectivising way". Sciences provide the prime example of the objectifying way. This way involves the formation of hypotheses about the world that can be tested in controlled experiments. Inquiries informed by the subjectivising way are by contrast typically found in the humanities and arts. The subjectivising way requires sensitive attention to the particulars of lived human experience. The arts can enrich life but, from the perspective of the objectifying way, the focus the arts place on individual moods and emotions discredits them as reliable routes to truth about reality (Hepburn, 2001). The objectifying way thus seeks to strip away all traces of human subjectivity from the pursuit of knowledge, instead focusing on "the quantifiable objective qualities handled by the sciences" (2001: 26). Hepburn claims that scepticism about the truth-revealing capacities of art is founded in a general "disparagement of subjectivity as such" (1990: 191). Those inclined to disparage art are likely those who accept that the objectifying way is the only reliable way to reality. Hepburn (1990, 2001) questions these dualistic thought models and concludes that the arts and the sciences can both generate truthful understanding of reality. Hepburn believes that human subjectivity underpins all knowledge-seeking practices, concluding that "in art, as outside it, the sub-jectivising way can be a cognitive path" (1990: 196). Naess and Hepburn both then denounce the idea that *only* objective and scientific knowledge is valu-able. As we shall now see, they both nonetheless also believe that, if subjective human experiences are to reliably help would-be knowers understand reality, they require thoughtful reflection and education.

5 Educating for Ecosophy and the Aesthetic Appreciation of Art and Nature

How does Naess think people might learn to develop their own ecosophies? He suggests that *ecophilosophy* is appropriate to the "university milieu" (1990: 36) as it involves examination of problems common to the disciplines of ecology and philosophy. However, he also indicates that studying ecophilosophy and forming an ecosophy are not synonymous. He states that we "study ecophiloso-phy, but to approach practical situations involving ourselves we aim to develop our own ecosophies" (1990: 37). Naess emphasises that developing one's own ecosophy does not mean creating it from scratch by oneself. Instead "it is enough that it is a kind of total view which you feel at home with, 'where you philosophically belong'" (1990: 37). Naess's relational understanding of reality has the merit of imbuing spontaneous human emotion and subjectivity with value. Naess does not however advocate that those who are concerned about the environmental crisis blindly follow feeling. He maintains that outbreaks of feeling "do little more than express what a person likes or dislikes. Value standpoints", in contrast, "are reflections in relation to such reactions" (Naess, 1990: 64). Naess therefore argues that followers of the deep ecology movement should receive training in making their value standpoints clear so that they can meaningfully engage in dialogue with those who adhere to different value standpoints.

Naess argues that an education that supports the aims of deep ecology
will "counteract the excessive valuation of things with a price tag" (1986: 21),
accord deep respect for the whole biosphere and concentrate on moderating
consumption and living more simply. Naess also remarks that outdoor education should discourage "conventional goal direction" (1990: 179) in nature and
things like being skilful or better than others or having the fanciest equipment.
Instead it should encourage children to identify widely with non-human life
through rich and varied interactions in nature. Naess (1990) was thoroughly
suspicious of the widespread practice of schools examining students individually too. He felt this encouraged overly competitive and egoistic values, not
deep ecological ones. While Naess generally emphasised the importance of
philosophy and/or religion for the formation of personal ecosophies, he also
maintained that artists and writers might be the most influential participants
in the deep ecology movement. He suggests that artistic and poetic expression of deep ecological values might have greater communicative potential
than the insights from professional philosophy (Naess, 1986). What Naess gestures towards, Hepburn makes clear: thoughtful engagement with the arts can
inspire new perceptions, thoughts, values and actions, often better than communication via propositions in written or spoken language alone. He remarks
that "new insight, new truth-discovery, in art come as a *collusion* between artist and spectator" (Hepburn, 1990: 186–187). Significantly, "the indirectness of
communication is ... the most powerful means of not simply communicating
propositional content but of achieving a concomitant, perhaps abrupt, re-
orientation of perception and thought" (1990: 186–187).

According to Hepburn (2001), aesthetic appreciation of art and nature can
be trivial or serious. One trivial approach to aesthetic appreciation involves
distorting the art or nature in question and falsely representing how it really
is. Another trivial approach is simply being unreflective and uncritical about
the sensory information that comes from the aesthetic entanglement. What
matters in any serious aesthetic appreciation is the level of thoughtful engagement and spectator *collusion* with the artwork or natural environment. Hepburn explains that art and nature can be unthinkingly and trivially perceived
or attended to with seriousness, "with full and thoughtful attention" (2001: 1).
To exemplify the difference between trivial and serious appreciation of nature
he considers two different experiences of the fall of a leaf in autumn. If the
spectator observes the leaf fall without thought the full significance of the
moment is lost; it "must be robbed of its poignancy, it's mute message of summer gone" (2001: 3). However, leaf veins can also be suggestive of blood veins
in other species, "symbolising continuity in the forms of life ... this autumn is
linked to innumerable other autumns" (2001: 3).[4] The arts can educate moral

sensibilities too, perhaps especially film. Sinnerbrink argues that cinema can "elicit ethical experience by aesthetic means" (2016: 20). He claims that films do not generally invoke ethical experiences solely via abstract thought about a moral problem or dilemma. Instead cinema can enable experientially thick explorations of subjectivity, as film images and narratives engage spectators in multiple ways including their senses, emotions, imagination as well as powers of reason. He rightly points out that, though films can be ideological and manipulative, they also have the aesthetic capacity to be ethically transformative when they broaden the ethical horizons of spectators and challenge any ideological prejudices they may have via images, sounds and narratives on screen. Hepburn similarly believed that, while there is no necessary connection between art and ethics, great artworks can be appreciated seriously when they enable a rapprochement between the moral and aesthetic spheres. When this happens "some momentous moral vision is brought alive through the agency of great art" (2001: 59). Serious appreciation of art or nature and "aesthetic education" seem to be synonymous for Hepburn.

Hepburn says that "an aesthetic education is an introduction to countless alternative possibilities for feeling" (1972: 488) where the new possibilities of feeling transcend the shallow clichés of ordinary life and instead ring deep and true. Likewise, art and nature are appreciated seriously when they lead those who engage with them to think and feel in previously unimagined ways. Serious aesthetic appreciation can elicit new reactions, but also new action and the formation of new values (Hepburn, 1990). Art can be most rewarding and educational, Hepburn says, when it presents highly concrete images that prompt spectators to see otherwise elusive truths about the world, truths that spectators of art can make their own. Hepburn comments that, though "we may often be content to experience in art a succession of alternative ways of seeing the world ... there is no doubt that we also particularly cherish the presentation of a perspective that we can make our own" (1990: 187). Furthermore, new views on the world are "especially prized if the perspective – a highly particularised complex, let us say, of fact, value, emotion, attitude – is normally elusive, barely accessible to us, and the work of art greatly increases its accessibility" (1990: 187). What we can learn from Naess and Hepburn then is that a balanced education is not confined to inculcating scientific knowledge or climate-fixing skills. Instead, it involves exploration of ecological values as well as serious aesthetic appreciation of the arts and nature. In what remains of this chapter I argue that *Embrace of the Serpent* presents an "elusive, barely accessible" world to viewers of the film. It is a world of moral and aesthetic vision rich with educational possibilities.

6   Embracing the Serpent

Set in the Colombian Amazon, *Embrace of the Serpent* is a quietly magical and
mysterious film. It is loosely based on the travel diaries of the German ethnolo-
gist Theodor Von Martius and the American botanist Richard Evan Schultes.[5]
Von Martius and Schultes made separate journeys down the Amazon in search
of the yakruna plant – Von Martius at the turn of the twentieth century and
Schultes some thirty years later. The former was searching for the plant to cure
his unnamed illness of the body. The latter travelled because he had an illness of the soul – he had forgotten how to dream and hoped the plant would
help him remember. The two journeys in the film are connected together by
Karamakate, one of the last members of the Cohiuano people. Karamakate
accompanies both explorers on their quests for the yakruna. As a young man
Karamakate agrees to travel with Von Martius, hoping he will help him find
the other last members of the Cohiuano. Before agreeing to travel with him he
insists that Von Martius "respect" the jungle and not cut any roots or eat any
meat or fish until the rains come. Von Martius consents to these rules. However, in a starving, delirious and tragicomical state Von Martius later spears a
fish on an arrow and bites into it raw. As he is doing this he screams to Karamakate that the river is full of fish and that he cannot end them. After Von Martius collapses, Karamakate comments, "You have no discipline. You will devour
everything". When they eventually find the other Cohiuano, Karamakate is
appalled to see they are ignoring their traditions and cultivating the yakruna.
Enraged, Karamakate burns all the yakruna.
    It is initially less clear why Karamakate decides to travel with Schultes. How-
ever, over the course of their journey together it becomes evident that Karamakate intends to teach him how to understand the Cohiuano way of life, a way
of life that respects the forest and the river and the living things in them. When
Schultes remarks that "I devote my life to plants" Karamakate replies: "That's
the most reasonable thing I have heard a white man say". In a pivotal scene
Karamakate asks Schultes how many edges the river has. Schultes answers that
it has two. Karamakate asks how he knows this and Schultes says, "It's easy. One
plus one equals two". Karamakate resists:

> You are wrong – the river has three, five, one thousand edges – a child
> can easily understand that but not you. The river is the anaconda's son.
> We learn it in our dreams but it's the real truth. More real than what you
> call reality.

Karamakate explains that, for the Cohiuano, knowledge is generated from
dreams induced by the yakruna. When taken to the last yakruna plant Schultes

confesses he intends to cultivate its potential for high quality rubber to help with the American war effort. Karamakate insists that Schultes cannot use it for weapons and killing. Instead Schultes needs to ingest the yakruna and become one with it. Karamakate imploringly says, "I wasn't meant to teach my people; I was meant to teach you". Karamakate prepares the last yakruna for Schultes to imbibe. After taking the yakruna Schultes dreams.[6] Most of the film is shot in black and white. However, in the climactic dream sequence it explodes into colour. In his dream Schultes sees Karamakate, who has a glowing mouth and massive, iridescent eyes. Has he dreamed a different way of being? Has he seen the world through Karamakate's eyes?[7] At the close of the film he wakes and looks on in wonder as butterflies dance around him – much like Karamakate was doing when Schultes first met him.

What might we learn from this haunting film? While it eschews linear interpretation, according to the director Ciro Guerra, in Amazonian mythology a giant anaconda carried alien beings to Earth. These beings stopped in the Amazon and showed people how to live – how to fish and hunt. When the beings departed, the anaconda became the Amazon river. The beings left behind them sacred plants including the yakruna. Guerra explains that when you use yakruna

> the serpent descends again from the Milky Way and embraces you. That embrace takes you to faraway places; to the beginning where life doesn't even exist; to a place where you can see the world in a different way. I hope that's what the film means to the audience. (Guillén, 2016)

I think the film does ask spectators to see the world with different eyes. It invokes evaluation and reflection in ways that resonate deeply with the work of both Naess and Hepburn. The film questions assumptions about objective and scientific knowledge being the only path to a true grasp of reality. As we have seen, Naess and Hepburn also open up similar questions in their work. Importantly, *Embrace of the Serpent* illustrates really well how and why arts and especially film-based interventions can come to matter in education generally and STEAM programs specifically. As Sinnerbrink puts it, "cinema is where cultures across the globe can find imaginative ways to address, reflect upon, question, and explore some of the most important moral-ethical and cultural-political issues of our times" (2016: 16). More than anything *Embrace of the Serpent* exemplifies that film has the aesthetic potential to generate ethically transformative educational experiences. The film invites spectators to broaden their ethical horizons and learn from Karamakate. It invites them to reflect upon their relationship with and attitude towards the non-human world. Viewers of the film may also experience a sharp deep ecological challenge to human-in-environment ideology. Given the extent of the environmental crisis such experiences and challenges are arguably needed now more than ever.

The film is dedicated to the lost peoples of the Amazon. It unsparingly sheds light on the devastation wrought by rubber barons on indigenous people as well as the Amazonian ecosystem. Naess's principles of bio-spherical egalitarianism, diversity and symbiosis, and anti-class posture are clearly opposed to such colonial and ecologically shallow practices. The film takes viewers on a journey into nature and Hepburn suggests that journeys in art and nature may be especially educative of human subjectivity (Hepburn, 1990; MacAllister, 2018). He also holds that great art encourages alternative ways of seeing the world that were not previously accessible to the spectators of that art (Hepburn, 2001). *Embrace of the Serpent* brilliantly brings to life parts of the Amazon and ways of living with nature that are very remote from most of those who live in the West. The film offers viewers an opportunity to think about human–environment relations in alternative and more ecophilosophically fruitful and aesthetically serious ways. Notably, *Embrace of the Serpent* has the possible pedagogical advantage of opening up these issues for reflection via the relatively accessible medium of film and not the more abstract language of philosophy.[8] For all these reasons I think *Embrace of the Serpent* would be an ideal film for students in STEAM programs to watch, discuss and think deeply about. While I would recommend it as a resource for prompting reflection on the environment and sustainability in schools, the film has wide educational potential. They may not take up the invitation but all who watch it are asked to reflect on their value priorities. The film may even confront some educators and education policy makers with a deep ecological question: Do they want to help the next generation merely fix climate change and then carry on, business as usual, or do they want the next generation to embrace the serpent?

Notes

1   While writing this chapter I was interrupted by hundreds of joyous school children together marching past my office on the Royal Mile down to the Scottish Parliament. This recent climate change strike and the many others like it across the world inspired by Greta Thunberg (2019) are a reminder that students can teach "grown-ups" about how to collectively respond to the environmental crisis.

2   Locke (1969) expounded this distinction. He thought secondary qualities are not in the objects themselves. They are only powers to produce sensations in persons. Primary qualities are in the objects themselves.

3 Naess called this "ecosophy T". His ecosophy is in no small part inspired by Spinoza (Naess, 1990).

4 Spinoza's idea that god is nature, and that nature is a whole, informs both Naess's (1990) and Hepburn's views on the connectedness of all of nature. Hepburn says that "a serious aesthetic approach to nature is close to a Spinozistic intellectual love of God-or-Nature in its totality" (Hepburn, 2001: 6).

5 In real life Theodor's surname was Koch-Grünberg.

6 The yakruna plant is a fictional creation. However, indigenous people in the Amazon basin do drink an ayahuasca brew made from the caapi vine to help them dream.

7 Mark Kermode (2016) suggests the film inverts the dark representation of the Amazon in *Fitzcarraldo* and *Apocalypse Now* and instead turns it into "a crucible of light, as seen from the perspective of the indigenous Amazonian tribespeople".

8 This chimes with Naess (1986), who thought that artists may be the most powerful advocates for deep ecology. However, STEAM educators thinking about using this film may also want to think about using some of Hepburn's and Naess's ideas to stimulate deeper discussion about the film. I think they would help here.

References

Ghosh, P. (2019, May 10). Climate change: Scientists test radical ways to fix Earth's climate. *BBC News*. Retrieved July 26, 2019, from https://www.bbc.co.uk/news/science-environment-48069663?intlink_from_url=https://www.bbc.co.uk/news/topics/cmj34zmwm1zt/climate-change&link_location=live-reporting-story

Guerro, C. (Director). (2015). *Embrace of the serpent* [Motion picture]. Buffalo Films, Columbia.

Guillén, M. (2016) *Embrace of the serpent*: An interview with Ciro Guerra. *Cineaste, 41*(2). Retrieved July 26, 2019, from https://www.cineaste.com/spring2016/embrace-of-the-serpent-ciro-guerra/

Hepburn, R. (1972). The arts and the education of feeling and emotion. In R. Dearden, P. Hirst, & R. Peters (Eds.), *Education and the development of reason* (pp. 484–500). London: Routledge-Kegan Paul.

Hepburn, R. (1990). Art, truth and the education of subjectivity. *Journal of Philosophy of Education, 24*, 185–198.

Hepburn, R. (2001). *The reach of the aesthetic: Collected essays on art and nature*. Aldershot: Ashgate.

Kermode, M. (2016, June 12). *Embrace of the serpent* review – You will be transported. *The Observer*. Retrieved July 26, 2019, from https://www.theguardian.com/film/2016/jun/12/embrace-of-the-serpent-observer-review

Locke, J. (1969). *An essay concerning human understanding.* London: Fontana-Collins.

MacAllister, J. (2018). Ronald W. Hepburn on wonder and the education of emotions and subjectivity. *Journal of Scottish Thought, 10*, 123–138.

Naess, A. (1973). The shallow and the deep, long-range ecology movement: A summary. *Inquiry, 16*(1–4), 95–100.

Naess, A. (1980). Environmental ethics and Spinoza's ethics: Comments on Genevieve Lloyd's article. *Inquiry, 23*(3), 313–325.

Naess, A. (1984). A defence of the deep ecology movement. *Environmental Ethics, 6*(3), 265–270.

Naess, A. (1986). The deep ecology movement: Some philosophical aspects. *Philosophical Inquiry, 8*(1–2), 10–31.

Naess, A. (1990). *Ecology, community and lifestyle: Outline of an ecosophy* (D. Rothenberg, Trans. & Ed.). Cambridge: Cambridge University Press.

Sinnerbrink, R. (2016). *Cinematic ethics: Exploring ethical experience through film.* London: Routledge.

Thunberg, G. (2019, May 24). Young people have led the climate strikes: Now we need adults to join us too. *The Guardian.* Retrieved July 26, 2019, from https://www.theguardian.com/commentisfree/2019/may/23/greta-thunberg-young-people-climate-strikes-20-september

Watson, R. (1983). A critique of anti-anthropocentric biocentrism. *Environmental Ethics, 5*(3), 245–256.

CHAPTER 11

Linking the Missing Links: An Artful Workshop on Metamorphoses of Organic Forms

Jan van Boeckel

Abstract

This chapter offers an account of a workshop in arts-based learning called "Metamorphoses of Organic Forms". This detailed description of a particular practice may inform a discussion of ways in which artful approaches, in general, may come to matter in STEAM education, with implications for both educational research and practice. Added to that, the chapter argues that such art-based practices can also be relevant more widely in the context of sustainability education, such as on the theme of climate change. Precisely because the content of the art workshop at hand is not *prima facie* linked to it, there is an unexpected potential to take up such a tangential theme in an unusual way. Typically, participants feel invigorated to enter new territory – both spatial and mental. On a meta-level, the session can also be seen as a practice in facing complexity, uncertainty, not knowing. The chapter suggests that such artful educational practices have intrinsic merit if we are to equip new generations with skills to live in and endure "post-normal times".

In the workshop "Metamorphoses of Organic Forms", participants are invited to imagine how forms in nature might either evolve or disintegrate over time. The workshop lends itself to follow-up lessons in biology and natural history. The outcome is not given. Participants go through a shared process step by step, following a sequence that is outlined for them as they go along. They are encouraged to imagine how natural phenomena might grow or decay in time and they do this in a series of short sessions where they sculpt works in clay. Such a practice in art-based environmental education is arguably a form of "poor pedagogy". This educational activity is primarily and fundamentally an open-ended process. Rather than requiring an extensive methodology, its practice requires participants to surrender themselves to a process that will be unique each time it is performed. Such a practice is an expression of a view on education that is not centred on the transmission of knowledge but rather looks at attention as education and the education of attention.

Keywords

art-based – Bateson – imagination – Ingold – metamorphosis – open-ended – sustainability education

1   Introduction

In general, it is not easy to pinpoint when and how innovative arts-based educational practices may come to matter in new and critical configurations of STEAM education. A first problem here is one of attribution: which impacts can actually be traced *back* to artistic interventions? The way art "works" upon us (as part of what Freud called "primary process" – i.e., actualising a free flow of psychic energy) is often "below the surface": subliminal, unspoken, implicit and indirect. A second, related, issue is how one deals with the epistemological ramifications of *open-ended* artful engagements: the goal of such undertakings may be mostly unknown beforehand. Meanings tend to emerge precisely in the process itself, not necessarily only in its outcome. This often literally *unheard* of approach to knowledge making may, unwontedly, give the impression – both to its participants and observers – that the creative activity is less, or not at all, structured. Such an assessment, however, would not adequately do justice to the pedagogical intricacies of reconfigured approaches in STEAM education like this one. What is more, such art-informed educational activities (I will argue here) can have the additional (and essentially *implicit*) aim of enhancing the competencies of learner participants to adequately face some of the challenges that the future is likely to hold for us. In this chapter, I will try to shed some light on aspects of the "hidden design" of the workshop "Metamorphoses of Organic Forms". Indeed, there may be some resonance with the words of Lord Polonius in *Hamlet*: "Though this be madness, yet there is method in it."

In this chapter, I explore how a particular kind of art making with clay can be of relevance in the context of both science and sustainability education with young people and adults. Here art is not included as "the icing on the cake" (to make things playful or attractive) or as mere illustration of the scientific data to which we tend to lend most weight, but as a *point of departure* in a process of exploration and coming to a new understanding of the world. But I will begin with an observation on the very materiality of this embodied activity.

To many people, there is something deeply satisfying to working with clay. As a material, it is drawn from the earth, literally from below our feet. For millennia, our predecessors have worked their hands in the soil. Clay can be moist and malleable as butter, but also hard and dry as rock. When working with it, there is a subtle exchange between the grainy medium and the flesh of our body. When the clay is cold, it warms up due to our kneading. And the longer we work with it, the dryer it becomes and eventually our skin becomes slightly dehydrated. Humanity has had a long relationship with clay. As a material, it *is* earth.

For British sculptor Antony Gormley, art is the best tool we have for trying to understand our place in the world. Speaking about working imaginatively with clay, he says, "whether we call it art or not, there is something absolutely wonderful just about this activity, as a form of thinking and feeling *through* just doing, *through* making!" (Gormley, 2019). However, this intimate connection with clay has become less relevant to most of us. As grown-ups, most of us leave it untouched; we do not play with it any longer. Gormley has reflected on this rupture:

> When you give six-year-olds a piece of paper and a pencil or a lump of clay, they don't think, they just *do*. They make something, they draw something. At a certain point in our lives, we begin to self-censor our expression in this area, an area which I believe is a fundamental human characteristic. (Gormley, as quoted in Van Boeckel, 2013: 319)

In much of our present-day education, embodied, sensory experience has all but disappeared. According to Finnish architect Juhani Pallasmaa, however, embodiment is not a secondary experience; rather, human existence is fundamentally an embodied condition. As he argues in his book *The thinking hand* (Pallasmaa, 2009), the head is not the sole locus of cognitive thinking; our senses and entire bodily being directly structure, produce and store silent existential knowledge. In short, the whole human body is a knowing entity. The creative capacity to imagine, to liberate oneself from the limits of matter, place and time, "does not hide in our brains alone, as our entire bodily constitution has its fantasies, desires, and dreams. All our senses 'think' and structure our relationship with the world" (Pallasmaa, 2009: 17). Acknowledging this corporeal epistemology and the central role of bodily perception is the point of departure for the workshop described in this chapter.

2   Metamorphoses of Organic Forms

Dozens of times and with different groups I have facilitated an art workshop that I have come to call "Metamorphoses of Organic Forms" (MOOF), and that is much inspired by the work of Gormley. In it, participants mould a series of

organic forms in clay, and artfully imagine how these might grow or disintegrate as time passes. It is a *framed* open-ended process – meaning that the
outcomes of the activity remain open-ended though the consecutive phases
participants go through are framed (Van Boeckel, 2013: 302). It is not open in
the sense of "anything goes"; rather, the process follows a certain predetermined "protocol" (Masschelein, 2012), simultaneously leaving room, during
each of the sequential steps, for probing and improvisation by participants.[1]
The MOOF art-making event thematises processes of growth and unfolding, as
well as processes of withering and decay.

The first time (to my knowledge) that such a workshop was hosted, albeit a
more basic version, was in 2006 during the course "Art in Place" at Schumacher
College in the United Kingdom. Antony Gormley, one of the visiting teachers,
led it at the time. In the years that followed, I developed the activity further,
adding several new elements to it. During the art-making event, there are times
of surrendering to the process, undergoing it, and conversely, of creatively acting upon the material (cf. Dewey, 1987). When working with clay, the imagination of the subject, as Gormley put it, is allowed to make impressions on a
receiving material, "both as *investigator* (the curious mind), and as *producer*
(the creative mind)" (Gormley, 2009).

A typical MOOF workshop has ten participants. At the beginning of the
session, participants are invited to together create a circle of clay balls on the

FIGURE 11.1   Clay balls the size of apples are put in a circle on the ground

ground, each ball at a distance of about 30 cm from the following one. Every participant is asked to mould four clay balls the size of a big apple and to spread these out evenly at the circumference of the circle. Thus a continuous circular chain of forty clay balls is created. I ask the participants to stand apart on the outer edge of the circle, at equal distances from each other, so there is one clay ball at the feet of each participant, and three clay balls between him or her and the next person. Meanwhile I have put some prints on the ground, copies of black and white photographs made by Karl Blossfeldt in the early nineteenth century, and enlarged images of seeds recently made by Svjetlana Tepavcevic (2017).

Now all is ready for the art-making event to really take off.

3   Phase I: "Growth or Decay?"

What follows is a guided process which I take the participants through step by step. They will simultaneously create several artworks and they do this in silence. I invite them to start by picking up the clay ball that is right in front of them and to mould it into an organic form. The form that they make could be either natural-realistic or imaginative, but it should somehow be reminiscent of (or refer to) a form that *could* actually exist in nature. It can be small or big, flat or round; the choice is theirs. It could conjure up associations with a plant or an animal, an insect, mushroom, or even a bacterium – all is well as long as the organic form that they create reminds us (if even only vaguely) in some way of a living species. Participants spend about five minutes making this form while standing or sitting at the periphery of the circle. I then ask them to put the sculpted clay form back on the same spot where the ball was initially picked up. When all are standing upright again, I request them to walk a few steps, rotating clockwise along the circumference of the circle, until they come to the organic form that their neighbour on their left has finished a moment ago. I then ask them to attend carefully to that form at their feet. They may want to pick it up or just look at it, while bending forward on their knees. However, they should not change its shape in any way. When a few moments have passed I invite them to imagine what kind of shape this form might evolve into, if it were to develop further. This could be in the course of the passing of an hour, a day, a week, or even a month. They have to decide upon the length of the time interval themselves. How would this form look, when revisited later? Would it expand, blossom, or – in contrast – start to wither, to fall apart? They can take it in *either* direction: to unfolding *or* to decay. Again, this imaginative contemplating is done without talking to each other.

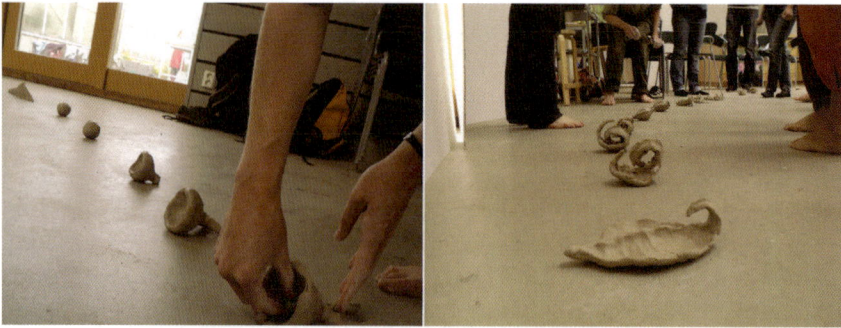

FIGURE 11.2   Determining the direction in which the organic forms will develop further in
time

I then request each participant to pick up a *second* ball of clay, on the left
of the moulded organic form that is already there. And then my invitation to
them is that they sculpt from this fresh ball a new shape that will express how
they decided that the original organic form (sculpted by one of the other participants) would develop in time. As before, the new form, when finished, is
put back on the ground in its original position. Once again, the participants are
then asked to move positions along the circle, in clockwise fashion, until they
come to what are now *two* moulded organic forms (both part of an emerging
sequence) that were left behind for them by two of their fellow participants
who previously worked at this section of the circle.

The participants are then asked to make a new, *third* form at this location in
which they take the already present sequence of organic forms a step ahead,
in the direction they surmise it is evolving in time. If the first form was for
example a clay sculpture that suggested the form of a mushroom, and the second figure looked like an older mushroom in the process of falling apart, then
a new, third form may well be a mushroom that has totally collapsed – with
perhaps some parts of its head broken off into separate pieces. When this third
work is finished, I ask the participants to again move positions (moving clockwise) along the edge of the circle of emerging clay works.

4   Phase II: "Missing Links"

If done correctly, each participant now finds him or herself in front of one of
the ten last remaining clay balls, dispersed at equal distances around the edge
of the circle. These are in fact located in between the original *first* piece of a
sequence of developing organic forms on the left-hand side of the participant
concerned, and the *last* piece of another, almost completed sequence of forms

on the right. I now invite the group members to lift this unworked ball in front of them up, suggesting to them that this left-over chunk of clay is to become a "missing link" between the two disparate sequences. What kind of form, I ask, could possibly forge a bridge between the sequence on their left, and the other sequence on their right? How could one make the "jump" between the two, through inserting a new, "hybrid" clay form? If the two sequences are very dissimilar (e.g. a series of disintegrating mushroom forms on the left and the sequential unfolding of a flower bud on the right), then the participant has to figure out what kind of shape could possibly be "in between". As all participants face this challenge and work it out, the circle of forty budding or withering organic forms becomes continuous and complete. When finished, all original apple-sized clay balls have been transformed into new organic forms somewhere on a trajectory in time. I ask the participants to slowly walk along the periphery of the circle, and to study in silence how each sequence of three forms has been created in successive steps and is then followed by a "missing link" that forges a bridge to a new and different sequence of forms.

The next step is that I ask participants to relocate the "missing link" form that they just made about half a meter inward, towards the centre. Together, these ten "missing links" then comprise a new and smaller circle, concentric with the original outer one. Everybody is now invited to fetch a new chunk of clay from me and to mould a fresh ball, again the size of an apple, which each of them is to position exactly in between the "missing links" already placed on the floor. I then ask them to find themselves a place somewhere along the edge of this inner circle, where they are no longer in front of the one "missing link" that they made themselves some moments ago. When standing in front of a new clay ball in between two "missing links", they are encouraged to imagine a (*meta*)link, connecting the "missing link" object on their left to the "missing link "object on the right. What shape, I ask, would be an adequate expression *half way* between these two odd forms? Eventually this inner circle – consisting of "missing links" and "links-*between*-missing-links" – starts to become complete.

5   Phase III: "Social Sculpture"

Meanwhile, I have put a big lump of rough fresh clay (weighing several kilograms) in the very centre of the circle. This is the prelude to the final phase of the artistic group activity. I invite the participants to move one last time, now to the very centre of the circle. There, I ask them to collectively work in silence on the mass of new clay and to make what I call (with a hint to Joseph Beuys) a "social sculpture" together. The idea is that they try, in this group artwork, to give a three-dimensional expression to what each of them has experienced thus far, in and through the whole process. When they together sculpt the big common clay piece in the centre, they can add parts to forms that others create, but they are requested not to modify them. At a certain moment, usually after about ten minutes, I determine that the art-making part of the MOOF workshop is finished. I then encourage participants to move around a bit and to look carefully at all the fantastic forms that have evolved throughout the art-making event. They are stimulated to ask each other questions like: "What caused you to take the metamorphosis of the organic form that I made into *this* particular direction?" Or, "What do you think of the way I imagined what the next step would be in the emerging sequence?" Now, at last, words *can* be used.

FIGURE 11.3   Working together on one "social sculpture"

In the end, all disperse at the fringes of the outer circle and find a comfortable position to sit, overlooking the clay landscape of organic shapes and forms with the common sculpture at its centre. Being the facilitator of the session, I initiate a conversation with open questions such as: "How was it for you to experience this?" or: "What do you *see* in front of you?" This often evolves into a most animated conversation; people can be full of excitement about having been part of this demanding but also rewarding process. Because of the accumulated flow of energy in the group, what I have referred to elsewhere as a presence of "light in the eyes",[2] this lively conversation can involve deep reflection and highly original thinking. I usually ask people to comment on what the difference to them is between the very start of the process, with all its unfamiliarity, and its final stage, when they worked together intimately on one common sculpture, negotiating in silence, through gesture and body language, how it is best to evolve. The dialogue may then further develop into addressing questions like, "Is it conceivable that the experience of an imaginative, embodied and artistic investigation of organic forms such as practised in this workshop, can be a fruitful way of learning about nature and ecological relationships, in addition to merely science-based understandings? And if so, in what ways?" Or: "Did the practice of a workshop such as this one have an impact on the development of your material sensitivity to the ways in which you perceive and tune in with the shared world of human and non-human relations?" Subsequently, I also try to connect to themes that on first glance have *no* apparent relation to the whole experience. I may ask, for example, "Does this experience make sense to you in the context of the theme of sustainability, or with respect to how we find novel ways to face the climate crisis? And, again, *if* so, in what way?"

6   Expanding the Workshop to Other Domains

In the wake of my own facilitation of this clay workshop over the years, other people have facilitated it in their own ways, such as Scottish anthropologist Tim Ingold, who prefers to call it, perhaps more accurately, an exercise in "*morphogenesis of organic forms*" (Ingold, personal communication, 2017).[3] It does not take much effort to see that there are multiple ways in which the MOOF workshop would lend itself to follow-up lessons in biology and natural history (e.g. botany and zoology), as it would for example allow further exploration of what processes of metamorphosis or morphogenesis in nature are about, or of how the (now dated) notion of "missing links" figured in early evolutionary thinking.

The art-making activity itself could also be elaborated in new directions. Participants could for example be invited to imagine (and create in clay) organisms that are in symbiosis with (or a parasite to) another imaginative organism that has been crafted previously by someone else in the group. Or there is the option to link the MOOF workshop with a (Batesonian) apprehension of evolution, where the unit of survival is always the "organism-*in*-its-environment" (Bateson, 1972: 451). What would it look like in clay, an environment that would accommodate (and itself be co-dependent on) the individual organic form that another group member just created? How would they together *co*-evolve in time? Botanical and other natural forms are always in transformation and interdependent on each other; yet this is just one epistemological layer that can be accessed in and through the MOOF workshop.

Next to delving into aspects that touch on (evolutionary) biology   through working with processes of metamorphosis and morphogenesis – there are also more heterogeneous elaborations that can be given to this artful workshop. As said, the often rather lively follow-up conversation can provide openings to take up a theme like climate change. To pursue such an incongruous thematic expansion as a sequel to it is by no means obvious. But *if* one opts for this, one can build, interestingly, on the common circumstance that things "have shifted" in the sense of presence, the overall mindset, of the participants when they have moved from the first timid engagements with the rough clay to more elaborate and imaginative artistic activities later on. They also make a sheer physical move, from being first bodily dispersed on the outskirts of the outer circle, to entering the inner circle in a following step, and finally to working collectively on *one* clay work within the confined space at the centre.

Here are two reflections by participants:

> My experience of the clay workshop is that we had these three different stages. First we worked with only the constraint of the biological form and our own creativity and imagination, then more and more constraints followed, fixed tasks and also responding to the work of someone else. It went from complete openness to more and more constraints. It made me realise that it is easier to be creative within the constraints, whereas I was struggling a bit with the completely open. It was harder for me to just begin. Probably the most important skill that young people can learn today is cooperation. And this activity is definitely helpful there.[4]

For another participant, the change happened in the opposite direction:

> What I experienced in the workshop was this tension between trying out something, and simultaneously knowing that it is never going to be as good as I want it to be because I am not good with the clay. Once I got past that initial friction, there was a support structure that helped me become part of it and that led me into a community of fellow travellers facing the same challenges. The next steps became gradually easier, more spontaneous, reciprocal and mutually supportive, until the point where you lose the sense of individual intention and you just participate. For me, it relates directly to the work I am doing of finding a structure for ordinary citizens to come to terms with the different problems we are facing as society. How people can play a bigger part than just through their individual actions, as part of a great collective whole.

As said above, I look at this art-based activity with clay as a primarily and fundamentally open-ended form of meaning making. The outcome is not given, though the participants follow certain sequential steps that frame the process. Through inviting participants to engage in an imaginative, hands-on creative process, it aims to afford new, embodied rather than merely cognitive appreciations and understandings of relationships between biological phenomena. As such, it is a form of art-based environmental education, a way of learning which, according to Meri-Helga Mantere (who coined the concept in 1995), aims to develop environmental understanding and responsibility "by becoming more receptive to sense perceptions and observations and by using artistic methods to express personal environmental experiences and thoughts" (Mantere 1995: 1). Such educational innovations centre on embodied art-making activity, as practised in the clay workshop, thereby affording a fundamental remaking and re-configuring of our attention to the materiality of the world and engendering a heightened sensitivity to the kinds of spatial and temporal dynamics that come into play in the process.

Tim Ingold (thereby following Jan Masschelein) emphasises the *two* root origins of the word "education". One is, in Latin, *educare*, with connotations of rearing, of bringing up. This form of education foregrounds "instilling knowledge *in* to the mind of novices". The other form is *educere*, that comes from *ex* (out) and *ducere* (to lead): "leading novices *out* into the world" (Ingold, 2013b: 7). Here, the idea of education is not primarily the transmission of knowledge, but rather the education of *attention* (Ingold, 2018: 31). In such learning processes, the factor of uncertainty inevitably gains more prominence, as I will discuss further below.

7   The Ability to Inhabit Uncertainty

On a December day in 1817, Romantic poet John Keats wrote a letter to his brothers in which he expressed his theory of "negative capability". Asking himself what quality went to form a "man of achievement" such as Shakespeare, he came upon the view that such a person is, first and foremost, "capable of being in uncertainties, Mysteries, doubts, without any irritable reaching after fact and reason" (Keats' Kingdom, 2019). Basically it is the ability to accept that not everything can be resolved. Keats had a high regard for receptive intuition, for which the intellectual self could be standing in the way. Negative capability has been defined as "the ability to contemplate the world without the desire to try to reconcile contradictory aspects or fit it into closed and rational systems" (Keats' Kingdom, 2019). This capability, I believe, is something that can be nourished through an art workshop such as Metamorphoses of Organic Forms. There are several instances where participants are encouraged to dwell, at least for some moments, in the doubt about how to go on. Again and again they are faced with new challenges. It is only by immersing oneself in the activity, "without any irritable reaching after fact and reason", that they later perhaps begin to grasp some of the possible meanings it may have – which are different for each individual participant.

The protocol for such a workshop could of course have been different; as the facilitator, one could, for starters, have explained *why* one is expected to make a naturalistic or imaginary organic form and to what purpose. To me, however, there resides a meaning in *not* disclosing the aim. Participating, then, involves surrendering oneself to the process, without knowing how or where it will go. I invite each member of the group to work out imaginatively how a form made by someone else may change in time, either towards its blossoming, its maturation, or towards its decay, its death. The clay objects that are made are always original – something is suddenly there and it grows further in new forms through the successive imaginative sculpturing by others, each work acquiring a new expression. Any given artwork brings its own connotations and associations which will be different from person to person, and new interpretations may continue to reveal themselves over time, adding up to each other. In artistic activities – practiced individually or in groups – there can be room for different meanings. One has licence, so to speak, to elongate a state in which one is being confronted with opposing viewpoints, with ambiguity. And indeed this happens because one, as an embodied being, is thinking and feeling *through* making, *through* doing (Pallasmaa, 2009; Ingold, 2013a), suspending an (in other cases more predominant) one-sided cognitive engagement with the world.

Gregory Bateson held that encountering paradoxes is a basic part of life and of evolution, a thought that is concisely expressed in the title of Stewart Brand's (1973) interview with him, "Both sides of the necessary paradox". For Bateson, a paradox is a contradiction in which you take sides – *both* sides. One half of the paradox proposes the other. Dwelling a little longer with paradoxes, and not opting for one side at the expense of the other too soon, is like embarking on a sort of voyage, in his view: "you come out knowing something you didn't know before, something about the nature of where you are in the universe" (Bateson, as quoted in Brand, 1973: 35). Paradox, in Bateson's view, is healthy; the truth for him is always one of complexity. Psychologist Carl Rogers defines openness towards new experience as the opposite of the psychological attitude of defence. For him it involves a "lack of rigidity and a permeability of the boundary lines of the spheres of concepts, perceptions, and hypotheses". It means a tolerance of ambiguity, where ambiguity exists. This signifies, says Rogers, "the ability to receive very conflicting information, without forcing the closure of the given situation" (Rogers, as quoted in Pitruzzella, 2009: 28–29).

An important aspect of the MOOF workshop is to put the participants, as it were, on the "wrong foot", a sporting term. You suggest with your movements that you will kick the ball in a certain direction, and your opponent believes it will go there. But then at the last moment, you kick the ball quickly with your foot in the opposite direction, and your opponent finds him or herself standing on their wrong foot – unable to adapt to the abrupt and unforeseen change. Understood more broadly, the other is intentionally put into an unexpected or difficult situation. He or she will be expecting a certain outcome, but you predetermine that that result is not bound to happen. This intervention, the organised surprise, tends to cause confusion, and in some cases also frustration. The other person may feel that they are trapped into a situation that is not of their choosing and over which they do not have control. For many participants, this new way of relating to the artistic process is at first completely new, foreign and frightening. When I practise (what I call) "wrong footing" in art-based environmental education activities (cf. Van Boeckel, 2013: 219, 378), deliberately causing defamiliarisation, I try to evoke participants' imaginative capacity, which they will need to face and overcome this unexpected threshold.

8   Fantastic Binominals

How can we foster imagination in education? This is a theme that Italian children's author Gianni Rodari explores in *The grammar of fantasy* (1996). In all his pedagogical projects, Rodari underlined the importance of the social context: different types of children can collaborate and use their imaginations together. An impetus to do so, he found, is to entice them to develop stories, whereby they uncover new skills as they go along. A catalytic intervention to set such a process in motion that Rodari came up with was the juxtaposition of two entirely unrelated words: the first word must be sufficiently strange or different from the other. The unusual coupling triggers the imagination to establish a relationship between the two. For our mind aims to construct a new, *fantastic* whole, "in which the two foreign elements can live together" (Rodari, 1996: 12). Two words that are utterly at odds with each other can still always be linked, says Rodari, and thus they become a fertile way to guide the imagination further:

> In reality one electrical pole is not enough to cause a spark; it takes two. The single word "acts" only when it encounters a second that provokes it and compels it to leave the track of habit and to discover new possibilities of meaning. To live means to struggle. (1996: 12)

It is this tension that is important to Rodari. If one takes the word pair of, say, horse and dog, it would be a simple association within the same zoological classification of four-legged animals. In such cases the imagination remains indifferent: it does not promise anything exciting. This leads Rodari to his concept of a "fantastic binominal", of two words having a distance between them. Rodari gives the example of the words "dog" and "closet". Such a combination, propelled by chance, can be an exciting stimulus. In this way the whole ground is shifted; one word is thrown into a completely unrelated context. Words are not taken in their colloquial meaning, but freed from the verbal chains that hold them together on a daily basis. They are estranged or, as Rodari puts it, "thrown against one another in a sky *that has never been seen before*" (1996: 13, emphasis added). In that way, he suggests, they are in the best possible condition for generating a story. Or, one could say in the context of this book, they can initiate art creativities in domains that seem at odds with imaginative artful engagement such as much of contemporary science education.

Just like Rodari, Bateson was very fond of a kind of thinking that looks for associations that combine phenomena in metaphoric terms. Elaborating on this, Bateson (1991) would bring up the contrast between two types of syllogisms. The first one is called a "syllogism in Barbara", and goes like this:

> Men die.
> Socrates is a man.
> Socrates will die.

Bateson's alternative was what he termed a "syllogism in grass":

> Grass dies.
> Men die.
> Men are grass.

The common response to the latter syllogism would be that it "does not hold water". It could only be condoned if it were the lyric lines of a poet, but regarded as utter nonsense when stated by a biologist. Bateson, however, felt that such a "syllogism in grass" was actually truer to the way he thought himself, as it uses the language of metaphor: "while not always logically sound, it might be a very useful contribution to the principles of life. Life, perhaps, doesn't always ask what is logically sound. I'd be surprised if it did" (1991: 240–241). The syllogism in Barbara identifies Socrates as a member of a class; this kind of syllogism deals with subjects, nouns, things. The grass syllogism, in contrast, is concerned with the equation of *predicates*: "that which dies is equal to that other thing which dies" (1991: 241). This is the way poets think. Bateson believes that the syllogism in grass is the way organisms manage to organise themselves:

> It became evident that metaphor was not just pretty poetry, it was not either good or bad logic, but was in fact the logic upon which the biological world had been built, the main characteristic and organizing glue of the world of mental process. (1991: 241)

To me, the use of the language of metaphor – which Bateson saw as an organising principle both in nature and in his own thinking – is also intrinsic to the kind of art-based environmental education that I facilitate. For, as an artist educator, I often seek ways to encourage participants to discover similarities between things that appear to be utterly foreign to one another. Participants can be encouraged to dwell a little longer with what appears to be contradictory, paradoxical or nonsensical, such as statements like "men are grass". The poetry of the incomprehensible can be both the starting point and the outcome of meaning making in a creative process that aims to meet the natural environment from a fresh perspective, not clouded by one's presuppositions. From the perspective of analogy, men are indeed grass – to the extent that what unites both is an underlying and shared pattern of the living world. It takes effort to find this "pattern that connects", as it often is not readily discernible at an obvious level.

Dutch novelist Jaap Robben explains why, in general, children are much better at engaging with this way of thinking:

> Children are much less restrained by the "rules of life". So they fantasize two truths that they *do* understand, between which there is something that they *don't* understand. With their fantasy they then make that all into one whole. If you do that as an adult, you are crazy, or you're taken to a mental hospital. But for a child it makes sense. One doesn't need to know it all, but one can make one's *own* connections between facts. (DWDD, 2017; author's transcript and edited translation)

Overcoming one's initial hesitation or resistance to having to bring together what is seemingly unrelated, and does not seem to make sense, is one of the principles at work in the MOOF art making activity. The invitation to participants to sculpt an imaginative organic form that acts as a "missing link" between two forms utterly at odds with each other seems pointless, even ridiculous, and when they try to do it they do not have any help. As various participants have mentioned, they would never do such a thing on their own. But once they *do* surrender themselves to the process, it is like entering a new territory.

My practice of "wrong footing", of inviting students to unexpectedly make a "missing link" or to switch to creating a common sculpture collectively, is like a gentle disturbance in what they were just getting habituated to. In his book *Letting art teach*, Gert Biesta (2017) discusses the value of interruption. For Biesta (2017: 86), the educational gesture is the act of showing, of focusing the attention of another human being on something "outside", with the suggestion that there is something that the teacher believes may be important for the student to pay attention to. (Here we can see clear correspondence with the understanding of education as *educere*, of leading students out into the world.) This gesture, says Biesta, interrupts where someone is, what someone is doing or wants. The point of education, he insists, is not that students focus on what they fancy or desire to focus on, but that they are turned in a particular direction.

9   A Poor Pedagogy

A MOOF workshop requires from participants an attitude of receptivity, of "attending to one's own attending". Another activity to which such a guided artistic process can perhaps be compared, in that respect, is the practice of walking and not knowing where it will lead you. As part of his courses in "world-forming education", Belgian philosopher of education Jan Masschelein would ask his students to walk day and night along arbitrary lines drawn on city maps, crossing at random neighbourhoods. For him, such experiments in "e-ducating the gaze" are part of what he calls a "poor pedagogy" (Masschelein, 2010). The key is its grounding in an exploring, open-ended activity. Masschelein is interested in how we can turn the world into something "real", how to make the world "present". Here, education is about being exposed to the world. By foregrounding the act of walking, we question the act of taking a position, a standpoint. The walker's attention comes not from having arrived at a position but from being pulled away from it, from displacement (Masschelein, 2010: 46). Ingold comments:

> to walk is to be commanded by what is not yet given but *on the way* to being given ... It is not, then, that the walker's attention is being educated; rather the reverse: his education is rendered attentive, opened up in readiness of the "not yet" of what is to come. (Ingold, 2015: 136)

Both Masschelein and Ingold seem to fear that a unilateral focus on the stern deployment of a fixed methodology runs the risk of turning means into ends: divorcing knowledge-as-content from ways of coming to know, enforcing a kind of closure that is the very antithesis of the opening up to the present which a poor pedagogy offers. The kind of education that Biesta, Ingold and Masschelein advocate focuses on being present in the present to what presents itself. For this, both acceptance and attention are needed to be able to read what is happening today. It implies a kind of curiosity that is not driven by the "will to know" but by a caring attitude to what is happening now. Further, it is not driven by the willingness to merely accumulate knowledge. In an attitude of caring, we open up to our current conditions of living together. Such education is about being in the world, being exposed, being out of position, or being captured by questions of living together (Simons & Masschelein, 2009). The price of being present in such a way, says Ingold (2015), is vulnerability, but its reward is an understanding, founded on immediate experience, that goes beyond knowledge.

10   A New Conversation on Climate Change?

We need an artistic turn in sustainability science and research, says Sacha Kagan (2017: 151). In the face of a threat like climate change, one of the challenges is how to work wisely with intricate combinations of knowing and not-knowing, relative certainties and uncertainties, hard limits and open possibilities. It requires a deepened understanding of what resilience really implies. For Kagan our current predicament calls for "the necessity to learn from the unexpected" (2017: 153). Kagan's term for this is "serendipitous learning". We need experiences that train the capacity to perceive and interpret the world in complex ways, and such learning *"requires* artful qualities" (Kagan, 2017: 153, emphasis added). Psychologist and educator Maureen O'Hara argues in a similar vein that what we need today is a cultivation of "the necessary capacities of mind to live well in an unavoidably uncertain world" (2005: 2). In our time, she says, we need the capacity to hold many opposing ideas at the same time, and we have to resist the desire for easy certainty and premature closure. We need to invent new kinds of socialising experiences, so that people learn to see the world through new eyes and to take in its complexity without becoming overwhelmed by it:

> We need to cultivate intuition and appreciation of the non-rational; not as substitutes for reason and skepticism, but as a complement to them.

> We need to cultivate both/and thinking, enhance our capacity for holis-
> tic perception, gestalt awareness, network logic and pattern recognition.
> Along with a capacity to focus, we need to be at home with fuzziness
> and a wide-angle view. We will need to balance a fear that we have not
> enough information with the problems of having too much. People will
> need to become comfortable in a world of fluid boundaries, understand-
> ing the world as a continuous web of relationally connected integrities.
> (O'Hara, 2005: 7)

What is the relevance of an artful activity such as the MOOF workshop and
sustainability education, or more broadly, learning to be at home with fuzziness and a wide-angle view? Such relationships are not necessarily explicit or
obvious. Perhaps we should start by first appreciating what happens to participants on a very basic, corporeal level. What happens is that people often
feel mentally and physically invigorated through doing the workshop. They
have just been together as a group in a completely different way than usual. By
consequence, any conversation that takes place immediately afterwards on a
theme like climate change or living in an increasingly uncertain world immediately tends to become more animated and interesting. If the participants
were invited to start the workshop by partaking in a group conversation on a
sustainability theme, then chances would be high that they would contribute
more expected and "socially desirable" statements. But if, before entering into
such a conversation, they have first engaged with an activity that is intensive
and embodied, and they have felt that they, through the art making, have been
in a "new territory", there is at least the likelihood that this experience will
have caused their ways of thinking to become more "stretched" as well, possibly leading to the input of more original perspectives in the ensuing dialogue.

In artistic processes, there are always a lot of things happening in the so-
called "in-between space", where things are not always explicit. The in-between
space is like the imaginary jump in time that takes place between one created
organic form and the next. One does not know exactly what has happened in
this interval: it needs to be filled in by one's imagination.

But there is also *another* in-between space, and that is the physical space
between the bodies of participants: as the workshop unfolds the participants
move slowly more and more to the centre. Part of each participant is busy finding a link between "missing links". But in the meantime, they and the other
participants also move closer to each other as a group. The bodily engagement
is different and this partly helps to prepare them for being ready to make the

common sculpture later together in the confined and more intimate central space.

One of the participants in a MOOF workshop reflected on the experience like this:

> I definitively think it wouldn't work if you'd laid out the whole plan. If you have a sense of where we are headed, then you have expectations of where it is going to go. And then when it doesn't match your expectations, you are disappointed before you even get to its conclusion. By only revealing the next step when you actually are there, you don't focus on the big picture of what it is becoming. At some point you invited people to go around the circle and to see the whole. Mostly, as a participant you just focus on the one small thing that you actually can affect. I like that, because people can get paralyzed by the size of the challenges of living today and the things they feel they need to change. What I am interested in is how you can make it easy for people to take those first steps, how they can find others who are in a similar situation so that they can support each other in this. What the workshop did was that you had to build on other people's work. You had to acknowledge that we work together. For me, this losing of a sense of ownership, forgetting which bits are yours, just looking at the whole, is all of value.

I began this chapter with Antony Gormley's reflections on the impact of working with the materiality of clay, and I will end by quoting him:

> As a material, [clay] is earth ... This is about reconnecting flesh with earth, through touch ... It is strange and powerful that something connected to landscape and geology, distant both in terms of time and space, comes into your intimate, subjective zone when formed by the hand, first being worked on at arm's length before being brought into the inner orbit of the maker's body. You work on the clay in this zone between the place of speech and the heart, before placing it away from you and, once again, standing apart. (Gormley, as quoted in Van Boeckel, 2013: 330)

On a metaphysical level, the participants in the project brought a material close to themselves that was "forgotten", because clay resides, literally, *below* the surface of things. "In a post-religious and post-political ideological vacuum", Gormley asserts, "the issue is the recovery of an agency. Whether we recognise it or not, each of us is an agent; making the world out of the earth" (as quoted in Van Boeckel, 2013: 331).

Notes

1 A protocol to Masschelein is a clear guideline which one follows that has no clear "end", no destination. It is a kind of path, he says, that leads nowhere; it is like a cut that opens onto a world. The protocol thus helps, he explains, to suspend too-familiar stories. Basically, it "offers a certain chance that something will appear and communicate, that something will be disclosed" (Masschelein, 2012: 367).

2 In my lecture entitled "A pedagogy of the light in the eyes", at CEMUS, in Uppsala, Sweden, 21 January 2019. This lecture is the basis of a forthcoming paper.

3 Morphogenesis literally means the "beginning of shape", derived from Greek *morphê* (shape) and *genesis* (creation). It is the biological process that causes an organism to develop its shape. It is one of three fundamental aspects of developmental biology along with the control of cell growth and cellular differentiation, unified in evolutionary developmental biology.

4 The quotations from participants in a MOOF workshop presented here were recorded in Sweden in the spring of 2019. I have edited them slightly for readability.

References

Bateson, G. (1972). *Steps to an ecology of mind.* New York, NY: Ballantine.

Bateson, G. (1991). Men are grass: Metaphor and the world of mental process. In R. E. Donaldson (Ed.), *A sacred unity: Further steps to an ecology of mind* (pp. 236–242). New York, NY: HarperCollins.

Biesta, G. (2017). *Letting art teach.* Arnhem: ArtEZ Press.

Brand. S. (1973, November). Both sides of the necessary paradox. *Harper's Magazine,* 20–37.

Dewey, J. (1987 [1934]). *John Dewey: The later works, 1925–1953, Vol. 10: 1934: Art as experience* (J. A. Boydston, Ed.). Carbondale, IL: Southern Illinois University Press.

DWDD. (2017, March 23). Hier is … Adriaan van Dis – Jaap Robben. *De Wereld Draait Door.* Retrieved July 8, 2019, from https://dewerelddraaitdoor.bnnvara.nl/media/371392

Gormley, A. (2009). *Antony Gormley: Interview with Paulo Herkenhoff.* Retrieved July 8, 2019, from http://www.antonygormley.com/resources/download-text/id/159

Gormley, G. (2019). *How art began* [Motion picture]. BBC, United Kingdom. My transcript.

Ingold, T. (2013a). *Making: Anthropology, archaeology, art and architecture.* Abingdon: Routledge.

Ingold, T. (2013b). The maze and the labyrinth: Walking and the education of attention. In: M. Collier, C. Morrison-Bell, & A. Robinson (Eds.), *Walk on: From Richard Long to Janet Cardiff* (pp. 7–11). Sunderland: Art Editions North, University of Sunderland.

Ingold, T. (2015). *The life of lines.* Abingdon: Routledge.

Ingold, T. (2018). *Anthropology and/as education.* Abingdon: Routledge.

Kagan. S. (2017). Artful sustainability: Queer-convivialist life-art and the artistic turn in sustainability research. *Transdisciplinary Journal of Engineering & Science, 8,* 151–168.

Keats' Kingdom. (2019). *Negative capability.* Retrieved July 8, 2019, from http://www.keatsian.co.uk/negative-capability.php

Mantere, M.-H. (1995). Foreword. In M.-H. Mantere (Ed.), *Image of the earth: Writings on art-based environmental education* (pp. 1–2, M. Barron, Trans.). Helsinki: University of Art of Design.

Masschelein, J. (2010). E-ducating the gaze: The idea of a poor pedagogy. *Ethics and Education, 5*(1), 43–53.

Masschelein, J. (2012). Inciting an attentive experimental ethos and creating a laboratory setting: Philosophy of education and the transformation of educational institutions. *Zeitschrift für Pädagogik, 58*(3), 354–370.

O'Hara, M. (2005, November). *The challenge for education in uncertain times.* Paper presented at the General Assembly of the World Academy of Arts and Sciences, Zagreb, Croatia. Retrieved from http://maureen.ohara.net/pubs/zagreb_final.pdf

Pallasmaa, J. (2009). *The thinking hand: Existential and embodied wisdom in architecture.* Chichester: Wiley.

Pitruzzella, S. (2009). *The mysterious guest: An enquiry on creativity from arts therapy's perspective.* New York, NY: iUniverse.

Rodari, G. (1996). *The grammar of fantasy: An introduction to the art of inventing stories* (J. Zipes, Trans.). New York, NY: Teachers & Writers Collaborative.

Simons, M., & Masschelein, J. (2009). Towards the idea of a world university. *Interchange, 40*(1), 1–23.

Tepavcevic, S. (2017). *Svetlana Tepavcevic.* Retrieved August 21, 2019, from http://www.svjetlanat.com/home.html

Van Boeckel, J. (2013). *At the heart of art and earth: An exploration of practices in arts-based environmental education* (PhD dissertation). Aalto University, Helsinki.

PART 4

STEAM Reconfigurings in Practice

..

Introduction to Part 4

Pamela Burnard and Laura Colucci-Gray

Sympoiesis is a process of ecological relationality, that "takes seriously organisms' *practices*, their *inventions*, and experiments crafting interspecies lives and worlds" (Haraway, 2016: 68, emphasis added). This rhizome emerges from the line of organisms coming into 'being and becoming' in a space of entanglement and rupture, of growth and transformation. Like the towers of knowledge of a castle in the sand, creative practices bring new configurations and understandings, yet these are temporary, changeable and fluid. We are also reminded however that "creativity and curiosity characterise the experimental forms of life of *all kinds of practitioners,* not only the humans" (Haraway, 2016: 69, emphasis added).

This part offers accounts from research and pedagogical practice (practice as research), seeking to grapple with the opportunities offered by STEAM as a site of trans-corporeality. Each contribution provides examples of practices and "thinking with" particular theorists to surface ways of being, ways of learning and ways of thinking, that are stimulated and reinforced through inter- and transdisciplinary offerings of arts and sciences. The precise action of re-making subjects in and through research, and the iterative reconfiguring to which earlier chapters refer, are explored in ways that see teaching and learning in critically different ways: as sites of trans-corporeality for future-making education.

Chapters in this part span from illustrations of "practice as research" (see particularly Chapter 13, Kristof Fenyvesi et al.; Chapter 14, Nicola Walshe et al.;

© KONINKLIJKE BRILL NV, LEIDEN, 2020 | DOI: 10.1163/9789004421585_016

Chapter 16, Catherine Francis) to reflections and theorising on "research as practice" (see particularly Chapter 12, Lindsay Hetherington et al.; Chapter 15, Erik Fooladi; Chapter 17, Carolyn Cooke).

This part advances and stimulates thinking-through-practice and practice-as-research for enacting STEAM in everyday teaching and learning contexts.

Reference

Haraway, D. (2016). *Staying with the trouble. Making kin in the Chtulucene.* Durham, NC: Duke University Press.

Creative Pedagogy and Environmental Responsibility: A Diffractive Analysis of an Intra-Active Science|Arts Practice

Lindsay Hetherington (with Kerry Chappell, Hermione Ruck Keene and Heather Wren)

Abstract

This chapter explores the entanglement of research and practice, offering an account of science|arts practice in which research-driven "features of creative pedagogy" were used within an action research project to engage young people with the problem of ocean plastics. Thinking with Barad's theory of agential realism, we explore the ongoing emergence of new matter and meaning for the young people, teachers and researchers engaged in this transdisciplinary practice-research.

One component of a large H2020-funded project exploring creativity in science/arts transdisciplinary practices across Europe was a study of action research in six UK secondary schools with science/art teacher pairs. This chapter draws on research conducted within one school in which the issue of plastics in the ocean was explored with 52 students aged 14–15 within an "arts-science project", to develop the young people's ideas about environmental responsibility understood, explored and expressed together through science and art.

An approach to researching emergent and creative pedagogies which brings agency to the fore within a material-dialogic, intra-active understanding of (post)human creativity was used. Data gathered through mixed methods, including questionnaires, interviews and photographs, and selected via "glow moment" assemblages, were analysed with and through theory using diffractive analysis to iteratively unfold data, theory, research and practice. This stance embodies a material-dialogic approach, with research, theory and "data" in dialogue.

In the chapter, a sequence of diffractions is described, responding to initial questions posed by the book editors: "When/where/how do objects/subjects of inquiry, and embodiment, come to matter in STEAM (re-)configurings in practice?" These diffractions unfold the emergence of matter and meaning through intra-active material dialogue in a science|art practice, raising questions from/ for practice about the concept of ethics, trusteeship and responsibility in environmental education.

Keywords

action research – agential realism – Barad – creative pedagogy – diffraction – embodied dialogue – environmental responsibility – intra-action – new materialism – transdisciplinarity

1   Introduction

> There are many things in the human body and materials that are works of art, and science is almost like learning about the art. (Student, age 14–15)

In this chapter, I offer an account of an iterative unfolding of research and practice in which a science|arts transdisciplinary practice[1] surfaced, for those involved, different ways of thinking about school subjects, about environmental responsibility and about themselves. At the same time, I engage critically with a relational understanding of research and practice to explore the opportunities offered by STEAM transdisciplinarity to think "research practice" differently. I take a diffractive analytical approach (Barad, 2007) to read insights from a specific example of science|arts school practice and theories of creativity through one another. In so doing, I produce "an emergent series of readings as data and theory make themselves intelligible to each other" (Mazzei, 2014: 742). This chapter therefore reflects a living inquiry in which the researcher's intra-action[2] with data and theory is a creative and emergent process of meaning making about science|arts creative pedagogy. I respond to the questions "How/where/when do objects/subjects of inquiry matter in STEAM (re-)configurings in practice?", and "How/where/when does embodiment matter in STEAM (re-)configuring practices" in the context of STEAM environmental education practice with a creativity and "future-making" orientation. My response to these questions is informed by our previous theoretical and empirical work exploring science|arts creative pedagogies as part of the CREATIONS project (Chappell et al., 2019). The chapter begins with an explanation of the CREATIONS project. I outline the research-based "features of creative pedagogy" which informed the practice explored in this chapter, and the theorisation of creativity which developed and unfolded through the project and in subsequent work that draws diffractively on ideas from Barad (2007). This enables a strong foundation on which to ground STEAM practices (Colucci-Gray et al., 2017). I then outline the diffractive methodological approach used in analysing data and theory together, before turning to the specific practice-based example at the core of the chapter. Following a short description of the example, I offer a sequence of "diffractions", in which I explore the science|arts practice in an iterative response to questions emerging from engaging with theory and previous analyses. This is, in itself, a transdisciplinary approach, where transdisciplinarity is understood as drawing on different disciplinary ideas and ways of knowing in order to respond to ongoing questioning. As such, it exemplifies a different way of approaching both research and practice through science|arts creativity. I close the chapter with a deliberately speculative diffraction, opening a space for teachers and researchers to continue to engage diffractively with the ideas shared.

2   Creativity and Creative Pedagogies

The data I draw on in this chapter was captured in the context of the CREATIONS project, a large H2020-EU funded program aiming to develop arts-based creative approaches for science education. Working across eleven countries, the project was situated in the context of the growing STE(A)M education movement with the aim of engaging more students with science. Research conducted as part of this project included: (1) an exploration of the role of dialogue and materiality/embodiment in science|arts pedagogy across four cases in three participant countries (Chappell et al., 2019); (2) European educators' perspectives on creativity in science (Hetherington et al., 2019b); and (3) monitoring students' creativity in science|arts contexts (Conradty & Bogner, 2018; Thuneberg, Salmi, & Bogner, 2018). Underpinning this work was an extensive literature review and workshopping process in which a set of eight features of creative pedagogy were developed (Chappell et al., 2015) and used to design teaching and learning activities for approximately 100 different science|arts activities across Europe, including the one explored in this chapter. The eight features are: dialogue; empowerment and agency; interdisciplinarity (which became transdisciplinarity during the life of the project); possibilities; risk, immersion and play; ethics and trusteeship; balance and navigation; and individual, collaborative and communal activities for change. Throughout this project, we expanded and developed our theoretical understanding of creativity in STE(A)M education. A brief diversion to outline our theoretical stance is therefore necessary before connecting it to practice in this chapter.

Influential in defining creativity and creative pedagogy in STEAM studies is a "democratic" approach to educational research and practice that recognises the everyday creativity of all children, whilst acknowledging that novelty may apply only to the creator/s (Banaji, Burn, & Buckingham, 2006; Craft, 2001, 2013; Kaufman & Beghetto, 2009). Teaching creatively is distinct from teaching for creativity (fostering creativity in students), and in combination these two processes enable co-participative approaches where students' perspectives guide learning (Jeffrey & Craft, 2004). Creative teaching is not oppositional to the teaching of knowledge, skills and understanding (Cremin & Barnes, 2014), but the role of the teacher is shifted from the "sage on the stage" (with the teacher transmitting knowledge to the learner) to a "meddler in the middle" (McWilliam, 2008), with the teacher engaging in the dynamic of learning with the learners, as part of an improvisational educational relationship (Sawyer, 2011). This argues for the importance of relationality in creative pedagogy: a key theoretical notion in interpreting the features of creative pedagogy used within and developed through the research.

Informing the CREATIONS project research was a definition of creativity in science education, developed by building on and refining an earlier definition within EU-funded science education projects[3] via literature reviews of creative pedagogy research and co-creation via international workshops (Chappell et al., 2015). Creativity in science education was defined as:

> Purposive and imaginative activity generating outcomes that are original and valuable in relation to the learner. This occurs through critical reasoning using the available evidence to generate ideas, explanations and strategies as an individual or community, whilst acknowledging the role of risk and emotions in interdisciplinary contexts. (Chappell et al., 2015: 61)

Both the CREATIONS definition and the features of creative pedagogies developed through the project and its antecedents were founded in respect for professional wisdom, recognising practitioners' wealth of expertise both in their teaching and in their disciplinary knowledge and skills. Derived against a background of inter- and transdisciplinary work in creative pedagogies, their ongoing materialisation within the research is part of an emergent phenomenon through meaningful engagement in a responsible, professional educational relation (Biesta, 2004).

In the broader literature on creative pedagogies described above and, indeed, in the CREATIONS definition itself, there is a dominantly humanist conception of creativity in research and practice. Our recent research is moving away from this (whilst acknowledging its influence) as we are increasingly engaged with new materialist theorising (Chappell, 2018; Hetherington et al., 2019c). Therefore, the articulation of the relevant features in this chapter is rooted in a new materialist stance. Broadly, this is in response to the synergies we find between the embodied, relational dialogic stance at the heart of Chappell and Craft's (2011) earlier articulation of creativity and our theorising of creativity, which acknowledges the enmeshed (from Braidotti, 2013) or entangled (from Barad, 2007) nature of human–other-than-human relationships[4] in order to be able to creatively respond to the educational challenges of rapid and unpredictable change. Chappell's (2018) (posthumanising) creativity situates embodied dialogue at its heart, with objects, environments and humans intra-acting as embodied, agentic and entangled actants. Creativity is dispersed through the intra-action rather than humanly centred. As such, the "becomings" that emerge through creative, material-dialogic intra-actions are also dispersed through the emerging phenomena. Ethics is re-configured as emergent and relational.

However, in re-configuring creative pedagogies through relational new materialist or posthumanist lenses, we need to go further and consider also the temporality of creative intra-action: in Barad's (2007) terms, spacetimemattering. As (2018) points out, learning theories often associate learning with either "building on" earlier foundational knowledge or "breaking with" previous naïve understandings, and therefore do not exist in temporal isolation. Neither does creativity: as highlighted earlier, creative pedagogy is not oppositional to the teaching of knowledge and skills and, indeed, creativity cannot be separated from the disciplinary context(s) in which it is enacted. However, creativity in education, albeit activity creating outcomes that are original *to the learner*, is often associated with novelty and therefore with learning that breaks with previous ideas and understandings – the "aha!" moments. Barad (in conversation with Juelskjær & Schwennesen, 2012) explains that the notion of dis/continuity is helpful here. Using the both/and logic typically found in posthumanist and new materialist theorising, Barad sees creativity as a "dis/continuity": *both* continuous *and* discontinuous with past and future as part of an ongoing entangled material-discursive intra-action with spacetime.

> [C]reativity is not about crafting the new through a radical break with the past. It's a matter of dis/continuity, neither continuous nor discontinuous in *the usual sense. It seems to me that it's important to have some kind of way of thinking about change that doesn't presume there's either more of the same or a radical break. Dis/continuity is a cutting together-apart (one move) that doesn't deny creativity and innovation but understands*

> *its indebtedness and entanglements to the past and the future.* (Barad, in conversation with Juelskjær & Schwennesen, 2012: 16, emphasis added)

STEAM transdisciplinarity is one way of (re)configuring educational practices that engage with this dis/continuous understanding of creativity to teach *for* creativity (Jeffery & Craft, 2004). In our previous work, we have described our perspective on transdisciplinarity that draws dynamically and openly on ideas and processes from any discipline to respond to questions asked (Chappell et al., 2019, drawing on Morgan, 2000). We shifted to the term transdisciplinarity rather than interdisciplinarity, or the integration of disciplines, because for us it implies a sense of disciplinary equality that is not necessarily the case in interdisciplinary practices where one discipline supports the learning in the other. In transdisciplinary practice, then, creativity and innovation lie in the generation of and response to new questions whilst maintaining a connection to the ideas and processes embodied in existing, and ongoing, disciplinary knowledges, practices and creativities – acknowledging that creativity emerges and materialises differently in different disciplinary contexts (Colucci-Gray et al., 2017; Hetherington et al., 2019b). This leads to a question-driven approach to teaching for creativity through STEAM.

Resulting from our ongoing theorisation of creative pedagogies using new materialist ideas, we are also engaged in an iterative and emergent reconfiguring of the practice-oriented CREATIONS features, seeing creativity as a more-than-human, entangled and intra-active material dialogue within space and time. An emergent outcome from previous work (Chappell et al., 2019) that is relevant to the analysis in this chapter is that question-driven STEAM transdisciplinary practice is grounded in the idea that matter and meaning are mutually constituted in a material-dialogic space (Hetherington et al., 2019c). This has wider implications for the question-driven practice described above, because if what is emerging through intra-actions in the dialogic "gap" between temporarily bounded, entangled and intra-acting objects/subjects is *subjectivities* – rather than unique human subjects/minds – then practice is continually (re-)configured through unique *assemblages* of teachers, students, ideas and materials as they respond to emergent inquiry questions by drawing on intra-acting disciplinary practices. This approach to STEAM transdisciplinary inquiry in practice is an embodied/material process.

Our starting point for the diffractions through which we explore these questions in this chapter is therefore that *entangled matter/meaning/subjectivities emerge and are dynamically (re-)configured through embodied material-dialogic intra-actions in STEAM transdisciplinary inquiry.*

The chapter does not follow the familiar format for reporting empirical research, but instead exemplifies a process that Barad (2014) calls "cutting together-apart", as the entangled phenomena within the research assemblage (the researchers, the theories, the participants [through their words/creations/survey responses], and the methodology) intra-act. This diffractive approach is appropriate in researching creativity and future making in education, given its complementarity with the emergent and open-ended theoretical stance of the work. It is chosen in anticipation of opening a space for teachers, students and researchers to explore seeing, doing, feeling, talking, thinking and materialising responsible, anticipatory science|arts creative pedagogy in environmental education.

I now turn to the diffractive methodology, followed by a short description of the specific practice-based context from which the data in this chapter is drawn. I then engage with the diffractive process by exploring and intra-acting with strands of theory and data within the research assemblage, uniquely cutting them together-apart in a process that is itself emergent and creative.

3   Diffractive Methodology

The relational theoretical stance we developed through the life of the CREATIONS project led us to a diffractive methodology, to enable a creative response to the dynamic settings of arts|science practices we were engaging with (Chappell et al., 2019). The concept of diffraction, as a methodology developed by Barad (2007, building on Haraway, 1997), highlights how different methodological "cuts" are performed (Van Der Tuin, 2011), which interrupt and dissect the object of study in co-productive ways such that methods, data, the object/s of study and the researchers are cut together-apart in a single move to materialise new meanings (Barad, 2014). In our approach to diffractive methodology, we draw on the concept of assemblages, made up of intra-acting elements that are productive of new matter/meaning (Fox & Alldred, 2015). The primary unit of analysis, the assemblage, is composed of data selected through the agentic intra-action of data and researcher/s together. MacLure (2013), drawing on Deleuze and Guattari, refers to "moments that glow" to describe data/theory that pushes itself forward into the assemblages, provoking a response. Assemblages are formed and re-formed as the analysis proceeds, questioning and responding and questioning as new methodological cuts are made, new knowledge created, and new questions generated. In this way, theory and data are read through one another in a challenging process that does not seek closure but acknowledges the complexity of the study (Mazzei, 2014; Uprichard & Dawney, 2016).

Typically, this analytical approach draws on qualitative data but avoids "coding" it, resisting the reduction and representation that a more typical analytical stance offers (St Pierre, 2011). However, following Uprichard and Dawney (2016), we suggest that the entanglement of mixed methods and mixed analytical techniques offers another form of intra-activity and the materialisation of meaning, and therefore the findings of quantitative analysis of survey data and thematic coding of large numbers of qualitative survey responses can be drawn into a diffractive research assemblage, as we do here (Hetherington, 2019). Diffractive analysis shifts our attention away from the human "subject" of the research and towards the agentic role of both theory and materiality in research (Lenz Taguchi, 2009). We assert that this approach has both rigour and legitimacy that does not derive from a sense of replicability, or representation through thick description, but instead arises from the synergy between questions, theoretical framework design and analysis (Onwuegbuzie & Johnson, 2006) alongside meticulous documentation of the processes through tracing and mapping intra-actions between data, theory and questioning (Lenz Taguchi, 2016). Through this diffractive process, the research emerges – materialises meaning – in intra-activity. It is not representational but is part of a living inquiry and an ongoing reconfiguring. In this way, diffractive methodology itself can be seen as part of a unique research assemblage, emerging and developing in response to the ongoing study.

In the study at hand (described in more detail in the next section), data was collected by the teachers involved in the project using a pre- and post-questionnaire (designed by the teachers) that explored pupils' perceptions of art, science and their relationship to environmental responsibility through short qualitative responses, alongside pupils' self-report on their identity as a scientist and/or artist and a Likert-style question rating their interest in science and art on a 5-point scale. Artefacts produced by the pupils and photographs of their activities were also collected, and the teachers involved were recorded explaining their perceptions of the project to other teachers and University of Exeter researchers involved in the broader science/arts research project. Questionnaire data was analysed quantitatively and qualitatively, producing a summary of the students' perceptions using descriptive statistics and themes drawn from coding of students' open-ended responses, to produce a written summary of questionnaire findings. Excerpts from this summary, alongside direct quotations from the questionnaire responses, quotations from the teachers' descriptions, and photographs of artefacts and objects generated through the activity, were used within the analysis where they pushed themselves into the analysis as "glow moments" (see above). This inclusion of questionnaire data was therefore not about data integration and synthesis in a way that could be seen as oppositional to the diffractive approach taken (St. Pierre & Jackson, 2014). This is because the coding of qualitative responses does not replace their potential inclusion as separate "glow moments" within the assemblage. Instead, the coding itself is treated as another piece of data which can diffract through the theory/other data. In a sense, the coded data enables the exploration of entangled phenomena where boundaries are temporarily drawn around the [group of pupils-questionnaires] as an entangled complex learning system, as well as around individuals, acknowledging the nested levels of complexity within the materialising learning system (Hetherington, 2019).

4   The Practice Context: Science|Arts|Environmental Education

The practice we explore in this chapter was one of the science|arts activities developed using the CREATIONS features of creative pedagogy (Chappell et al., 2015) as part of a wider research project. Science and art teacher pairs in six UK secondary settings worked with researchers from the University of Exeter to engage in research that involved them in designing and researching a science/arts interdisciplinary activity using the features. Teachers from all sites came together three times with the university research team, initially to frame the project, midway through the project to share progress and inspiration, and at the end of the project to share outcomes and explore implications both in their own practice and more widely. The projects the teachers created varied substantially, showing the diverse creativities associated with the generative, emergent and contextualised nature of teachers' intra-actions with theories of creative pedagogy, their disciplines and each other (see Chappell et al., 2019 for a diffractive analysis including two of these case studies not explored here).

In this chapter, we draw on data generated in one of these sites, a secondary mixed-gender faith school serving a diverse urban community in central England, where the focus was placed on science|arts creative pedagogies to explore environmental issues. For the activity, 52 pupils aged 14–15 participated in a day-long interdisciplinary science|arts project in which a range of activities were set up in different rooms within the school. Pupils were invited to explore metals, plastics, dyes and textiles from the perspective of both disciplines, and to explore the issue of plastic in the ocean through both art and science. Some pupils took inspiration from the day into their ongoing textiles projects, and images of early outcomes from these projects were included in the dataset. It is quite rare for creativity to be linked to education for sustainability and/or environmental education: a literature review conducted for a different project (Hetherington et al., 2019a) suggests that, where links in existing studies are

found, environmental education and sustainability are often used as a context
to teach "skills" of problem-based learning and creativity, or creativity is seen
as a required skill to be taught to foster environmental responsibility.

5   Diffraction 1: When/Where/How Do Objects/Subjects of Inquiry Matter in STEAM (Re-)Configurings of Practice?

Inspired by Areljung's (Chapter 7, this volume) use of active verbs to explore
dynamic, material phenomena with young children, Renold and Ringrose's
(2019) description of their JARring methodology, and a particular photograph
from the data set in this study (Figure 12.1), a "netting" approach was developed to respond diffractively to the first question. These diffractions emerged
through my intra-actions with the data assemblage and must therefore be
influenced by my disciplinary perspective as a science educator: had one of
the other members of the Exeter team engaged in this analysis from their arts
backgrounds, the emergent responses would be different.

FIGURE 12.1
Net of plastics, data
artefact

A net is defined in the *Oxford English dictionary* (2019) as "an open-meshed material made of twine, cord or something similar" that can be used to catch fish or other animals, or people/objects as a safety net or in a trap, or with a support structure to catch balls in a goal, or as a communications network as in a shortened term for the internet. In this diffraction, I undertook "netting" as a means of enacting an "agential cut" to bring glowing theory and data together in a specific orientation with which we explored the enmeshed and entangled images and theoretical concepts. To achieve this, I created a net out of knotted string and laid it out on a table. I dropped cut-out "glow moment" images and quotations onto the net, lifted it, and pinned the paper pieces to the net where they were captured. I then laid the net flat onto a large sheet of paper, orienting the data pieces so they could be seen, before annotating them in coloured pen as an initial layer of responses to our key question (Figure 12.2).

FIGURE 12.2   Netted glow moments

The netting of glow moments for this first assemblage brings to the fore the reconfiguring of objects/subjects within the science|arts day exploring ocean plastics. "Everyday" material objects (plastic bottles, pieces of fabric) and "everyday" methods (a hairdryer) were put to work via a combination of scientific processes (the breaking and making of polymer chains, combustion, melting and freezing of solder) and artistic processes (sculpting of warmed plastics,

"There are many things in the human body and materials that are works of art, and science is almost like learning about the art"
- Student quote
(re-)configuring objects
Spacetimemattering

FIGURE 12.3 Jellyfish sculpture created from plastic bottle

painting, plaiting and sewing of plastic bags and fabrics) to create new matter/meaning. New objects were created that were themselves works of art (the plastic jellyfish image in the centre of the net, Figure 12.3), and new understandings of science, art and of the students themselves emerged (changing interest levels in science and art, Figure 12.4).

One of the features of creative pedagogies we have been working with through the creations project is "transdisciplinarity", which we understand to be drawing on ideas and processes from any discipline in order to answer the questions being asked: in effect, this is about transdisciplinary practice as a form of inquiry. As Kerry put it in the quotation in the assemblage from a research project meeting with the teachers (Figure 12.5), the pupils are engaging in an ongoing process of "curious questioning".

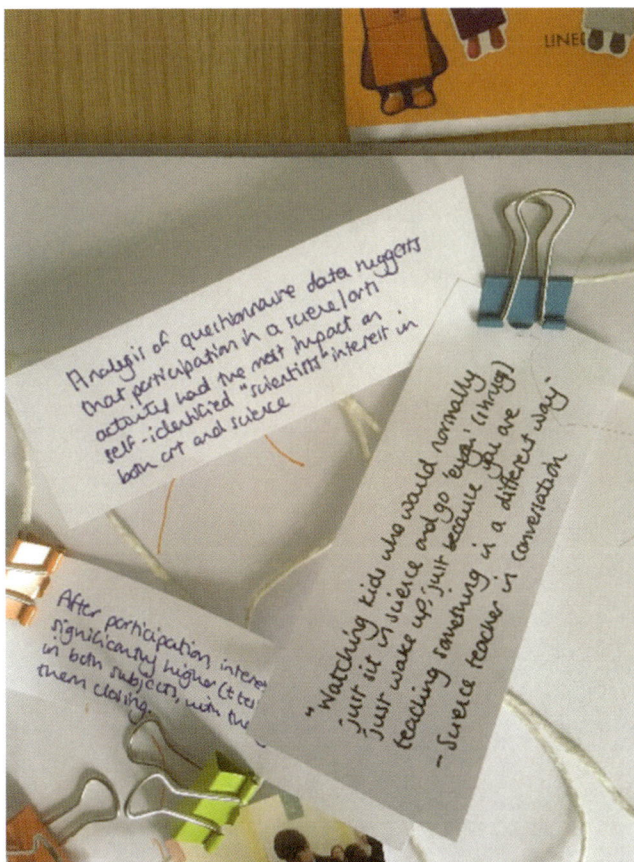

FIGURE 12.4   Data excerpts from questionnaire analysis and teacher research conversation,
noting changes in students' behaviour and perception of Art and Science

STEAM practices may be interdisciplinary, involving the weaving together of
different disciplines such that they support each other but retain their boundaried nature (Harris & de Bruin, 2018), and this appears to be at least partially
the case here with the production of a GCSE Textiles portfolio. However, as
Kerry points out, the student is reaching for science or arts knowledges and processes as needed to respond to her continually emerging "curious questions".
At the same time, we can also view transdisciplinarity using Barad's theoretical lens of entanglement and the ongoing (re)configuring of the disciplines as
temporarily or fluidly boundaried phenomena. The glow moments captured
in the net are suggestive of such an entangled, transdisciplinary reconfigur
ing of material objects, subjectivities, and the disciplines of science and art
as they are continually (re)created and embodied through ongoing entangled
intra-actions. As the pieces of data drawn from the thematic analysis and the

FIGURE 12.5   Data excerpt from Kerry during a research conversation with teachers, noting pupil's use of Arts and Sciences as she responds to her own question

textiles workbooks show (Figure 12.6), the pupils enacting this science|art practice associate creativity in both disciplines with *making*, with *colour* and with *inquiry*, but these manifest differently in each discipline. This is suggestive of creativity as a transdisciplinary practice that materialises within, and in the gaps between, disciplines.

This leads to another aspect of the question with which I began this diffraction: having engaged with the ongoing reconfigurings of objects/subjects – of entangled and embodied matter/meaning – in my exploration of the netted assemblage so far, I have not yet considered when/where/how this reconfiguring occurs in such science|art practices. The data excerpts in the assemblage come from a range of times and places and with different groups of human and other-than-human agents, and yet it seems impossible to pin down particular "whens", "wheres" or "hows" from this data: each excerpt contains some aspect of the ongoing materialisation of matter/meaning within this creative

FIGURE 12.6   Data excerpts showing pupils' intra-action with materials and association of
                creativity with making, colour and inquiry

science|arts work, whether in pupils' conversations with teachers, working
with particular processes, creating artefacts, responding to questionnaires,
researchers analysing questionnaire data, or teachers and researchers engaging in dialogue about the research. Rather than try to answer this aspect of the
question with respect to each element of the practices in this case (which readers can interpret themselves as they engage diffractively with the data assemblage presented), I instead return to theory to help me explore and respond to
the question, reconfigured in light of my first diffraction through new materialist theoretical concepts of entanglement and transdisciplinarity.

6   Diffraction 2: (Re-)Configured Question: When/Where/How Do
         Entangled and Embodied Matter/Meaning/Objects/Subjectivities
         Emerge and Dynamically Reconfigure in an Environmental
         Science|Arts Education Practice?

Zooming in on a corner of the net (Figure 12.7), I find some images that sprang
out as relating to our conceptualisation of embodied dialogue and material-
dialogic space. Within a relational ontology, the concept of embodied dialogue

FIGURE 12.7   Data excerpts within the net, showing 'embodied, material-dialogic spaces'

has increasingly become, to us, a crucial feature of creative pedagogies in transdisciplinary practices. Related to Barad's concept of intra-action, we have elsewhere (Chappell et al., 2019), developing an earlier conceptualisation of "living dialogic space" (Chappell & Craft, 2011), articulated in detail how embodied dialogue can contribute to the enactment and materialisation of creative transdisciplinary pedagogies. Further, in Hetherington et al. (2019b, 2019c) we explore how bringing theory from Barad and Bakhtin together can help us consider where and how such an embodied dialogue can occur. Citing Shotter (2013), Carlile et al. (2013) also note how the work of these two theorists can be usefully brought together as they both work with a relational ontology. Dialogic theory holds that dialogue can only occur when there is an "other" with whom a dialogue can proceed – where there is no difference, no other, then there can be no dialogue (see Wegerif, 2019). However, dialogue need not be between human subjects: the material/non-human other also contributes a "voice" in the dialogue. For Barad, objects cannot pre-exist their intra-action but are produced by and productive of it *by means of that intra-action*. Dialogue is possible between these temporarily boundaried, temporarily "othered", agentially intra-active entities. Wegerif (2019) uses a helpful concept in his discussions of dialogic theory: dialogic space. Dialogic space is a shared, relational space that emerges in a dialogue. Chappell and Craft (2011) termed the dialogic spaces that are produced in creative pedagogical practices "living dialogic spaces" in order to encapsulate their fluidity and dynamism as those engaged in creative dialogue respond to and create (with) each other. Hetherington et al. (2019c) explore the materiality of dialogic space where other-than-human and embodied human voices are foregrounded with/in the dialogue.

The elements of data in the assemblage that I home in on in this diffraction suggest to me that the material and embodied reconfigurings in this science|arts|environmental practice took place in what could be considered a living material dialogic space. Pupils, teachers, materials and ideas were brought together in a physical and ideational space (as shown in the photograph of teacher, student and plastic in dialogue in the school hall in Figure 12.7), where "science and art combines our imagination and reality" (as the student quoted in the assemblage put it). People, materials and ideas flowed in and out of this space as they moved around the different classrooms during the science|arts day and onwards into their lives and other lessons, changing things and being changed as the entangled, temporarily boundaried intra-acting entities (by which we include groups of pupils, or pupil-objects) shifted and moved both through physical space and time. Barad might call the phenomena produced in this living material-dialogic space "spacetimemattering" (Barad, 2007: 142). The importance and relevance of the idea that living material-dialogic space stretches and flows through time is shown through the photograph at the bottom of the assemblage (in Figure 12.7). Taken on an action research project day in which the six science and art teacher pairs from each school visited the University of Exeter for a day to work with the project research team, sharing and discussing their own research in the context of the wider creations project framework, the photograph shows what we came to call the "sharing table" at the end of a discussion of three teacher pairs' work. It is interesting to see the materials the teacher brought to share and discuss: graphs of outcomes from the questionnaires along with photographs of students' work from the case that we are exploring in this chapter physically bring together approaches that are commonly associated with "scientific" or "arts-based" methodologies but stretch beyond disciplinary boundaries and associations as they are brought through space and time to intra-act in response to our creative research inquiry. The artefacts from the case we explore in this chapter lay over and are overlain by artefacts from other projects, with the teachers' and researchers' bodies just visible around the edge of the table. The artefacts (material-dialogic objects that "came to matter" in the project) therefore extend the phenomena produced within the dialogic spaces on the science|arts day, stretching the material-dialogic space through time and bringing them into new dialogues with new artefacts, objects and people in an ongoing creative research process as well as a pedagogical one.

The where/when/how question of entangled and embodied (re)configurings of objects/subjects in a science|arts transdisciplinary practice could therefore be answered: through embodied/material dialogue, within a living material-dialogic space. The importance of this space as fluid, dynamic and shifting through time as well as physical and ideational space is foregrounded in the diffractive assemblage produced through the "netting" process, linking images and quotations from the project day through to the teacher-researchers' dialogues on the research sharing table and Kerry's quotation from the analytical conversation at the research meeting. In the context of a science|arts day that was intended (on the teachers' part) to engage pupils in thinking about environmental responsibility, and therefore future making, the importance of space, time and materiality together highlighted in diffraction 2 leads us to a new question: In a creative science|arts transdisciplinary practice about ocean plastics, in what ways does environmental responsibility come to matter?

7   Diffraction 3: In a Creative Science|Arts Transdisciplinary Practice about Ocean Plastics, in What Ways Does Environmental Responsibility Come to Matter?

The notion of environmental responsibility holds within it a sense of temporality: responsibility towards the environment with/in and of which we are a part both in the present and the future. In my last diffractive response, I reached a point where the analysis of the practices suggested the importance of material-dialogic space extending through time within creative pedagogical practice and research: a dialogic spacetimemattering. Taking this as a starting point, I again used the "netting" process to bring together a data assemblage responding to the question of how, in this practice, environmental responsibility came to matter. As with the previous diffraction, the whole net is shown in Figure 12.8, with zoomed in photographs to show the data excerpts more clearly as the diffraction proceeds.

FIGURE 12.8   The 'net' produced for diffraction 3

In the questionnaires completed before and after the science|arts day, the pupils were asked for their ideas about whether scientists and artists had a responsibility to protect the environment. Data excerpts show that their reasoning drew on their ideas about scientific knowledge, collective and individual responsibility, communication and creativity, in responses that, for me, are about exploring the agency of "scientists" and "artists" to protect the environment, with questions of "Who can act?" and "In what ways?" To respond to the question prompting this third diffractive piece, then, we turn to the CREATIONS feature of creative pedagogies: empowerment and agency.

In the context of a humanising perspective on creative pedagogy with which we began our work on the CREATIONS project, agency and empowerment are important for both teachers and students to be able to work creatively. Agency is commonly understood as the "capacity to act" and it could be argued that, in order to be creative, freedom to choose one's actions is a necessity. In an educational context, the freedom for teachers and students to take risks and play with possibilities is rooted in the idea that they have agency over what and how they learn. However, agency can be understood not simply as an individual, human capacity but as a relational performance within an entangled assemblage of material and human actors, where agency is enacted "intra-actively" (Barad, 2007). Intra-actions enact "agential cuts" which determine the boundaries between phenomena and thus make objects or concepts (phenomena, for Barad) meaningful. Creativity through embodied/material dialogue occurs as boundaries between objects/concepts are creatively performed by agential intra-action within an entangled, living dialogic space that acts to open out new possibilities.

A relational view of agency suggests relata[5] within a living material-dialogic space that also has a temporal dimension. Emirbayer and Mische (1998) describe the temporal nature of agency as formed of a "chordal triad" of past, present and future influences acting together in the moment of agentic action. Thus, agency has a "projective" dimension, in which agents act towards an imagined future, a "practical-evaluative" dimension in which present conditions are taken into account, and an "iterational" dimension in which past experiences informing action are considered. This is a useful framing for the way in which actants relate to experiences across time as well as space. However, Emirbayer and Mische's is a solely human perspective on agency and also assumes that the future can be envisioned and extrapolated.

Turning to our data assemblage, it seems that, at the outset of the day, many of the pupils associated the capacity for environmental protection with scientists' knowledge, and appeared to suggest that artists' responsibilities are part of a collective sense but did not offer a specific responsibility rooted in the discipline (excerpt from questionnaire analysis summary, Figure 12.9, and quotation "It is everyone's responsibility to look after the environment", left, Figure 12.8). Taking Emirbayer and Mische's (1998) conceptualisation of temporal agency, this could be explained by the idea that, as a result of their (past) knowledge, scientists are able to envision the future and act in the present, based on that knowledge. However, this begs the question of how agency can be enacted without reference to any special knowledge, not least under conditions of real uncertainty about the future, as are currently faced in relation to Earth's responsive global climate change. This could be addressed through Hetherington's (2012) development of a further dimension of agency, "creative agency", which comes into play under conditions of radical uncertainty when the future cannot be envisioned and, instead, agency must be enacted to open the space of what is possible without knowledge about what the outcome of that action might be. It could be argued that, through the science|arts day, pupils increasingly engaged with the need for creative as well as iterational agency in terms of environmental responsibility. However, this was still situated firmly within a human perspective.

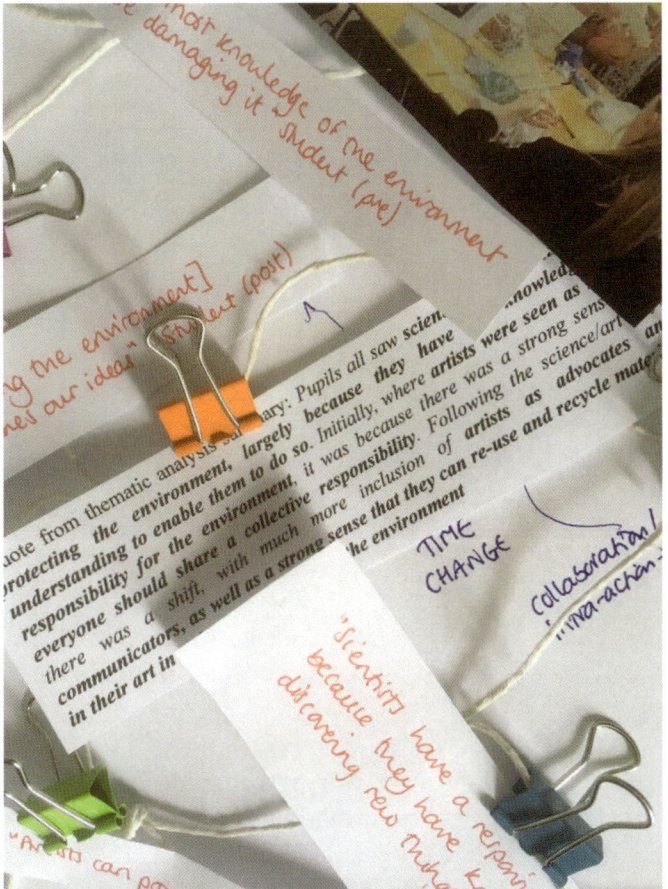

FIGURE 12.9   Data excerpt highlighting pupil perspectives on environmental responsibility, captured through thematic analysis of questionnaire data

In the data assemblage, we also see excerpts from the students' work during the day, intra-acting in a transdisciplinary sense with plastic materials and each other within a material-dialogic space that, as argued above, creates new objects and subjectivities in practice. In the netting, these excerpts are brought into relation with quotations from pupils' perspectives at the end of the day that appear to indicate some change in their subjectivities in relation to environmental responsibility. There is an acknowledgement of interdisciplinary and transdisciplinary creativity that "propels ideas forward" in time, with "new discoveries" (Figure 12.10) that, whilst unknown, might help protect the environment in a creative orientation to the unknown future. This shift in perspective resulting from the material-dialogic creative practices appears to show one way in which environmental responsibility comes to matter: as embodied pupils physically and dialogically intra-act within an interdisciplinary and at

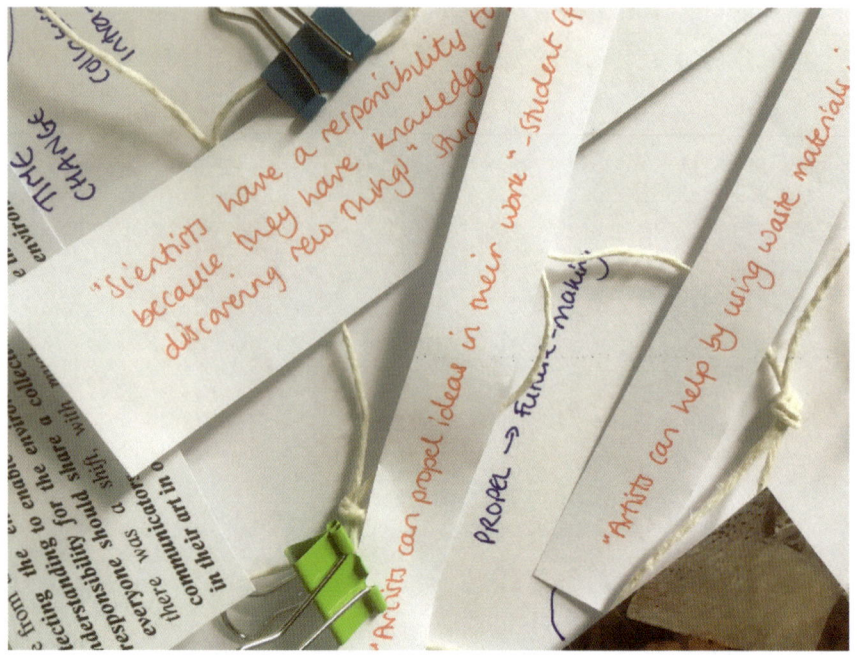

FIGURE 12.10   Data excerpts showing pupil association of environmental responsibility with
the future, and with discovery

times transdisciplinary practice, new objects/subjectivities are made in relation to environmental responsibility. The pupils began to recognise that artists
can, through art, contribute directly to environmental protection through their
use of waste materials in the way the pupils did themselves on the day, but they
also recognised the communicative potential of such science-art outcomes,
and the creative potential in bringing the disciplines into relation.

With the material intra-actions visible in the data assemblage bringing our
attention to embodied and material practices in how environmental respon-
sibility comes to matter in science|arts|environmental education practice,
it seems that a materialist dimension is needed with respect to the creative,
temporal nature of relational agency. How can we put to work the notion of
agential intra-action, and the agential "cut", as a temporally emergent phenomenon? If past, present *and future* are part of an entangled agential material-
discursive cut, what does this mean for responsible agential intra-action (for
us, in the context of environmental responsibility), where emergent phenomena are radically new, radically unpredictable? Returning to Barad's notion of
dis/continuity, the intra-active agential cut reconfigures the entangled past,
present and future – reconfigures spacetimematter – and constrains *but does
not determine* future possibilities (Barad, 2007: 177). The agential cut both

opens and closes possibilities, leading to a "dis/continuity between past and future that resists both acausality and determinism" (Barad, 2007: 178). Like creativity, the emergent future can be both radically new, innovative and not *determined* by the past (discontinuous) whilst also being *constrained* by the past (continuous). The both/and logic of the dis/continuity highlights how creative agential intra-action includes entanglements with (using Emirbayer and Mische's terminology, these would be "orientations to") the past, the present, the envisionable future *and* the emergent future.[6] In a sense, environmental responsibility comes to matter in science|arts pedagogical practices through the enactment of this dis/continuity. The pupils' ideas about environmental protection emerged and materialised as they explored scientific knowledge, artistic knowledge and how they can contribute creatively together through intra-action within a material-dialogic space that stretches and flows through time.

8   Diffraction 4 …? Ethics and Trusteeship and SpacetimeMattering

In this sequence of diffractions of theory and data drawn from science|arts practice, I have developed the idea of the temporality of material-dialogic space in practice. I have also explored how a creative, temporal dimension to agency within a relational, materialist frame is necessary in reconfiguring creative, inter- and trans-disciplinary practices for education about environmental responsibility. For me, the notion of a temporal material-dialogic space is similar to Barad's (2007) spacetimemattering, but more helpful as an inspiration for developing pedagogical practice via the "hook" of the more familiar dialogic, creative pedagogy. Having explored environmental responsibility with this theory-data through the notion of agency, I am left with questions for further diffractive reading of this data in relation to the "ethics and trusteeship" feature of creative pedagogy, not least in the context of the dynamic nature of the Earth's global systems of which we are a part. It may be that, in respect of creative educational practices, there is a call not just to reconfigure objects/ subjectivities but also to reconfigure anticipatory futures (Osberg, 2018) through intra-action within a fluid and dynamic material-dialogic space, and I leave this final diffractive thought to open a space for teachers and researchers to take forward:

> Ethicality is part of the fabric of the world; the call to respond and be responsible is part of what is. There is no spatial-temporal domain that is excluded from the ethicality of what matters. Questions of

responsibility and accountability present themselves with every possibility; each moment is alive with different possibilities for the world's
becoming and different reconfigurings of what may yet be possible.
(Barad, 2007: 182)

9   Material(ising) Science|Arts Creativities in Environmental
Education Research And Practice

In the series of diffractions in this chapter I have connected and entangled
new materialist theory, a review of creativities research, and action research
practice in which science|arts material-dialogic creativities emerged and
came to matter in exploring the issue of ocean plastics. In doing so, I have
developed theoretical and practical ideas together, opening a space for teachers to engage with them in their own exploratory STEAM (re)configurings of
practice. The chapter does not offer step-by-step guidance for practice, but
instead invites and inspires teachers to engage, experiment and improvise
with material objects, ideas and disciplines together in question-driven transdisciplinary STEAM creative inquiry to explore environmental responsibility.
The diffractions in this chapter suggest practices that open out fluid, dynamic
material-dialogic spaces in which materials, processes and ideas drawn from
arts and sciences are brought into relation with teachers and students in order
to respond creatively to questions about environmental challenges such as
the issue of ocean plastics. The temporal, physical and ideational nature of
a living material-dialogic space enabled by such a STEAM (re)configuring of
practice is crucial to enacting agency in future-making educational practice
and research, as it values both innovation for the future (materialising creative agency) and disciplinary knowledges that embody the past (materialising
iterational agency) in an ongoing ethical, responsive practice.

Acknowledgements

I would like to acknowledge the teachers Cora Gartland and Anne Morgan,
whose practice-based research is diffracted through theory in this chapter, and
the University of Exeter CREATIONS project team: Dr Kerry Chappell, project
lead; Dr Hermione Ruck Keene and Heather Wren. Although I took the lead on
the data analysis and writing for this chapter, the project as a whole and our
ongoing theoretical work is a relational, dialogic team effort.

Notes

1   The practice explored in this chapter was part of an action research study conducted as part of the CREATIONS project, funded by the EU under the H2020 scheme.
2   The term intra-action within Barad's (2007) agential realism, rather than the more familiar interaction, is used to highlight that boundaried entities do not pre-exist any intra-action, but are continuously made and remade through entangled material-discursive relationships.
3   Creative Little Scientists (Cremin et al., 2015) and CREAT-IT (Craft et al., 2016).
4   Although they are distinct theoretical notions, Braidotti's (2013) concept of enmeshing and Barad's (2007) notion of entanglement sit within a similar position in the arguments made throughout this chapter. For simplicity, and because Barad's agential realism is the dominant new materialist theorisation drawn into this diffractive analysis, entanglement is used throughout the remainder of the chapter.
5   The term "relata", taken from Barad, refers to the objects/subjects that emerge through relations. An agential realist ontology "does not take separateness to be an inherent feature of how the world is. But nor does it denigrate separateness as a mere illusion, an artefact of human consciousness led astray.
6   I use "emergent" here in the sense of "strongly emergent", where the emergent future is not determined by the past. This contrasts with "weak emergence" in which it would be theoretically possible to determine future outcomes with sufficient data and computing power (Osberg & Biesta, 2007).

References

Banaji, S., Burn, A., & Buckingham, D. (2006). *The rhetorics of creativity: A review of the literature*. London: Arts Council England.

Barad, K. (2007). *Meeting the universe halfway: Quantum physics and the entanglement of matter and meaning*. Durham, NC: Duke University Press.

Barad, K. (2014). Diffracting diffraction: Cutting together-apart. *Parallax, 20*, 168–187. https://doi.org/10.1080/13534645.2014.927623

Biesta, G. J. J. (2004). "Mind the gap!" Communication and the educational relation. In C. Bingham & A. M. Sidorkin (Eds.), *No education without relation* (pp. 11–22). New York, NY: Peter Lang.

Braidotti, R. (2013). *The posthuman*. Cambridge: Polity Press.

Carlile, P. R., Nicolini, D., Langley, A., & Tsoukas, H. (2013). *How matter matters: Objects, artifacts, and materiality in organization studies*. Oxford: Oxford University Press.

Chappell, K. (2018). From wise humanising creativity to (posthumanising) creativity. In K. Snepvangers, P. Thomson, & A. Harris (Eds.), *Creativity policy, partnerships and practice in education* (pp. 279–306). Cham: Springer. https://doi.org/10.1007/978-3-319-96725-7_13

Chappell, K., & Craft, A. (2011). Creative learning conversations: Producing living dialogic spaces. *Educational Research, 53*, 363–385. https://doi.org/10.1080/00131881.2011.598663

Chappell, K., Hetherington, L., Keene, H. R., Wren, H., Alexopoulos, A., Ben-Horin, O., Nikolopoulos, K., Robberstad, J., Sotiriou, S., & Bogner, F. X. (2019). Dialogue and materiality/embodiment in science|arts creative pedagogy: Their role and manifestation. *Thinking Skills and Creativity, 31*, 296–322. https://doi.org/10.1016/j.tsc.2018.12.008

Chappell, K., Hetherington, L., Ruck Keene, H., Slade, C., & Cukurova, M. (2015). *D2.1 The features of inquiry learning: Theory, research and practice.* Bayreuth: Creations Project, University of Bayreuth.

Colucci-Gray, L., Trowsdale, J., Cooke, C. F., Davies, R., Burnard, P., & Gray, D. S. (2017). *Reviewing the potential and challenges of developing STEAM education through creative pedagogies for 21st learning: how can school curricula be broadened towards a more responsive, dynamic, and inclusive form of education?* British Educational Research Associates.

Conradty, C., & Bogner, F. X. (2018). From STEM to STEAM: How to monitor creativity. *Creativity Research Journal, 30*, 233–240. https://doi.org/10.1080/10400419.2018.1488195

Craft, A. (2001). Little c creativity. In A. Craft, B. Jeffrey, & M. Leibling (Eds.), *Creativity in education* (pp. 45–61). London: Continuum.

Craft, A. (2013). Childhood, possibility thinking and wise, humanising educational futures. *International Journal of Educational Research, 61*, 126–134. https://doi.org/10.1016/j.ijer.2013.02.005

Craft, A., Horin, O. B., Sotiriou, M., Stergiopoulos, P., Sotiriou, S., Hennessy, S., ... Conforto, G. (2016). CREAT-IT: Implementing creative strategies into science teaching. In M. Riopel & Z. Smyrnaiou (Eds.), *New developments in science and technology education* (pp. 163–179). Cham: Springer. https://doi.org/10.1007/978-3-319-22933-1_15

Cremin, T., & Barnes, J. (2014). Creativity and creative teaching and learning. In T. Cremin & J. Arthur (Eds.), *Learning to teach in the primary school* (3rd ed., pp. 467–481). New York, NY: Routledge.

Cremin, T., Glauert, E., Craft, A., Compton, A., & Stylianidou, F. (2015). Creative little scientists: Exploring pedagogical synergies between inquiry-based and creative approaches in early years science. *Education 3–13, 43*, 404–419. https://doi.org/10.1080/03004279.2015.1020655

Emirbayer, M., & Mische, A. (1998). What is agency? *American Journal of Sociology, 103*, 962–1023. https://doi.org/10.1086/231294

Fox, N. J., & Alldred, P. (2015). New materialist social inquiry: Designs, methods and the research-assemblage. *International Journal of Social Research Methodology, 18*, 399–414. https://doi.org/10.1080/13645579.2014.921458

Haraway, D. (1997). *Modest_Witness@Second_Millennium. FemaleMan_Meets_OncoMouse: Feminism and technoscience*. London: Routledge.

Harris, A., & de Bruin, L. R. (2018). Secondary school creativity, teacher practice and STEAM education: An international study. *Journal of Educational Change, 19*, 153–179. https://doi.org/10.1007/s10833-017-9311-2

Hetherington, L. E. J. (2012). *"Walking the line between structure and freedom": A case study of teachers' responses to curriculum change using complexity theory* (PhD thesis). University of Exeter, Exeter.

Hetherington, L. (2019, August 26–30). *Entangling methods: Implications of new materialist theory for mixed methods in STE(A)M educational research*. Paper presented at the ESERA Conference, Bologna, Italy.

Hetherington, L., Chappell, K., & Dillon, J. (2019a). *Ocean connections: UK national state of the art report* (Deliverable No. IO1:1). Exeter: University of Exeter.

Hetherington, L., Chappell, K., Keene, H. R., Wren, H., Cukurova, M., Hathaway, C., Sotiriou, S., & Bogner, F. (2019b). International educators' perspectives on the purpose of science education and the relationship between school science and creativity. *Research in Science & Technological Education* [Preprint]. https://doi.org/10.1080/02635143.2019.1575803

Hetherington, L., Hardman, M., Noakes, J., & Wegerif, R. (2019c). Making the case for a material-dialogic approach to science education. *Studies in Science Education, 54*, 141–176. https://doi.org/10.1080/03057267.2019.1598036

Jeffrey, B., & Craft, A. (2004). Teaching creatively and teaching for creativity: Distinctions and relationships. *Educational Studies, 30*, 77–87. https://doi.org/10.1080/0305569032000159750

Juelskjær, M., & Schwennesen, N. (2012). Intra-active entanglements – An interview with Karen Barad. *Kvinder, Køn & Forskning, 1–2*, 10–23. https://doi.org/10.7146/kkf.v0i1-2.28068

Kaufman, J. C., & Beghetto, R. A. (2009). Beyond big and little: The four C model of creativity. *Review of General Psychology, 13*, 1–12. https://doi.org/10.1037/a0013688

Lenz Taguchi, H. (2009). *Going beyond the theory/practice divide in early childhood education: Introducing an intra-active pedagogy*. Oxon: Routledge. https://doi.org/10.4324/9780203872956

Lenz Taguchi, H. (2016). "The concept as method": Tracing-and-mapping the problem of the neuro(n) in the field of education. *Cultural Studies ↔ Critical Methodologies, 16*, 213–223. https://doi.org/10.1177/1532708616634726

MacLure, M. (2013). Researching without representation? Language and materiality in post-qualitative methodology. *International Journal of Qualitative Studies in Education, 26*, 658–667. https://doi.org/10.1080/09518398.2013.788755

Mazzei, L. A. (2014). Beyond an easy sense: A diffractive analysis. *Qualitative Inquiry,* *20,* 742–746. https://doi.org/10.1177/1077800414530257

McWilliam, E. (2008). Unlearning how to teach. *Innovations in Education and Teaching International, 45,* 263–269. https://doi.org/10.1080/14703290802176147

Morgan, N. (2000). Notions of transdisciplinarity. In M. A. Somerville & D. J. Rapport (Eds.), *Transdisciplinarity: Recreating integrated knowledge* (pp. 38–41). Oxford: EOLSS.

Onwuegbuzie, A. J., & Johnson, R. B. (2006). The validity issue in mixed research. *Research in the Schools, 13,* 48–63.

Osberg, D. (2018). Education and the future: Rethinking the role of anticipation and responsibility in multicultural and technological societies. In R. Poli (Ed.), *Handbook of anticipation* (pp. 1–20). Cham: Springer. https://doi.org/10.1007/978-3-319-31737-3_88-1

Osberg, D., & Biesta, G. J. J. (2007). Beyond presence: Epistemological and pedagogical implications of "strong" emergence. *Interchange, 38,* 31–51. https://doi.org/10.1007/s10780-007-9014-3

Plauborg, H. (2018). Towards an agential realist concept of learning. *Subjectivity, 11,* 322–338. https://doi.org/10.1057/s41286-018-0059-9

Renold, E., & Ringrose, J. (2019). JARring: Making phEmaterialist research practices matter. *MAI: Feminism and Visual Culture, 4.* (Colucci-Gray et al., 2017; Hetherington, 2019) Retrieved August 2, 2019, from https://maifeminism.com/introducing-phematerialism-feminist-posthuman-andnew-materialist-research-methodologies-in-education/

Sawyer, R. K. (2011). *Explaining creativity: The science of human innovation.* Oxford: Oxford University Press.

Shotter, J. (2013). Reflections on sociomateriality and dialogicality in organisation studies: From inter- to intra-thinking. In D. Nicolini, A. Langley, & H. Tsoukas (Eds.), *How matter matters: Objects, artifacts, and materiality in organization studies* (pp. 32–57). Oxford: Oxford University Press.

St. Pierre, E. A. (2011). Post-qualitative research: The critique and the coming after. In N. K. Denzin & Y. S. Lincoln (Eds.), *Sage handbook of qualitative inquiry* (pp. 611–635). Thousand Oaks, CA: Sage.

St. Pierre, E. A., & Jackson, A. Y. (2014). Qualitative data analysis after coding. *Qualitative Inquiry, 20,* 715–719. https://doi.org/10.1177/1077800414532435

Thuneberg, H. M., Salmi, H. S., & Bogner, F. X. (2018). How creativity, autonomy and visual reasoning contribute to cognitive learning in a STEAM hands-on inquiry-based math module. *Thinking Skills and Creativity, 29,* 153–160. https://doi.org/10.1016/j.tsc.2018.07.003

Uprichard, E., & Dawney, L. (2016). Data diffraction: Challenging data integration in mixed methods research. *Journal of Mixed Methods Research, 13,* 19–32. https://doi.org/10.1177/1558689816674650

Van Der Tuin, I. (2011). "A different starting point, a different metaphysics": Reading Bergson and Barad diffractively. *Hypatia, 26,* 22–42. https://doi.org/10.1111/j.1527-2001.2010.01114.x

Wegerif, R. (2019). Dialogic education. In G. W. Noblit et al. (Eds.), *Oxford research encyclopedia of education.* Oxford: Oxford University Press. https://doi.org/10.1093/acrefore/9780190264093.013.396

Learning Mathematical Concepts as a Whole-Body Experience: Connecting Multiple Intelligences, Creativities and Embodiments within the STEAM Framework

Kristóf Fenyvesi, Saara Lehto, Christopher Brownell, Lena Nasiakou, Zsolt Lavicza and Riikka Kosola

Abstract

Mathematics and science education are still strongly based on the concept of mind–body dualism, in which mind and body are viewed as separate entities. Learning mathematics is most often regarded as a solely intellectual activity, which involves only the brain. The "Maths in Motion" modules described in this chapter were collaboratively written and field tested by experts in dance/movement, educational researchers and mathematics education researchers. neuropsychological research has shown that physical activity correlates positively with cognitive skills. This chapter describes six activities, linking them to theories of multiple intelligences, multiple creativities and multiple embodiment. Each activity presents STEAM-integrated mathematics educational practices, which highlight methods of "embodying" mathematical concepts through physicality and kinaesthetic engagement, imagination and creativity. Our goal is to present outlines of these multidisciplinary and multisensory learning programs, which open up new dimensions for students, teachers and parents by offering the simultaneous experience of structural, spatial, rhythmic and symbolic dimensions of mathematics through body movement. The main body of this chapter describes these modules and some of the theoretical underpinnings of their creation. They represent the results of an international Erasmus+ educational project, called "Maths in Motion".

© KONINKLIJKE BRILL NV, LEIDEN, 2020 | DOI: 10.1163/9789004421585_018

Keywords

dance – Dienes – embodied learning – Gardner (kinaesthetic intelligence) – mathematics education – Maths in Motion – Burnard (multiple creativities) – multiple intelligences

1   Why Maths in Motion? An Introduction

The project Maths in Motion (MiM) brought together several experts from the fields of mathematics, dance and education, who all shared the perspective that dance and mathematics have something in common, and that dance would, therefore, be an excellent aid in mathematics education.[1] Medicine, neuroscience, learning theory and contemporary philosophy all have foci that include unity of the human body and brain. These are inseparably linked (Kolb & Kolb, 2015; Novak, 2017); thus, this perspective is demonstrated within the research. Educational neuropsychology provides evidence that physical activity is positively associated with cognitive skills. The academic performance of children improves with physical activity, and evidence suggests that regular physical activity links to structural and functional changes in the brain that can play a primary role in achieving better intellectual results (AFIS, 2019). Despite these findings, mathematics and science education is still regularly based on a variety of mind–body dualism wherein the learner is expected to employ their mind only and dissociate themselves from the body with students in mathematics classes typically sitting at their desks, expected "to use their brain only". They are being told to exclude all the external stimuli from their attention and instructed to focus "only on the task in front of them". Our practices are based on the conviction that a more intentional focus on embodied mathematics education is therefore needed.

Indeed, studies of embodied mathematics education yield positive results. Anderson (2015) found that integration of dance and movement in mathematics instruction for students diagnosed with learning disabilities, emotional or behavioural disorders, attention deficits, and hyperactive disorders can play a key role in increasing their mathematical performance. Novak (2017) demonstrated that body movement and dance can enhance learning and the understanding of mathematical concepts. Ruiter, Loyens, and Paas (2015) showed that incorporating embodied methods using the whole body can lead to better learning results than methods that merely use thinking or even drawing. Overall, structural, spatial, rhythmic and symbolic dimensions of mathematics can be learned through body movement and presence (Gerofsky, 2011; Katai, Toth,

Neogen, & Adorjani, 2014; Renesse, Ecke, Fleron, & Hotchkiss, 2016; Sung, Ahn, & Black, 2017). The MiM project was built upon the core of this research. The project also greatly benefited from the work of several dance, mathematics, learning and embodiment experts, like Schaffer (Schaffer et al., 2001; Schaffer & Stern, 2010), Renesse et al. (2016), Gerofsky (2011) and Bingham (2007).

MiM relies on a coaching model of teaching that proposes three core schema or roles for teachers to adopt. This model assumes that the teacher will take on the role of coach – what some have colloquially termed the "guide on the side" – rather than the distributor of information – "sage on the stage" – who establishes practice goals similar to a sports team coach for daily workouts. We summarise these differences here: 1. Teachers guide through questioning rather than inform via telling. 2. Learning mathematics is a journey of discovery, not the acquisition of a static body of knowledge. 3. Mistakes are inevitable in this framework, and they represent learning opportunities, not failures to achieve. In this we link to the broader growth mindsets theory described by Boaler and Dweck (2016; see also Dweck, 2008).

MiM activities connect directly to bodily-kinaesthetic intelligence to embody mathematical concepts regardless of the effect upon logico-mathematical intelligence. This is accomplished through placing the student/participant in an environment where this activity and intelligence is valued. As Gardner points out, "we are the kind of species that can learn to carry on those activities that are valued by our culture" (1999). The MiM activities described below are aimed at an equitable treatment of bodily-kinaesthetic intelligence; they are what Gardner (1999) might call "intelligence fair".

The work of Gardner and associates in the field of intelligence, specifically related to the concept of Multiple Intelligences (MI), has received criticism for its devolution into ideas that are encapsulated in the "learning styles" literature. This linkage has been debunked and, equally importantly, refuted by Gardner himself. These "learning styles" devolve the theory to once again favour a single intelligence, which is contrary to the core of multiple intelligences (Terada, 2018). The MiM activities discussed below make an effort to incorporate specifically bodily-kinaesthetic intelligence, as Gardner describes. In doing so, we initiate a dialogue between bodily-kinaesthetic intelligence and other components of multiple intelligences, intentionally expanding the process of mathematics learning to incorporate multiple intelligences and multiple creativities.

Through applying dance/movement as problem solving, bodily-kinaesthetic intelligence is called into play to make sense of and embody various mathematical concepts. Mirror transformations, a challenging topic in the basic mathematics curriculum, will have been experienced in the body of each student when they partner together then attempt to reflect the movements of another. Consider how the mind must construct a knowledge of two points that move closer to an axis of reflection, after the body has had to move a fingertip towards its "mirror image" in the other person. Thus, concepts of equal rates of change become embedded as well.

While Burnard's (2012) theory of "multiple creativities" has emerged within research into musical practices theory, we see parallels between it and arts-based education, including creative body movement and dance, and through movement and dance in the learning and doing of mathematics. Burnard's theory of multiple creativities diverges from Gardner in that it focuses on practices during learning and originally focused solely on learning and teaching music through performances in a variety of skill areas. We see a connection to these practices within mathematics instruction. We describe a few of these below. Our analysis is based on the "practice-based framework" of multiple creativities, as it was presented in Burnard (2012: 223). Burnard's practice-based framework for multiple creativities differentiates between modalities, forms of authorship, practice principles, domains, fields and persons as the main variables in the practical configuration of multiple creativities. Modalities include the tools, technologies and media used in the learning process. Forms of authorship include agency, distribution of roles, negotiation, and forms and levels of contribution to the creative process. Practice principles mainly refers to the goals of production, the nature of interaction and participation. Domains involve elements of culture. Fields include "sociocultural" or "technological" creative processes, and can imply specific forms and principles of practices. The factor "persons" can refer to individuals and communities.

Regarding modalities, the approach to using different tools in the creative process is largely different in how we train maths teachers than how we train artists and art teachers. The former may only have been given a single pedagogical tool (typically a transactional model based on lectures typical of Western schooling in the twentieth century) without an overview and opportunity for the experience-oriented trial of various experimental mathematics pedagogies, while the arts teachers have been introduced to a very large spectra of approaches, tools and techniques, cultural positions and philosophies (from Renaissance through to contemporary periods, etc.). This also differs from physics teachers, who are aware of modern physics that includes both quantum and relativistic modes of thought, while primarily instructing classical or Newtonian concepts. The variety of content here would drive alterations in pedagogy. The use of technologies also varies. Many technologies may be available to teachers, but they may not have a true opportunity to implement or explore how these technologies can fundamentally shift the content to be considered. Take for example the concept of logarithms: even as recent as fifty years ago extensive curricular time was spent on these powerful computational tools. Students would be taught a variety of ways to access values from tables and to substitute these values into an extensive calculation. However, in the 1980s the handheld calculator rendered logarithm tables, and the calculation tools of logarithms, essentially obsolete. Then, with the advent of the graphing calculator, the nature of logarithms as functions came to the fore in the curriculum. The vital role of natural logarithms in calculus requires some awareness of these tools but the technology has altered their importance entirely. This said, teachers still spend a great deal of time on the calculation aspects of logarithms.

Within the bodily-kinaesthetic intelligence there are already technologies with which human movement can be tracked, recorded, transformed into various datasets and even instantly analysed. Some of these include analogue and digital pedometers, motion sensors, tracker software combined with GeoGebra, Micro:bit, fitness wristbands and smart watches, and PocketLab.[2] This latter device is the focus of a research project underway at Fresno Pacific University in California, USA, where Christopher Brownell is collaborating with faculty members in the Kinesiology and Bio-Mechanics Departments to make use of PocketLab to study human movement from a kinematics and physics perspective. Here the science faculty are interested in the forces at work within the body during movements, while Brownell is connecting these ideas to mathematics teaching and the integrated perspectives of STEAM education.

Regarding forms of authorship, typically within a mathematics classroom the question "Whose mathematics are we working out?" is never asked. Certainly, teachers and project-based learning can bring in elements of the historical figures associated with concepts, but rarely are students the discoverers of mathematical knowledge and this way become the authors of their "own mathematics". Students gain agency and ownership of concepts, definitions and patterns that they have experienced through movements choreographed to encode them into the bodily-kinaesthetic intelligence of the learner. This is in stark contrast to a curriculum of predetermined definitions and understandings. Here students can be brought into the process of constructing the definitions or concepts within mathematics. In this, students do not need to have definitions repetitively stated by or for them; rather they have constructed their own understandings within their body, providing a variety of muscle memory which is then available for reflection to systematically building up a concept.

As described above, MiM was a collaborative effort between teachers, teacher educators, mathematics education experts and mathematicians. These collaborators sought to create lessons and experiences that enhance "possibility thinking" (see Burnard et al., 2017) within the participants. Through a focus upon questioning, play, immersion, innovation and risk taking, participants are encouraged to tap into the multiplicity of creative practices they already possess, and form new ones to fit the new situations that arise. Similarly to Burnard et al. (2017), we applied Woolery's "arts-based perceptual ecology" (ABPE) framework to understand how to create the possibility spaces for STE(A)M education. Seeking to immerse participants in an ABPE, as characterised by direct experience, magic and play, intuition, imagination, art making and the language of patterns (Woolery, 2006), elements of a parallel world (a magic world) are created by the students and the teachers through their own bodily movement. In the "Dragon's World" activity children are invited into a new realm, created through imagination, a unique and unusual world, where mythical creatures also have problems to solve. In this case, kinesthetic and sensory experiences inspired imagination, art and role playing become the modality and motivational source of problem solving. Furthermore, students come to "know" in their bodies what a mirror transformation is, and how angles are formed, deformed and combined by involving their intuitions and physical space. Here they see through their own senses what these mathematical constructs can accomplish and describe.

As Cuoco, Goldberg and Mark (1996: 382) describe in their influential work, *Habits of mind: An organizing principle for mathematics curriculum*, mathematically powerful students should be visualisers, specifically of continuous change. The MiM modules require all participants to actively visualise the shifts in their bodies, the environment they are in, and the limitations of their personal space. This habit is said to "cut across many other [habits]" as worrying about how geometric objects change is the central idea within a dynamic geometry. Tools such as GeoGebra – an open educational resource in the form of a dynamic geometry environment – have taken hold in classrooms all over the world. Consider though that the human body in motion is the genesis of much of humanity's understanding of change within space, and the effects of changes of space upon objects embedded in it.

Zoltan Dienes' ideas on multiple embodiment, specifically his perceptual variability principle and the interdisciplinary principle (Dienes, 1973; Benedek, 2018) are incorporated within the MiM modules. When teachers focus on finding multiple embodiments for a variety of mathematical concepts, they assist students to collect a larger variety of perceptions for those concepts. By sharing experiences based in both movements and evocative objects within the group, then returning to reflective abstraction later, students embody the concepts at hand. Both the variety of experiences and the group setting are within Dienes's conceptualisation of the variability principle (Benedek, 2018).

As Benedek (2018) has convincingly pointed out, Dienes's views on multiple embodiment are an important predecessor of today's widespread theories of "embodied mathematics" and "embodied cognition". These theories were introduced by Lakoff and Núñez (2000), who emphasised the role of linguistic and cognitive psychological consequences of bodily experience in the origins of mathematical conceptualisation. Benedek (2018) describes the direct connections between dance and playful mathematics learning through activities in the background of Dienes' original mathematics pedagogy, which recognised the mathematics learning potential in human movement and dance choreography.

The Dienesian interdisciplinary principle is the bedrock upon which MiM is constructed. These modules display a variety of modalities, or threads, that get deployed in the lessons. The variations in form, time and symbols are inherently mathematical within the Dienesian principles. Based on these considerations, we find connections between Gardner's multiple intelligences, Burnard's multiple creativities, and Dienes' multiple embodiments in the Mathematics in Motion pedagogical framework within the modules.

2   Methodology

The methodology of the MiM project was co-created by an international group of teachers, dancers, science communication experts, researchers and mathematicians. The development took place between 2017 and 2019 (Olde Vechte Foundation, 2019). Fifty-six teachers and more than 200 students implemented these activities and methods during this development period. *Maths in Motion: The toolkit*, a book in which the framework of this project is published, contains results from evaluations of this project (Nasiakou, 2018).

Maths in Motion: The toolkit contains six learning modules, and summaries of the activities are included in this chapter. All modules were created during MiM training events in Ommen, the Netherlands by diverse groups of experts from the fields of dance, mathematics and education. Each module targeted a specific group of students and was tested according to approximate age groupings such as kindergarten, elementary school, middle school and high school.

During the MiM development events, an international group of teachers, mathematics education specialists and dance pedagogists gathered together for a five-day residency in the Netherlands. This was a creative camp. The first day featured a series of movement experiences, tasks and problem-solving situations guided by the dance pedagogists; this lasted approximately 8 hours and was characterised as fun and playful. The second day was led by the maths educators, who had experience with various forms of mathematics learning through body movement models. The third day the larger group was split into six smaller groups, where each worked on their own modules focused on mathematics education through movement. This was the format for the final 2.5 days, with a final sharing of activities.

After three months the modules were tested in the teacher participants' own schools in different countries with the participation of all members of the international group that created the original modules. After field testing these modules with children, the children were asked to reflect upon the activities in the module. This feedback and all the field experiences were considered and the modules refined.

3   MiM Modules

All the MiM modules follow a shared structure of a warm-up, a main part and a closing session. The warm-up has several purposes: to lure the participants into engaging in their learning, warming up their bodies, enhancing creative movement and placing the participants in a playful mood. Similar to Anderson's (2015) findings, these actions were effective in improving attitudes towards mathematics.

In the main part, learners explore and gain a deeper understanding of mathematical concepts through the movement of their bodies. In this stage the experience provokes the insights and reactions needed to move towards learning in a more conscious way. This can be achieved through different embodied activity components, which offer the frame for an experiential process of translating mathematical vocabulary into embodied vocabulary and vice versa. Some embodied activity components are:
– using one or more of the senses to observe and interact with the world
– being aware of certain parts of the body and body positions
– being in a particular location
– moving from one point to another
– studying objects from various physical perspectives

- moving certain parts of the body
- experiencing different qualities of a movement
- moving with spatial relationship to, and in interaction with, other participants
- interacting with concepts through objects and elements of the world.

The MiM methodology employs interaction (Moerman, 2016) and discovery (Mosston & Ashworth, 2002). These imply seeing/perceiving mathematics not as a product, but as a process. Therefore participants are supported by concentrating on their engagement and progress.

Every MiM closing session includes acknowledgment, reflection and sharing. Acknowledgement is achieved by the learners presenting their creations and the results of their work through movement. Herein the whole group comes together for an opportunity to inspire and be inspired.

During this acknowledgment phase, the teacher employs the questioning/guiding model described above, following Kolb's experiential learning theory model (Kolb & Kolb, 2015). The reflection is a crucial part of the learning process because, "[w]hen students make connections between physical experience and abstract thinking, their understanding is more resilient and can stretch to fit in new situations" (Schaefer et al., 2001: 13). Sharing thoughts and ideas with the whole group supports the teacher's understanding of participants' learning and empowers the learners to get new insights through other people's reflections.

The goal of MiM is primarily to enhance mathematics education. However, we acknowledge that a much higher purpose is to be strived for when combining two disciplines. Employing the arts as tools for mathematics education may be common, but an equal balance between the two is best. Dance and mathematics should both benefit from the multidisciplinary context, as Moerman (2018) pointed out in the Bridges Mathematics and Art Conference in 2018. For example, the paper by Schaffer, Thie, and Williams (2018) from the same conference shows that mathematics can also be used as a tool to benefit dance. Although the core work in MiM aims to strengthen mathematics education, several aspects of the MiM modules offer exciting methods for the use of dance artists as well. For example, in Module 1: Dancing Snowflakes, the learning goals (symmetries, geometry, creative movement, cooperation, problem-solving skills, coordination of movement and creativity) are all useful tools for dancers and choreographers. Thus, it could be viewed as a module for teaching dancers choreographic skills.

The arts allow us to express what is important but cannot be captured in words – at least not in poetry or prose. As the dancer Isadora Duncan is reported to have remarked, "If I could say it, I wouldn't have to dance it". Movement, dance included, engage the whole person in the learning process. The

emotional connections that come while moving and acting out various concepts serve to encode, perhaps within the whole nervous system, the ideas and
meanings carried within the experience. We cite the so-called learning standards framework (also known as the backbone of STEAM education) within
which South Korean students are expected to form an emotional connection
to the problem they are being asked to solve. In this, engagement becomes
personal.

4   Module 1: Dancing Snowflakes

The first 30-minute module titled "Dancing Snowflakes" is a set of participatory and experience-oriented activities about rotational symmetries, geometry
and creative movement. Along with these, the module reinforces cooperation,
problem-solving skills and general creativity. Participants experience geometry and symmetry as part of a more extended symmetric figure and create a
movement-based performance piece: a short dance that explores rotational
symmetries. We have adapted the activity known as "Threesies" described in
chapter 5 of the book *Math dance* with Schaffer and Stern (Schaffer et al., 2001).
Schaffer and Stern also explore different kinds of symmetries more deeply in
chapters 5 and 6 of their book.

4.1   *Warm-Up*
The warm-up learning goals are exploring mirror symmetry (reflection), working together with a partner, learning to observe and copy others' movements,
communicating through movement, getting comfortable with touch, awaken-
ing creativity for body motion, and exploring different possibilities for body
positions with a partner.

4.1.1   Warm-up Activity 1
Teachers ask students to form pairs to investigate mirroring each other's
motions. After describing the activity, the teacher plays a selection of slow
melodic music. One person in each pair is designated "leader" and she leads
while the other follows as a mirror image of the leader. After some time the
teacher will call out, "switch". At this time the leader and the follower switch
roles without stopping their motion; the pairs try to keep their movements
continuous despite the switches. The goal for the team is to find a state of constant flow and attention where neither leads nor follows, but both are attuned
to their joint movement (Figures 13.1 and 13.2). The participants are asked not to
talk during this exercise but to fully concentrate on the actions of their bodies.

FIGURE 13.1   DMirroring exercise introduced by the workshop leader. (Maths in Motion
activity led by experience workshop at IC Codogno School, Italy in 2018)

FIGURE 13.2   Mirroring exercise. (Maths in Motion activity led by experience workshop at IC
Codogno School, Italy in 2018)

4.1.2   Warm-up Activity 2, Rotational Symmetry

After working with reflectively symmetric movement, the focus shifts to rotationally symmetric motion. Now, when the leader lifts the left part of her body, the follower lifts the left part of his body as well. The concept of rotational symmetry is introduced here. Then the roles are switched. As before, the goal remains that each pair become attuned to each other so that their symmetric motions are fluid and not interrupted by shifting roles.

4.1.3   Warm-up Activity 3, Bodily Connections

Participants work in triplets to find different means of connecting three people. Different kinds of links are encouraged using first arms and legs and then whole bodies. This activity is a modified version of Schaffer and Stern's (2010) activity "How many ways to shake hands?" After the exercise, each group is asked to show their favourite connection. In the discussion, different artistic aspects of these relationships become the focus. Attention is given to the mathematical and symmetric properties of the connections created.

4.2   *Main Part*

The learning goals in the main part are exploring and learning about rotational symmetries, working in a larger group, and solving problems with bodily connections. The participants can experience how to move from one position into another as a group, learn about developing a choreography, learn to memorise moves, move in synchronisation with others, learn to observe geometric figures in their bodies, and so on.

4.2.1   Main Part Activity 1, Rotational Symmetries

In groups of six, participants are asked to start by forming a circle facing inward so as to be able to see each other and hold hands. With slow ambient music in the background, the groups are asked to find different positions that have rotational symmetry for the group. Groups are then asked to find ways to move from one such formation into another. If groups are creatively stuck, the teacher will provide prompts that are designed to engage creative problem solving (Figure 13.3).

4.2.2   Main Part Activity 2, Everyone Is a Choreographer

Once creativity is flowing, the groups are asked to form a short dance based on their symmetry ideas. Groups get to pick their favourite positions and moves and decide how the different symmetries flow from one into another, how the dance starts and ends, and how their different movements emerge from each other. Groups are asked to memorise and practise their choreographies.

FIGURE 13.3   Maths in Motion dancing snowflake activity led by experience workshop at IC
                Codogno School, Italy in 2018 (photograph by Giada Totaro)

4.3   *Closing*

The learning goals of the closing session are to achieve artistic satisfaction
through performing and watching the produced symmetry dances, bringing the mathematical ideas inside the activities to the forefront, and further
exploring the phenomenon.

4.3.1   Closing Activity 1, Acknowledgement

All groups are asked to perform their symmetry dances for the others to see.
Filming from above (this highlights and makes visible the inherent symmetries
in the dances), after consent by the groups is given, everyone gets a chance to
see and discuss how the symmetries work and what the artistic effect of the
dance is.

4.3.2   Closing Activity 2, Reflection

A series of interest groupings will be sought out through discussion, then individuals will choose which interest group they will attend. They discuss what
they experienced and felt during the activity, and what mathematical concepts
and skills they learned during the exercise. Suggestions for further study from
both or either mathematics or artistic points of view will naturally be generated from these interest group discussions.

4.3.3   Closing Activity 3, Sharing

Groups share their thoughts and ideas with everyone.

5   Module 2: Get Angled!

"Get Angled!" is a participatory and experience-oriented module about angles, their measurement and problem solving. The emphasis is on discovering the conditions wherein three angles form a triangle. In this lesson, participants experience creative movements in groups of two and three and come up with solutions for tasks using their innate body knowledge.

5.1   *Warm-Up*
The learning goal in the warm-up is to explore several different types of triangles using parts of the body, from the largest to the smallest.

5.1.1   Warm-up Activity 1, Different Levels
Teachers ask students to form different postures with their bodies on each of the three levels: bottom, middle, and top. The postures can include crab kick, gorilla hop and so on (Figures 13.4 a, b, c).

FIGURE 13.4   Maths in Motion different levels exercise by SciCo, Greece. (a) Low level; (b) middle level; (c) high level

5.1.2   Warm-up Activity 2, Shape Triangles
Participants form triangles with different parts of their bodies. Teachers suggest that participants look for the smallest and the largest such triangles.

Suggestions are also made to investigate "How many triangles can be formed with different parts of the body?"

5.1.3   Warm-up Activity 3, Secret Triangles

All participants stand in the room free from chairs. Each participant chooses two others without letting them know. While moving, each participant attempts to be always at equal distances from their chosen participants.

5.2   *Main Part*

The learning goals in the main part are, first, to represent different types of angles with the span of the arms; second, to understand in a creative, embodied way that three random angles do not necessarily form a triangle; and third, to discover the property that the sum of the angles of a triangle is constant.

5.2.1   Main Part Activity 1, Span of the Arms

A rope is placed across the centre of the workshop space in a straight line, separating it into two zones. On one side of the line is the "Acute Zone", the other the "Obtuse Zone". Participants can freely and independently experiment with forming acute angles with outstretched arms while moving about within the Acute Zone. They are just as free to experience making obtuse angles with the span of their arms within the Obtuse Zone. However, when moving across the delineated zone's boundary, participants must freeze on the line in a right angle until another participant's supplementary right angle comes to join them. The two supplementary right angles now total 180 degrees and both participants are released from the line, and are allowed to flow freely and independently into the other zone. If the workshop space has corners that are architecturally right angles, then participants can go to these corners to use them as 90-degree reference points. Participants place themselves into the right-angled vertices, stretch out their arms to get their bearings as to what is 90 degrees, and then step away, adjusting their arms to be sure their arm angles are greater than a right angle in the Obtuse Zone and less than a right angle in the Acute Zone.

5.2.2   Main Part Activity 2, Triangles Attempt

Once participants have practised changing the span of their arms for different types of angles, they are asked to freeze in space and keep the angle they have. Without moving their arms, they form triplets with two other participants and try to form a triangle using their predetermined angles formed by the position of their arms. Teachers will lead discussions that guide participants to articulate the discovery that not all triplets of angles will automatically form triangles.

5.2.3   Main Part Activity 3, the 180 Degree Zone

Participants in groups of three have to figure out a solution to the following problem. The rope or a line on the floor represents an angle of 180 degrees. Teachers ask the students, in groups of three, to form three angles with their arms that fit precisely inside this 180-degree angle. Can they make a triangle with these angles? What does this tell them about triangles? In one possible strategy, one participant steps on the rope splitting the room and holds his/her hands wide open (parallel to the rope). The second team member steps next to the first and together they form an angle, stretching their arms to form two angles with an overall sum of 180 degrees. The third member goes between the other two, making them reduce their angles in order to keep the overall sum of 180 degrees. Without moving the positions of their hands, participants now move to form a triangle with the sides formed by participants' arms. They observe that the three angles ideally form a triangle.

5.3   *Closing*

The closing learning goals are to provide the different groups the opportunity to articulate their ideas, to learn other solutions, and to summarise the given task.

5.3.1   Closing, Acknowledgement

All groups are asked to perform their solution as a sequence of different body sculptures. In these demonstrations, the participants start from the attached rope on the floor and end as an embodied triangle.

5.3.2   Closing, Reflection

The groups (here again, separate participants into groups with different interests) discuss and describe what each participant learned, experienced and felt during the activity, focusing on what specific mathematical concepts were embodied. Groups can discuss the different possibilities for further study from a mathematical or an artistic viewpoint.

5.3.3   Closing, Sharing

Groups share their thoughts and ideas with everyone.

6   Module 3: Monkeys and Elephants

"Monkeys and Elephants" is an experience-based module suitable for early childhood education. Rhythmic patterns and a visual pattern notation for the rhythms are introduced through singing, acting, dancing and play. The activity helps children to learn the difference between a long and a short duration of notes in music and composition of rhythmic patterns in music and poetry.

6.1   *Warm-Up*

The warm-up learning goals are to make students familiar with the song and to learn about the different movements, steps and pawprints of two different animals: a monkey and an elephant. In particular, elephants take slow and long steps (Figure 13.5) while monkeys take short, quick steps.

6.1.1   Warm-up Activity 1, Walk Like an Animal

For this activity, it is good to use a song with which the children are familiar. Start by just singing the song walking in a circle. Then stop to describe elephants using terms such as big, heavy and massive, with slow and thunderous steps. Sing the song again, now walking or dancing in the circle imagining you are an elephant, taking slow, weighty, swaying steps. After the elephant is familiar, repeat the same discussion and singing now considering a monkey, which makes quick, short, energetic steps. Elephants will step only on the full beat, and monkeys also on the half beats. Encourage everyone to add different attributes of the animals, to use their whole bodies and imagination to create the movement of the different animals.

FIGURE 13.5   Walking like an elephant. Monkeys and Elephants module led by experience
workshop at a kindergarten in Codogno, Italy in 2018 (photograph by Giada
Totaro)

6.1.2   Warm-up Activity 2, Pawprints

Take some time to discuss the pawprints of monkeys and elephants. Monkeys have small paws, and one piece of paper always fits two of those. Elephants have large paws, and only one elephant pawprint fits on one sheet of paper. The teacher can prepare the pawprints in advance or this part of the module could incorporate another activity: discussing, drawing and colouring the pawprints (Figures 13.6 and 13.7).

FIGURE 13.6   Discussing the pawprints of monkeys and elephants. Activity led by experience workshop at a kindergarten in Codogno, Italy in 2018 (photography by Giada Totaro)

FIGURE 13.7   Discussing and drawing the pawprints of monkeys and elephants. Activity led by experience workshop at a kindergarten in Codogno, Italy in 2018 (photograph by Giada Totaro)

6.2 *Main Part*

The learning goals of the main part are to learn to step in a particular rhythm, to understand the difference between a long and a short note in the music, and to understand the connection between the rhythm and a visual representation of it. Here we see the emphasis shifting to include how to abstract patterns the children experience, an inherently mathematical process.

6.2.1 Main Part Activity 1, Stepping in Rhythm

Come back to the circle and sing the familiar song again, now asking everyone to look at the teacher's feet and mimic the steps. Sing and walk until everyone gets the rhythm. The idea is to walk in the rhythm of the song based on the long and short syllables/notes in the music.

6.2.2 Main Part Activity 2, Small Rhythm Paths

Bring the monkey and elephant pawprint papers and create small paths on the floor. They should be simple, for example, elephant, monkey, monkey, elephant (slow [long], fast [short], fast [short], slow [long]). As there are always two monkey prints or one elephant print on one piece of paper, one piece of paper then represents either two fast (short) steps or one slow (long) step. Ask the children to try walking these paths in the correct rhythm, practising different small path patterns (Figures 13.8 and 13.9).

FIGURE 13.8   Creating small paths on the floor. Activity led by experience workshop at a kindergarten in Codogno, Italy in 2018 (photograph by Giada Totaro)

FIGURE 13.9   Practising walking small paths on the floor. Activity led by experience workshop
at a kindergarten in Codogno, Italy in 2018 (photograph by Giada Totaro)

6.2.3   Main Part Activity 3, Creating the Song Path
Once everyone is comfortable with the idea of paths, this task will gather
the whole group to create collaboratively a pathway for the complete song.
Sing the song in small bits and solicit from the students where the elephant
(slow/long) and the monkey (fast/short) steps should go. All students will have
pawprint papers to bring to the path construction. Once the pathway is ready,
it should be tested by the children walking and singing along it. This phase
will, by necessity, include several iterations where the path tested will not fit
the song. These "mistakes" will be turned to learning and refining exercises,
reinforcing the growth mindset (Boaler & Dweck, 2016).

6.3   *Closing*

Here, we suggest several possible extension activities. These take the basic concepts from the main part and provide different avenues of exploration:

- Walk and Sing a Highly Repetitive Song: Walk and sing the path in Pachelbel's *Canon in D.*
- Create Your Own Paths: Divide the children into groups, and ask each group to create a small path for the other groups to walk/sing.
- Repeating Paths: Introduce to the students several repetitive paths (e.g., slow, fast, fast, slow, fast, fast; or fast, fast, fast, slow ...). Have the students repeat these paths with their bodies, and construct rhymes to accompany themselves.
- Constructing Abstractions of Paths: Guide the students who may be ready to build patterns using building blocks, Cuisenaire rods, or drawings on paper.

7   Module 4: Dragon's World

Dragon's World is an imaginative and experience-oriented activity, suitable for elementary school. The activity empowers creativity, teamwork, problem solving and appreciation of each other. During the activity, students learn to create and present maths stories with movement and practise solving calculations with 2–3 mathematical operations.

This activity needs several teachers and a theatrical setting or a place for creating a magical atmosphere somewhere outside the classroom environment. Outdoor settings are encouraged: the school's garden or a nearby park can be perfect. Before the activity starts, teachers decorate the space to resemble a dragon forest and dress themselves as dragons (Figures 13.10 and 13.11). They practice dragon moves and sounds, which they can perform to support their students in their transformation into dragons. They also hide dragon eggs (two-piece plastic eggs are often found during spring holidays in the northern hemisphere) in the dragon forest, one per student, in spots marked with colourful, shiny pieces of paper or foil, pinwheels, or such like. The eggs each contain a treat, a picture of an animal and a table of numbers.

7.1   *Warm-Up*

The warm-up learning goals are for the participants to imagine themselves as different creatures through the use of their imagination, and collaborating with others to carry out simple tasks. In an introduction, students are invited to imagine themselves becoming dragons.

FIGURE 13.10
Teachers are preparing the dragon forest in Şcoala Gimnazială nr. 20, Galati, Romania

FIGURE 13.11
Teachers are dressing up and acting as dragons in Şcoala Gimnazială nr. 20, Galati, Romania

A teacher holds a hula-hoop and says: "Through this hula hoop, you will enter into a magic world". Students step through and once "inside" they have entered into this realm. Now, the teacher says, "Once you've gone through that door you will need to see differently, hear differently, feel differently". While saying this, teachers can gently massage their eyes, ears and skin respectively to encourage the students to imagine their eyes, ears and skin are morphing into those of a dragon. Guide students in exploring how their new senses are behaving differently, how different their skin feels, the heat from their breath, the altered vision of a dragon, and so on.

7.1.1   Warm-up Activity 1, Practising Egg Hunt

Students practise an egg hunt by accomplishing a few simple tasks, for example find a tree, or go to the rock (Figure 13.12). After accomplishing each small task, groups change their leaders. They can create a ritual for the change of leader (Figure 13.13).

FIGURE 13.12   Practising egg hunt as dragons in Şcoala Gimnazială nr. 20, Galati, Romania

FIGURE 13.13   Stepping through the magic threshold to become dragons in Şcoala Gimnazială
nr. 20, Galati, Romania

7.2   *Main Part*

Here, creating mathematical stories is introduced. Students learn both to create stories around mathematics and to investigate the hidden mathematics within a given story. Students will practise calculations requiring several operations in the context of creative work.

7.2.1   Main Part Activity 1, The Real Egg Hunt

Tell a story about a dragon mother who laid eggs (as many as there are students) last night, but when she came to the nest today, all the eggs had disappeared. The task of the small dragons is now to find the missing eggs. Each dragon may bring one egg back. You may ask questions of the students who are quick at finding their eggs: How many places did you have to go before you found your egg? How many leaders have we had so far? How many eyes, ears and tails do you have?

Once everyone has found their egg, open them all. The animal pictures inside the eggs sort the students into groups; all the cats are in one group, all the dogs in another, and so on. Distribute the photos in such a way that there are about five students in each group. Make sure all the papers found inside the eggs are kept safe.

7.2.2   Main Part Activity 2, Maths Story Performed by Teachers

After returning all students and eggs to a suitable space, teachers perform a rehearsed theatrical mime of a maths story with the egg. The mother dragon can have seven eggs; then four other dragons can each bring one egg to the mother and then a thief comes and steals three eggs. After the mime the class discusses the maths behind the story. How many eggs were there to begin with? How many dragons brought a gift egg? Discuss until you come up with the formula of the story: $7 + 4 - 3 = 8$ (Figures 13.14 and 13.15).

FIGURE 13.14   Eggs brought back to the dragons' cave in Şcoala Gimnazială nr. 20, Galati, Romania

FIGURE 13.15   Teachers' mime performance of the maths story in Şcoala Gimnazială nr. 20, Galati, Romania

7.2.3   Main Part Activity 3, Creating Your Own Maths Stories

The students are now asked to return to their animal groups. Each member in the same group received the same table of numbers and symbols. The group is now asked to come up with their own mathematical story based on the numbers (for example 10, 3, 2, 8, 5) and symbols (for example +, -, =) they found in their eggs. Teachers provide support and encouragement where needed.

7.2.4   Main Part Activity 4, Performing the Stories

Each group gets to perform their maths story by movement, and other students get to figure out the formula behind the story.

7.2.5   Main Part Activity 5, Recreating Stories in Formulae

Students create the story in the form of a mathematical sentence that relates the facts depicted in the mimes performed by other groups, then display them upon a flipchart or personal whiteboard.

7.3   *Closing*

7.3.1   Closing Reflection

As a closure for this lesson, students are asked to describe what happened, how the mimes could tell a story without words and still be translated into maths sentences also without words.

7.3.2   Closing Activity 1, Becoming Human

In the end, each dragon steps back through the magical threshold, becoming a normal human again. They can also receive a certificate or a passport-like stamp as a sign that they have visited the dragon world.

7.3.3   Closing Activity 2, Student Evaluation of Task

Use the eggs to evaluate student attitudes towards the activity by asking students who feel happy afterwards to place their egg into the basket, while those are not happy should place their egg outside the basket. Several mathematical expressions may then be formed, for example, the total number of eggs, minus the eggs outside equal the eggs inside.

Of note here is an explicit use of the ABPE process of including "magic". Students are expected to employ their imagination, create a parallel world inside the world they live in, follow the patterns of expected behaviour for this new world, and still apply mathematical insights from their so-called real world. In so doing, students are employing a wealth of creativities to encode the mathematical concepts that are embedded in the module.

8   Module 5: Negative Numbers, Positive Learning

The activity "Negative Numbers, Positive Learning" is designed to teach negative numbers in lower secondary education. The focus is upon embodying
growing and diminishing numbers in creative ways to provide visceral experiences and elicit emotions in the students. Creating concrete and experiential
structures for the abstraction that is the integer line, coupled with embodying
scales for measurement, are the core mathematical concepts of this activity.

8.1   *Warm-Up*
These warm-up experiences focus on the concepts of bigger and smaller, growing and shrinking, along with using your imagination and your body. The goal
is to become comfortable expressing growth (whether that be positive or negative) with your own body.

8.1.1   Warm-up Activity 1, Shrinking Words
Start the activity by having the whole class standing in one big circle (or two
smaller ones if the class is too large). In turn, everyone says his or her name.
After the first round, the second round starts, this time everyone saying their
name minus one letter, so the name "Nora" would become "Nor" and "Marcus"
would become "Marcu".

8.1.2   Warm-up Activity 2, Growing and Shrinking Your Body
As a teacher, mime a ball or another shape that you hold in your hands. Make
sure to handle it a little so everyone can see what kind of an object it is. Pass
the object to your left or right in the circle. This student is to mime collecting
this object and manipulating it in space. Each student can change the shape of
the object before giving it to the next in the circle. Hold eye contact while the
imagined object is passed around. When the shape goes around for the second
time, make a rule that it has to be growing all the time. When it returns to you
for the third round, now the shape will shrink. When it comes back to the start,
gather it and pretend to eat it.

   Play this game again with a twist; this time, you become the shape you wish
using your whole body. The shape passes from one student to the next as before;
the next student mimicking the object the previous student has become and
changing again to something else.

8.2   *Main Part*
Students will embody the integer line and the concepts of positive and negative numbers along with scale.

8.2.1   Main Part Activity 1, Form a Line of Integers
All the students grab hands in one big line (not necessarily a straight line) that
circles or twists around the room. Give each student a number, which they
put on the floor in front of them. The middle student (if an even number of
students, then choose the younger of two nearest the middle) is assigned the
number 0. All students in one direction from 0 get numbers 1, 2, 3 and so on,
and the students in the other direction from 0 get numbers –1, –2, –3 and
so on.

8.2.2   Main Part Activity 2, Moving on the Integer Line
Introduce a system of tapping. Taps on the shoulder are positive, taps on the
lower leg are negative. If you get tapped three times on the shoulder, you
should become three bigger (+3), if you get tapped 5 times on your lower leg,
you should become five smaller (–5).
    Start a tapping game on your integer line. Tap one student a number of
times on his or her shoulder or lower leg. The tapped student has to move that
many places in the correct direction along the integer line. If they were tapped
on the shoulder, they have to be growing or shuttling toward the positive end;
if tapped on the lower leg, the student will have to be shrinking or moving
towards the negative end when they move. The shrinking and growing can be
done in any way the student wishes: walking, jumping, dancing, turning, as
long as they grow or shrink according to their direction and the magnitude of
the number of taps.
    Once the growing or shrinking student finds their new spot, the student
previously standing there becomes the next tapper (Figure 13.16).

8.2.3   Main Part Activity 3, Warm and Cold
For this part, you will need music that sounds and feels cold and music that
sounds and feels warm. Play the cold music first and experiment how it feels to
move with the cold music. Everyone imagines getting colder and colder until
they freeze like statues (Figure 13.17). (Instruct the students to remember the
location where they are now.)
    Next, play the warm music (*Flight of the bumble bee* perhaps). Now students
can play with how it feels to get slowly warmer and warmer. Encourage students to move around in the space while they are getting warmer. Eventually
everyone melts and remains lying on the floor.
    Every student now gets a piece of painters tape attached to the floor on the
place they melted. They are asked to give a temperature of how hot they are,
and they should write that on the painters tape, for example +34. Everyone also
gets another piece of painters tape and are asked to find the place where they

froze and put some tape there then mark the temperature they felt there, for example –15.

8.2.4   Main Part Activity 4, Find Zero

Each student now has a melting point and a freezing point in the room. They should imagine a line between those points and figure out where zero is on it. The whole class can reflect on the questions: How many different measuring scales were used? Why do we need different scales? Were all the choices of scales correct?

8.2.5   Main Part Activity 5, Creative Time

This final exercise is the most creative. Students form groups of 4; their task is to create exercises with negative numbers. Provide them some materials like string, painters tape, coloured markers, scissors and paper. In this exercise students will create anything they imagine given that it meets the constraint of being based on negative integers.

FIGURE 13.16   "Moving on the Integer Line" activity in Şcoala Gimnazială nr. 20, Galati, Romania

FIGURE 13.17   "Warm and Cold" activity in Şcoala Gimnazială nr. 20, Galati, Romania

8.3   *Closing*

In the closing part, students reflect on what they learned and provide feedback regarding their conceptual understanding of the focus of the actions.

8.3.1   Closing, Sharing
All the groups share their creations, and others can try out their exercises.

8.3.2   Closing, Discussion
Lead a discussion about the activities, how everyone felt, and what they experienced and learned.

8.3.3   Closing, Evaluation
The students can give an evaluation of how they liked the activities. If they liked them a lot, they become large; if a student did not like the activities, they become small.

9   Module 6: Dance of the Shapes

This module is suitable for upper secondary students. The focus is upon the coordinate system, symmetries, and reflecting across or with respect to a line.

Further learning goals are collaborative problem solving, teamwork, leadership and creativity.

9.1   *Warm-Up*

In the warm-up students get comfortable moving and find different methods of movement and expression of their bodies. They learn to create shapes using their bodies. They also are introduced to the action of mirroring each other within a coordinate system.

9.1.1   Warm-up Activity 1, Different Body Parts

Accompanied by lively music, students move and dance freely in the space. They should pay attention to different parts of the body and how they can move: head, arms, fingers, knees, feet and so on. They experiment with drawing different shapes in the air using first their fingers and arms, then different parts of their bodies. These objects could be anything imaginable or geometric shapes: triangles, lines, circles and so on.

9.1.2   Warm-up Activity 2, Body Supports

Ask students to form pairs. The couples are to create different body postures by leaning against each other and supporting each other in different ways.

9.1.3   Warm-up Activity 3, Mirroring in Couples

While sitting on the floor, pairs of students are asked to mirror or reflect each other. After starting from the floor, three levels are introduced: low (on the floor), middle (kneeling or sitting), and high (standing up). The pairs are asked to mirror each other on each of the three levels.

9.1.4   Warm-up Activity 4, The Coordinate System

Prepare in advance a coordinate system on the floor of a big room with an x-axis and a y-axis. Again, in pairs, the students get an x-coordinate and a y-coordinate and are asked to find their common, but unique to them, place on the coordinate system.

9.2   *Main Part*

Here, students learn how to reflect each other's movements across a line. Further, they explore mirroring shapes with respect to a line and then forming a rotational symmetry using the two lines of the coordinate system as mirroring lines.

9.2.1   Main Part Activity 1, Symmetry with Respect to a Line

Ask students to pair up again. This time only one student stands at one point on the plane. Ask each pair to mirror each other using one of the axes as a symmetry line. They can choose to use either the x-axis or the y-axis so that everyone has space to move. One of the students leads while the other follows. Make sure all the pairs experiment with moving in this space and that they understand how mirroring works while moving around. Then change the roles of the leader and the follower. Encourage the students to form different poses and move in various and creative ways from one place to another.

9.2.2   Main Part Activity 2, Mirroring Two Points

Ask two pairs to join together so that they form a quadruple. Now two leaders on one side of the line find two points (they now form a line segment) and the two followers have to arrange themselves in a corresponding reflection. Once a few formations like this have been tried out, the pairs can start moving around, all the time keeping reflective symmetry.

9.2.3   Main Part Activity 3, Mirroring Triangles

Next ask three pairs to join so that six students can form two triangles of points. One triple mirrors the movements of the other triple on the other side of the axis, again maintaining the reflective symmetry. The teacher should draw attention to the reality that the location of three students creates one triangle on one side, and the other students form a mirrored triangle on the other side. Again, switch roles of leaders and followers.

9.2.4   Main Part Activity 4, Mirroring Triangle Dances

The groups get some time to plan small "dances" of 5–10 moves in their symmetric triangles. The teacher should encourage the teams that may still be struggling and ask everyone to practise their dances. Afterward, each group will perform their dances for the others.

9.2.5   Main Part Activity 5, Symmetry with Respect to Two Lines

Four groups of three are now joined, and each group gets their sector of the coordinate system. One group starts by forming a triangle with poses. Another group over the x-axis then assumes mirroring poses using the x-axis as the symmetry line. A third group then mirrors the second group, this time using the y-axis as their symmetry line. The fourth group displays a reflection of the third using the x-axis as a symmetry line. The groups can notice that the first group and the fourth group are also in symmetry with respect to the y-axis. Different poses and triangles should be formed with different leaders, and the groups can try out moving and dancing simultaneously as well.

9.3   *Closing*
Closing the activity, students will reflect on what they learned and provide feedback about the activity.

9.3.1   Closing, Sharing
Create a circle and sit down. Lead a discussion about whether everyone liked the activity and what they learned. The teacher should probe for student perceptions of difficult or easy-to-grasp concepts, perhaps asking, "Did you learn more about the coordinate system?" or "What did you learn regarding reflections/mirroring?"

10   Discussion and Conclusions

The MiM project's team members are already using the approach and the project's own toolkit, *Maths in Motion: The Toolkit* (Nasiakou, 2018) in formal and informal learning situations and teacher education. MiM has been demonstrated in several locations worldwide including the world's largest mathematics and arts community's meeting, the Bridges Math Art Conference in 2019. Though no scientific analysis has been applied, we summarise some themes from the feedback received from both students and teachers. In general, the MiM project is received with enthusiasm, interest and curiosity. Teachers (both school teachers and university maths educators) feel that the teaching ideas and methods in MiM are new, creative and functional. Most comment that they are eager to try something like this in their own teaching. Many workshop participants comment on the importance of embodied learning. One aspect of this is simply the desire to have more movement in classrooms in general (not necessarily dance or even maths or education related, just getting students to move more). However, at the recent Bridges conference – a convening of many experts and researchers within this field – there were many statements of interest in mathematics and dance themes. The consensus was that there is not enough work done in this field and that more research is needed both in the mathematics-art and mathematics education fields. It was further noted that these practices align closely with the integrated (STEAM education) focus that is becoming widespread in the EU and around the globe.

The feedback we receive during our experiments suggests that our approach of highly supportive and engaging actions provides motivation which effectively contributes to STEAM-oriented (Colucci-Gray et al., 2017) mathematics education. The MiM approach can address the development of Gardner's (1983) multiple intelligences and Burnard's (2016) multiple creativities together with Dienes' multiple embodiment (Dienes, 1960, 1973; Benedek, 2008) through movement-based learning strategies.

Our next goals include integrating our approach into multidisciplinary and multisensory learning programs, and we would seek to further explore the potentials of sports-based mathematics learning and to employ technology (e.g., tracker software, GeoGebra, Micro:bit, fitness wristbands, electronic textiles, soft robotics, pedometers) for motivation and data collection in movement-based mathematics learning programs in general.

MiM has also inspired projects incorporating dance and mathematics in artistic works. MiM team members are working on dance, choreography and productions based on the connection between dance and mathematics. We find this an intriguing direction for development as well.

Revisiting and synthesising the theories of Gardner, Burnard and Dienes within a collection of movement-based mathematical experiences provides a rich opportunity to examine how the arts can be placed at the core of a STEAM approach to learning. Herein students' bodies and sensory experiences and objects (dragons' eggs, arms, hands and feet, and manipulatives) become intertwined and entangled with mathematical concepts. We would argue that these experiences elicit the emergence and construction of both artistic knowings and mathematical constructs. This approach deserves further study that relies directly upon the collaborative efforts of teachers with diverse expertise, artists and STEAM specialists.

10.1   *Further Research*

To date this project has undertaken little formal research upon the impact of these modules on student engagement, comprehension, long-term retention of concepts and practices. To gain more understanding of the mechanisms at work the team will first seek to design several research projects around these modules.

The modules themselves are undergoing a process of revision before being launched again. These modules are not the only materials the collaborators have in mind to write: more ideas from geometry, combinatorics and number theory are being discussed. This further research could focus both upon traditional scholastic benefits and the larger goals of STEAM integration. Clarifying and more completely stating the synthesis of multiple intelligences, creativities and embodiments into a cohesive theory is a goal of this work.

Acknowledgements

This chapter is one of the results of the three-year "Maths in Motion" Erasmus+ project, supported by the European Commission in the framework of Strategic Partnership for Innovation in School Education. The following organisations are participating in the realisation of the project: Olde Vechte Foundation, The Netherlands; Experience Workshop, Finland; Fun Mathematics, Bulgaria; SciCo, Greece; IC Codogno, Italy; Scoala Gimnaziala No. 20 Galati, Romania; and Balletskolen Holstebro, Denmark.

Notes

1   Maths in Motion was an international, educational Erasmus+ project, supported by the European Commission (see Olde Vechte Foundation, 2019). We would like to note that the name of our project, Maths in Motion, might get confused with a similar term "Math in Motion" which is widely used for projects combining mathematics with a variety of fields including music, visual arts or origami. However, we felt it was critical to keep the name of our Erasmus+ project, funded by the European Commission.

2   See GeoGebra (https://www.geogebra.org/), Micro:bit (https://microbit.org/) and PocketLab (https://www.thepocketlab.com/).

References

AFIS. (2018). *Active, fit and smart – Effects of physical activity and fitness on the cognitive prerequisites of learning.* Jyväskylä: University of Jyväskylä. Retrieved July 27, 2019, from https://cibr.jyu.fi/en/research/projects/afis

Anderson, A. (2015). Dance/movement therapy's influence on adolescents' mathematics, social-emotional, and dance skills. *Educational Forum, 79*(3), 230–247.

Benedek, A. G. (2018, May 23–26). *Embodied conceptions of mathematical understanding in the twentieth century: The emergence of Zoltan P. Dienes's principles and their origin.* Paper presented at the History of Mathematics and Teaching of Mathematics Conference, Miskolc, Hungary. Retrieved July 27, 2019, from http://real.mtak.hu/80683/1/Benedek_Paper_A4_format_v13_u.pdf

Bingham, A. D. (2007, February 22–27). *Teaching transformations of functions using modern dance: An experiment pairing a modern dance class with college algebra.* Paper presented at the Conference on Research in Undergraduate Mathematics Education, San Diego, CA.

Boaler, J., & Dweck, C. S. (2016). *Mathematical mindsets: Unleashing students' potential through creative math, inspiring messages and innovative teaching.* San Francisco, CA: Jossey-Bass.

Burnard, P. (2012). *Musical creativities in practice.* Oxford: Oxford University Press.

Burnard, P. (2016). Rethinking "musical creativity" and the notion of multiple creativities in music. In O. Odena (Ed.), *Musical creativity: Insights from music education research* (pp. 27–50). Farnham: Ashgate.

Burnard, P., Dragovic, T., Jasilek, S., Biddulph, J., Rolls, L., Durning, A., & Fenyvesi, K. (2017). The art of co-creating arts-based possibility spaces for fostering STE(A)M practices in primary education. In T. Chemi & X. Du (Eds.), *Arts-based methods in education around the world* (pp. 245–279). Gistrup: River Publishers.

Colucci-Gray, L., Burnard, P., Trowsdale, J., Cooke, C. F., Davies, R., & Gray, D. S. (2017). *Reviewing the potential and challenges of developing STEAM education through creative pedagogies for 21st learning.* London: British Educational Research Association.

Cuoco, A., Goldberg, E., & Mark, J. (1996). *Habits of mind: An organizing principle for mathematics curriculum.* Boston, MA: Harvard University Press.

Dienes, Z. P. (1960). *Building up mathematics.* London: Hutchinson Educational Company.

Dienes, Z. P. (1973). *Mathematics through the senses, games, dance and art.* Windsor: National Foundation for Educational Research.

Dweck, C. S. (2008). *Mindset: The new psychology of success.* New York, NY: Ballantine Books.

Gardner, H. (1983). *Frames of mind: The theory of multiple intelligences.* New York, NY: Basic Books.

Gardner, H. (1999). The happy meeting of multiple intelligences and the arts. *Harvard Education Letters, 15*(6). Retrieved July 27, 2019, from https://www.hepg.org/hel-home/issues/15_6/helarticle/the-happy-meeting-of-multiple-intelligences-and-th

Gerofsky, S. (2011). Seeing the graph vs. being the graph. *Integrating Gestures: The Interdisciplinary Nature of Gesture, 30*(4), 245–256.

Hong, O. (2017). Education in Korea: Current policies and future directions. *Asian Research Policy, 8*(2), 92–102.

Katai, Z., Toth, L., Neogen, S. A., & Adorjani, A. K. (2014). Multi-sensory informatics education. *Informatics in Education, 13*(2), 225–240.

Kolb, A. Y., & Kolb, D. A. (2015). Learning styles and learning spaces: Enhancing experiential learning in higher education. *Academy of Management Learning & Education, 4*(2), 193–212.

Lakoff, G., & Núñez, E. R. (2000). *Where mathematics comes from.* New York, NY: Basic Books.

Moerman, P. (2016). Dancing math. In E. Torrence et al. (Eds.), *Bridges Finland: Conference proceedings* (pp. 269–276). Phoenix, AZ: Tessellations Publishing. Retrieved July 27, 2019, from http://archive.bridgesmathart.org/2016/bridges2016-269.pdf

Moerman, P. (2018). Dance, art, math, education – An eternal triangle. In E. Torrence et al. (Eds.), *Bridges Stockholm 2018: Conference proceedings* (pp. 347–350). Phoenix, AZ: Tessellations Publishing. Retrieved July 27, 2019, from https://archive.bridgesmathart.org/2018/bridges2018-347.pdf

Mosston, M., & Ashworth, S. (2002). *Teaching physical education* (5th ed.). Boston, MA: Benjamin Cummings.

Nasiakou, L. (Ed.). (2018). *Maths in motion: The toolkit.* Ommen: Olde Vechte Foundation. Retrieved July 27, 2019, from https://oldevechte.com/wp-content/uploads/2019/01/MATHS-IN-MOTION-digital-book.pdf

Novak, M. (2017). *Case studies listening to students using kinesthetic movement while learning to graph linear functions* (PhD thesis). Kent State University. Retrieved July 27, 2019, from https://etd.ohiolink.edu/pg_10?0::NO:10:P10_ACCESSION_NUM:kent1498162366548228

Olde Vechte Foundation. (2019). *Maths in motion.* Retrieved August 7, 2019, from https://oldevechte.com/international-projects/partnership/maths-in-motion/

Renesse, C. V., Ecke, V., Fleron, J. F., & Hotchkiss, P. K. (2016). *Discovering the art of mathematics: Dance.* Westfield, MA: Discovering the Art of Mathematics, Westfield State University. Retrieved July 27, 2019, from http://www.artofmathematics.org/books/dance

Ruiter, M., Loyens, S., & Paas, F. (2015). Watch your step children! Learning two-digit numbers through mirror-based observation of self-initiated body movements. *Educational Psychology Review, 27*(3), 457–474. doi:10.1007/s10648-015-9324-4

Schaffer, K., & Stern, E. (2010). Workshop on mathematics and dance. In G. W. Hart & R. Sarhangi (Eds.), *Bridges Pécs: Conference proceedings* (pp. 551–554). Phoenix, AZ: Tessellations Publishing. Retrieved July 27, 2019, from https://archive.bridgesmathart.org/2010/bridges2010-551.pdf

Schaffer, K., Stern, E., & Kim, S. (2001). *Math dance with Dr. Schaffer and Mr. Stern.* Santa Cruz, CA: MoveSpeakSpin.

Schaffer, K., Thie, J., & Williams, K. (2018). The mathematical center of attention, its attributes and motion analyses in dance choreography. In E. Torrence et al. (Eds.), *Bridges Stockholm 2018: Conference proceedings* (pp. 273–280). Phoenix, AZ: Tessellations Publishing.

Sung, W., Ahn, J., & Black, J. B. (2017). Introducing computational thinking to young learners: Practicing computational perspectives through embodiment in mathematics education. *Technology, Knowledge and Learning, 22*(3), 443–463.

Woolery, L. A. (2006). *Art-based perceptual ecology as a way of knowing the language of place* (PhD thesis). Antioch University, Yellow Springs, OH.

CHAPTER 14

STEM to STEAM as an Approach to Human Development: The Potential of Arts Practices for Supporting Wellbeing

Nicola Walshe, Elsa Lee, Danielle Lloyd and Ruth Sapsed

Abstract

The National Science Foundation conceived the term STEM with an emphasis on the links between economic prosperity and knowledge-intensive jobs that are dependent on science and technology. As such, traditionally STEM subject initiatives have aligned with and facilitated a largely economic conceptualisation of human and social development. It seems likely that the wellbeing crisis that we are experiencing in the West is linked to this. This is compounded by the rising influence of technology which has facilitated what is sometimes called the indoorisation of children, and the raised levels of parental concern about safety. From this follows an associated sense of disenfranchisement for children, with consequences for their wellbeing and happiness.

This chapter begins with an overview of the impact of STEM on wellbeing, arguing that a focus on human development after Sen and Nussbaum is a more holistic approach to understanding wellbeing. In this understanding, wellbeing arises from an *entanglement* of threads representing the different elements of an individual's life, such as their physical health, their social networks, their access to wild, natural and outdoor spaces, and so forth. This chapter focuses specifically on this access to wild, natural and outdoor spaces (using the arts and arts-based research to mediate this access) to consider how the capability approach provides a foundation for a broadly conceived notion of wellbeing that incorporates environmental sustainability, social justice and future economic wellbeing. Nussbaum's list of capabilities is used as a framework with which to analyse focus group data from artists working with the arts-based charity Cambridge Curiosity and Imagination (CCI). The chapter concludes by considering how working with artists as co-researchers and how the co-development of artwork between children and artists might expose a more holistic understanding of the entangled roles of art and wild/natural/outdoor spaces in the wellbeing of young people. In so doing the chapter adds to conceptualisations of childhoodnature which seek to demonstrate that children

© KONINKLIJKE BRILL NV, LEIDEN, 2020 | DOI: 10.1163/9789004421585_019

and nature are inextricably linked through shared characteristics such as free-dom and a non-linear view of time.

Keywords

access to nature – arts – capabilities – children's wellbeing – eco-capabilities – entanglement – Nussbaum – Sen – STEM – wellbeing

1   Introduction

The National Science Foundation conceived the term STEM with an empha-sis on the links between economic prosperity and knowledge-intensive jobs that are dependent on science and technology (National Academy of Sci-ences, 2007). As such, traditionally STEM subject initiatives have been devel-oped with a utilitarian approach, aligning with and facilitating a largely economic conceptualisation of human and social development. It seems likely that the wellbeing crisis that we are experiencing in the West is linked to this (WHO, 2016). This is compounded by the rising influence of technology which has facilitated what is sometimes called the indoorisation of children (e.g. Frumkin et al., 2017; Louv, 2008), and the raised levels of parental con-cern about safety (e.g. Malone, 2007). From this follows an associated sense of disenfranchisement for children, with consequences for their wellbeing and happiness.

    The study of nature has often been seen as a STEM practice, for example through environmental science (e.g. Sümen & Çalışıcı, 2016) and design and technology (Pitt, 2009). Indeed the environment has been touted as a mecha-nism for maintaining the relevance of STEM (e.g. Bybee, 2010). However, this limits its potential to understand how humans relate to it and its importance to human flourishing. In seeing the study of nature and the human–nature relationship instead as a STEAM practice, we may be able to achieve a much broader and deeper understanding of the significance of the human–nature relationship. The impacts of STEAM practices might be deepened through pay-ing attention to epistemological framings of posthumanism. Posthumanism is increasingly being used as a mode for thinking about environmental and sustainability education research (e.g. Clarke & Mcphie, 2016; Gannon, 2017; Lindgren & Ohman, 2018; Rautio, 2013). It rejects an anthropocentric view of nature, advocating an understanding that nature and humans are intimately entwined (Malone, 2015). Whilst this view is not uncontested (Lee et al., 2018), such a shift could lead to educational practices that facilitate global efforts to overcome the crisis in wellbeing, particularly amongst children and young people, that teachers are increasingly under pressure to address. By using arts-based research methods within STEAM practice and focusing on the interdisciplinarity of human–nature relations, we may be able both to understand environmental and sustainability problems *and* to address them.

1.1   *STEM and Wellbeing*

STEM literature predominantly refers to wellbeing through a neoliberal lens, such that its value is measured in terms of economic and financial wellbeing; for example, a number of macroeconomic studies have argued the case for a clear link between student achievement on science and maths tests and per capita gross domestic product (GDP) growth, supporting the widely held belief that STEM education is central to the production of economic prosperity and wellbeing (e.g. Hanushek et al., 2008; Osborne, 2000; Roschelle et al., 2011). Marginson et al. (2013: 13) argue that "STEM is a central preoccupation of policy makers across the world", as for example in Europe (e.g. Rocard et al., 2007; House of Commons Committee of Public Accounts, 2018), Australia (e.g. Office of the Chief Scientist, 2013, 2014), and the USA (e.g. Committee on STEM Education, National Science and Technology Council, 2013). Consequently, underpinned by the belief that STEM skills are crucial for a country's productivity, government investment has focused on promoting STEM subjects, particularly among minority groups (e.g. Byars-Winston, 2014). This utilitarian approach represents an instrumentalist philosophy of education (Carr & Kemmis, 1986; Simonneaux & Simonneaux, 2012), aligning with and facilitating an economic conceptualisation of development and wellbeing.

However, wellbeing is a much more complex term than this economic, neoliberal framing suggests. This complexity is about more than breadth (in terms of what dimensions of human life are included); it is also about how those dimensions are entwined and *entangled* and how they constellate across time too. To be able to understand the breadth of wellbeing, we bring Amartya Sen's work on capabilities into play, whilst to try and understand how these notions intra-act and *entangle* we use a posthumanist perspective, drawing on the work of Karen Barad (2017) amongst others. We then go on to suggest that a way to both grow and understand wellbeing is through working with artists and arts based research methods; methods that enable a fuller expression of the entanglement of different dimensions of wellbeing across and through an individual's experience.

2   Capabilities as an Approach to Human Development and Wellbeing

Amartya Sen describes human capabilities as a "a person's ability to do valuable
acts or reach valuable states of being" (1993: 30). Capabilities are a broad range
of human *functionings* that go beyond the notion of subjective and economic
wellbeing. Capabilities are future oriented, aiming to provide humans with real
opportunities to achieve a state of physical, emotional, intellectual and existential wellbeing in life (Delors et al., 1996), whatever an individual considers
valuable (Sen, 1980). Sen's work challenges dominant models that assert that
a nation's quality of life improves when GDP increases. Evidence shows that a
simplistic measure based on GDP is problematic because significant inequalities persist within many nations despite economic growth. In other words, the
benefits of economic growth are not enjoyed by all citizens – its distribution
is disproportional, resulting in an unequal landscape of economic prosperity.
Sen proposes that it is more useful to assess a nation's development by looking at the *capabilities* of its citizens. The capabilities approach looks at each
individual not in terms of actual contribution or achievement (for example
to economic growth), but rather their potential (Robeyns, 2006). Sen's theory
is the starting point for the human development approach: the idea that the
purpose of development is to improve human lives by expanding the range of
things that a person can be and do, such as to be healthy and well nourished, to
be knowledgeable, and to participate in community life. Thus human development becomes the process of enlarging a person's capabilities to function, the
range of things that a person could do and be in her life, expressed as expanding choices (Sen, 1989).

   There is a longstanding debate in the capabilities literature about the
necessity of enumerating a list of capabilities, questioning whether there is
a universally applicable and identifiable list of capabilities that all individuals have the potential to access, in spite of circumstance. Sen argues for the
importance of public participation and dialogue in arriving at valued capabilities for each situation and context (e.g. 1992, 1999, 2002); he leaves his framework deliberately vague, because of the importance to him that communities
decide what capabilities count as valuable. Nussbaum (2000), on the other
hand, argues the case for a universal, cross-cultural list of central capabilities
for human flourishing, even one that is provisional and open to debate. She
identifies ten central human capabilities which would need to be present for
a fully good human life: life; bodily health; bodily integrity; senses, imagination and thought; emotions; practical reason; affiliation; other species; play;
and control over one's environment (Nussbaum, 2000: 78–80). Others, such
as Fattore, Mason, and Watson (2007), develop this list further by creating a

capabilities index specifically for children, pointing out that a person's capabilities may be compromised by decisions made on behalf of that person, specifically young children (Underwood et al., 2015). Sen suggests that education ought to enhance freedom, agency and wellbeing by "making one's life richer with the opportunity of reflective choice" for a life of "genuine choices with serious options" (1992: 41), and enhancing "the ability of people to help themselves and to influence the world" (Sen, 1999: 18). In this way, the process of identifying capabilities entails some form of participatory and inclusive dialogue, however conceptualised (Saito, 2003). Overall, Sen's capability approach is based on human agency, meaning that a person is responsible for their own life and their own goals that matter to them. This is significant within a context in which agency has widely been acknowledged as being important to wellbeing (e.g. Hojman & Miranda, 2018; Welzel & Inglehart, 2010), particularly the wellbeing of children (Fattore, Mason, & Watson, 2007).

The belief that capabilities influence wellbeing has been tested in a number of studies: for example, Van and (2012) found capabilities to be a successful alternative measure for wellbeing (using life satisfaction as an interpretation of wellbeing); M and Headey (2013) suggest that both subjective and objective wellbeing are the outcome of the interaction process between capabilities and choices; and Anand, Hunter and Smith (2005) found a significant relationship between subjective wellbeing and capabilities.

Our forthcoming publication will explore the way in which the aforementioned lists of capabilities map onto sustainability as it emerges from the United Nations' Sustainable Development Goals. We have been able to show that there is a strong synergy between what the Sustainable Development Goals are trying to achieve and what the capability approach is trying to achieve. It is also important to note here that Sen's capability approach holds that the natural world is important to human wellbeing (Anand & Sen, 1994); although this is significant, it does attribute instrumental value to nature, considering how it can be of benefit to people-centred development (Watene, 2016), rather than having its own intrinsic value (Sneddon, Howarth, & Norgaard, 2006). However, the literature on this is not consistent; for example, Nussbaum's (2000) central capabilities include respect for other species and nature, whilst Ballet, Koffi, and Pelenc (2013) suggest that human wellbeing should be considered equal to the preservation of natural resources.

This latter position is an invitation for thinking with a posthuman perspective about the role of wild, natural and outdoor places in the establishment and maintenance of positive subjective wellbeing. If we consider people to be a part of nature (Haraway, 2015; Taylor, 2013, 2017) (as well as being apart from it, as has been argued elsewhere, e.g. Bonnet, 2012; Lee et al., 2018), entangled and implicit in its fate, then we have to accept that a threat to nature (such as climate breakdown) is also a threat to humanity and that this is likely to have a very significant impact on our mental health and wellbeing. From this point of inherence, it becomes necessary for us to think about our wellbeing as entwined with that of the rest of the biosphere, and our fate as implicit in the fate of the biosphere. However, it also becomes clear that the process of indoorisation and disenfranchisement of childhood that has happened over the past few decades has involved a disjuncture, resulting in a sense of separateness and a heightened awareness of what Bonnet (2012) and others refer to as the exceptionalism of humanity from nature. This sense of disjuncture might serve the purpose of an anthropocentric existence that treats the planet as a resource or a service (language like "resource depletion" and "ecosystem services" are indicators of this kind of thinking), and something we are in control of. However, the sense of wellbeing and happiness that is derived from being a part of something greater than ourselves, of being an inherent but tiny part of a beautiful and awe-inspiring biodiversity, is not at all served by this disjuncture.

At this point it is worth noting that we use the term "place" in a highly relational, entangled manner, as we have written about elsewhere in relation to this research (Lee et al., 2018). So we are not thinking simply about a geographical, physical location, but about a place that is loaded with meaning emerging from the way that a physical location has been experienced through encounters within it. These encounters bring with them memories of previous events and other creatures that have shared those encounters in that place, as well as the inherited memories and stories of the place that are commonly known. Our conceptualisation of place aligns with that of others such as Massey (1994), Basso (1996), Fettes and Judson (2010), and Clarke and Mcphie (2016).

3   Looking to the Arts to Develop Capabilities and Wellbeing

Now to the other major thread of our research: the potential of the arts for wellbeing. There is evidence that arts education can improve both wellbeing and social inclusion (e.g. Karkou & Glasman, 2004; Kinder & Harland, 2004; Walshe, Lee, & Smith, forthcoming), as well as developing children's capabilities (Zitcer, Hawkins, & Vakharia, 2016). Arts-based approaches have been found to support the development of several of the qualities on Nussbaum's (2000) list of capabilities: for example, arts performance through kinaesthetic forms such as dance and theatre have a demonstrated impact on bodily health and bodily integrity (Stuckey & Nobel, 2010); practice in the visual arts has been shown to increase one's development of imagination and thought (Burchenal & Grohe, 2007); and a considerable body of research addresses the role of arts participation in developing emotional skills (e.g. McRobie, 2014; Nussbaum, 1995). Despite this compelling evidence, individuals with low socioeconomic status continue to have less access to the arts than their more affluent counterparts (National Endowment for the Arts, 2015) and the arts are increasingly marginalised in school curricula (National Society for Education in Art & Design, 2016; see also Cultural Learning Alliance, n.d., for further evidence of the way that arts provision has been diminished in British curricula).

What emerges from this discussion of the role of arts and access to natural, wild, outdoor places is a narrative of a childhood experience that is increasingly impoverished and segregated, a child as a thread pulled out of a greater entanglement of nature and stretched into the singular, individualised linearity of a STEM-focused education. In other words, if we imagine the living and non-living elements on our planet each as a shifting and moving thread and nature as the entanglement that results from their interactions, and if we accept that each element is dependent on each other element for its wellbeing and continuance and that it exists in a constant state of responsiveness, then we can see that the thread that represents the child, when it is pulled out of this whole to be regularised and socialised into the routines of the adult human world, becomes impoverished and transformed. What is more, what remains as nature is similarly weakened by the removal and transformation of this element of itself. A better experience of childhood might support a child to become increasingly entwined into their dwelling place, using all forms of expression and exploration at their disposal to create the entwinement and entanglement of becoming; encouraged and guided through a much broader, richer set of STEAM-like practices to inhere in the world they share with other similar and different creatures. What we mean by STEAM-like practice (in contrast to a STEM-focused education) is that the learning that a child experiences might involve the child's imagination and their artistic, adventuring characters in exploring questions about the world using the knowledge and approaches of the scientific method without determining what or how that exploration takes place. Such practices nurture the child's sense of awe and wonder whilst also enabling them to learn more about the world and about how we have come to know what we know already, including learning about the scientists and the artists who have contributed to this knowledge. In this way, the child will be able to benefit from a knowledge-rich curriculum (in line with current policy in England) without allowing that knowledge to overpower their capacity for creativity and curiosity.

The work of arts-based charity Cambridge Curiosity and Imagination (CCI) aims to address this challenge. By creating opportunities for children's creative adventures in local, familiar and (if possible) wild outdoor places, CCI seeks to empower young people (and encourage others in their wider community) with the agency to act in relation to the spaces that matter to them. This empowerment, through the growing of capabilities, may potentiate improved wellbeing, particularly in contexts of economic and social deprivation. In the next section we will discuss some empirical work which demonstrates the potential of CCI's practice to achieve these ends, focusing on extracts from our data that show how this kind of work can develop capabilities that align with the human capabilities approach.

4   Exploring Capabilities in the Light of STEAM Practice: A Case Study of Cambridge Curiosity and Imagination (CCI)

The empirical work for this chapter was undertaken as part of an ongoing exploratory ethnographic case study of CCI which aimed to produce thickly described data of an ethnographic nature within a constructivist, interpretivist framework (Whitehead, 2004). The data we are going to discuss here focus specifically on how the STEAM-like practices of CCI, when viewed through the lens of capabilities theory, provide suggestions for the way that capability theory (as a proxy for wellbeing) can more comprehensively include the concept of nature. CCI brings together artists, educators, parents and researchers with a shared passion for how the arts and nature can transform lives, and a belief in the power of democratic forms of community activism (sometimes termed "artivism"). Children are at the heart of CCI's work. It practises a carefully considered and articulated approach that is committed to deep listening, thoughtful collaboration and artistic co-creation (Lee et al., 2018). Common to all of CCI's projects is a focus on developing a sense of agency and voice for all through engagement with the arts, often in nature (Denmead, 2011). Artists work as independent consultants with CCI so this work comprises only part of their professional activity. Using purposive sampling, we invited seven CCI artists to be involved in the research; these comprised all the artists currently or recently working on CCI projects and included some founding artists. In addition, the CCI founding and assistant directors were involved in the research and also became part of the writing team for some of the publications emerging from the research. This latter point is identified here as it speaks to the themes of this book section around how *entanglements* of researcher and researched arise until the notion of objectivity in research becomes superfluous and a deeper understanding of subjectivity and intra-activity takes over and concretises a negotiated approach to understanding what is being investigated.

Our study initially comprised a "talk and draw" focus group interview with the CCI artists, with conversation focusing on three elements: nature, children and place. This was followed by individual interviews with the same artists. The two directors of CCI completed a semi-structured questionnaire comprising open questions that was designed after the artist interviews to elaborate on the emerging data. The focus group and interviews were audio recorded and recordings subsequently transcribed. The transcriptions were sent to the artists for verification, some of whom made minor amendments which were duly incorporated. The amended transcriptions were submitted to a process of *a priori* coding using the capabilities list as a coding template (Table 14.1). Artist drawings were analysed alongside focus group and interview transcriptions using content analysis (Rose, 2005). To support the internal validity of the research and increase the reliability of our conclusions, data analysis was undertaken independently by two researchers and emerging findings discussed with a third colleague who was present during the interviews.

The results of the analysis suggest that artists articulate the capability "senses, imagination and thought" most frequently both within individual and focus group interviews. In particular, many of the artists reflected on using practice that sparks children's imagination. For example in the focus group Debbie stated: "I would go in and make, like, a dome or something like that out of willow, and then because it's not a defined thing, the kids can imagine what it is". Imagination is a key point: Secker et al. (2017) state that play, imagination and learning improve mental wellbeing. In the focus group, Debbie articulated a belief that they (as artists) were key to helping children imagine: "you are creating a container for their imaginations". When talking about the senses, Caroline commented:

> For instance, I did a little lesson on the colour yellow ... so I brought in a huge, soft, yellow blanket, and I wanted the children to feel the colour. So I invited them to hide under the cover, to wrap themselves around the cover and it really worked. They love it; they love that.

This highlights the importance of experiential learning and using the senses in order to learn and develop (Nussbaum, 2000). This experiential aspect of wellbeing is common within the literature (e.g. Kolb, 1984; Dewey, 1959) and was reiterated by the other artists.

In addition to developing senses, imagination and thought, the artists discussed how they developed the children's ability to work with and have concern for other humans. Susanne described how children working with her "gain

TABLE 14.1   List of capabilities used for a priori coding, with examples of text assigned to each code

Capability	Description	Example quotations from artists
Senses, imagination and thought	To be able to use senses, imagination and thought, informed by education and involving freedom of expression	"I really enjoy that kind of floating off into the imaginative space of unnatural nature" (focus group). "burnt-out bit of metal that a young child picked up, and it was in the same quality as picking up a leaf, and she said, 'Look, a burnt witch's house'" (focus group).
Autonomy	To have ownership or control over aspects of one's life	"But what is nice, and this is where this thing was interesting for me, is that the ... children have the power – and this is an important word for me" (focus group).
Affiliation	To be able to live with and towards others, to recognise and show concern for other humans, to engage in social relations, to be treated with respect and dignity	"I think their sense of their own value is felt often very quickly through the project, and the longer we can work with them the more that is sustained" (Deb). "I think it's important to feel that you are part of a community and like the reality of school life is existing in a wider context and for you to start to see a little bit beyond that" (Elena).
Emotions	To love and care for those who love and care for us, to grieve at their absence. To not have emotional development harmed by fear and/or anxiety.	"with the playground we want to change it from a place where we set fire to things to a place which we love, and you're going to change the perception of the place" (Debbie).
Mental wellbeing	To be mentally healthy	"A lot of the workshops I've done when I've asked for feedback, a lot of the children have written or said the word 'safe'" (Susanne). "I find that actually, little by little, those children are able to gain confidence because you've given them the chance to be and to have a place" (Caroline).

(cont.)

TABLE 14.1   List of capabilities used for a priori coding, with examples of text assigned to
each code (*cont.*)

Capability	Description	Example quotations from artists
Religion and identity	To be able to live by a religion or not by a religion and to be able to live according to one's own identity	"I think more and more for me I am really concerned that they re-imagine themselves, they have a sense of who they could also be" (Deb).
Play	To be able to play, laugh and participate in recreational activities	"I invited them to hide under the cover, to wrap themselves around the cover and it really worked. They love it; they love that" (Caroline).
Bodily integrity and safety	To have protection from violence of any sort	None identified.
Bodily health	To have good health, enough food and sufficient shelter	"the area in which the school is is described as being the worst place to live in Britain, and it's well-known as having had more heroin use per head than anywhere else" (Caroline).
Life	To be able to live to the end of a human life of normal length and not having a life so reduced that it is not worth living.	"the area in which the school is is described as being the worst place to live in Britain, and it's well-known as having had more heroin use per head than anywhere else" (Caroline).
Other species	To be able to live with concern for and in relation to animals, plants and the world of nature	"I wanted that language of perspective and seeing through an animal's eyes" (Deb).

SOURCES: NUSSBAUM (2000), BIGGERI (2007), DI TOMMASO (2006), ADDABBO,
TOMMASO AND FACCHINETTI (2004) AND SEN (1993)

often different insights into each other, because sometimes [they] work with other children that they didn't work with before". Additionally, they described that children have shown concern and empathy for other students, reflecting studies which show that art supports the development of emotional skills (e.g. McRobie, 2014). Susanne illustrated this:

> Then one boy cried, I remember, and he had been a bit outside all the groups. You could see there was a main group that hung out together, then this boy, like the "king" of this group, went and actually encouraged him and helped him.

Affiliation through collaborative approaches to practice is another key point of the artists' work; this was demonstrated by Sally who explained how she prioritises "collaboration and partnership ... I aim and intend always to work alongside children, alongside the teachers, alongside any of the participants that I happen to be working with". Through their discussion a strong sense of artists valuing the children emerged; for example, Susanne suggested that "I think they feel they are heard and that we really value what they say and that we are taking seriously the things they have to say from their imagination". Deb agreed, stating: "I think their sense of their own value is felt often very quickly through the project, and the longer we can work with them the more that is sustained". This is particularly the case for children who do not usually find school easy: "I will often have really valued something from a child and then discovered that that child is the child that is always in trouble or whose handwriting is terrible or ... But you know, that kind of contrast". These artists' practices of working together and valuing children are part of developing the affiliation capability; they contribute to showing concern for other humans, engaging in social relations, and being treated with respect and dignity.

Also of particular note through the artist discussions was the capability of autonomy; for example, Debbie emphasised the importance of this in the focus group:

> I was talking about the [town] project as well, one of the really crucial things about that was to give the teenagers a bit of ownership of the place that they were seeing ... once they've got their own involvement in making the space that they want to use, stuff like that, then it becomes more valuable to them ... so something that kind of wasn't theirs became theirs in a real way.

Sally developed this, suggesting that ownership empowers the children: "that acknowledgement and valuing of what they've then named something ... that's really empowering isn't it? That the children then have a sense of ownership, of claiming the space". Fattore, Mason, and Watson (2007) argue that having a sense of autonomy is important for children's wellbeing; we suggest that the empowerment of children through CCI's truly child-led, artistic practice in nature may be of further benefit as it develops intrinsic motivation (Douglas & Jaquith, 2009) which, in turn, contributes to growth of further capabilities.

While this is just a brief analysis, we have illustrated how using Nussbaum's adapted list suggests that environmental and sustainability education practices that incorporate art pedagogies may be a useful way to conceptualise a more holistic approach to wellbeing. We now move on to the final part of the chapter which considers how engaging children in defining a list of their own capabilities and developing these through participatory arts practice in nature might support a more holistic, embodied and relational growing of wellbeing. This growth can be sustained across a lifetime through setting up affecting experiences that can "flash up", to borrow a term from Barad (2018), when life trajectories present challenges to wellbeing in the future and can form part of a person's resilience in the face of these.

5   The Potential of Eco-Capabilities for Supporting Children's Wellbeing

Along with Barratt Hacking, Barratt, and Scott (2007), we see children as significant stakeholders in their local environment with an equitable right to participate in its current and future development. Barratt and Barratt Hacking (2003) have found that children experience high levels of frustration about the state of the local environment. They find it hard to engage with their environment and this lack of agency means that they are subsequently powerless to effect any changes in it (see also Spencer & Woolley, 2000; Barratt Hacking et al., 2006; Barratt & Barratt Hacking, 2003; Irvine et al., 2016). Seeing this as crucial to the current and future wellbeing of people and planet, and inspired by GeoCapabilities, a multimillion pound project funded by the National Science Foundation and the European Union's Comenius Programme (e.g. Uhlenwinkel et al., 2017; Walkington et al., 2018), we use the term *eco-capabilities* to describe how children define what is important to them, particularly in terms of environmental sustainability, social justice and future economic wellbeing (i.e. the three pillars of sustainability). With a focus on the wellbeing of children living in areas of high deprivation, we suggest there is a potential to contribute to contemporary academic and societal conversations about children's disconnect from nature, their wellbeing (or lack thereof) and the role of the arts at the intersection between the two. A future project aims to do just this; taking a participatory approach, we will work with primary-aged children through workshops in schools to explore wellbeing and nature, introducing the concept of *eco*-capabilities. We will use this as a platform from which to elicit from children a list of eco-capabilities that would make them happy or give them greater wellbeing, and ask children to assess themselves against their list: to what extent do they feel they will be able to achieve these? We then aim to explore how the children's perceptions of these eco-capabilities change through working with the CCI artists in nature, based on co-planned interventions or adventures in their local area. This is in line with the view that attachment to place is linked to a child's identity and wellbeing (Twigger-Ross & Uzzell, 1996; Green & White, 2007). An essential aspect of this project is the collaboration with the teachers of the classes that we engage in the research; drawing on their expert knowledge will enable us to greatly enhance the data that we collect. We also aim for this work to provide these teachers with a means of developing their own creative practice and ideas for enlivening the curriculum through the STEAM-like practices that CCI artists use. To extend these opportunities to teachers external to the project, we will also be developing resources and convening teach-meets to share this practice.

This project has been developed in consultation with CCI over the past two years and during this time there has been much cross-fertilisation of ideas between practitioners in CCI and the researchers. This is evident in the increasingly explicit focus on wellbeing in CCI's work alongside the deepening intensification of interests of the researchers in arts-based practices and research. Thus a knot of researcher and researched has emerged which has enhanced and heightened our shared knowledge of the potential benefits for wellbeing that this sort of work has, but the intimacy between us also has implications for our capacity to make the familiar strange, thus threatening our ability to notice and thoroughly appreciate the influences of the work that we are about to undertake. However, being aware of this increasing entanglement is important because it may enable us to consciously exclude ourselves from it in an attempt to understand the implications of the work from a more removed perspective. In essence, we might pull the thread of our involvement in the knot of practice between children, artists, teachers, place and researchers away temporarily to see what unravels and is revealed when we do so.

6   Conclusions

Within this chapter, we have conceptualised wellbeing through the capability approach and used this as a mechanism for exploring how the interdisciplinary practice of using art in nature might support positive wellbeing. Using this approach, we have been able to reflect on the ways in which artistic practice in nature, particularly that of CCI, might be one mechanism to address the crisis in wellbeing that has been identified by policy makers and practitioners across a range of sectors (e.g. Public Health England, 2018). Whilst a focus solely on STEM, as conceptualised through a neoliberal lens of economic and financial wellbeing, may in fact contribute to the problem of decreased wellbeing and mental health, the insertion of art for STEAM practice presents potential solutions from which both school-based and broader practitioners can learn and develop. As such, we suggest that arts-based practices might be powerful mediators in addressing the neoliberal drivers of STEM, facilitating deeper epistemological and theoretical understanding of what being a part of nature means for human wellbeing. In particular, it is possible that a posthuman onto-epistemic framework might deepen the way we conceptualise the holism of wellbeing, helping us to view it as a trans-corporeal entanglement of human and environment (Alaimo, 2016). This may help us, in turn, to overcome some of the problems with a reductionist view of wellbeing that tries to attribute different elements of wellbeing to different elements of lifestyle (e.g. McGillivray, 2007; Scott, 2012). As part of our plans to investigate eco-capabilities further we will, therefore, seek ways to explore how the eco-capabilities that the children identify are *entangled* with each other and with elements of the environments in which they move and act. Further, we will consider the mechanisms through which STEAM practice which engages children with their local places (Massey, 1994), as exemplified by CCI, can develop these eco-capabilities in the children, and what this might mean for teachers seeking to support children to find ways to develop holistic, positive mental health and wellbeing throughout their lives.

References

Addabbo, T., Di Tommaso, M. L., & Facchinetti, G. (2004). *To what extent fuzzy set theory and structural equation modelling can measure functionings? An application to child well being* (CHILD Working Paper No. 30/2004). Turin: Centre for Household, Income, Labour and Demographic Economics. Retrieved August 18, 2019, from http://www.child.carloalberto.org/images/wp/child30_2004.pdf

Alaimo, S. (2016). *Protest and pleasure: New materialism, environmental activism, and feminist exposure*. Minneapolis, MN: University of Minnesota Press.

Anand, P., Hunter, G., & Smith, R. (2005). Capabilities and well-being: Evidence based on the Sen-Nussbaum approach to welfare. *Social Indicators Research, 74*(1), 9–55.

Anand, S., & Sen, A. (1994). *Sustainable human development: Concepts and priorities* (UNDP Human Development Report Office 1994 Occasional Papers). New York, NY: United Nations Development Programme. Retrieved August 18, 2019, from https://ssrn.com/abstract=2294664

Ballet, J., Koffi, J.-M., & Pelenc, J. (2013). Environment, justice and the capability approach. *Ecological Economics, 85*, 28–34.

Barad, K. (2017). What flashes up: Theological-political-scientific fragments. In C. Keller & M.-J. Rubenstein (Eds.), *Entangled worlds: Religion, science, and new materialisms* (pp. 21–88). New York, NY: Fordham University Press.

Barratt, R., & Barratt Hacking, E. (2003). Rethinking the geography national curriculum: A case for community relevance. *Teaching Geography, 18*(2), 29–33.

Barratt Hacking, E., Barratt, R., & Scott, W. (2007). Engaging children: Research issues around participation and environmental learning. *Environmental Education Research, 13*(4), 529–544.

Barratt Hacking, E., Scott, W. A. H. S., Barratt, R., Talbot, W., Nichols, D., & Davies, K. (2006). Education for sustainability: Schools and their communities. In J. Chi-Kin Lee & M. Williams (Eds.), *Environmental and geographical education for sustainability: Cultural contexts* (pp. 123–138). New York, NY: Nova Science Publishers.

Basso, K. (1996). *Wisdom sits in places: Landscape and language among the Western Apache*. Albuquerque, NM: University of New Mexico Press.

Biggeri, M. (2007). Children's valued capabilities. In M. Walker & E. Unterhalter (Eds.), *Amartya Sen's capability approach and social justice in education* (pp. 197–214). New York, NY: Palgrave Macmillan.

Bonnett, M. (2012). Environmental concern, moral education and our place in nature. *Journal of Moral Education, 41*(3), 285–300.

Burchenal, M., & Grohe, M. (2007). Thinking through art: Transforming museum curriculum. *Journal of Museum Education, 32*(2), 111–122.

Byars-Winston, A. (2014). Toward a framework for multicultural STEM-focused career interventions. *Career Development Quarterly, 62*(4), 340–357.

Bybee, R. W. (2010). Advancing STEM education: A 2020 vision. *Technology & Engineering Teacher, 70*(1), 30–35.

Carr, W., & Kemmis, S. (1986). *Becoming critical: Education, knowledge and action research*. Philadelphia, PA: Falmer Press.

Clarke, D. A. G., & Mcphie, J. (2016). From places to paths: Learning for sustainability, teacher education and a philosophy of becoming. *Environmental Education Research, 22*(7), 1002–1024.

Committee on STEM Education, National Science and Technology Council. (2013). *Federal science, technology, engineering, and mathematics (STEM) education: 5-year strategic plan. Committee on STEM Education National Science and Technology Council*. Washington, DC: National Science and Technology Council. Retrieved August

18, 2019, from https://ntrl.ntis.gov/NTRL/dashboard/searchResults/titleDetail/
PB2013108885.xhtml

Cultural Learning Alliance. (n.d.). *Evidence*. Retrieved August 18, 2019, from
https://culturallearningalliance.org.uk/evidence/

Delors, J., Al Mufti, I., Amagi, I., Carneiro, R., Chung, F., Geremek, B., ... Nanzhao, Z.
(1996). *Learning: The treasure within. Report to UNESCO of the International Commission on Education for the twenty-first century*. Paris: UNESCO.

Denmead, T. (2011). Being and becoming: Elements of pedagogies described by three
East Anglian creative practitioners. *International Journal of Thinking Skills and Creativity, 6*(1), 57–66.

Dewey, J. (1959). Experience and education. New York, NY: Macmillan.

Di Tommaso, M. L. (2006). *Measuring the wellbeing of children using a capabil-
ity approach: An application to Indian data* (CHILD Working Paper No. 5/2006).
Turin, Italy: Centre for Household, Income, Labour and Demographic Economics.
Retrieved August 18, 2019, from https://ideas.repec.org/p/wpc/wplist/wp05_06.html

Douglas, K. M., & Jaquith, D. B. (2009). *Engaging learners through artmaking: Choice-
based art education in the classroom*. New York, NY: Teachers College Press.

Fattore, T., Mason, J., & Watson, E. (2007). Children's conceptualisation(s) of their wellbeing. Social Indicators Research, 80(1), 5–29.

Frumkin, H., Bratman, G. N., Breslow, S. J., Cochran, B., Kahn Jr., P. H., Lawler, J. J., ...
Wood, S. A. (2017). Nature contact and human health: A research agenda. *Environmental Health Perspectives, 125*(7). doi:10.1289/EHP1663

Fettes, M., & Judson, G. (2010). Imagination and the cognitive tools of place-making.
Journal of Environmental Education, 42(2), 123–135.

Gannon, S. (2017). Saving squawk? Animal and human entanglement at the edge of the
lagoon. *Environmental Education Research, 23*(1), 91–110.

Green, A. E., & White, R. J. (2007). *Attachment to place: Social networks, mobility and
prospects of young people*. Warwick: Joseph Rowntree Foundation.

Hanushek, E. A., Jamison, D. T., Jamison, E. A., & Woessmann, L. (2008). Education and
economic growth: It's not just going to school, but learning something while there
that matters. *EdNext, 8*, 62–70.

Haraway, D. (2015). Anthropocene, capitalocene, plantationocene, chthulucene:
Making kin. *Environmental Humanities, 6*, 159–165.

Hojman, D. A., & Miranda, A. (2018). Agency, human dignity and subjective well-being.
World Development, 101, 1–15.

House of Commons Committee of Public Accounts. (2018). *Delivering STEM skills for
the economy: Forty-seventh report of session 2017–2019*. London: House of Commons.
Retrieved August 18, 2019, from https://publications.parliament.uk/pa/cm201719/
cmselect/cmpubacc/691/691.pdf

Irvine, R. D. G, Lee, E., Strubel, R., & Bodenhorn, B. (2016). Exclusion and reappropria-tion: Experiences of contemporary enclosure among children in three East Anglian schools. *Environment and Planning D: Society and Space, 34*(5), 935–953.

Karkou, V., & Glasman, J. (2004). Arts, education and society: The role of the arts in promoting the emotional wellbeing and social inclusion of young people. *Support for Learning, 19*(2), 57–65.

Kinder, K., & Harland, J. (2004). The arts and social inclusion: What's the evidence? *Support for Learning, 19*(2), 52–56.

Kolb, D. A. (1984). *Experiential learning: Experience as the source of learning and devel-opment* (Vol. 1). Englewood Cliffs, NJ: Prentice-Hall.

Lee, E., Walshe, N., Sapsed R., & Holland, J. (2018). Artists as emplaced pedagogues: How does thinking about children's nature relations influence pedagogy? In A. Cutter-Mackenzie, K. Malone, & E. Barratt Hacking (Eds.), *Research handbook on childhoodnature: Assemblages of childhood and nature research* (pp. 1–24). Cham: Springer. doi:10.1007/978-3-319-51949-4_78-1

Lindgren, N., & Öhman, J. (2018). A posthuman approach to human–animal relation-ships: Advocating critical pluralism. *Environmental Education Research* [Preprint]. doi:10.1080/13504622.2018.1450848

Louv, R. (2008). *Last child in the woods: Saving our children from nature-deficit disorder.* Chapel Hill, NC: Algonquin Books.

Malone, K. (2007). The bubble-wrap generation: Children growing up in walled gardens. *Environmental Education Research, 13*(4), 513–27. https://doi.org/10.1080/13504620701581612

Malone, K. (2015). Theorizing a child–dog encounter in the slums of La Paz using post-humanistic approaches in order to disrupt universalisms in current "child in nature" debates. *Children's Geographies, 14*(4), 390–407. https://doi.org/10.1080/14733285.2015.1077369

Marginson, S., Tytler, R., Freeman, B., & Roberts, K. (2013). *STEM: Country compari-sons: International comparisons of Science, Technology, Engineering and Math-ematics (STEM) education. Final report.* Melbourne: Australian Council of Learned Academies. Retrieved August 18, 2019, from https://dro.deakin.edu.au/eserv/DU:30059041/tytler-stemcountry-2013.pdf

Massey, D. (1994). *Space, place and gender.* Oxford: Blackwell Publishers.

McGillivray, M. (2007). Human well-being: Issues, concepts and measures. In M. McGillivray (Ed.), *Human well-being: Concept and measurement* (pp. 1–22). Helsinki: UNU Wider.

McRobie, H. (2014, March 7). Martha Nussbaum, empathy and the moral imagination. *Open Democracy.* Retrieved August 18, 2019, from https://www.opendemocracy.net/5050/heather-mcrobie/martha-nussbaum-empathy-and-moral-imagination

Muffels, R., & Headey, B. (2013). Capabilities and choices: Do they make sense for understanding objective and subjective well-being? An empirical test of Sen's capability framework on German and British panel data. *Social Indicators Research,* 110(3), 1159–1185.

National Academy of Sciences. (2007). *Taking science to school: Learning and teaching science in Grades K–8.* Washington, DC: National Academies Press. Retrieved August 18, 2019, from https://www.nap.edu/read/11625/chapter/1

National Endowment for the Arts. (2015). *2015 annual report.* Washington, DC: National Endowment for the Arts. Retrieved August 18, 2019, from https://www.arts.gov/ sites/default/files/2015%20Annual%20Report.pdf

National Society for Education in Art and Design. (2016). *The National Society for education in art and design survey report 2015–16.* Wiltshire: NSEAD. Retrieved August 18, 2019, from http://www.nsead.org/downloads/survey.pdf

Nussbaum, M. (1995). *Poetic justice: The literary imagination and public life.* Boston, MA: Beacon Press.

Nussbaum, M. (2000). *Women and human development: The capabilities approach.* Cambridge: Cambridge University Press.

Office of the Chief Scientist. (2013). *Science, technology, engineering and mathematics in the national interest: A strategic approach.* Canberra: Australian Government. Retrieved August 18, 2019, from https://www.chiefscientist.gov.au/wp-content/ uploads/STEMstrategy290713FINALweb.pdf

Office of the Chief Scientist. (2014). *Science, technology, engineering and mathematics: Australia's future.* Canberra: Australian Government. Retrieved August 18, 2019, from https://www.chiefscientist.gov.au/wp-content/uploads/ STEM_AustraliasFuture_Sept2014_Web.pdf

Osborne, J. (2000). Science for citizenship. In J. Osborne & M. Monk (Eds.), *Good practice in science teaching: What research has to say* (pp. 46–67). Berkshire: Open University Press.

Pitt, J. (2009). Blurring the boundaries – STEM education and education for sustainable development. *Design and Technology Education: An International Journal,* 14(1), 37–48.

Public Health England. (2018). *Wellbeing and mental health: Applying all our health.* London: Public Health England. Retrieved August 18, 2019, from https://www.gov.uk/ government/publications/wellbeing-in-mental-health-applying-all-our-health/ wellbeing-in-mental-health-applying-all-our-health

Rautio, P. (2013). Children who carry stones in their pockets: On autotelic material practices in everyday life. *Children's Geographies,* 11(4), 394–408.

Robeyns, I. (2006). The capability approach in practice. *Journal of Political Philosophy,* 14(3), 351–376.

Rocard, M., Csermeley, P., Jorde, D., Lenzen, D., Walberg-Henriksson, H., & Hemmo, V. (2007). *Science education NOW: A renewed pedagogy for the future of Europe.* Brussels: European Commission. Retrieved August 18, 2019, from https://ec.europa.eu/research/science-society/document_library/pdf_06/report-rocard-on-science-education_en.pdf

Roschelle, J., Bakia, M., Toyama, Y., & Patton, C. (2011). Eight issues for learning scientists about education and the economy. *Journal of Learning Sciences, 20,* 3–49.

Rose, G. (2005). *Visual methodologies.* London: Sage.

Saito, M. (2003). Amartya Sen's capability approach to education: A critical exploration. *Journal of Philosophy of Education, 37*(1), 17–33.

Scott, K. (2012). *Measuring wellbeing: Towards sustainability?* London: Routledge.

Secker, J., Heydinrych, K., Kent, L., & Keay, J. (2017). Why art? Exploring the contribution to mental well-being of the creative aspects and processes of visual art-making in an arts and mental health course. *Arts & Health, 10*(1), 72–84.

Sen, A. (1980). Equality of what? In S. M. MacMurrin (Ed.), *The Tanner lectures on human values* (pp. 195–220). Salt Lake City, UT: University of Utah Press.

Sen, A. (1989). Women's survival as a development problem. *Bulletin of the American Academy of Arts and Sciences, 43*(2), 14–29.

Sen, A. (1992). *Inequality reexamined.* Oxford: Oxford University Press.

Sen, A. (1993). Capability and well-being. In M. Nussbaum & A. Sen (Eds.), *The quality of life* (pp. 30–53). Oxford: Clarendon Press.

Sen, A. (1999). *Development as freedom.* Oxford: Oxford University Press.

Sen, A. (2002). Globalization, inequality and global protest. *Development, 45*(2), 11–16.

Simonneaux, J., & Simonneaux, L. (2012). Educational configurations for teaching environmental socioscientific issues within the perspective of sustainability. *Research in Science Education, 42*(1), 75–94.

Sneddon, C., Howarth, R. B., & Norgaard, R. B. (2006). Sustainable development in a post-Brundtland world. *Ecological Economics, 57,* 253–268.

Spencer, C., & Woolley, H. (2000). Children and the city: A summary of recent environmental psychology research. *Child: Care, Health and Development, 26*(3), 181–198.

Stuckey, H. L., & Nobel, J. (2010). The connection between art, healing and public health: A review of current literature. *American Journal of Public Health, 100*(2), 254–263.

Sümen, O. O., & Çalışıcı, H. (2016). Pre-service teachers' mind maps and opinions on STEM education implemented in an environmental literacy course. *Educational Sciences: Theory & Practice, 16,* 459–476.

Taylor, A. (2013). *Reconfiguring the natures of childhood.* London: Routledge.

Taylor, A. (2017). Beyond stewardship: Common world pedagogies for the Anthropocene. *Environmental Education Research, 23*(10), 1448–1461.

Twigger-Ross, C. L., & Uzzell, D. L. (1996). Place and identity processes. *Journal of Environmental Psychology, 16*(3), 205–229.

Uhlenwinkel, A., Béneker, T., Bladh, G., Tani, S., & Lambert, D. (2017). GeoCapabilities and curriculum leadership: Balancing the priorities of aim-based and knowledge-led curriculum thinking in schools. *International Research in Geographical and Environmental Education, 26*(4), 327–341.

Underwood, K., Chan, C., Koller, D., & Valeo, A. (2015). Understanding young children's capabilities: Approaches to interviews with young children experiencing disability. *Child Care in Practice, 21*(3), 220–237.

Van Ootegem, L., & Verhofstadt, E. (2012). Using capabilities as an alternative indicator for well-being. *Social Indicators Research, 106*(1), 133–152.

Walkington, H., Dyer, S., Solem, M., Haigh, M., & Waddington, S. (2018). A capabilities approach to higher education: Geocapabilities and implications for geography curricular. *Journal of Geography in Higher Education, 42*(1), 7–42.

Walshe, N., Lee, E., & Smith, M. (forthcoming). Supporting children's wellbeing with art in nature: Artist pedagogue perceptions. *Journal of Education for Sustainable Development, 13*(1).

Watene, K. (2016). Valuing nature: Māori philosophy and the capability approach. *Oxford Development Studies, 44*(3), 287–296.

Welzel, C., & Inglehart, R. (2010). Agency, values, and well-being: A human development model. *Social Indicators Research, 97*(1), 43–63.

Whitehead, T. L. (2004). *What is ethnography? Methodological, ontological and epistemological attributes* (CuSAG Working Paper Series). College Park, MD: Department of Anthropology, University of Maryland.

WHO. (2016). *World health statistics 2016: Monitoring health for the SDGs.* Geneva: World Health Organisation. Retrieved August 18, 2019, from https://www.who.int/gho/publications/world_health_statistics/2016/en/

Zitcer, A., Hawkins, J., & Vakharia, N. (2016). A capabilities approach to arts and culture? Theorizing community development in West Philadelphia. *Planning Theory and Practice, 17*(1), 35–51.

CHAPTER 15

Taste as Science, Aesthetic Experience and Inquiry

Erik Fooladi

Abstract

This chapter explores STEAM from a transdisciplinary perspective where sense/ory experiences are made explicit in the process of teaching and learning. In dialogue with John Dewey's last complete work, *Art as Experience*, possibilities of engaging a wider array of sensuous perceptions in the interface between sciences and arts are explored. Two innovative teaching activities are described and discussed where taste (ambiguity intended) and acts of tasting play key roles. Theory and research-based knowledge is sought put to work, thus shedding light on possibilities and challenges for teaching of, and through, inquiry in the interface between subject domains with distinct practices and epistemologies. Through rich descriptions, looking closely and paying attention to details and specifics, simplistic and overly optimistic descriptions of STEAM initiatives are sought avoided. Departure is taken from some major challenges in science and STEM education, ultimately seeking to open a space where some challenges in arts education may also be met. Finally, challenges, frictions and the possible transformative power of such integration for the respective subjects is discussed.

Keywords

aesthetic experience – arts – Dewey – inquiry – science – STEAM – taste – transdisciplinary

1   Introduction

Numerous approaches to science education have been proposed to meet challenges of relevance and the role of science in an "education for all". Examples are STS (science, technology, society), problem-based approaches and, indeed, STEAM. Aikenhead (2006) and Gilbert (2006), from their respective perspectives of humanistic science education and context-based science education, have described a problematic gap between, on the one side, science as taught in school and, on the other, learners' lives outside the classroom. This gap, they contend, results in lack of transfer of knowledge from the classroom to other situations as well as a lack of experienced relevance of STEM subjects (for others voicing similar arguments, see e.g., Calabrese Barton, Furman, Muir, Barnes & Monaco, 2007; Roth & Lee, 2004). Aikenhead's (2006; 2015) notion of humanistic science education emphasises the need to take the students' perspectives, valuing the students' cultures and social settings, as opposed to seeking to "assimilate" the students into the subculture of science: The main purpose of science/STEM education cannot be to educate future scientists and technologists, "pipeline" or preprofessional notions of science education, but rather to provide a science education relevant for all. Gilbert (2006) provides a possible strategy to meet this challenge: explicitly contextualising science into everyday or relevant situations. The consequence of such contextualisation of science content is that the teacher's perspective must turn from seeking to make a given predefined content appear relevant to the learners, to asking: which science content and practices are relevant in dealing with this specific question/situation? Taught content, be it declarative knowledge ("science facts") or procedural knowledge (scientific methods and ways of thinking), should be sought on a need-to-know basis, only when it is relevant to shed light on the issue under study. The *context*, rather than the *content*, becomes the starting point. Consequently, not only scientific knowledge but also knowledge from other domains, of extra-situational nature, may be of importance and should be considered when carrying out context-based teaching.

2   On Senses and Taste

> "Sense" covers a wide range of contents: the sensory, the sensational, the sensitive, the sensible, and the sentimental, along with the sensuous. It includes almost everything from bare physical and emotional shock to sense itself   that is, the meaning of things present in immediate experience. (Dewey, 1980: 22)

As humans we have five senses with their concomitant potential for sense experiences (ambiguity intended, cf. quotation above). In the Western philosophical and aesthetic traditions, however, there appears to be an implicit sensory hierarchy, with priority given to sight and hearing as "the higher senses" whilst olfaction/smell, taste and somatosensation/touch are considered "lower senses" (Korsmeyer, 2004). In the work herein, I bring sense experiences other than sight and hearing to the forefront of scientific and aesthetic inquiry. Specifically, I seek to show how the sense of taste, seldom used explicitly or consciously in education, can be a doorway into both science and aesthetic experience. Inspired by Gregory Bateson's (1972) notion of metalogue, a conversation about a subject where the structure of the conversation itself sheds light on the subject, I set off with a narrative to illustrate the role taste can play in science and aesthetic experience, and conversely, the role science can play in aesthetic experiences. This provides a bridge to the subsequent empirical material from two STEAM-oriented classroom cases. The chapter concludes with a general discussion of possibilities, challenges and implications inherent in the two cases as well as in transdisciplinary teaching that employs a broader set of senses than only sight and hearing. I now turn to the rich description of an example that I believe illustrates Aikenhead's and Gilbert's points concerning the role of scientific knowledge and how it is contextualised. The context, or social circumstance (Gilbert, 2006), is something so apparently mundane and trivial as a cup of coffee in a coffee bar.

2.1   "I Really Wish I Had a Gas Chromatographer at Home"

This statement was made by a barista during a taxi ride we had together some years ago. It was a peculiar comment from an individual whose highest scientific education according to himself was upper secondary school. How did the barista come to know what a gas chromatographer is? How did he conceptualise that this piece of advanced scientific instrument could be put to relevant use by a barista? I will try to shed light on how I conceptualise this barista's interest in rather advanced scientific and socio-scientific knowledge through the following imagined but realistic dialogue between him and a customer in the coffee bar later that day:

Customer (C):   Is today's coffee single-origin?

Barista (B):   Yes, it is from a farmer cooperative in the Yirgacheffe region, Ethiopia.

C: Is it fair trade? The package doesn't say ...?

B: It's not certified fair trade, no. It's direct trade between the cooperative and our roastery. If farmers want to be certified as fair trade, they must pay a fee to the fair-trade program. In return they get 25% above market price. But the coffee would still go through up to seven steps from farmer to your cup, each one taking out some profit. When *we* buy the coffee *directly*, the only intermediary between the farmer and you is the roastery., & we pay up to five times market price because we collaborate with the farmers to get beans of highest possible quality. The berries of the coffee plant don't ripen all at the same time; you've got to return to the plant several times [pointing to a poster on the wall showing various stages of coffee bean growth]. You want to avoid unripe green and yellow berries, as well as overripe and partially rotten ones, because they give off-flavours to the coffee. We pay the farmer more to compensate for the added effort and lower volume as they must discard under-/overripe berries. Some large-scale producers just strip the whole shrubs in one go, getting a mixture of green, yellow, red and overripe berries. Then they roast the coffee darker to burn away the off-flavours. But at the same time, they sacrifice the characteristics of that specific coffee.

C: Yeah, the beans from that other coffee brand are really black ...

B: Roasting is about finding a balance between raw green beans at the one extreme, and charcoal at the other. The lighter you roast, the more of the character is retained., & the roasting profile, the temperature *history* the beans experience, makes a difference. So, we roast this coffee a bit differently than that Colombia over there. But profile is a matter of taste as well, although I don't see the point in paying five times market price for a great coffee and then roasting all the character out of it.

C [tasting the coffee]: Wow, this was really something special! Really fruity, almost like a tea. It smells a bit like strawberry, almost. But less tart than the Kenya I got the other day.

B: Yes, I find it high on sweetness. But still juicy, with strawberry, jasmine and citrus aromas. Some of this comes from the beans themselves and some from the processing.

C [reading the label]: "Process: natural?"

B: The berries lie to dry on raised beds for several weeks, flesh on. The flesh turns into a dry shell and is removed mechanically. Some areas have little access to water, so wet processing where the berries are de-pulped and soaked in water to ferment for a day or three is not always an option. Many South and Central American coffees are washed, so they get a different flavour profile. But some areas, especially in Africa, simply haven't got access to that much water. It's a question of climate and resources, ... and taste, I guess., & coffee plant variety, of course. This one is Ethiopian Heirloom.

C: So, how would you brew this one?

B: I prefer pour-over. I use a slightly coarser grind because I find that the water tends to go slower through for very light roasted coffees. That way I don't over-extract, I avoid bitterness but still retain the fruitiness.

C: But I like the bitterness ...

B: OK, if you like, I'll grind it a little finer. The particles will be smaller, and you'll get a more complete extraction. You might lose some transparency, it won't taste as clean. Or I could make you the Brazil which is a washed coffee of different variety and style, with more chocolate, toast and tobacco aromas?

C: I'll go for the Ethiopia. It would've been interesting to do a blind tasting with different grinder settings, though.

B   [brewing]: We haven't done that for this one.

B   [after a pause, still brewing]: We're a bit worried these days because the average temperatures in the tropics have been rising steadily over years. Yirgacheffe coffee is often grown in the forest among other species at around 2000 metres, not like the large plantations in the Americas where you have long rows of coffee plants and some palms for shade. In a few years, the conditions might not be suitable for this cooperative to grow coffee anymore. The farmers will have to move, maybe, or find something else to grow.

2.2   *Discussion of the Narrative: Dimensions of Taste*

The list of science-related topics in this dialogue is long: plant physiology, agriculture, climate and climate change, aqueous solutions, extraction, chemical reactions, socio-scientific issues, scientific inquiry methods. However, the fact that there is science to be found in coffee and coffee production is not the main point. What separates this dialogue from many teaching/learning situations is the *trajectory* in which science is approached, and the role it plays in the dialogue. Returning to Gilbert's (2006) context-based perspective and Aikenhead's (2006) humanistic science education, the question of interest is not whether science can be found within the issue, but whether it makes a difference, without taking hegemony of the context. After all, few customers enter a coffee bar for a science lesson; the purpose and centrepiece of the dialogue is that singular cup of coffee. Still, science is instrumental in understanding, talking about and even appreciating the coffee. Some scientific knowledge is present in the foreground – sustainability, plant physiology, and extraction – whilst other aspects are accessed only in deliberate interaction with the experience of tasting. Furthermore, when the customer brings up blind tasting, a scientific method in itself but also inextricably linked to the aesthetic aspects of tasting coffee, the aesthetic experience becomes a doorway to a scientific practice.

In this narrative, "taste" appears in different forms/dimensions, of which I choose to draw out three[1]: (1) taste as a physiological sense perception, such as bitterness; (2) taste as an act of analysis, evaluation or judgement, be it descriptive or normative; and (3) taste as an act of perceived aesthetic experience (enjoyment, disgust, existential, sublime, etc.).

Dimension 1, comprising descriptions of the basic tastes, sweet, sour, bitter and so forth, is traditionally encountered as declarative science knowledge in science classrooms, taught as part of human physiology. In this dimension, however, the learner need not be much more than a passive spectator of their own senses, often abstracted and decontextualised from the contexts where tasting normally occurs: eating and drinking. Taste is a noun, something to be observed; "the sense of taste". In dimensions 2 and 3, taste takes the function of a verb for possible types of actions. Dimension 2 may be framed as a method of scientific inquiry from the domain of sensory science (Meilgaard, Civille, & Carr, 1999; Martens, 1999), a seemingly uncharted territory for most science educators. The conception of taste as an act of analysis may, however, also include aesthetic judgement: "off-flavours", "high on sweetness" and so on. Thus, boundaries between "scientific" and "aesthetic" are blurred; it is not clear where the scientific ends and aesthetic starts and vice versa. Still, such acts of tasting facilitate an external purpose. They hold extrinsic meaning, namely that of evaluation of a product. In dimension 3, the experience itself is the main purpose, such as the customer's expression of surprise and enjoyment: "Wow, this was really something special!" This perspective is seldom met in science education but is often met in arts education and philosophy through discussions of extrinsic versus intrinsic meaning (e.g. Jackson, 1998), and aesthetic autonomy versus heteronomy (e.g. Varkøy, 2015). I will return to this aspect in the discussion of the two classroom cases.

2.3   Dewey on Art and Aesthetic Experience

> As long as art is the beauty parlor of civilization, neither art nor civilization is secure. (Dewey, 1980: 344)

Dewey's notion of art is broad, partially overlapping with what is often termed crafts. With Dewey the distinction between the two is not always clear, and contrary to (e.g.) Kant, he seems to resist drawing sharp lines between the two. Dewey uses pottery as an example of this fluid boundary, where objects of former daily use later become artefacts for display in galleries. Since the days of Dewey, the arts have expanded and developed to include amongst others performance art, conceptual art (e.g. ready-mades, c.f. Marcel Duchamp's urinal piece "fountain"), photography and possibly gastronomy (see Korsmeyer, 2004, for a discussion on gastronomy as art). Indeed, Dewey anticipated and welcomed such change, and was critical of a static conservationist notion of aesthetic value (e.g. Dewey, 1980: 303, 306). He also operates with a broad notion of aesthetic experience across multiple contexts, not exclusively associated with formal arts. He does, however, not expand much on this latter aspect except to link it to his notion of "*an* experience"; a coherent experience running to fulfilment, as opposed to "mere" experience. He exemplifies *an* experience to include such things as "the zest of the spectator in poking the wood burning on the hearth" (Dewey, 1980: 5). For *an* experience to be aesthetic, it must be one of expressive nature with intrinsic meaning, consummatory and final, and not solely of a practical or utilitarian purpose (Jackson, 1998: 29). Aesthetic experiences hold an emotional character and may well occur outside the formalised arts. Unfortunately, after introducing this notion of aesthetic experience he appears to leave this perspective of "mundane aesthetic experiences" and limit his in-depth discussions to arts and crafts. As demonstrated in the coffee narrative, I focus on experiences that are not necessarily associated with the formal arts but seek to expand on aspects that Dewey did not seem to explore in depth. Whether the experience qualifies as *an* experience is not only a product of the perceived object but one that occurs in the interaction between the thing sensed and the sensing individual. The aesthetic is not inherent in the object; it is transactional (Jackson, 1998: 3). The one and same object may elicit an aesthetic experience or not when perceived by an individual; it is the nature of the encounter which defines whether the experience is aesthetic. Conversely, "[t] here [may be] experience, but so slack and discursive that it is not *an* experience. Needless to say, such experiences are anesthetic" (Dewey, 1980, emphasis in original). In the coffee bar narrative, the customer could have consumed the coffee for her habitual dose of caffeine on the way home without further attention to the experience. The very same cup of coffee would be ingested, the same aroma compounds would reach her nose, the same tastants would make receptors in her mouth fire off taste signals to the brain. But there would not be *an* experience in Dewey's sense.[2] On the other hand, the coffee as *an* experience could become a memorable one, an "experiential object" (Jackson, 1998: 24), to be referred to in retrospect and savoured for the rest of her life. This way, aesthetic experiences may form a "background" to take the shape of, or be filled by, expressive meaning for later use (Dewey, 1980: 264; Uhrmacher, 2009: 622). For this person, the characteristic strawberry aroma in some coffees may for ever be associated with "Yirgacheffe" as a general concept. Like the famous madeleine cakes of Marcel Proust, the mere scent may evoke a stream of reflections about coffee region, harvest strategies, farmers struggling due to global warming, roasting profiles, grinding, pleasure, particle size-dependence of hot water extracts and so on. Conversely, knowledge can modulate and enrich future aesthetic experiences: The knowledge of characteristics of Ethiopian coffee and all that follows from it can add layers of depth to the aesthetic experience the next time the customer recognises it in a cup of coffee. Expectations are evoked by the mere sight of a bag of Ethiopian coffee: "How would this coffee from Sidamo compare with the Yirgacheffe I got that time at the coffee bar?" Finally, what if the narrative *had* gone as earlier described but the customer found the coffee utterly unpalatable? Would it then have been an aesthetic experience? Dewey would probably answer confirmatory, because "[w]hether the necessary undergoing phase is by itself pleasurable or painful is a matter of particular conditions. It is indifferent to the total esthetic quality, save that there are few intense esthetic experiences that are wholly gleeful" (Dewey, 1980: 41). Even though an aesthetic experience may be one of pleasure or beauty, it may just as well be one of discomfort/disturbance or even disgust, of mixed feelings, puzzlement, or of neutral observation, whilst still not devoid of emotions.[3] As succinctly described by Østergaard (2017) from the perspective of science education and Fossum and Varkøy (2012) from music education, aesthetic is not equivalent with, or limited to, neither beauty nor pleasure. Most likely, such reduction based on an everyday language notion of "aesthetic" would be considered fallacious from a Kantian (Fossum and Varkøy, 2012), Deweyan, as well as more recent theory on aesthetics (this is particularly present in feministic perspectives, see Korsmeyer, 2004).

2.4   *Some Words of Clarification*
Herein, I use the word "perception" to denote a distinct sensory impulse whilst "experience", in line with Dewey, is used to denote a more holistic and complete experience. Dewey also introduced the word "impulsion" to denote a more outward-oriented movement by the perceiver, a

> movement of the organism to which special impulses are auxiliary, ... the turning toward light of the body as a whole, like the heliotropism of plants, as distinct from the following of a particular light by the eyes. ... the initial stage of any complete experience. (Dewey, 1980: 58)

Dewey's use of "impulse" is in my understanding similar to what we from a physiological perspective would denote a "perception", in Dewey's words more "specialized and particular". Furthermore, I use "taste" rather than "flavour", although the latter would be formally correct since any act of putting something in one's mouth is a multisensory experience, instantaneously engaging all our senses: aroma/smell, texture/touch, visual cues such as colour or shape, hearing such as crunching and so forth (Auvray & Spence, 2008). "Taste", however, bears much broader connotations than that of the mouth: "personal taste", "good taste", taste in a Kantian sense and so forth. My conflations and reductions herein are intentional, and inspired by Wittgenstein (2009), I trust that the meaning of "taste" will be given by its use in context. This allows for a smoother discussion with theory and other research, thus opening a space for discussing encounters between scientific and aesthetic notions of taste. Only when explicitly required, I use "flavour", "aroma", "texture" and so forth. Since Dewey's broad notions of what may count as art and aesthetic are also taken herein, I will allow "aesthetic(s)" to replace "art" in the acronym STEAM. By centring the discussion around aesthetic rather than art, a more general philosophical discussion of what qualifies as art is avoided or postponed, to be discussed elsewhere (e.g. questions such as "Can a barista be called an artist?"). I choose to centre the perspectives on STEM education mostly towards the sciences and will not probe deep into issues of mathematics or technology education, although at least mathematics education would be a possible avenue as may be visible from the two cases described below.

In the following, I turn to two classroom cases where the perspectives from the narrative and discussion above are transferred to classroom settings, at the same time seeking to maintain a balance between the analytic and aesthetic, and between science and arts.

3   Case 1: The Cookie Project (STEAM Leaning towards Science)

The first case is a teaching sequence designed by pre-service teachers as part of an undergraduate course on context-based inquiry teaching (Herranen et al., 2019). It is an inquiry project about leavening agents in cookies, with multiple possible learning goals depending on the chosen emphasis (chemical substances or reactions, acids/bases and pH, design and conduct of open experiments, development of concepts related to taste, sensory awareness and perceptual acuity, baking, etc.). The starting point is that when we bake cookies, we have access to three different chemical leavening agents to produce gas, usually carbon dioxide, and thus raise the baked product. Questions posed as motivation for inquiry were: What happens if we replace one leavening agent with another? And more generally, why do we need three different leavening agents in the kitchen at all: couldn't we make do with one? The teaching sequence was designed for and tested with Finnish students of age 13–15 but has also been carried out in chemistry lessons with a Finnish upper secondary class of music and plastic arts specialisation, as well as in home economics pre-service teacher education. The practical part of the sequence is of primary interest and is described in the following.

3.1   Part One: A Classical Chemistry Lab Activity (2 Hours)

The three leavening agents are not only food ingredients but may also be considered from a purely chemical perspective. We assume that the purpose of using leavening agents is to make the baked product rise, to produce gas:

– baking powder: a composite product based on sodium hydrogen carbonate ($NaHCO_3$) and one or two solid acids. It requires liquid to react to produce carbon dioxide (CO_2).
– baking soda: pure $NaHCO_3$. It requires an acidic ingredient (juice, buttermilk, etc.) and liquid to react and produce CO_2.
– hartshorn salt: pure ammonium hydrogen carbonate (NH_4HCO_3). Upon heating, it decomposes to the gases ammonia (NH_3), CO_2 and water vapour, hence functioning also in drier doughs.

The three leavening agents were tested for which conditions and with which additional ingredients they would produce gas: cold water, warm water, reaction with various acidic ingredients (lemon juice, citric acid powder, vinegar). For each parallel, the experiment was conducted by putting a teaspoon of leavening agent into a balloon, placing the balloon over the neck of an Erlenmeyer flask with water or another ingredient, and emptying the balloon contents into the flask. Gas evolution could be monitored by the degree to which the balloon inflated (Figure 15.1). This would give hints to necessary conditions when using the various leavening agents.

This experiment is open as it is prone to many variations, but chemically the result is closed/predefined, and it is justifiable to say that the activity falls within one of many notions of inquiry (Herranen et al., 2019). One may conclude from the experiment that chemistry can give an answer to why, or how, leavening agents are used, namely: if your recipe contains an acid, use baking soda. If your dough is rather dry, use hartshorn salt. In other cases, baking powder is a good bet (Table 15.1).

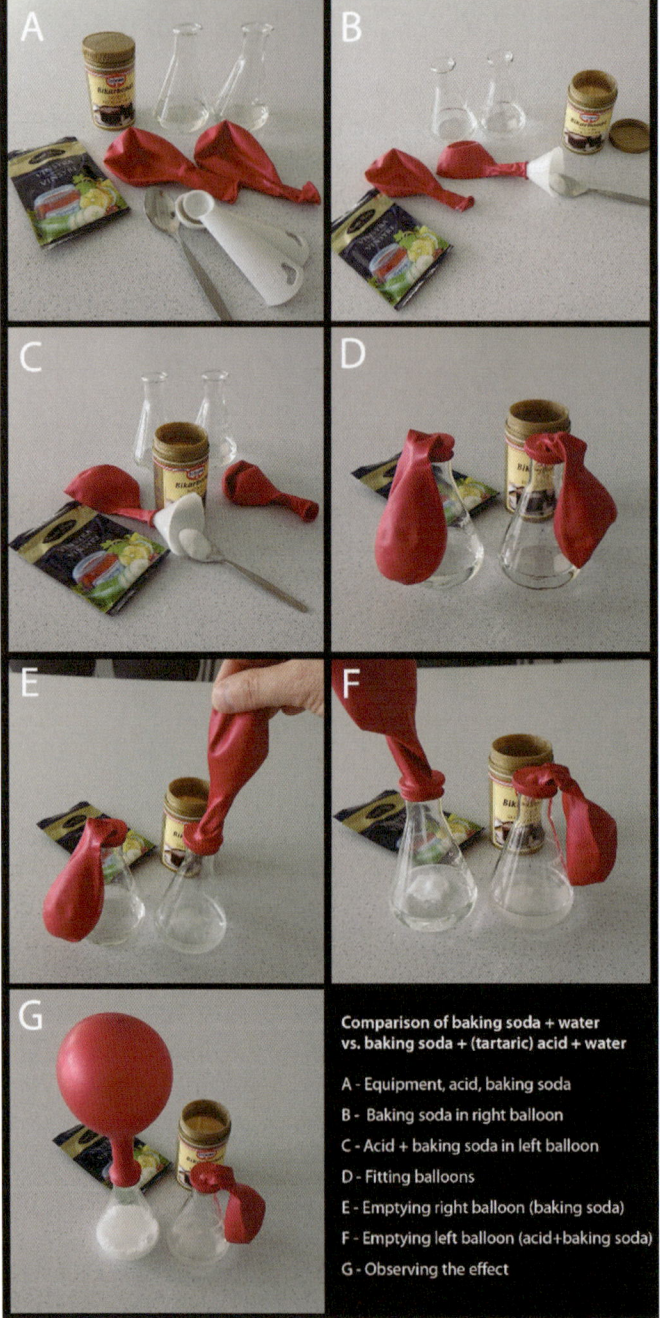

FIGURE 15.1   Testing leavening agent action in the lab, here baking soda in cold water with and
without a solid acid

TABLE 15.1   Results from chemistry lab activity showing under which conditions and with which other ingredients the three leavening agents may function (+ = gas production; – = no gas production; +/– = a little gas production; ? = ambiguous result)

	Baking powder	Baking soda	Hartshorn salt
Cold water	+/–	–	–
Warm water	+	–	?
Lemon juice	+	+	?
Vinegar	+	+	?
Citric acid (solid)	+	+	?
Etc.	...	...	...

3.2   Part Two: Baking and Blind Tasting Cookies (Homework or Cooking Class + 2 Hours)

In this part, students were asked to bake cookies at home, or in cooking class, using the exact same recipe and procedure while varying the leavening agent. Each group was asked to bake two batches of cookies with two different leavening agents. This way, variations between groups could be controlled for (Table 15.2).

TABLE 15.2   Task distribution for cookie baking homework to test effect of leavening agent

	Baking powder	Baking soda	Hartshorn salt
Group A	🍪	🍪	
Group B	🍪		🍪
Group C		🍪	🍪
Etc.			

The student groups brought the cookies to school for blind tasting. When setting up a blind tasting one must decide which characteristics should be evaluated. In this case the teacher had anticipated possible variations in aspects such as sweetness, bitterness (unreacted carbonates taste bitter), lightness and darkness of colour, softness/hardness, porosity and nutty flavour. The students were asked to individually evaluate the cookies according to precisely defined characteristics and mark off their judgements in a table: "Which of the three is sweetest?", "Which of the three is darkest in colour?", "Which is most bitter?" and so on. Only at the very end, the students are asked to judge which they personally prefer.[4] Thereafter, the teacher takes up the results by hand raising: "How many thought cookie A was the sweetest?" and so on. The numbers are written on the whiteboard (Table 15.3).

TABLE 15.3   Example of results from blind tasting of cookies (names of columns are revealed after conducted the blind tasting)

	Baking powder	Baking soda	Hartshorn salt
Sweetest	24	0	18
Most bitter	9	16	12
Brownest/darkest	12	23	13
Lightest	21	5	21
Etc. (e.g. height)	...	...	...
Most preferred	19	9	15

Individual and subjective experiences, even barely noticeable differences, materialise as collective judgements and gain a more objective character. Qualitative can become quantitative, and differences perceived by individuals as marginal, or even barely noticeable, become trends when we are many. As the teacher takes the votes and writes them on the board, the results materialise in front of everyone to be discussed and reflected upon. Still, each student's personal experience is a valid one; there is no ultimate right or wrong, but patterns emerge that may be interpreted., & although the patterns may be similar from one class to another, the results will be unique every time the activity is carried out. Notably, the results in Table 15.3 indicate that the leavening agents do not primarily/only affect how much a baked product rises, but also other characteristics such as taste, colour and texture.

3.3   Discussion of Case 1

The most striking observation from this activity is that the proof of the pudding is literally in the eating, namely the act of tasting. The lab experiment alone provides results that appear sensible from a chemical point of view, but ones that are very different from those found when the cookies are actually baked. The leap from the apparently relevant lab experiment to the effect on the cookies is so great that it is unlikely that it could have been foreseen.

Indeed, the present author, browsing food science literature and conferring with a food science professor, has not been able to uncover the reasons for all the differences in products effected by the leavening agents. One clue, however, lies in the fact that Maillard browning reactions are pH dependent (e.g. Lersch, 2008). These colour- and flavour-producing reactions are accelerated in basic/ alkaline conditions and retarded in acidic conditions, thus indicating a reason for some of the results, while some differences are still not well accounted for. Hence, the activity is to be considered one of open inquiry where even food scientists may not have all the answers.

In science laboratories tasting is usually forbidden, but here the result of the lab experiment was at best incomplete, and at worst misleading. We had to move out of traditional school science to find answers for an issue that is inherently scientific, & we must draw on methods that are uncommon in the science class but may be familiar to the home economics teacher, well versed in judging products from a craft-based practice such as baking. Viewing leavening agents as chemicals, although they are rightly so, rather than ingredients leads to a lack of transferability between science class and life outside school. If we stopped at the lab experiment and the student brought this knowledge home to test, the most likely conclusion would be that science does not give us much useful information, but on the contrary may even lead to false conclusions. The insight that leavening agents may have a direct effect on Maillard reactions in cookies was only available subsequent to baking and tasting. Creativity is here conceptualised as the search for explanations, hypothesising retrospectively from the unforeseen results. It is knowledge-bound, but not solely from a scientific perspective. In open inquiry, choices are made throughout the process, based on creative thinking, scientific knowledge and crafts-based/experiential knowledge. Which properties should we evaluate in the blind tasting? How should we set up the experiment and distribute tasks? Which type of cookies will be best suited for the experiment? It is up to the teacher to decide which choices to leave to the students and which to be made by the teacher on behalf of the class. Nevertheless, each choice requires creative work on the part of either the teacher, the students or both.

As Gilbert and Aikenhead argue, science education must demonstrate its contextual credibility. In this case, credibility is not achieved unless one moves out of the lab and into the kitchen. The apparently trivial and non-academic act of tasting is shown to be scientifically pivotal. At the same time, this teaching sequence exemplifies the diversity of inquiry (Herranen et al., 2019). Context-based inquiry becomes an arena where aesthetic judgement, on equal terms with scientific practices, plays a significant role in building scientific understanding and knowledge, both declarative and procedural. Furthermore, drawing on sensory science, judgement of good versus bad and liked versus disliked is suspended, allowing time for reflection, before the students are asked to take a stance about which they would prefer themselves. The choice of *which questions to ask* when tasting something makes the whole difference, and thereby "a matter of taste" is redefined to become something collective that can be talked about rather than purely subjective and tacit.

4 Case 2: Crossmodal Correspondences in "the Porridge Activity" (STEAM Leaning towards Arts)

Neuroscience has shown that our senses work in a concerted manner, physiological sense perceptions being fused into complex multisensory ones. Such *crossmodal correspondences* operate via cognitive associations between senses, for example the colour red is associated with sweetness, sour taste is associated with high-pitch dissonant sounds, bitter taste with angular rather than rounded shapes and so forth (e.g. Spence, 2011). Drawing on these phenomena that we experience every day, but do not necessarily reflect upon, the second case describes an experimental teaching activity (Fooladi, 2018) in a small school in rural Norway featuring teachers Paul and Matthew (pseudonyms) and a mixed first to third grade class of age 6–9. The activity was inspired by one of the teachers' attendance at an event featuring a dish, porridge, from a cultural historical, scientific and multisensory perspective. In the lesson, learning goals were not predefined as we wanted to openly explore possibilities inherent in such activities. The empirical material consists of sound recording and photos from the teaching activity and two subsequent interviews with the teachers. The following narrative describes the sequence that lasted about 45 minutes.

> One day, Matthew brings food with him to class: two different types of porridge, an important cultural historical dish in the Nordic countries. One is a whole-grain oat porridge (A), the other a smooth spelt porridge (B), both mild and sweet tasting. He tells the students that they shall do an activity where they will explore how our senses may work together. He says it is common that we make connection between our senses, such as between what we hear and what we taste, and that these connections can be shared among people. They are to taste the porridges, and someone shall play the piano. The question for the class is to explore whether it is possible to play soundtracks to each of the two porridges so that those people tasting will recognise which soundscape represents which

porridge. After all, many composers say that their music is descriptive of things other than the music itself. Is it possible to hear those other things in the music? If so, can you create music that matches the taste experience, or even communicate a flavour experience through music? Matthew asks if anyone wants to take the piano and, although not a piano player, third grader Maria volunteers. She goes with Paul to another room with a piano, bringing a portion of the first porridge with her. She tastes it and reflects on how to convey her flavour experience using only the piano, trying out her ideas on the instrument. Her only available language is the music; no words of explanation can be uttered until after the experiment. Back in class, Maria sits at the classroom piano. The other students have helped themselves to a small portion of each porridge, ready to listen attentively while tasting. Without a word, Maria starts playing the music, lasting about 30 seconds.[5] Matthew asks the students to make their individual choices without telling anyone. They have three options: does the music correspond best with porridge A, porridge B or none/both? Or perhaps they do not feel there is any connection between sound and flavour at all (synonymous with the "none/both" choice)? The students are invited, one at a time, to come to the kitchen and point at the porridge they experience corresponds best with the music. Maria then tastes porridge B and the process is repeated.

The data has thus been collected using Maria's porridge-inspired musical performances and the students' personal sound–flavour associations. The teachers present the results to the class. It appears that many students share Maria's sound–flavour associations. The teachers are puzzled by the fact that many students seemed to have clear notions of how the porridges and music corresponded, and that Maria had no hesitations or problems conveying her sensory experiences via the piano. Subsequently, they could talk about this being a way we can explore things in similar ways to some scientists, that artists, scientists and chefs sometimes work together to explore or produce multisensory experiences, and that we in our own lives can make music and explore our own sensory experiences.[6]

During the subsequent interview, the teachers mentioned that one parent told that their child had talked about the porridge they had for dinner one day. He said the dinner porridge resembled one of those they had at school earlier. How so, the parents had asked. The child, a second language student, had problems putting into words the flavour, texture or experience of the porridge. He chose to describe it by mimicking playing the piano in a certain way as he had seen and heard Maria do for one of the porridges at school.

4.1   *Discussion of Case 2*

Although we do not necessarily reflect upon this in our daily doings, our perceptions of the world are fundamentally multisensory, and often it is difficult to discern where one sense ends, and another starts. Is it the smell, taste, texture or sound that makes a bite of apple what it is? As opposed to synaesthesia, a condition found among a small percentage of humans where one sensory stimulus elicits, often involuntarily, a perception in another sensory modality, crossmodal correspondences are *associations* experienced by all humans and have multiple sources of origin. Whilst synaesthesia is often idiosyncratic, crossmodal correspondences are often shared among individuals or within cultures and environments (Deroy & Spence, 2013).

In the described activity, students were invited to use their senses to move from subjective and individual experiences to a collective result that could be discussed both in the frame of aesthetic experience, and as data from/for scientific inquiry. The meeting of scientific counting and measuring with an aesthetic non-countable intuitive response, or in Maria's case musicianship, became an integrated whole. Scientific inquiry and aesthetic inquiry played co-equal roles, neither being subservient nor dominant (Bresler, 1995). The students' experiences, and the teachers' questions, concerned the aesthetic aspects of sound and flavour; it was an open inquiry for which no textbook can give an answer, but where empirical neuroscience may give hints (Spence, 2011). Sensory awareness, or perceptual acuity (Jackson, 1998: xiii, 5), was promoted as listening became a conscious and deliberate *action* in an Arendtian sense, a human activity with its own ends, as contrasted to the cyclical and never-ending Arendtian *labour* or instrumental *work* (Varkøy, 2015). This echoes Dewey's notions of *an* experience: "Such an experience is a whole and carries with it its own individualizing quality and self-sufficiency. It is *an* experience" (Dewey, 1980: 35, emphasis in original). Maria's improvisation is clearly creative in nature, but so also are the other students' attentive listening and tasting as they make their intuitive crossmodal connections (*viz.* choices). I envisage that this type of inquiry activity could be developed into further creative inquiry using the results from the experiment to produce further artistic expressions. Now that the students have identified links between flavour and sound, these links can be used to produce multisensory works of crafts and arts. What about a soundtrack to be played with a dish to enhance or modify the experience of a dish? As visualised in Figure 15.2, integration may be achieved with a natural oscillation between inquiry and creation, and between emphasis on science and arts where neither one is subject to instrumental use by the other. The distinction between scientific and art creativity is blurred as they both take analytic as well as productive qualities.

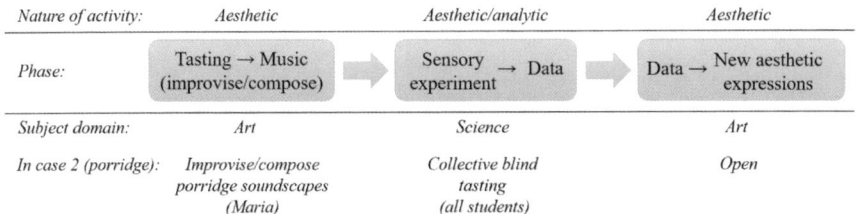

Nature of activity:	Aesthetic	Aesthetic/analytic	Aesthetic
Phase:	Tasting → Music (improvise/compose)	Sensory experiment → Data	Data → New aesthetic expressions
Subject domain:	Art	Science	Art
In case 2 (porridge):	Improvise/compose porridge soundscapes (Maria)	Collective blind tasting (all students)	Open

FIGURE 15.2   Conceptualisation of oscillation between aesthetic and analytic in creative inquiry activities building on crossmodal correspondences as modelled by Case 2

5   Challenges: Sensory and Disciplinary Power Relations, and Transdisciplinarity

As described initially, the Western academic and philosophical tradition carries power relations concerning the "higher" versus the "lower" senses. Korsmeyer (2004) describes this as vision and hearing being considered cognitive, intellectual and masculine, associated with art (and probably science), whilst taste, smell and touch are considered bodily, feminine and associated with crafts. Albeit often hidden or overlooked, philosophy of art and aesthetic theory consequently carry a gendered manner of thinking: "taste, for example, has never secured a foothold in philosophy, nor have eating, food, and drink (except in some moral discussions where moderation is advised)" (Korsmeyer, 2004: 7). Even in food education, Leer and Wistoft (2018: 343–345) have showed that children's taste is seen as "a tool to push children toward 'hegemonic nutrition' [in order] to modify children's eating habits, which are considered very poor". Taste becomes a tool for an external purpose, neither suited as a modality for gathering information of a refined nature, nor for deep or elevated aesthetic experiences. Hence, educators wishing to include sensory modalities other than vision and hearing in teaching should not be surprised if they find this to be an upstream struggle. Case 1, the cookie activity, however, demonstrates how our inherent tendency to give priority to mind over body, and the general over the particular (Korsmeyer, 2004: 84), may become a pitfall even from a purely scientific perspective. Both cases 1 and 2 illustrate that taste may provide both refined and vital information in scientific inquiry, as well as aesthetic experiences with their own inherent value. What appears trivial and mundane might hide much sophistication. Only as a result of skewed power relations is it seen as less relevant or significant than "art proper" or "science proper". Working explicitly with the "lower senses" might contribute to alleviating this skewness.

In context-based approaches the issue under study will more often than not transcend disciplinary boundaries, with concomitant risk of reductionisms or skewed disciplinary power relations. Bresler (1995) describes such skewed power relations as a "subservient style of integration", whilst Ramadier (2004) describes interdisciplinarity as a situation where one discipline takes charge and others are forced to submit to, or appropriate, models and thinking of the former.

For example, for music education, it would lead to reduced benefit if it was to sacrifice its distinctive character and submit to the aims, thinking and philosophy of science education (e.g. Varkøy, 2013), and vice versa. Case 1 above demonstrates the risk of reductionism as result of a narrow unidisciplinary perspective. Seeing leavening agents from the lab point of view leads us to miss out on important factors, ultimately leading the whole issue astray. According to Ramadier (2004), multidisciplinary approaches, characterised by "multiple unidisciplinarities" where separate disciplines work side by side with their respective models and tools, bear the same risk of reductionism because the issue at hand is still limited by disciplinary boundaries. The benefits of unidisciplinarity, interdisciplinarity and multidisciplinarity, according to Ramadier (2004), are reduced friction and avoidance of paradoxes, but they come at the cost of skewed power relations and loss of understanding due to reductionism. In schools, the result is a risk that what is learned will lack experienced relevance, transferability and credibility. A transdisciplinary approach, on the other hand, seeks to preserve various disciplinary perspectives and confront them with each other. Paradoxes and conflicts may arise but are confronted in dialogue. Rather than seeking consensus, the main goal is the search for articulations thus "avoid[ing] reproducing fragmentary models typical of disciplinary thinking" (Ramadier, 2004: 434). "Different realities" and ways of thinking are acknowledged, at the same time challenging all parties to readjust their perspectives. I thus believe that Ramadier (2004) offers a more refined and realistic description of transdisciplinarity than descriptions such as "all-working-happily-together" or "dissolution-of-subject-domains-into-one" (e.g. Costantino, 2018).

The two cases herein provide fertile ground for transdisciplinary collaboration. Case 1 implies meetings between science and food (home economics), case 2 between science, food (home economics) and music. In the latter, the interface between science education and music education may bring forth questions and frictions concerning instrumentalism, the inherent value of aesthetic experience and listening to music, as opposed to "using" this experience for an external purpose. Extrinsic meaning meets intrinsic, aesthetic autonomy meets aesthetic heteronomy. What is the "use" of these links between flavour and sound? Perhaps the question of "use" is not relevant at all because the experience carries its own inherent value. Maybe we can manage to juggle both perspectives at the same time, accepting the paradox that an experience or action may have both an extrinsic and intrinsic meaning at the same time. Perhaps the arts can help science see the aesthetic aspects of what science has before seen as purely instrumental, and maybe systematic and creative scientific practices can add new dimensions to art practices. Clearly, context-based approaches challenge teachers not only on practical issues such as timetable planning, but also their knowledge-bound creativities because identifying all relevant perspectives of the context under scrutiny is itself a creative practice that requires one to move out of one's own discipline and take the perspectives of others.

6   Outlook

The coffee bar narrative and the two cases show how taste may play a central role in context-based inquiry, taking its departure from the issue/context rather than the subject content. Art is not reduced to a tool for science learning, and neither is science used as legitimation for art in societies influenced by productivity-oriented ideologies. A common objection to context-based teaching is that it may result in incomplete coverage of curriculum content. This argument operates under the assumption that "conventional" coverage-oriented approaches ensure learning, which is not necessarily the case. On the contrary, reviews by Bennett, Lubben and Hogarth (2007) and King and Ritchie (2012) indicate that context-based approaches may be at least on a par with coverage-oriented ones. A challenge in STEAM initiatives, however, is to seek issues and contexts where sciences and arts can meet on equal terms, but where both still benefit on their own terms. Herein, I show that such "third spaces" may be found in the context of taste. In the two activities, different *types* of judgements are passed as compared with those commonly seen in science class (right/wrong) and perhaps even in arts classes. To Dewey, there is no clear separation between the aesthetic and the intellectual and he stated that it is unfortunate that there is no English term that "covers the act of production and the act of appreciation combined as one thing ... And yet, production and consumption should not be seen as separate" (Leddy, 2016). Further, Dewey urges us to reawaken our sensibilities, helping us to see once again what we have come to overlook (Jackson, 1998: 27). I would claim that this may also be turned the other way around: Reawakening our sensibility to sense experiences that we easily overlook, and which are often subdued, may transform otherwise mundane and unnoticed perceptions into aesthetic experiences that may be savoured and used as knowledge when reconfiguring STEAM for future-making education.

Notes

1   Other taxonomies, or sets of dimensions, of taste are obviously possible. For a recent example, see Wistoft and Qvortrup's (2019) forthcoming book *Teaching Taste*.
2   Notably, the word "consumed" is also charged in this respect, not necessarily leading one's thoughts towards aesthetic experience but rather ingestion, consumption, digestion, nutrition, etc. (see Leer & Wistoft, 2018).
3   Even some restaurants, such as Mugaritz in Spain (www.mugaritz.com), seek to provoke their guests to think, expecting them to engage actively in the meal. By challenging the guests' notions of a meal and eating, the restaurant questions satiety, or even pleasure, as ultimate purposes of a meal.
4   An alternative and more dialogical version is that the students do a non-blind tasting in groups and discuss the characteristics, differences and similarities between the respective columns in Table 15.2. Task distribution for cookie baking homework to test effect of leavening agent. This will not be a blind tasting but adds the dimension of discussion and argumentation.
5   See supplementary material for sound clips and experimental results (https://www.hivolda.no/fooladi-suppl-taste-in-steam).
6   Crossmodalism is indeed a field of artistic and scientific synthesis. See supplementary material for examples (https://www.hivolda.no/fooladi-suppl-taste-in-steam).

References

Aikenhead, G. S. (2015). Acculturation. In R. Gunstone (Ed.), *Encyclopedia of science education* (pp. 7–9). Dordrecht: Springer.

Aikenhead, G. S. (2006). *Science education for everyday life: Evidence-based practice.* New York, NY: Teachers College Press.

Auvray, M., & Spence, C. (2008). The multisensory perception of flavor. *Consciousness and Cognition, 17*(3), 1016–1031. doi:10.1016/j.concog.2007.06.005

Bateson, G. (1972). *Steps to an ecology of mind.* New York, NY: Ballantine Books.

Bennett, J., Lubben, F., & Hogarth, S. (2007). Bringing science to life: A synthesis of the research evidence on the effects of context-based and STS approaches to science teaching. *Science Education, 91*(3), 347–370. doi:10.1002/sce.20186

Bresler, L. (1995). The subservient, co-equal, affective, and social integration styles and their implications for the arts. *Arts Education Policy Review, 96*(5), 31–37. doi:10.1080/10632913.1995.9934564

Calabrese Barton, A., Furman, M., Muir, B., Barnes, J., & Monaco, S. (2007). Working on the margins to bring science to the center of students' lives. In S. M. Ritchie (Ed.), *Research collaboration: Relationships and praxis* (pp. 173–187). Rotterdam, The Netherlands: Sense Publishers.

Costantino, T. (2018). STEAM by another name: Transdisciplinary practice in art and design education. *Arts Education Policy Review, 119*(2), 100–106. doi:10.1080/10632913.2017.1292973

Deroy, O., & Spence, C. (2013). Why we are not all synesthetes (not even weakly so). *Psychonomic Bulletin & Review, 20*(4), 643–664. doi:10.3758/s13423-013-0387-2

Dewey, J. (1980 [1934]). *Art as experience.* New York, NY: Perigee Books.

Fooladi, E. (2018, August 13–17). *Making use of all five senses in the intersection between scientific and aesthetic practices – The case of "The porridge music experiment".* Paper presented at the 18th IOSTE Conference, Malmö, Sweden.

Fossum, H., & Varkøy, Ø. (2012). The changing concept of aesthetic experience in music education. *Nordic Research in Music Education Yearbook, 14*, 9–25.

Gilbert, J. K. (2006). On the nature of "context" in chemical education. *International Journal of Science Education, 28*(9), 957–976. doi:10.1080/09500690600702470

Herranen, J., Kousa, P., Fooladi, E., & Aksela, M. (2019). Inquiry as a context-based practice – A case study of pre-service teachers' beliefs and implementation of inquiry in context-based science teaching. *International Journal of Science Education.* doi:10.1080/09500693.2019.1655679

Jackson, P. W. (1998). *John Dewey and the lessons of art.* New Haven, CT: Yale University Press.

King, D., & Ritchie, S. M. (2012). Learning science through real-world contexts. In B. J. Fraser, K. Tobin, & C. J. McRobbie (Eds.), *Second international handbook of science education* (pp. 69–79). Dordrecht: Springer.

Korsmeyer, C. (2004). *Gender and aesthetics: An introduction.* New York, NY: Routledge.

Leddy, T. (2016). *Dewey's aesthetics.* Retrieved May 31, 2019, from https://plato.stanford.edu/archives/win2016/entries/dewey-aesthetics/

Leer, J., & Wistoft, K. (2018). Taste in food education: A critical review essay. *Food and Foodways, 26*(4), 329–349. doi:10.1080/07409710.2018.1534047

Lersch, M. (2008). *Speeding up the Maillard reaction.* Retrieved May 31, 2019, from https://blog.khymos.org/2008/09/26/speeding-up-the-maillard-reaction/

Martens, M. (1999). A philosophy for sensory science. *Food Quality and Preference,* *10*(4), 233–244. doi:10.1016/S0950-3293(99)00024-5

Meilgaard, M. C., Civille, G. V., & Carr, B. T. (1999). *Sensory evaluation techniques* (3rd ed.). Boca Raton, NY: CRC Press.

Østergaard, E. (2017, August 21–25). *Only beauty? Aspects of an aesthetic-sensitive science education.* Paper presented at ESERA 2017 Conference, Dublin.

Ramadier, T. (2004). Transdisciplinarity and its challenges: The case of urban studies. *Futures, 36*(4), 423–439. doi:10.1016/j.futures.2003.10.009

Roth, W.-M., & Lee, S. (2004). Science education as/for participation in the community. *Science Education, 88*(2), 263–291. doi:10.1002/sce.10113.

Spence, C. (2011). Crossmodal correspondences: A tutorial review. *Attention, Perception, & Psychophysics, 73*(4), 971–995. doi:10.3758/s13414-010-0073-7

Uhrmacher, P. B. (2009). Toward a theory of aesthetic learning experiences. *Curriculum Inquiry, 39*(5), 613–636. doi:10.1111/j.1467-873X.2009.00462.x

Varkøy, Ø. (2013). Technical rationality, techne and music education. In P. Burnard (Ed.), *Professional knowledge in music teacher education* (pp. 39–50). London: Routledge.

Varkøy, Ø. (2015). The intrinsic value of musical experience. A rethinking: why and how? In F. Pio & Ø. Varkøy (Eds.), *Philosophy of music education challenged: Heideggerian inspirations* (pp. 45–60). Dordrecht: Springer.

Wistoft, K., & Qvortrup, L. (2019). *Teaching taste.* Illinois: Common Ground Research Networks.

Wittgenstein, L. (2009 [1953]). *Philosophical investigations* (4th ed., G. E. M. Anscombe, P. M. S. Hacker, & J. Schulte, Eds.). Malden, MA: Wiley-Blackwell.

On Sensorial Experiences at the Beach: Thinking with Haraway to Explore an Unfolding Sensory Knowing of Marine STEAM

Catherine Francis

Abstract

An increasing realisation and acceptance of the impact of climate change has raised the profile of STEM and learning for sustainability in educational systems across the world. However, despite arguably some of the most encouraging policy in the world, teachers in Scotland often remain thwarted by the pragmatics of schooling and furthermore they may lack personal or professional conviction to take learning outside. In their defence, teachers in Scotland are working with a school population and ways of learning increasingly removed from nature and the specificity of place. This chapter describes the author's attitude to teaching and learning, which has always been to "get stuck in" and face issues "head on". Therefore, creating an opportunity from this pedagogical challenge was an obvious response. Donna Haraway's curiosity is likewise piqued by the entanglements between *beings* and *becoming*, implicating such response-ability. Her passionate use of art and story describes the delicate, yet tenacious, webs of implicit relationality humans find themselves within. Haraway's theorising of *the worlding game on Earth*, a game the children and the author played out each week at the beach, develops understandings of the value of alternative ways of learning which can occur when citizen scientist meets artist in a littoral *contact zone*. This chapter explores Haraway's writing, in parallel with a description of a lived inquiry, to extend and deepen understanding of how sensorial encounter can complement rather than counter or polarise experiences of the other and of other learning.

Keywords

beach clean – contact zones – entanglement – Haraway – learning for sustainability – litter – outdoor learning – relationality – senses – encounter

1   Responding to Pedagogical Challenge and Climate Change

My attitude to teaching and learning has always been to get stuck in and face issues head on. Creating and inventing opportunities from pedagogical challenge is my spontaneous and innate response. This has ranged from a nuanced shift in my behaviour to a dramatic step change. Some changes have occurred almost instantaneously, whereas others have evolved gradually over time. However, arguably, we are collectively facing a far greater challenge for which change is demanded, which is to live through the Anthropocene (IPCC, 2014). During a time of increasing awareness of and growing concern about the effects of climate change and the implications for current and future generations of life on Earth, education has been identified as a source of salvation (Orr, 2004). It is suggested that a combination of policy and grassroots action may be the most promising way forward (Sterling, 2002). The regulatory body for teachers in Scotland, the General Teaching Council for Scotland, insists that teaching learning for sustainability (LfS) is the responsibility of all teachers (GTCS, 2012), and Scottish curriculum and policy documents identify and promote teaching of environmental and sustainability education within a Curriculum for Excellence (Education Scotland, 2004, 2016). The language used in such Scottish documents is perhaps amongst the strongest used across the world (Christie et al., 2014). Beyond Scotland, in August 2018 Swedish pupil Greta Thunberg began the school strike for climate movement. Such grassroots activism is gaining momentum in many countries, especially amongst the young. Children are demanding change and they demand it urgently. Thunberg (2019: 10.49) tells us policy and politics are not working: "We can't save the world by playing by the rules, because the rules have to be changed. Everything needs to change and it has to start today".

Thunberg refers to the rules governing our everyday lives which in turn determine the ways we treat our environment and what we expect from it. This book similarly mounts a challenge to the rules shaping teaching and learning, which hinge upon a society's hegemony of knowledge and understanding. I suggest the rules of teaching and learning could be challenged were we to shift our understanding of what constitutes knowledge and understanding, especially if the processes become valued as much as the products. Today's rules of teaching and learning are generally designed from an almost exclusively anthropocentric and Western perspective of the adult human. No doubt the rules are designed, in good faith, to deliver an education so that future flourishing is ensured for all learners. However, as Thunberg warns, there may not be a future for us.

Perhaps it is alongside these young, passionate humans that we might finally effect a necessary environmental response. I propose creating an enlightened teaching force eager to embrace a richer learning journey. I suggest this enlightenment can be made possible by sharing the thinking, theorising and storying contained within this book. This chapter exemplifies a current opportunity for teachers to bend the rules and explore the future-making of education, now.

1.1   *Responding with Nature*

I began teaching in 1988, the year the International Panel on Climate Change (IPCC) was set up to provide independent scientific advice on climate change (Uggla, 2010). I was teaching before any global acknowledgement of the Anthropocene or heightened concern for climate change had prompted any curricular considerations. Grassroots action, although evident, was perhaps not as accessible or accepted as it is now. Today my hope is that the sort of pedagogical decisions I made quietly, day to day, for the past thirty years, will now be recognised as important. They are important not only as a means of learning, but in forging the links between children and planet, so that each may flourish in the future. My teaching then, as now, is predicated upon a belief in and trust that nature, in a state of perpetual change yet constancy, has the capacity to lead the learner on a path of discovery. Because of this, I have consciously allowed room, temporal and spatial, for nature to exert her full effect on young learners. Critically, I have always tried to encourage the children to see and feel nature as their ally or teacher rather than mere resource. Nature is neither merely a venue, or place, in which to learn. Shakespeare likens the world to a stage upon which men and women are players; I would have the world (i.e. nature), the children and I co-responding as friendly, joyful and curious playmates. Neither is set within, above or below the other, but rather we are as one. In living and teaching this aspiration, I inadvertently challenged the hegemony of pedagogy and learning in science which assumes human superiority over nature (Kopnina, 2014).

1.2   *Responding to the Context*

This chapter explores the playful connections forming between nature, the children and myself which occurred during a term's work of learning at the beach. The beach lessons were planned ostensibly to: address science experiences and outcomes (Education Scotland, 2004); encompass areas of learning for sustainability (Education Scotland, 2016); and demonstrate General Teaching Council for Scotland (GTCS) requirements (GTCS, 2012). I was alternatively intent on providing opportunities for the children's sensory exploration of the beach with a view to prompt a Carson-esque wonder of nature (Carson, 1998). In doing so I envisaged positive mutual connection growing between children and nature. Each Tuesday morning, for eleven weeks, my class of eight-year-old children made walking excursions to the local beach. Once there, we engaged in a variety of activities: environmental art, beach combing, sand modelling, rock pooling, watercolour painting and scavenger hunting.

Co-incident with our beach visits, *Blue planet II* was broadcast on the BBC. The final episode, amongst other content, explicitly laid the blame for the depletion of marine life and degradation of the Earth's hydrosphere unequivocally at the feet of the human race. The plight of marine mammals in the face of increasing plastic pollution was highlighted. I used clips from episodes earlier in the series to illustrate the role of kelp in our oceans and seas, and each week many children would speak about that week's episode.

Part way through our eleven-week block of visits my class asked if they might complete "a litter pick". It was not on my agenda or even my radar. I suspect it was inspired by a recent *Blue planet II* episode and the fact that my class from last year had completed a beach clean event. I could acquiesce to their demands or not: I was their teacher. I chose to agree, although I was secretly disappointed that the hegemony of steward or carer of nature and natural places was to be potentially reinforced within such a project, carefully conceived to realign students within, rather than situate them as custodians of, nature.

In a moment of creativity and invention, I decided that, in acknowledging and respecting the children's ideas and opinions, I could also afford an opportunity to jolt their senses into greater connection with litter in the hope they might take better notice of it. The children had challenged me in the course of their learning, and I determined to challenge their relationship with the other.

Mindful of Barad's mattering of matter, my intention was to expose "the ongoing ebb and flow of agency" (2003: 817) between humans and litter within nature. I intended the pupils to learn more deeply of the process of littering and the impact of it upon nature. I wanted to move the children from collecting, classifying and clearing up to an aesthetic appreciation of litter in the hope that the process and product of our activities would make them wonder ... all sorts of things. I decided to change the rules of what counted as learning in science and I looked forward to their response.

1.3   *Responding with Haraway*

Haraway's (2016) curiosity is piqued by the entanglements between beings and becoming, associated with the capacity to respond. She explores a feminist ethic of response-ability in terms of an ecological relationality between "all kinds of practitioners, not only the humans" (2016: 68). I find myself enraptured by her passionate use of art to describe the delicate, yet tenacious, webs of implicit relationality within which not only humans find themselves. I enjoy her enlightened storying of staying with the trouble (2016), and of response-ability. I consider her descriptions reminiscent of my steadfast inclination to facilitate pedagogical change, often in the face of adversity.

Persistently and strenuously applied, I came to understand that my personal and pedagogical responses are forged within a feminist ethic of democratic co-respondence or adaptation based on regard for and respect of the other, or nature. In English, to hold another with regard is to respect them; however, the French origin of *regard* is to look at or to see. I interpret *regard* as encompassing sensing beyond sight. A holistic sensing of the other includes sound, taste, smell and touch, and together they synergistically allow for a more nuanced understanding of the other and of self. This understanding exposes a learning opportunity more complex, dense or powerful than I first thought or imagined.

To return to Haraway's appeal to stay with the trouble, there is an implication of a continuity of contact between the components of the issue. As such, the playmates, constituting a scenario, are perceived to dance around with one another rather than have one partner leading or instigating an apparent parking, fixing or removal of the other. As I read further, I was intrigued by the simplicity yet complexity of Haraway's concept of *contact zone*. She describes herself with her companion dog becoming in an "encounter in a contact zone fraught with power, knowledge and technique, moral questions – and the chance for joint, cross species invention that is simultaneously work and play" (Haraway, 2007: 8). I suspected this was the phenomenon unfolding at the beach between the children and the litter. I wondered, if one were to invite or regard the non-human other to include purportedly inert and apparently inanimate litter, one could employ more of Haraway's thinking: "Species interdependence is the name of the worlding game on Earth, and that game must be one of response and respect. That is the play of companion species learning to pay attention" (Haraway, 2008: 102). Here, although litter does not perhaps directly respond to the human child in a sentient manner, it certainly elicits a response from the child. It plays with the child; it shapes the child's world and invites them to pay attention.

Brombin interprets a contact zone to be characterised by "individual and collective well-being that is based on proximity and sharing, on emotional involvement, and creative expression" (2015: 476). This eloquent description arose from her examination of the relationship between the food produced at an ecovillage and the residents therein. In a similar manner, I consider the contact zone existing between litter and humans co-existing within a specific shared location.

As I continued to theorise about the nature of contact zones, I was struck by the contrasting, yet powerful, human experiences of disgust, fear or love of nature. The oxymoronic fearsome beauty of nature has been commented on by others (Kahn, 1997) and it jolts sensibility. I recently witnessed such a depiction of cruelty and violence between human and nature evidenced in beautiful, magnificent, oversized statues in the Royal Botanic Gardens of Copenhagen. I know Denmark does not have the monopoly on statues of people slaughtering wild animals either. I found myself drawn to these statues in the park and, in a like manner, from the first visit to the beach, I saw children drawn to rotting fish at the shoreline and towards the occasional filthy bag of dog poo. I was then prompted to consider a relationship between human and the other which could either fester or be fostered by these emotions. Both fester and foster suggest to me a closeness or relationality between bodies. Foster may imply an enfolding or nurturing relationship which draws bodies together positively, whereas fester describes an uncomfortable situation where continued contact has a potentially negative impact upon participants. Whether a relationship can be considered festering or fostered, it is undoubtedly a powerful one.

I suggest these opposing experiences need not be mutually exclusive; indeed, the synergy between them is all the more powerful for their contradiction. Contrasting perspectives offer to rupture any continuity of experience felt between human and nature and this was what served to inspire my response to the children's request to "do a litter pick". I determined to counter the experience of apparent disgust felt by the children towards the litter found on the beach. I decided to try to persuade the children that the litter was beautiful and to begin to wonder about its form and its presence on the beach. In order to persuade them, I decided to expand and explore the contact zone between the children and litter. Once the beach clean was completed, as far as the guidelines for the Great British Beach Clean (MCS, n.d.) were concerned, I planned to then take the litter back to school to extend and explore the contact zone between the litter and us.

2   Making the Change

2.1   *From Traditional Learning*
As a novice researcher embarking upon an academic career, yet working full time as a primary school teacher, I began my exploration of academic literature in the traditional manner: a literature review. A simple Google Scholar

search listed innumerable pieces of literature recording and reporting hours spent in nature by humans designated by age, nationality, class and occupation. There was data recording the proximity of schoolyards to wider green spaces. There was information claiming to measure the benefits of being in nature in terms of human mental and physical health and wellbeing. There was evidence offered on the dividends of outdoor learning in terms of leadership or self-esteem for the human participants. Although traditionally or historically valuable in terms of developing policy, allocating funds or setting and achieving goals, such largely quantitative information may have been initially appealing, but what of knowing about the actual lived experiences of individuals once outside with nature? What was the nature of these encounters with nature? As I read on, I was prompted to unpick learning events in nature ingrained in my memory; a combination of personal and professional learning began to surface. I began to realise that, not only was I part of the statistical boasts of Scottish primary education, but I possessed lived, emotional, embodied learning within me. A moment's contemplation allowed me to recognise that the kinaesthetic and emotional learning events felt more important to me. This was because I had been there, quite literally every step along the way, either by myself or as teacher of children.

2.2   *To New Learning*

I realised that, through my altruistic attempts to share my love of nature with children, I had tacitly gathered an inventory of situated, personal and professional, pedagogical knowledge through thirty years in and out of the classroom. Particular children's particular embodied reactions outside in particular spaces and places were known to me. I felt I knew what worked and what did not. Although not infallible, I considered I had developed a sensitivity or sensibility to see these things. This might be otherwise expressed as sense-ability akin to Haraway's (2012) response-ability. Importantly, Haraway's description of response-ability imbues "a praxis of care and response" (2012: 302). The things, processes and products which appeared to catch a child's attention also caught mine. Although one can never argue a complete understanding of how nature might move another, I was sensitive to the possibilities and opportunities nature laid in our path. Making weekly visits to the beach with my class of eight-year-olds brought us into contact with phenomena such as: the clumps of drooping snowdrop heads alongside the footpath; the collection of roughcast, barnacle-covered rocks; a strandline composed of decaying seaweed; and sand, blasting against one's skin, whipped up by the wind along a flat beach. They all excited the dimensions of the human sensorium, be that a child's or mine. My quest for knowing or understanding had shifted from the written, published accounts of academia to the felt, organic, day-to-day lived experiences of humans.

I reasoned that knowing the beach, the litter and self through a stereotypical beach clean event, no matter how well intentioned, would only reaffirm the ownership of the environs with incumbent responsibility for its upkeep. Litter would be collected, sorted, perhaps collated, disposed of and forgotten about. In the rush to clear up the mess of others, where was there time to wonder?

I conceived the mandala activity as a direct result of a felt need to slow down the process of the highly prescriptive citizen science litter pick. I wanted the children to ponder the otherness of litter through a fuller sensory engagement with it. I wanted the children's senses to be more than piqued; I wanted to extend the children's knowing beyond simply picking up and putting down. I wanted them to wonder where the litter had come from beforehand, what it was doing now and what was about to happen to it next. I thought initially by just extending the temporality of the encounter, real or imagined, the surfacing within the contact zone would increase. Physics tells us the size of the surface area of one material against another is a determinant of the force of friction felt. However, it is not only the surface area of a body which determines the force felt; it is also dependent on the quality of those surfaces: Are they smooth or rough? Are they sticky? I suggest sight alone is a poor means by which to decipher a texture. I understood then that I needed to afford children time and space to engage with the litter using all their senses (except perhaps taste!). Whereas I thought I could perhaps rely on the children's festered or fostered relationship with the other to draw them in, I actively facilitated a temporally expansive and texturally dense human child and litter contact zone. In this way the children would be afforded a rich opportunity to make meaning of matter and matters as they made their mandala.

Descriptions of the two encounters between children and litter now follow. While they are presented sequentially as part of a linear text, I wish to invite the readers to 'view' the following two sections – Citizen science and Mingin mandala – not as counterparts or adversaries but in co-reliance and complementarity. The literary 'contact zone' of the two descriptions can thus be elongated through the reading of one section and then the other, with the attention swinging between the pictures: in some cases, showing the surveyor's eye, listing and cataloguing (Figures 16.1 and 16.2); in other cases, showing the makers' doings, sifting and re-arranging (Figures 16.3 and 16.4). The two descriptions which may appear separate are in fact 'lacing together' as the stories of the children's encounters at the beach unfold.

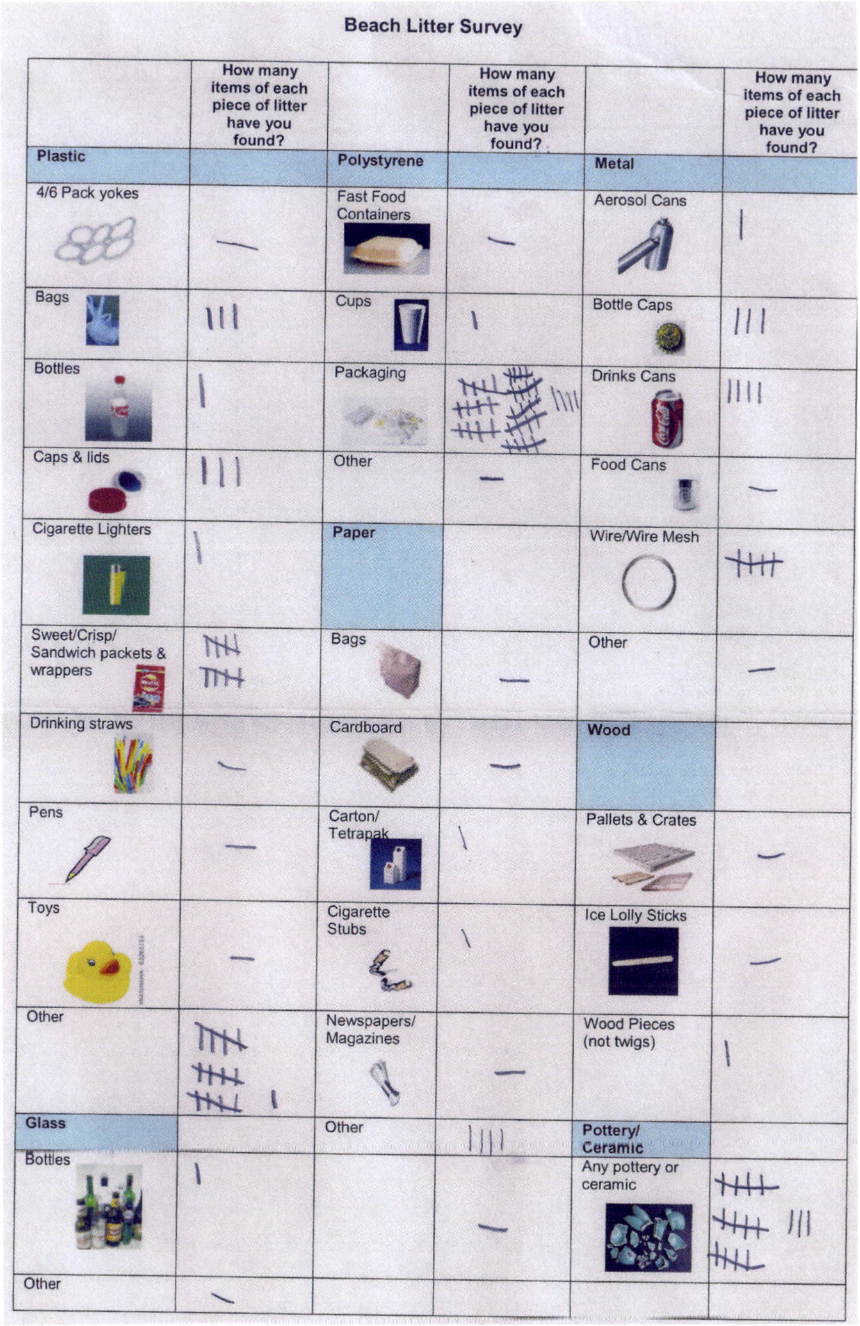

Beach Litter Survey

Plastic	How many items of each piece of litter have you found?	Polystyrene	How many items of each piece of litter have you found?	Metal	How many items of each piece of litter have you found?
4/6 Pack yokes	—	Fast Food Containers	—	Aerosol Cans	l
Bags	lll	Cups	l	Bottle Caps	lll
Bottles	l	Packaging	卌卌卌 卌卌 llll	Drinks Cans	llll
Caps & lids	lll	Other	—	Food Cans	—
Cigarette Lighters	l	**Paper**		Wire/Wire Mesh	卌
Sweet/Crisp/ Sandwich packets & wrappers	卌 卌	Bags	—	Other	—
Drinking straws	—	Cardboard	—	**Wood**	
Pens	—	Carton/ Tetrapak	l	Pallets & Crates	—
Toys	—	Cigarette Stubs	l	Ice Lolly Sticks	—
Other	卌 卌卌 卌卌 l	Newspapers/ Magazines	—	Wood Pieces (not twigs)	l
Glass		Other	llll	**Pottery/ Ceramic**	
Bottles	l		—	Any pottery or ceramic	卌 卌 卌 lll
Other	—				

FIGURE 16.1   Child-friendly, ranger-adapted beach litter survey sheet

Beach clean volunteer survey sheet

Date: ...... / ...... / ......

marine conservation society

Beach name: ....

Your name & email: ....

Just in case the organiser needs to query anything

Total **number** of rubbish bags collected: ....

Total **weight** of rubbish bags collected: ....

▪ To make your data count, **please enter actual values only** – 'lots', 'many', 'bag fulls' or '100s' can't be used.

What it's made of, and category no.

Keep a running tally as you collect your litter

0 Example	tally	total
Litter item ~~JHT JHT JHT JHT JHT~~ II		27

Add up your tally and enter your final total here

1 Plastic / Polystyrene	tally	total
4/6 pack yokes		
Bag ends		
Bags (e.g. shopping)		
Bags: Mesh (e.g. vegetable)		
Bags: Small (e.g. freezer / vegetable)		
Bottles / containers / drums: Other		
Bottles / containers: cleaner		
Bottles / containers: drinks		
Bottles / containers: toiletries / cosmetics		
Buckets		
Caps / lids		
Car parts		
Cigarette lighters / tobacco pouches		
Combs / hair brushes / sunglasses		
Containers: Food (inc. fast food)		
Crates		
Cups		
Cutlery / trays / straws		
Fertiliser / animal feed bags		
Fibreglass		
Fishboxes		
Fishing line (angling)		
Fishing net & net pieces: 0-50 cm		
Fishing net & net pieces: 50 cm +		
Floats / Buoys		
Foam / sponge / insulation		
Gloves (e.g. washing up)		
Gloves (industrial/professional)		
Hard hats		
Injection gun cartridge (e.g. sealant)		
Jerry cans		
Light / glow sticks (tubes with fluid)		
Lobster & fish tags		
Lobster / crab pots & tops		
Octopus pots		
Oil containers / drums: 0-50 cm		
Oil containers / drums: 50 cm +		
Oyster nets / mussel bags (inc. plastic stoppers)		
Oyster trays (round from oyster cultures)		
Packaging / plastic sheeting (industrial)		
Packets: Crisp / sweet / lolly (inc sticks) / sandwich		
Pens & pen lids		
Plastic / polystyrene pieces: 0 - 2.5 cm		
Plastic / polystyrene pieces: 2.5 - 50 cm		
Plastic / polystyrene pieces: 50 cm +		
Sheeting from mussel culture (tahitians)		
Shoes / sandals		
Shotgun cartridges		
Strapping bands		
String / cord / rope: thickness 0-1 cm		
String / cord / rope: thickness 1 cm +		
Tangled nets / cord / rope / string		
Toys / party poppers / fireworks / dummies		
Other (please specify)		

2 Rubber	tally	total
Balloons (inc string, valves, ribbons)		
Boots		
Tyres & engine belts		
Tyres used as fenders		
Other (please specify)		

3 Cloth	tally	total
Clothing / shoes / towels		
Furnishings		
Sacking		
Shoes (leather)		
Other (please specify)		

4 Paper / Cardboard	tally	total
Bags		
Cardboard		
Cartons (purepak e.g. milk)		
Cartons (tetrapak e.g. juice)		
Cigarette packets		
Cigarette stubs		
Cups		
Newspapers / magazines		
Other (please specify)		

5 Wood (machined)	tally	total
Corks		
Lolly sticks / chip forks		
Crab / lobster pots & tops		
Crates		
Fish boxes		
Paint brushes		
Pallets		
Other 0-50 cm (please specify)		
Other 50+ cm (please specify)		

6 Metal	tally	total
Aerosol / spray cans		
Appliances		
BBQs (disposable)		
Cans (drink)		
Cans (food)		
Caps / lids		
Fishing weights / hooks / lures		
Foil wrappers		
Lobster / crab pots & tops		
Oil drums		
Paint tins		
Scrap		
Wire / mesh / barbed wire		
Other 0-50 cm (please specify)		
Other 50+ cm (please specify)		

7 Glass	tally	total
Bottles		
Light bulbs / tubes		
Other (please specify)		

8 Pottery / Ceramics	tally	total
Construction material (e.g. tiles)		
Octopus pots		
Other (please specify)		

9 Sanitary	tally	total
Condoms		
Cotton bud sticks		
Tampons & applicators		
Toilet fresheners		
Towels / panty liners / backing strips		
Wet wipes		
Other (please specify)		

10 Medical	tally	total
Containers / tubes (inc. pill packets)		
Syringes & needles		
Other (please specify)		

11 Faeces (⚠ don't touch)	tally	total
Bagged dog faeces		

12 Pollutants	tally	total
Paraffin / wax pieces: 0-1cm		
Paraffin / wax pieces: 1-10cm		
Paraffin / wax pieces: 10cm +		
Other (please specify)		

Part of

The **Waitrose** Beach & River Clean-up

Marine Conservation Society, Overross House, Ross Park, Ross-on-Wye, Herefordshire HR9 7US
T 01989 567 807 E beachwatch@mcsuk.org
W www.mcsuk.org/beachwatch

Registered Charity No (England & Wales): 1004005
Registered Charity No (Scotland): SC037480
Company Limited by Guarantee No: 2550966
Registered in England VAT No: 489 1505 17

© Marine Conservation Society (MCS) 2017. All Rights Reserved
This page may be photocopied and reproduced for use as part of the MCS Beachwatch project, for all other uses seek permission from MCS.

Ruler (cm) 0 1 2 3 4 5 6 7 8 9 10 11 12

FIGURE 16.2   Beach clean volunteer survey sheet. (Source: Marine Conservation Society)

3   Citizen Science

Conveniently and co-incidentally to our series of visits to the beach, the annual
Great British Beach Clean event led by the Marine Conservation Society (MCS)
occurred. For over twenty years, the charity has collected information about
the types and quantities of litter on Britain's beaches. MCS (2018) reported that
some 15,000 volunteers took part in the beach clean in 2018 and that 8,550 kg
of litter was collected. The society presents their annual beach clean event to
schools as a citizen science-type exercise (Irwin, 1995; see Chapter 5 by Colucci-
Gray, this volume), ultimately requiring beach cleaning participants to upload
their litter finds to a nationwide database. Along with other teachers across
the UK, I registered the class online, made arrangements for parental helpers,
completed our school's obligatory risk assessment and downloaded the tally
charts to record our finds. I also contacted the local council ranger to ask if she
might like to accompany us to the beach and let us borrow her equipment of
child-sized gloves and litter pickers. She agreed.

On the day, dressed in their obligatory fluorescent vests and wellies, the children set off excitedly to the beach. Once at the beach, we gathered together
and met the ranger. She handed out the thick, uncomfortable gloves, bin bags
and mechanical litter pickers. She and I outlined the morning's activity. The
task was to find litter and collect it into large black plastic bags. Before placing it in the bags, the children were asked to classify and record the litter on a
prepared tally sheet attached to clipboards they were carrying. The sheet had
categories listed and pictures of the different types of litter typically found on
a British beach (see Figure 16.1). This was a more child-friendly and accessible
version of the one ordinarily provided by the charity (see Figure 16.2). I especially warned the children of the danger of some types of "litter". If they found
dog poo, for example, bagged or not, they were not allowed to pick it up.

The children walked up and down the beach, intent upon their task. There
were occasional shouts when something remarkable was found (a shoe for
example), but generally I thought the group was quite quiet this week. There
was little audible discussion within or between the teams of three, other than
occasional admiring comments from one team to another on a "big" find such
as a traffic cone. Most children were able to classify most things fairly easily
and, although some items were too large or heavy to be placed in the bags,
the children were nonetheless determined to remove them from the beach.
We made a collection of these oversize objects (such as the traffic cone and a
bucket) separately beside the ranger's van.

As I watched the children at the beach, I considered that in offering the children the chance to officially count and then remove the litter, as part of a national initiative, I had allowed them to fulfil their demand for action described earlier. They were afforded an opportunity for effective agency in the face of human desecration of the marine environment. I felt this was important in terms of building their scientific literacy (Roth & Lee, 2004) but, greater than this, I hoped I had avoided the inadvertent pitfall of inciting guilt and/or despair in the young learners as they learned about the litter during LfS (Sobel, 1998).

Whilst at the beach, I took the opportunity to talk to a couple of groups of children. Our conversations confirmed that they were having fun clearing up someone else's rubbish so that the sea creatures could live "happily". None of the participants could imagine throwing litter away into the ocean, yet they were all more than happy to clear up someone else's mess. The children told me they considered the litter had mostly come from the caravan park beside the beach from tourists, or from fishermen at sea, although they were less sure about how they could know this. One child suggested that people who littered did not know what they were doing, and that they did not understand about the other animals that lived at the beach. Another suggested that "people were uneducated who put litter in the sea"; she went on to assure me that she would never do such a thing.

A chasm appeared to exist between the people responsible for the litter and these children, essentially happy, clearing up the mess for and on behalf of all inhabitants of the beach. One group commented that, when the next tide came in, there would probably be more litter. This underlined for me that the root cause of the problem was not solved by a single beach clean, no matter how good it made you feel at the time. There were temporal, spatial, emotional and moral gaps nagging at me. I wanted to build understanding that it was not just a few "bad people" who were causing the mess.

After an hour of collecting, it was becoming clear not just to myself that the bags were getting rather heavy. There was too much litter for us to carry back to school easily. Some of the children and I had a dawning realisation that although we had considered our beach relatively clear of litter, we had collected quite a lot. I called the session to an end and we gathered once more at the ranger's van. As we were about to set off back to school, it became clear to the children that there were no bins to put our rubbish in and we would have to take it with us. Fortunately, the ranger offered to put the children's bags in her van whilst we walked up. We returned to school and the children went out to play.

Whilst at the beach, the children had collected and coded their finds, marking them off on tally sheets attached to clipboards as required. They then placed the litter into black bin bags. No one asked where the litter would go next. I, myself, had presumed that there would be bins at the beach or that

I would dispose of the litter, with the goodwill and assistance of the school janitor, later that day. Out of sight and out of mind, the rubbish would be dealt with. But it was not; it still existed; it was not gone. It was at school with us.

I took the bags into school and looked over the tally sheets. I realised that uploading the collected data to the internet and disposing of the rubbish into the school's bins did not reflect the ongoing nature or depth of the issue of litter in our marine environment. In a change of plan to the follow-up lesson, I delayed the disposal of the litter and asked the children to look again.

4   Mingin Mandala

Once back in school, I decided I wanted the children to look more closely at the litter or, more precisely, I wanted to shift their regard for the litter. To be honest, the children's demands for the litter pick had irritated me. I, in turn, wanted to irritate their sensory and aesthetic capacities so they might get to know the litter better and pay attention to it. I did not want to bow to the hegemony of the STEM citizen scientist dealing with a problem for the benefit of humankind. Although happy to encourage an ethic of care and compassion in any teaching and learning scenario, I was also acutely aware of trying not to exacerbate the inherent anthropocentricism of stewardship schemas especially when it came to LfS. I chose to stay with this trouble and took the litter into our classroom; I asked the children to re-meet it. I wanted the children to see beauty in the grotesque. In a moment of inspiration, I asked the children jointly to create art from our collected artefacts. I conceived the Mingin Mandala workshop.

With our collected finds emptied out of the black bin liners and spread over two long tables, I briefly told the children about mandalas and showed them a few pictures from the BBC's religion website on the interactive whiteboard. I got out the oversized sand tray (part of our normal classroom resources) and two children smoothed the sand ready for our placing of the litter.

At this point I made a conscious decision to encourage the children to physically handle the litter with bare hands in order to evaluate it. I wanted to give litter the chance to touch the children as they touched it, to enrich the physical contact zone. Without gloves, the sensorial experience of touch is deepened beyond understanding the size or weight of an object; I reasoned the children could now accurately gauge the strength, flexibility or slipperiness of an item. The litter and the children would also be at a maximum of arm's length, compared to their arms and added distance of the litter pickers. When a child stands at a school table, the hands conveniently just about touch it, facilitating easy picking up and putting down. I had never noticed nor thought this important before. Because the children and I were indoors, I was physically closer to them for longer. I could see and hear almost exactly what was said and done. Importantly, I also knew what litter we had on the tables, so was therefore confident the children could not physically hurt themselves when handling the litter.

The initial sounds the children made were different to those made at the beach, or at least I was able to hear them better. Ooohs and ahhhs were audible, positively and negatively. I noticed that generally, in the beginning, the children selected and handled the materials carefully or tentatively, but with apparent respect. I suspect it was not out of precious wonder though, but rather hesitating revulsion. Photos I took whilst the children were sorting in the classroom show faces contorted with disgust and revulsion (see Figure 16.3). Their noses are screwed up and their mouths grimacing. Some other children turned their faces and even their shoulders away from the litter; however, they still reached out to it. This contact zone was challenging; the children and litter were at the same time repulsed yet attracted to one another.

FIGURE 16.3   The children grimacing as they reach out to the litter in the classroom

As time passed, the children held the litter more in the palms of their hands and they looked closely at the pieces, some bringing them close up to their faces. They spoke about the texture and the lustre; they discussed where the objects should be placed in the mandala. They placed the pieces with care and with intention. Some pieces were placed and then re-placed, perhaps turned slightly or relocated to make sense with other pieces already there. Most of the placements they discussed with each other; I remained a silent observer. There was much animated chatter and exclamation throughout. There were many utterances of disgust but then also many of surprise and wonder. "I wonder how that got there?" was heard several times. Parts of shoes were of particular interest and they prompted the question: "Why would anyone want to throw this away?"

I observed the children working enthusiastically on the mandala for over an hour and then I was able to examine their feelings about the litter and the activity in their own words afterwards in a whole-class group discussion. We gathered around the completed mandala and talked at length about the sorts of litter we had used. The children explained their placing of various pieces and pointed out great detail of colour and shape due to the rusting or degradation of some pieces. The children took time to read to each other the small writing found on some pieces of plastic. They recognised the beer cans from the local supermarket and wondered why some of the pieces had actually been thrown away or lost. It felt like the children were properly enquiring into the origin of the litter and contemplating the place it currently held in relation to themselves. They contemplated the previous relationship the litter had held with others. It was exactly what I wanted them to learn; it was filling the gaps.

Confirmation of the immediate impact of a potentially extended contact zone came when I next suggested I send the children off to dinner, whilst I "threw away their *artwork*". There was consternation. The children wanted to share it with their friends and families, or perhaps show it in assembly, or maybe we could just keep it in our classroom a bit longer. I suggested it was just the old, disgusting litter we had found at the beach earlier that day. But the children had reclaimed it and were not so sure. They took photos (see Figures 16.4 and 16.5). The destination of the litter was now important to them; it mattered.

Significantly, after the mandala was finally disposed of some two weeks later (we chose to keep it in the classroom to show the other teachers and children and some mums and dads), many children chose photos of the mandala and its making as their special photos for inclusion in our class magazine; there were none chosen of the litter pick at the beach.

Later, an opportunity arose at the university for the children to contribute indirectly to a PhD conference. I was to lead outdoor activities for participants,

FIGURE 16.4
The finished mandala

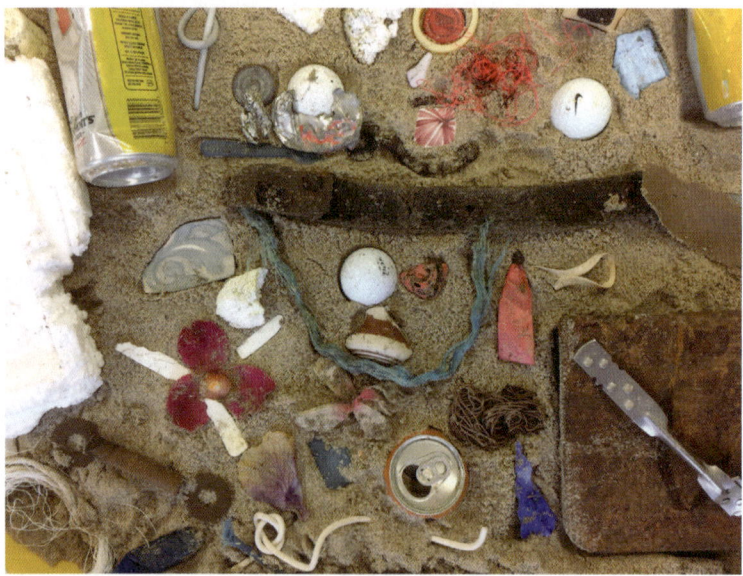

FIGURE 16.5   A close-up of the mandala

and I needed some inspiration for one of the workshops. On asking the children which activities from our term's work I should ask others to do, they identified a combination of litter picking and mandala making. Two comments from children were:

Make another Mingin Mandala so we can see everyone's faces. (Hilary)

Well the thing is if you are in Aberdeen, erm, there's, it's probably a bigger beach so, erm, you'll probably find more litter and you could make an even bigger picture. (David)

5   New Knowing

As I recorded the children's thoughts on their litter-picking efforts at the beach, I was primarily struck by their indignant reactions towards the litter and towards the absent people who had dropped it. They expressed powerful feelings of disgust, responsibility and care. They struggled to imagine why other people would drop litter, supposing that the "other" people must be ignorant of the damage they were causing and therefore did not care. There was no discussion of what to do with the litter once it was collected. It appeared, once collected, tallied and bagged, the litter was dealt with. The children's relationship with the litter was fleeting and it was actually very difficult to elucidate a clear relationality other than the idea that it was their responsibility to protect their beach and they had done it. The children had achieved the status of citizen scientist. I began to imagine that, of all the embodied, experiential opportunities I had offered the cohort over the term, this litter pick was the one which was offering direct response-ability and therefore connection with the other. After a short reflection during the walked journey back to school, I found this somewhat ironic because the children's bodies had been effectively physically most distanced from their environment. Despite the necessary barrier of protective gloves, high-vis jacket, warm clothes, waterproof wellies and finally a metre-long metal tool, the children's minds appeared to have reached out across the divide. Were they demonstrating "a praxis of care and response" (Haraway, 2012: 302) or was this a more anthropocentric attitude connected with nature conservation of old? Whatever it was, it was short lived. As the tide inevitably came and went, bringing more yet litter to the strandline, I surmised there was more learning to be had. Where was the sensory thrill of being and becoming in the world with this litter? Furthermore, how were they playing to pay attention, as Haraway (2008: 102) had mentioned, "of the worlding game on Earth"?

When it came to the mandala the strongest threads of discussion were: How did this litter get here? Who could have wanted to get rid of it? And most importantly: What do we do with it next? Interestingly, the problem of how to dispose of the "litter now turned artwork" was even problematic to the school cleaners. Usually intent on a tidy and clean classroom, even they showed some ambivalence about disposing of the work. The litter had in materiality remained the same but now it mattered what happened to it.

In bringing the litter in to our classroom environment from a marine environment, I was able to more closely explore the margins of the contact zone between bodies; in this case human and litter. I suspect the physical effort of separating litter from its original place (the beach) and welcoming it into our classroom is also an important element worthy of discussion; sadly, there are insufficient words here to do so. I suggest that collecting, sorting and disposing of litter at the beach, followed by data uploaded to a remote database from the classroom, reduces the temporal, spatial and moral possibilities of a contact zone shared by children and litter. In line with Colucci-Gray (Chapter 5, this volume), I suggest the praxis of this citizen science activity may only exacerbate the distance between child and other (litter, living other or place). Sensory contact is diminished: touching reduced (wearing gloves), smell negligible (outside and breezy) and vision curtailed (the litter is placed into a black bin bag almost as soon as it is found). Sensory contact is fleeting and ephemeral. In this instance there was little understanding of other developed beyond the oft-voiced idea that litter is disgusting and that only ill-intentioned, or ill-informed, people are capable of committing such a crime towards nature.

I do not want to suggest citizen science is "bad" science but, rather, I consider it incomplete. For example, in contrast to the MCS (2018) statistic that 559 items of litter per 100 m were found on Scottish beaches last year, our litter had lain more densely, collected on to a few tables and it smelt. Staff and children had often commented positively on our return to school that we smelt of the outdoors, as we walked up the corridor in our stocking feet to our classroom. But, smell (along with sand in the corridor and beach-combed treasure in the classroom) had also been a source of good humoured "banter" between the cleaning staff and me throughout this study. It struck me that smell had been an especially valuable embellishment to the embodied experiences of the children once back in the classroom this week. Whilst at the beach the smell from the litter was not noticeable, but once in the warm classroom it was negatively commented on by all. After all, I had arranged the sun-drenched classroom tables into two long rows, covered them thickly in newspaper and spread out the litter during playtime and now it stank!

In bringing the litter back to school to invade or infect our sanitised, child-centred learning environment, an extended opportunity for engagement with the other, through the senses, aesthetics and ultimately embodiment, was afforded. Now at table height, smelling and within bare-handed, easy arm's reach, the litter lay. It was out of context but where was its context other than here and now? I chose, on behalf of the children, to stay with the trouble of litter, to explore alongside them the entanglements between beings and becoming. I also afforded myself the chance to stay with the trouble of teaching and learning. The sensoriality of the litter in the classroom gave the opportunity for deepened and complex human response-ability. I felt that the litter now had time and space to tell its story and that the children could now not only hear the story, but also have time to enjoy and make sense of it. The children's comments and enquiries about the qualities, origins and final destination of the litter/art as they played with it and created their mandala were critical in my recognition of a renewed and embellished praxis of care and response. One comment about the amount of litter likely to be found across Scotland's beaches was perhaps admittedly an echo of the realisation voiced at the conclusion of the litter pick at the beach, but this time it was voiced with poignancy.

Unfortunately, generally in the hegemony of science and LfS in the West today, this kind of learning is perhaps considered either secondary or superfluous. I suggest, having teased apart some of Haraway's thinking, I have managed to identify, explore and make value of alternative ways of knowing. As I looked to the margins of learning, I found they moved, even as my gaze settled, and this was OK. The zone of contact between children and litter morphed and expanded as new being, becoming or learning surfaced.

6   Conclusion

I totally concur with the editors and other authors of this book, arguing that alternative ways of being and becoming lead from, and to, alternative ways of knowing. In sharing this story of pedagogical research as living enquiry, I hope to exemplify how tinkering with LfS can already offer a unique opportunity for all to engage critically with the teaching and learning processes of knowing, being and becoming. Our playful activities within marine STEAM allowed the children, me and the other to become more entangled. This, I believe, ultimately gave the opportunity for stories previously unheard to surface; matter now mattered. Although the concept of LfS and outdoor learning may have become more established within schools across the world, and schools have hesitatingly ventured outdoors more often, we must be careful not to repeat the hegemony of STEM learning. Given nature's predisposition to shift and adapt, perhaps in attempting to build a more secure connection with nature through LfS we could be in a perfect position to shift and adapt our understanding of learning also.

References

Barad, K. (2003). Posthumanist performativity: Toward an understanding of how matter comes to matter. *Signs: Journal of Women in Culture and Society, 28*(3), 801–831.

Brombin, A. (2015). Faces of sustainability in Italian ecovillages: Food as "contact zone". *International Journal of Consumer Studies, 39*(5), 468–477.

Carson, R. (1998). *The sense of wonder.* New York, NY: Harper Collins.

Christie, B., Beames, S., Higgins, P., Nicol, R., & Ross, H. (2014). Outdoor education provision in Scottish schools. *Scottish Educational Review, 46*(1), 48–64.

Education Scotland. (2004). *Curriculum for excellence: Sciences, experiences and outcomes.* Livingston: Education Scotland. Retrieved July 21, 2018, from https://education.gov.scot/Documents/sciences-eo.pdf

Education Scotland. (2016). *Vision 2030+: Concluding report of the learning for Sustainability National Implementation Group.* Livingston: Education Scotland. Retrieved August 4, 2019, from https://education.gov.scot/improvement/Documents/res1-vision-2030.pdf

General Teaching Council for Scotland (GTCS). (2012). *The standards for registration: Mandatory requirements for registration with the General Teaching Council for Scotland.* Edinburgh: GTCS. Retrieved March 12, 2017, from http://www.gtcs.org.uk/web/FILES/the-standards/standards-for-registration-1212.pdf

Haraway, D. J. (2007). *When species meet.* Minneapolis, MN: University of Minnesota Press.

Haraway, D. J. (2008). Encounters with companion species: Entangling dogs, baboons, philosophers, and biologists. *Configurations, 14*(1), 97–114.

Haraway, D. J. (2012). Awash in urine: DES and Premarin® in multispecies response-ability. *Women's Studies Quarterly, 40*(1–2), 301–316.

Haraway, D. J. (2016). *Staying with the trouble: Making kin in the Chthulucene.* Durham, NC: Duke University Press.

Intergovernmental Panel on Climate Change (IPCC). (2014). *Summary for policy makers. Climate change 2014: Impacts, adaptation and vulnerability – Contributions of the Working Group II to the fifth assessment report.* Geneva: IPCC.

Irwin, A. (1995). *Citizen science: A study of people, expertise and sustainable development.* London: Routledge.

Kahn, P. H. (1997). Developmental psychology and the biophilia hypothesis: Children's affiliation with nature. *Developmental Review, 17*(17), 1–61.

Kopnina, H. (2014). Nature, natural resources and valuation in the Anthropocene. *Visions for Sustainability, 2*, 21–35.

Marine Conservation Society (MCS). (2018). *25th Great British Beach Clean 2018 report.* Herefordshire: MCS. Retrieved August 9, 2019, from https://www.mcsuk.org/media/gbbc-2018-report.pdf

Marine Conservation Society (MCS). (n.d.). *Beach clean organiser guide.* Herefordshire: MCS. Retrieved August 12, 2019, from https://www.mcsuk.org/beachwatch/sites/ mcsuk.org.beachwatch/files/resources/Organiser%20guide%20new.pdf

Orr, D. W. (2004). *Earth in mind: On education, environment, and the human prospect.* Washington, DC: Island Press.

Roth, W. M., & Lee, S. (2004). Science education as/for participation in the community. *Science Education, 88*(2), 263–291.

Sobel, D. (1998, November 2). Beyond ecophobia. *Yes Magazine.* Retrieved August 12, 2019, from http://www.yesmagazine.org/issues/education-for-life/803

Sterling, S. (2002). *Sustainable education: Revisioning learning and change.* Bristol: Green Books.

Thunberg, G. (2019, February 13). The disarming case to act right now on climate change. *YouTube.* Retrieved July 01, 2019, from https://youtu.be/H2QxFM9yotY

Uggla, Y. (2010). What is this thing called "natural"? The nature–culture divide in climate change and biodiversity policy. *Journal of Political Ecology, 17,* 79–91.

On Methodological Accounts of Improvisation and "Making with" in Science and Music

Carolyn Cooke

Abstract

Donna Haraway calls us to create new ideas and new ways of thinking, and new kinds of stories to think with, because the old ones are failing to address the most pressing issues of our time. Such a shift relies on different concepts of what these terms mean, and creating new tools, concepts and ways of being with people, materials and environments. This chapter thinks with Haraway to explore how doing research differently in one research project (exploring teaching as an improvisatory act with music student teachers) has enabled the researcher to develop different stories about research, the role of a researcher and ultimately the role of a teacher. It challenges three interrelated assumptions about educational research and practice: the dominance of humanism, the linearity of process and the dominance of the linguistic. In their place, it explores research as improvisation, as *making with* materials, senses and forms. It considers how we can shift from a humanist, abstracted epistemology to a flattened onto-epistemology which focuses attention on being, on the entanglements of humans and materials, and on a pluralist knowing arising from all the senses.

Keywords

data – Haraway – improvisation – linear research – linguistic turn – methodology – posthumanism – research process – the senses in research – theme and variation

1   Introduction

> It matters what matters we use to think other matters with; it matters what stories we tell to tell other stories with … It matters what stories make worlds, what worlds make stories. (Haraway, 2016: 12)

© KONINKLIJKE BRILL NV, LEIDEN, 2020 | DOI: 10.1163/9789004421585_022

Central to Haraway's writings is the call to action that we need new ideas and new ways of thinking, and new kinds of stories to think with, because the old ones are failing to address the most pressing issues of our time. Such a shift relies on different concepts of what these terms mean, and creating new tools, concepts and ways of being with people, materials and environments. Haraway implores with us to re-see not only our practices and ways of living, but also how we can make with arts, science and social science methodologies together in new forms of research. She explores research practices which she describes as "art science activist worldings" (2016: 78), arguing that current research practices (with particular reference to "laboratory models of contemporary scientific practices") (2016: 64) fail us and what we need to do.

This chapter thinks with Haraway, to explore how doing research differently in my own research project (exploring teaching as an improvisatory act with music student teachers) has enabled me to develop different stories about my research, my role as researcher and ultimately how I perceive my role as a teacher.

2   What Does "Doing" Research Mean?

Over the last five years of my project I have been frequently asked, both within and beyond academia, how my research is going. This question is phrased in a number of ways including "Have you got all of your data now?", "Have you got a good group of participants?", "What methodology are you using?", "Have you got good stuff coming from the data?", or "How's the writing up going?" These questions often lead to me giving a vague and unsatisfactory response. These questions are not difficult, they are not unfair, but they do cause me problems because of the assumptions they contain, rooted as they are in the educational research paradigms arising from the social sciences, which have dominated our field, with particular assumptions about terms such as data, researcher, analysis and methodology.

The critiques of these research practices, coming most significantly from posthumanist literature (which in turn has developed from and with feminist literature, complexity theory and new materialism) gives us the opportunity to "change the story" (Haraway, 2016: 40) and, in doing so, change the relationships between subjects, knowledge and research. This changing of the story affords us the possibility of re-seeing, re-feeling and re thinking assumptions and practices in teaching, and in my case in music education. While critique of such assumptions and practices is well developed, it is only through changing the story that differences are made and explored, providing a way forward into the new, rather than just reflecting on and critiquing the present. Posthumanism, as a force for making difference, is a complex constellation of ideas, authors and theories, which as Taylor states "is resolutely interdisciplinary, post-disciplinary, transdisciplinary and anti-disciplinary" (2016: 7). Central to its momentum is its critique of educational research practices as a point of departure from the well-trodden story that currently exists in education. This current story of educational research and practice is grounded by three interrelated assumptions – the dominance of humanism, the linearity of process and the dominance of the linguistic – which we must now begin to challenge.

2.1 *Humanist Assumptions about Research and Practice*

As Haraway asks, "What happens when human exceptionalism and bounded individualism, those old saws of Western philosophy and political economics, become unthinkable in the best sciences, whether natural or social?" (2016: 29–30). Such a focus on humans and human-to-human relationships at the expense of all others is, as Taylor highlights, an outcome of the Western Enlightenment which, "via colonialism and science, generated a version of humanism grounded in the separation of, and domination by, a smallish section of 'mankind' from/of the 'rest of' nature, humanity, and nonhuman 'others'" (2016: 8). In this form, humanism is associated with particular forms of knowing, an epistemology which positions thinking as separate from bodies, nature and culture, and talks of singular truths and facts. This form of knowing is divided into disciplinary fields and is subject to disciplinary ways of being and researching. In music education this is exemplified in situations where knowledge *about* music is given higher value than other forms of knowing and is perceived as transferred from one human brain to another. As van der Schyff argues, quoting Bowman (2004), where music education relies on a cognitive, humanist assumption of training young people into being able to "accurately reproduce the pre-given relationships or 'meanings' ... it obscures music's 'participatory, enactive, embodied character' as well as its great pedagogical capacity to 'highlight the co-origination of body, mind, and culture'" (van der Schyff, 2015: 79–80).

While new materialism, and subsequently posthumanism, concepts which are elaborated in earlier chapters of this book (see for example, chapters 1 and 2, 5 and 10 amongst others) challenges these binaries of knowledge between us–them, culture–nature and human–animal, and feminism and arts-based research has developed notions of pluralist ways of knowing, humanist assumptions still dominate current understandings of what it means to do research. Accordingly, reporting on human thoughts and actions is hierarchically elevated and the mind of the researcher, and knowledge within it, is considered of most prominent importance. This is seen in the questions I am asked, where it is assumed that I am "reporting" on human responses and actions, where there is one truth that I am uncovering, with a separation between myself and the data which has been "collected". These are mirrored in the conversations I have had as a teacher where musical knowledge is considered bounded, separate and packaged for students to absorb. "The" knowledge is considered to be fixed and unchanged from their interaction with it and therefore the same for everyone.

2.2   *Assumptions about Linearity in Research and Practice*

Another set of assumptions exist in the questions asked of me, that the process of research is linear. Of particular challenge for a long time was the question of what methodology I have chosen. The difficulties of this question are highlighted by Weaver and Snaza (2017), who argue against what they term "methodocentrism", which they argue is "the belief that predetermined research methods are the determining factor in the validity and importance of educational research" (2017: 1055). They argue that choosing a methodology in advance, thus creating a linear pathway through a research project, "disenables research from taking account of problems and non-human actants that are presumed to be of no importance or value in existing social science research methodologies" (2017: 1055). It is this very ability to be responsive in-the-moment, to be response-able to problems and arising relationships, which Haraway talks of as "staying with the trouble" (Haraway, 2016: 1). Instead, goal-directed, teleological approaches to research and teaching are so embedded in our practices "that it has become conventional, reductionist, hegemonic, and sometimes oppressive and has lost its radical possibilities" (St.Pierre, 2011: 613). This is clearly seen in linear views of learning and progress in our education system, where intentions and expected outcomes create a linear journey between two fixed points, not knowing or knowing only a little, and knowing or knowing more. Unexpected outcomes, or outcomes that do not align with the curriculum (whether within or beyond a subject), are often "lost", although it is exactly in this difference that possibilities exist. This loss of radical possibility is what Haraway is referring to in her call for us to change the story, where we risk the story always being the same if we stick to our current ways of being researchers and teachers.

2.3   *Linguistic Dominance in Research and Practice*

Qualitative research practices in education continue to be regulated by representational forms of thinking, writing and doing, stemming from what is commonly referred to as the "linguistic turn" in which words and language are used to represent others' lived experiences. This again is mirrored in pedagogical practices where knowledge which is declarative, state-able, transferable and measurable dominates teaching. In music this has had a profound effect where writing about music, demonstrating verbal or written understanding, is of greater value to the system than "doing", as summarised by the headline "School music lessons: Not enough music" (BBC, 2012) based on a report by the English education inspectorate on 200 school music departments. In these lessons, musical knowledge was being "represented" but not always experienced. This representational view of knowledge also pervades research practices. As Maclure states, representation is an important part of research, and this critique is not to completely remove "representationalism", but it is to recognise what she describes as a "pervasive representationalism that has rendered material realities inaccessible behind the linguistic or discourse systems that purportedly construct or 'represent' them" (2013: 659). The key feature of such representationalism is a view of the researcher as someone who is able, through their own thinking capacities, to categorise and make judgements about others, ensuring truth is revealed and the resulting knowledge is fixed, transferable and abstracted. Fundamental to how this plays out in research is the view of what data is, what it looks like, and how it is to be interacted with. Assumptions that data is written, captured on paper, static once it has been collected, and separated from the researcher still shape expectations of what researchers do.

To rebalance the linguistic turn, posthumanism further develops the notion of the body and senses as central to understanding. This is described by Taguchi:

> This process of transcorporeal engagements, involving other bodily faculties than the mind, constitutes a rethinking of the very act of thinking that goes beyond the idea of reflexivity and interpretation as inner mental activities in the separate mind of the researcher. (2012: 267)

This shifts attention away from the interpretation of words and meanings and towards a re-balancing of the role of other senses in research and teaching, towards a knowing-in-being (Barad, 2007: 185) rather than knowing as represented through words. As Barad states, "We don't obtain knowledge by standing outside of the world; we know because we are part *of* the world" (2007: 185). This re-positions the researcher and teacher as living in and with the learning, not judging and assessing from the side-lines.

While these three critiques of research are well developed in some post-qualitative research[1]) circles, they have particular resonance with the question

"What does 'doing' STEAM research mean?" While a grammatically clumsy question, the doing is essential in reconfiguring research to be response-able to the demands of a changing environment, as stated by Haraway in her call to "make kin in lines of inventive connection as a practice of learning to live and die well with each other in a thick present" (2016: 1). This is reflected by Taylor's argument that posthumanism "invites us (humans) to undo the current ways of doing – and then imagine, invent and do the doing differently" (2016: 6), undoing binaries that have dominated research practices (e.g. theory–practice, body–mind, self–other, emotion–reason, human–nature) and "producing instead multiple and heterogeneous knowledge pathways that are radically generative for educational research" (2016: 7).

This creates a shift from epistemology (with its humanist focus and abstracted views of knowledge) to a flattened onto-epistemology which focuses attention on the being, the entanglements of humans and materials and a pluralist knowing arising from all the senses. This is where STEAM research and pedagogic practices can be seen as "joining in" with a world in which science and arts ways of being are already inherently entangled, where to artificially pull them apart, as previous incarnations of research practices have, is to stop ourselves being response-able to all that we are joining in with. The question then becomes what such research "doings" look, sound and feel like, recognising they will be different for each project undertaken.

3 STEAM Research as "Making With"

To change the stories we think and do research and practice with, particularly those with a humanist, linear and linguistic disposition, I have begun within my research project to think with the idea of "research as making with". This is an idea in the making itself, not a fully formed, fixed concept but one that is in motion (Taylor, 2016: 20). At the centre of this developing position is my own exploration of what it means "to make", which is also central to my doctoral project.

The distinction here between making and making with is significant. Making with is a making of relationships across and between matter; it is always inventing as a dynamic response. It is a making which is rooted not in a telling of past events, representing and interpreting, but staying in the present, exploring how the materials and relationships make with me at this moment in time. This is not a making of imposing ideas or a plan onto matter (Ingold, 2013a) but allowing ideas to surface between us (humans and materials) and stay, rather than being pushed aside as not important. It is embodied, a making with the hands, eyes and ears, and is a creative act which draws on pluralist ways of knowing and being.

This changes the story of research, meaning that it "cannot be 'about' something or someone", and "cannot be done or carried out" (Taylor, 2016: 20). Instead it is a performative view of research which "may only be activated, enacted, instantiated so that it strives to set in motion a 'cacophonous ecology'" (Taylor, 2016: 20). The ecology of my project involves not only the people, materials and interactions of the research but also the histories we all bring to each other, the lives we are living and the interactions we have beyond. This decomposes the idea of a project being a container, and contained; instead it is a living, ever-expanding entangled act. It is here that the synergy with improvisation is apparent, where "The spider spinning its web or the musician launching into the melody 'hazards an improvisation' … [where] to improvise is to join with the world or meld with it" (Ingold, 2011: 83–84). This is not a making whereby form is imposed, where the researcher decides on a methodology in advance and applies it, and it is not a making where matter is considered to be static or fixed, where research materials, whether conversations, videos, literature or my writing fragments, are an inert backdrop to the thinking and knowing, but instead is a making which "intervenes in worldly processes that are already going on … adding his own impetus to the forces and energies in play" (Ingold, 2011: 20–21).

This improvising, making as we go, joining in and inventing, is what Haraway (2016) terms "ongoingness", which not only changes the narrative of research, but also changes the story as to who and what a researcher is. It changes the temporality of "doing" and how material thinking is co-constituted with/in the matter itself. It repositions researchers as "makers", entangled in and with the materials, ideas, bodies and concepts of the project. It is a story of response-ability to the ever-changing entanglements of the research and of what Ingold terms "knowing from the inside" (2013a: 3), learning *with* not about, moving learning forward, not learning *from*, therefore creating an impetus to transform, not document (2013a: 3, 13).

5   Improvising Together

The illustrative examples used in this chapter are part of my doctoral project exploring the idea of teaching as an improvisatory act with music student teachers. Improvisation is defined broadly, including verbal, physical, material and sound responses. The project has developed with eight music student teachers in the last year of their teacher education course and their course leader. Although situated within a music education context due to the group, some of the activities and the disciplinary environments we met in, and the project's ideas, processes, teaching and research practices, literature and inter-actions with others (both human and non-human) is transdisciplinary. This was not obvious at the outset of the project but has developed during and in response to it.

At the core of the project's activities were two workshops in which we explored concepts of improvising and experiences of improvising, and impro-vised together, after which we spent three months playing with the notion of teaching as an improvisatory act via e-communications and in a final conver-sation and workshop. Central to these activities was the notion of "living" the research, where even in the planning stages of the project I was aware that I did not want to contain the research to on-course experiences, but to keep it responsive to whatever and wherever the group found synergies.

It was through these activities and the living of the ideas that we collectively put "bodies, things and concepts ... in[to] motion" (Taylor, 2016: 20). It was in this process of "making with" bodies, things and concepts, where everything was open to change and challenge and where all of us were taking the project with us into our lives beyond our time together, that the notion of making with became central to the project. This is explored in the rest of this chapter, focus-ing on making with materials, bodies, methodology and forms.

5.1   *Making with Materials*
Prior to the workshops in which we improvised with different materials and each other I had conceived of improvisation as a "way of being" with others and as a dynamic form of knowledge creation. What I had not fully appreci-ated was the way the materials of the improvisations would exert themselves into the project. Doing different types of improvisation with the research group and reading around posthumanist views of matter have led (and con-tinue to lead) to an appreciation of just how much matter matters, and a grad-ual reconceptualisation of the role of matter as an "active participant in the world's becoming" (Barad, 2007: 136). To appreciate the significant role mate-rials have made has involved me in deliberately "playing" with them, and the learning they have made.

The French word for play ("jeu") is broader than the English word "play", in that it encompasses the play of children, the act and manner of play-ing an instrument, and also the idea of there being room to manoeuvre (i.e. there is a little play in the steering wheel). To play with the research materi-als (whether playing like a child, playing them instrumentally or seeing the room for manoeuvre they create) involves multiple processes of doing, seeing each, as Archer and Kelen (2014) describe, as an opportunity to "encounter reality", as the "means by with we find ourselves and find each other beyond the noise of distraction" (Archer & Kelen, 2014: 200). The sequences of photographs, taken from the videos of the workshops, are included as an exploration of making with materials both with the research group (through the playdough and instrument improvisation experiences in the workshops) and into my own processes of working with the research materials.

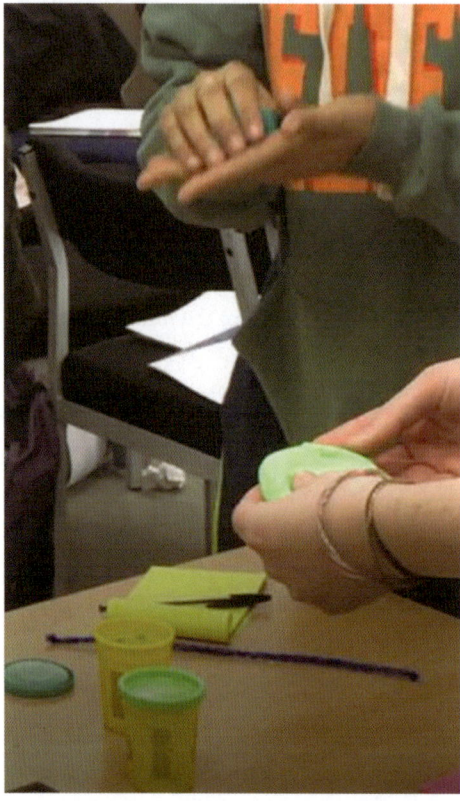

FIGURE 17.1
Go for it or hesitate?

This photo (Figure 17.1) was taken prior to the group establishing an explicit shared view about what product they were aiming to make. I wrote the following notes as I watched the video:

> *Rolling, squashing, making a ball, making a sausage, flattening out ...*
> *Careful and slow or quick and rhythmic ...*
> *Whole hand or just the tips of fingers ....*
> *Smell, feeling, laughing ...*
> *Comfortable, uncomfortable ...*

When the photo was alongside Taylor's (2016: 20) quotation "bodies, things and concepts ... in motion", I wrote:

Playing as activating the concept of improvising. Re-acquainting themselves with the material. Re-exploring previous ways of making with the materials, knowing the material will respond (many of the group made shapes they'd made in the past such as balls and sausages). Why the hesitation in making the materials move?

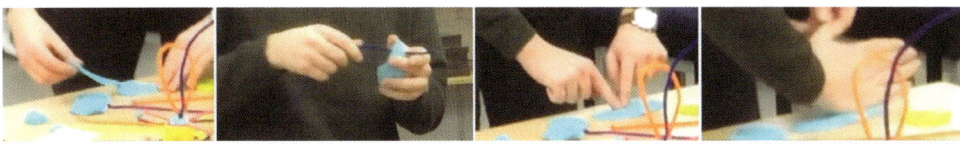

FIGURE 17.2   Material thinking

My notes in response to the playing sequence (Figure 17.2):

At first, seeing this as him exploring the materials for their potential, their affordances. Re-seeing this as the way in which the materials allow him to play, responding to his hand shapes, the pressures and pulls that he applies. Seeing the physical responses he makes to the shapes and weights, that the materials make and the role of the contact between surfaces (skin, play-dough, table, pipe cleaner).

FIGURE 17.3   Trying it out and "noodling"

I took these notes in response to two brief moments of exploration (Figure 17.3)

Taking a few seconds to explore, done so quickly others in the room may not have noticed, done in private with the material, done quietly and with reduced physical movements.

My notes continued:

"a purposeful purposelessness or a purposeless play. This play ... is an affirmation of life – not an attempt to bring order out of chaos nor to suggest

improvements in creation, but simply a way of waking up to the very life we're living …" (Cage, quoted in Hill, 2018: 59).
    A moment of "waking up" the body, the matter, the senses.

These photos are not being used as static representations of what happened at that time but have now become active materials which I play with. They ceased to be something to support the developing of ideas around improvisation and became *the* development in and of themselves. My notes are a performative space in which I see and re-see, allowing me to play with the pictures, ideas and my thinking. To play, following what is happening rather than imposing a fixed process onto the materials, involves attending to the materials, not to arrive at a particular perspective about what they mean but to "displac[e] one's gaze so that we are '(t)here' and the '(t)here' can present itself to us in its evidence and command us" (Masschelein, 2010: 44–45). Displacing one's gaze away from the humanist, linear, linguistic and away from immediate judgements and responses is not a one-step process, but a cycling of playful explorations which keep judgements suspended and perceptions dynamic.

Playing as a way of displacement involves not only making with the research materials in themselves, but making and re-making them in relationship with other materials (Figures 17.8 and 17.4). Making with the materials in relationship with different literatures, different materials from other parts of the project and my own experiences allows me to encounter the materials in different ways. Sorting, shifting, putting together, inserting something different, organising in lines, circles, piles or webs all involves a dynamic playfulness and a resistance to "fixing" meanings, akin to what Ruck and Mannion call "messy situational mapping" (2019: 12).

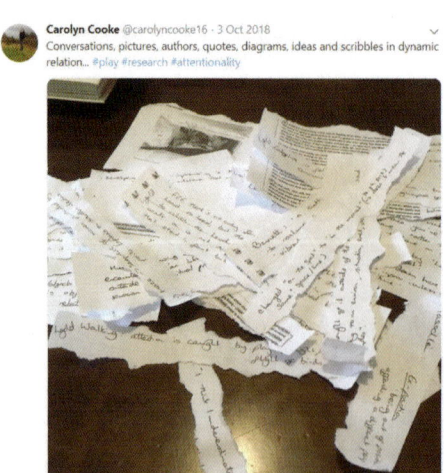

FIGURE 17.4   Playing with my research materials

The experience of playing with the research materials is not one-sided, where I play with them but they remain at a distance from me; rather in the process of making with them, I am engaged in what Haraway (2016) calls "making kin". It is not cyclical, inward-looking processing without purpose. Instead, making kin, as Niccolini, Zarabadi, and Ringrose (2018) describe, is "an active and mobile process of encounter which acknowledges and responds to what is carried (the fraught histories, damages, traumas and inequalities) and the risky connections inherent in such work" (2018: 336). Haraway herself argues that critical to making kin are the words "resignified, repopulated, and reinhabited" (2016: 216–217), where making with materials creates new ways of thinking, being and living.

5.2   *Making with Senses*

As a maker makes with materials, playing to their possibilities and their potentials, a maker also makes with their senses as they experience the encounter. This is not a making with senses in which they are considered in isolation, each telling us something different, "sliced up along sensory pathways by which they access it" (Ingold, 2013b: 320) but a complete bodily "inhabiting" in which we commit ourselves to fully joining in with the world (Ingold, 2014). Murris, drawing on Davies, talks of such encounters as "an intensity. A becoming that takes you outside the habitual practices of the already known" (Murris, 2016: 11). This moves us significantly beyond the idea of the "bounded" teacher, planning and delivering something static and fixed, to instead "inhabiting" and "encountering" the learning *with* the children.

This involves being attentive to how the senses make and create. Masschelein defines attention as related to care, being at, being present, listening to, going along with and implying a "kind of waiting ... [as related] to the [French] verb attendre" (Masschelein, 2010: 48). In my project this has involved making with senses in the workshops with the music student teachers and their course

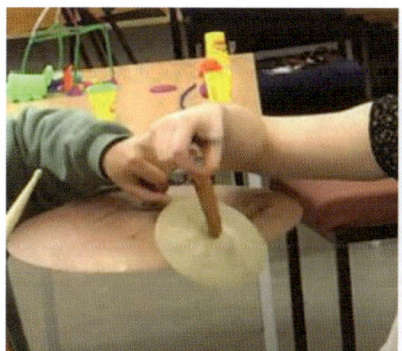

FIGURE 17.5   Touching ... slowly

leader, and also making with my own sensorial responses in the project. Avoiding a representative and interpretivist stance means recognising the impact of the senses in the research group's experiences of improvising, noting their recordings of sensorial reactions (of which there were many) and noting the moments in the workshops and conversations which were particularly sensorially charged, but not in an attempt to explain them or categorise them, but as a way into making with them.

My notes (Figure 17.7):

> *"To touch threatens bodily boundaries opening up different corporeal ontologies". "To touch is the opening of one body to another" (Springgay, 2018). When else do we bring hands, arms, skin together in playing instruments? Maybe in a piano duet? Otherwise our improvising, although musically together, is physically separate?*

The sequence of movement and sound from which these two still pictures are taken capture the slowing of time and the hesitant, awkward pauses which these two students took to explore the bringing together of their bodies, cymbals and therefore sounds. Relative to the creation of sounds that was going on around them, this sequence, which lasted for 8 seconds, was a highly charged sensorial moment as I looked on. Instead of reporting on the hesitation of the players as something separated from myself, I felt their awkwardness, their slow incremental movements towards each other and saw their facial reactions as side by side they gradually moved closer to each other. Allowing my own sensorial response, which was also making with the students and materials at the time, to be foregrounded is to trouble the sensorial hierarchy that has dominated educational research (that of sight) and to hold up the multisensorial world as a site of huge productive potential, making us re-see, attend differently, and make new ways of thinking.

At a later point, long after the workshop, I was reading Springgay's (2018) account of touch and immediately brought it together with these pictures, and a re-watching of the video in my messy mapping in PowerPoint (see Figure 17.9). The re-living of the moments in relationship with Springgay was to allow the sensorial responses noted at the time, and those experienced at this point to make with me, making me slow down and experience again, from a different place, allowing me to be attentional to a different view, and make a different set of questions than just reporting on and documenting what had occurred. This was not out of an attendance to categorisation and frequency, as many other research processes would do, but through a process of noticing what Maclure (2013) describes as "glow".

Maclure describes "glow moments" in her own work as being those which "generate sensations resonating in the body as well as the brain" (2013: 661) and which she further elaborates as when

> connections start to fire up: the conversation gets faster and more animated as we begin to recall other incidents and details in the project classrooms, our own childhood experiences, films or artwork that we have seen, articles that we have read. (Maclure, 2013: 661)

In my project such glow moments have occurred in much the same way as Maclure, forming the basis of themes which I have kept as a working document, refusing to fix them into existence and recognising that they continue to develop and respond to the project's material-sensorial experiences. However, they are not "moments" or "fragments", but are more distributed, where affective noticing leads to webs of associated materials and experiences from across the research project being joined together. Therefore, the term "theme" in this project is not a representation of a concept, but is, in musical terms, a complex web of melodic motifs, harmonies, rhythms, textures and timbres.

6   Making with Methodology

Elgar's *Engima variations*, the silhouetted cut-outs of trees in a craft shop window or playing with my son seem a strange answer to the question "What methodology are you using?" but the process of methodology in my project has been exactly that, a process, which has and is still developing in response to (or with) my lived experiences. I had not read Weaver and Snaza's (2017) critique of "methodocentrism" until quite far on in the project or read about methodologies as always "becoming" or "being methodologically in the mess" (Taylor, 2016: 17). I had, like most doctoral students, been through course processes which had required me to state my methodology and write about it in advance of "data collection". Even at my progress review in year 3 of my part-time studies I had written about a hybrid methodology bringing together arts-based research with critical reflective practices as I could not fully commit to something "off the shelf". While this felt uncomfortable at the time, as I felt I had not managed to present my project clearly and concisely in the expected format, I began to realise the potential of this situation once I had begun reading posthumanist literature and in particular Lather's notion of "methodology-to-come" (2013: 635), which is contingent on being response-able to what the project's experiences make.

Therefore, instead of imposing a methodology onto the project in advance, this project's methodologies have developed (and continue to develop) in parallel with the research experiences. As Ingold argues, this is about following "forces and flows of materials that bring the form of the work into being" (2013b: 317).

This has involved attentionality (Ingold, 2013b: 306) to what occurs along the way. This is not always easy, where intentions (driven by course procedures, time limitations and expected thesis structures) can easily overwhelm attentionality. To pay attention has not been about ignoring the original intentions of my methodological approach, ignoring the past histories and assumptions that I brought to the project, but instead taking time and making space(s) to make with what was occurring as a result.

I wrote in my notes:

> *The pictures I chose for the "hot responses" were chosen to help define improvisation as something broader than their assumptions of improv as jazz. I had conceived it as an experience to inform discussions and thinking once we went into the 3-month "living the research" phase. But actually, their responses have completely flipped my thinking – particularly the comments about hands, and hands together. That one comment is making me see and think about hands everywhere I look. Hands in their musical and playdough improv., use of hands in their initial conversations last month, how [my kids] use their hands together ...*

After this note, I started paying attention to hands, revisiting the initial conversations I had had with the group and attending to just how important the students' hands were in making "space objects" (Johnstone, 1979) as they made conversation with me. This was not initially part of my stated methodology; it is something that developed *with* the materials in the process.

FIGURE 17.6   Tromboning, clarinetting and guitaring

This in turn made me more attentive to the physical, influencing how I continue to "make with" ideas the students have set in motion. "It's about being right in there with the kids". This quotation, from a transcript of a final conversation, on first hearing was not that significant, but in light of the focus on the physicality of improvising has led to me making with it, exploring what this statement might mean from a physical perspective, bodies, hands, proximity, drawing heavily on my experiences of play with my children and my experiences of teaching that were occurring concurrently with the project at this point.

Designing methodology in this way, as "joining in with" and paying attention to what is being made, changes the idea of a research project from a container to "collective-producing systems that do not have self-defined spatial or temporal boundaries ... [and] are evolutionary and have the potential for surprising change" (Dempster, cited in Haraway 2016: 61). It challenges what "counts" as important and what is allowed to weave itself into the research and therefore I have begun to think less with the term methodology and more with the term "form".

6.1   *Making with Form*

From quite an early stage in my project I searched for a form, trialling writing out possible chapter titles, sequencing different parts of my "to be thesis" and proposing structures. As Ingold (2013a) notes, we are used to thinking of making as a project, which starts with an idea already conceived as to what the outcome will look like. Instead Ingold (2013b) quotes the artist Paul Klee in arguing for a re-seeing of form as a result of "a process of genesis and growth that give[s] rise to forms in the world we inhabit", with form as "movement, action [and] ... life" (Klee, quoted in Ingold, 2013b: 312). Form in Klee's sense is the setting up of the conditions which allow joining in to occur, where form becomes living.

As an educator working in systems bounded by intentions, success criteria and standardised practices and processes, adopting a view of form as something to make with, something to vary and develop, was a tension within the project for a long while. I was aware that during the project my planning for the workshops and conversations I had with the research group became less and less formal, leaving more spaces, gaps and pauses for the group to explore. This was noted by the group as one of the key difficulties in thinking about improvisation in the school classroom, where structures and pressures of time (whether individual lesson time or the pressure to "fit in the learning" for assessments) was a barrier to them having space and time to allow forms to develop. This was a tension we all felt – a balance between intention and attention, between form and freedom to recognise moments where forms were not productive or supportive, or where they gave impetus to paying attention to a different range of issues.

It was playing with terminology associated with improvising in music and listening to the radio (Elgar's *Enigma variations*) that made me attentive to theme and variation as being about this balance, and ultimately leading to me making with this form in my project. Randall-Page (2015) describes theme and variation as being "two sides of the same coin" where without the "underlying, ordering principles" of the theme there would be "undifferentiated chaos", while no variation would lead to stasis and "endless monotony" (Randall-Page, 2015). While Randall-Page is making this point in relation to nature, where theme and variation is a central principle of evolutionary development, he also sees the same process as underpinning evolutions in society and culture, stating that it is theme and variation "combined, the relationship between them [which] produces creativity both in the natural world and in art" (Randall-Page, 2015).

In contrast to some methodologies which could be seen as systematic and imposed onto the research materials, making with theme and variation as a form promotes movement and action, where the materials themselves make the form. Just as a composer might choose to work and develop new material from a harmony, rhythm or motif in a musical theme, making a new and different piece from it, research as making with form is similar. As Ingold states, "The movement of making does not lie in the relation between one thing and another ... but in a movement orthogonal to this relation" (2013b: 319). This is about seeing the dynamism, the openings, and the possibilities created in the interactions, how different classes, materials, contexts and ideas correspond, making something new. It is what is created at the juncture, which is not the sum of the relationship but the difference which is created as a result. This difference-driven making aligns with what some posthumanist researchers have termed diffractive research practices. Lather (2016), drawing on Rifkin and Taguchi, describes diffraction as "engagement towards a thinking otherwise ... [where] a new kind of object comes to attention: an object pulled out of shape by its framings and, equally importantly, framings pulled out of shape by the object" (Lather, 2016: 126). It is a way of making difference important where, as Taylor argues, it offers a more creative form of methodology "which opens ways of undoing traditional, humanist epistemic codes so we may do, present and write research differently" (2013: 692). However, as Lather (2016: 126) points out, this fundamentally challenges what it means to be a researcher.

7   Being a "Maker"

Changing the stories we do research with is to change *how we are* in research to escape from "majoritarian norms, subject positions, and habits of mind and practice" (Taguchi, 2012: 276). In this project I am acutely aware that making these shifts is not easy, often catching myself approaching or doing things with a humanist, linear or linguistic approach (Figure 17.7).

FIGURE 17.7   Facilitating or making?

My notes:

> *I was making with the research group in conversations but when it came to the physical making with the playdough and instruments, I sat and observed. Why did I do this? I wasn't learning with the materials and intra-actions but trying to understand and interpret. Maybe my teacher ways of being, in this room, with student teachers overrode my attention to the making!*

It is tempting to create a story here of not having engaged with posthumanist literature's challenges to terms such as researcher and data at this point and that I have now made this shift, but this is too simplistic. I find myself constantly having to fight myself and the pull of existing stories about research. The attraction of thinking about research as making, and therefore researcher as maker, is that it immediately changes how I am, what I see as my role, and the intra-actions I have with the project. I am making with materials, experiences, feelings, literature and ideas. I am creating, exploring and knowing-in-being. This involves being minoritarian (Taguchi, 2012) by "understanding the body as a space of transit, a series of open-ended systems in interaction with the material-discursive 'environment'" (Taguchi, 2012: 265), in which I interfere with the materials and ideas, and they interfere with me.

Making is not always an easy process. There are moments of tension, uncertainty and times where it would be easier and quicker to fall back into well-trodden ways of working, but these are the moments that can prove most productive and creative. As Springgay states, "thinking-making-doing asks us to consider how knowledge and learning are co-composed frictionally and through touching encounters" (2018: 60), where it is the interferences, the tensions, the friction that require makers to work with and create. Writing this chapter has given me an idea of how to respond to those questions I get asked about my research: "Have you got all of your data now?", "Have you got a good group of participants?", "What methodology are you using?", "Have you got good stuff coming from the data?", "How's the writing up going?"

I am making progress!

Note

1 Post-qualitative research is a term first used by St. Pierre (2011) to describe research practices that were beginning to reject and challenge the qualitative methodologies which were dominated by a humanist focus.

References

Archer, C., & Kelen, C. (2014). Dialogic pedagogy in creative practice: A conversation in examples. *Pedagogy, Culture & Society, 23*(2), 175–202.

Barad, K. (2007). *Meeting the universe halfway: Quantum physics and the entanglement of matter and meaning.* Durham, NC: Duke University Press.

BBC. (2012, March 2). School music lessons: Not enough music, says Ofsted. *BBC News.* Retrieved February 18, 2018, from http://www.bbc.co.uk/news/education-17226187

Bowman, W. (2004). Cognition and the body: Perspectives from music education. In L. Bresler (Ed.), *Knowing bodies, moving minds: Toward embodied teaching and learning* (pp. 29–50). Dordrecht: Kluwer Academic Publishers.

Haraway, D. (2016). *Staying with the trouble: Making kin in the Chthulucene.* Durham, NC: Duke University Press.

Hill, S. C. (2018). A "sound" approach: John Cage and music education. *Philosophy of Music Education Review, 26*(1), 46–62.

Ingold, T. (2011). *Being alive: Essays on movement, knowledge and description*. Oxon: Routledge.

Ingold, T. (2013a). *Making: Anthropology, archaeology, art and architecture*. Oxon: Routledge.

Ingold, T. (2013b). Making, growing, learning: Two lectures presented at UFMG, Belo Horizonte, October 2011. *Educação em Revista, 29*(3), 301–323.

Ingold, T. (2014). The creativity of undergoing. *Pragmatics and Cognition, 22*(1), 124–139.

Johnstone, K. (1979). *Impro: Improvisation and the theatre*. Oxon: Routledge.

Lather, P. (2013). Methodology-21: What do we do in the afterward? *International Journal of Qualitative Studies in Education, 26*(6), 634–645.

Lather, P. (2016). Top ten+ list: (Re)thinking ontology in (post)qualitative research. *Cultural Studies – Critical Methodologies, 16*(2), 125–131.

Maclure, M. (2013). Researching without representation? Language and materiality in post-qualitative methodology. *International Journal of Qualitative Studies in Education, 26*(6), 658–667.

Masschelein, J. (2010). E-ducating the gaze: The idea of a poor pedagogy. *Ethics and Education, 5*(1), 43–53.

Murris, K. (2016). *The posthuman child: Educational transformation through philosophy with picturebooks*. Oxon: Routledge.

Niccolini, A. D., Zarabadi, S., & Ringrose, J. (2018). Spinning yarns: Affective kinshipping as posthuman pedagogy. *Parallax, 24*(3), 324–343.

Randall-Page, P. (2013). On theme and variation. *Interdisciplinary Science Reviews, 38*(1), 52–62.

Randall-Page, P. (2015). *Theme and variation in nature and culture*. Retrieved August 14, 2019, from https://www.youtube.com/watch?v=tRjqFPwcJgY

Ruck, A., & Mannion, G. (2019). Fieldnotes and situational analysis in environmental education research: Experiments in new materialism. *Environmental Education Research* [Preprint]. https://doi.org/10.1080/13504622.2019.1594172

Springgay, S. (2018). "How to write as felt": Touching transmaterialities and more-than-human intimacies. *Studies in Philosophy and Education, 38*(1), 57–69.

St. Pierre, E. A. (2011). Post-qualitative research: The critique and the coming after. In N. Denzin & Y. Lincoln (Eds.), *The Sage handbook of qualitative research* (4th ed., pp. 611–626). Thousand Oaks, CA: Sage.

Taguchi, H. L. (2012). A diffractive and Deleuzian approach to analysing interview data. *Feminist Theory, 13*(3), 265–281.

Taylor, C. A. (2013). Objects, bodies and space: Gender and embodied practices of mattering in the classroom. *Gender and Education, 25*(6), 688–703.

Taylor, C. A. (2016). Edu-crafting a cacophonous ecology: Posthumanist research practices for education. In C. A. Taylor & C. Hughes (Eds.), *Posthuman research practices in education* (pp. 5–24). London: Palgrave Macmillan.

van der Schyff, D. (2015). Praxial music education and the ontological perspective: An enactivist response to Music matters 2. *Action, Criticism & Theory for Music Education, 14*(3), 75–105.

Weaver, J. A., & Snaza, N. (2017). Against methodocentrism in educational research. *Educational Philosophy and Theory, 49*(11), 1055–1065.

Un-Conclusions: Disentangling the Assemblage of Science and Arts Creativities for Future-Making Education

Pamela Burnard and Laura Colucci-Gray

1   Re-Turning

This assemblage of chapters embodies what Stengers (2007) calls an experimental achievement of "the power to wonder" about the science and arts inter-action question, as ways of knowing things differently. We have explored the entanglement of science and arts materialities, bodies, discourses and discursive practices as co-constitutive of STEAM education. It has been argued throughout that, in this our co-production of knowledge, we are – at least potentially – enacting the complex apparatus/dimensions of future-making education. Entanglements – of knowing, doing and being – bring ideas together across time, space and places of education. The re-configuring and mapping of this assemblage is no easy task.

The stories we tell in each chapter are of enactments of particular philosophical quests (Part 1), how we understand science (Part 2), how and why arts knowing in STEAM configurings come to matter (Part 3), and the possibilities and potential of practice as research (Part 4). The stories we tell in each chapter are at once provocative and important because they aim to engage you critically with the question of "futures". We seek to engage you with innovative ways of thinking about the complex, textured and (often contradictory) discourses of science and arts creativities vis-à-vis the future. Both arts and sciences are situated at the core of knowledge creation, shaping the cultural evolution of societies and their future-making practices. This is why we focus in particular on the confluence of such creativities with STEM disciplines: with the creative "arts" offering new insights into STEAM and its theorising in teaching and learning.

In developing new configurations of STEAM, this collection of new, previously unpublished chapters, concerns itself with inter-, intra-, trans- and multidisciplinary STEM education, STEAM education, science, arts and creativities. The writers employ different textual forms to create space for troubling, questioning, enacting and rethinking the materiality ("what matters") in STEAM configurations in teaching and learning, and their role in sustaining different and alternative futures.

This significance of this edited volume is that it enacts education research as part of our living enquiry, thus opening onto-epistemological matters in education, which features our troubling of politics, power and policy in STEAM (in Part 1), then moves onto why science matters in the re-positioning and re-theorising of STEAM (Part 2), and further expands the debate into why arts matter, dwelling further into affective and agentic aspects and materiality of arts-based educational innovations (Part 3). We end with critical encounters of STEAM re-configurings in practice (Part 4). This final set of chapters uniquely offer an assemblage of exemplary practice-based projects in which movement and disciplinary (and interdisciplinary) change occurs as a process of making. Here we see how value is placed on the experimental and material agency of invention and exchange between arts and science creativities in the configuration of critical practices of STEAM.

We recognise that what we have been doing across each aggregated part of this book is practising/embodying STEAM education as an ethical and political stance, which relates to how the material-discursive educational environment, with all its various agents and the plurality and diverging character of practices (Stengers, 2007), can be understood to be collectively response-able for, co-constitutive of and collaboratively enacting phenomena of STEAM education.

Each chapter brings theory and practice to the science and arts intra-action question through enactments of STEAM education, which are understood to emerge as effects of reconfiguring subjects (moving from a specific re-configuring of subjects: from silos into inter-trans-intradisciplinary phenomena) in an ongoing process of material-discursive mattering (Barad, 2007: 145–147). We have seen how children, youth and adults need to collaboratively engage in practices of intra-active engagements with science and arts creativities, where multiple re-configurings of STEAM education are allowed to be expressed, enunciated and actualised.

Each chapter seeks to trouble the role of method in conventional research and practice terms. Troubling the role of research method, like pedagogic practice, means we resist separating research and practice and engage in ethical, as well as ontological and epistemological, acts/enactments. Reframing "research-as-practice" and "practice-as-research" requires us to "trouble" the idea of educational innovation, including STEAM education. Instead of trying to define STEAM as a set of rulings and protocols, here we return to questions that have no answers, calling for an openness to living with uncertainty, to harness the generative power of creativity as a means to rupture as well as reconfiguring and mattering matter.

2   Why *UN*-Conclusions?

We know there is a critical need to create opportunities to convene and innovate across disciplines. We know there is a generative power of "unknowing"
in the meeting of disciplines. In putting to work the theoretical affordances
and possibilities of Donna Haraway's (1988, 1997, 2016) concepts of "entanglement" and "response-ability" (for an ongoing making and re-making of oneself
and future-making education) and Karen Barad's (1999) "agential realism", the
concept of "unknowing" offers generative power to an intentional exploration
of "un-conclusions". As knowers and unknowers, in this book, contributing
authors have shared their multiple realities in ways which diverge from existing accounts of ways to improve and innovate STEM. On the interplay of science and arts, we move to STEAM, between knowing and unknowing – forces
that no longer resist each other but rather are generative, productive and
interconnected as science and arts creativities in practice. The un-conclusions,
however, sit closer/reside in/involve tuning into a sustainability agenda that
can lead to educational innovation.

In this book, we have achieved a lot more than plunging into and reviewing
the burgeoning literature on STEM-to-STEAM (a task effectively achieved by
Colucci-Gray et al., 2016). In this edited book, the significant contribution has
been a distinctively posthumanist take which speaks directly and forcefully to
connect learning communities with demands/calls for new thinking and new
requirements for new teaching philosophies and practices within the context
of future-making education.

Within the context of employment, we know that artists, scientists and engineers approach their work in similar ways, with nearly the same set of creative
and conceptual tools. Scientific, artistic and technological processes and techniques are connected in the video-game industry in designing and creating
software. Scientific processes, whether for product development and manufacturing, software creation, or service delivery, are coupled with artistic processes in all professions where creating novel worlds and solutions is expected.
We also know that graduates must be attuned to the protean nature of an inter-
trans-intradisciplinary and digital world (i.e. STEAM). It is not just skills but
a mindset and a personality, and a hunger and appetite for lifelong learning.
Future-making education needs to be producing problem solvers and problem
finders, but also people who can make something with others – humans and
non-humans – entangled as we are within a world in ongoing and profound
transformation. Future-making education cannot rely on singular, stable and
unitary subjects. Future-making education needs to unravel, unsettle and
rupture, to get underneath the skin of diverse and multiple creativities, in the

uncertain terrain of unfamiliarity, that are compelling us to address complex societal questions. Are schools ready for these imperatives? Are universities ready for these imperatives? Are workplaces ready to enable and embrace science and arts creativities? Are we ready, as learners, educators, researchers and policy makers, to reconfigure STEAM education in sites of intra-action where difference is produced that enable future-making education?

3   Making Connections across the Book: A Rhizomic Disentanglement of Science and Arts Creativities

Outlined in *A Thousand Plateaus* (1987), Deleuze and Guattari's rhizome is introduced as a method of conceptual arrangement, a method of practice as research, a performance of thinking, a process of making and valuing responsiveness to context. A plateau is "any multiplicity connected to other multiplicities by superficial underground stems in such a way as to extend to form a rhizome" (Deleuze & Guattari, 1987: 22). A plateau forms an accordion-like compression of spaces, times, experiences and memories, that are intra-active, collective and progressive (Barad, 2007). The different thematics and dimensions which fold in and connect across our book offer insights into why and how arts and science creativities matter. In developing a rhizomatic understanding of this book we fold in to constitute/outline processes of mappings (as seen in Figure 18.1) that "can help us understand connections, linkages and offshoots in data in new ways" (Coleman & Ringrose, 2013: 13) which generate inspiration:

> Unlike a structure, which is defined by a set of points and positions, the rhizome is made only of lines: lines of segmentarity and stratification as its dimensions, and the line of flight or deterritorialization as the maximum dimension after which the multiplicity undergoes metamorphosis, changes in nature. (Deleuze & Guattari, 1987: 21)

Inspired by Anna Hickey-Moody's (2016) manifesto on the rhizomatics of practice as research and seeing this book as "draw[ing] on multiple fields and which piece together multiple practices ... entwining of contemporary creative practice and academic research landscapes" (2016: 169), we feature an iterative reconfiguration of remaking subjects in and through research as an intra-action. As Hickey-Moody (2016: 173–74) argues, rhizomatics is a method of conceptual and practical arrangement that initiates change. Making a rhizome is about generating questions, pulling things apart to see how they work and putting them together again in a different way to see what else they can produce. This re-making and re-seeing is what is featured in the Rhizomatic cross hatch shown below. Here we invite readers to ask what this mapping ruptures that supports their learning, their practice, academic work and teaching about STEAM education. What is in the sphere of discourse implying particular modes of assemblage in reconfiguring STEAM education for future-making education?

What this image or mapping of themes offers us is a difficult thing to describe because it is a complex, vulnerable and uncertain orientation to a new space and because it opens up the space and time between experiences and our responses to it. It opens us up to time and space, to experience and re-configure our ways-of-being-in-relation. An attentiveness to shifting relations, and an openness to the multiplicity and complexity of our entanglements, sets STEAM education in motion, so that we might materialise the possibilities for reconstructing teaching and learning for future-making education.

4   Future-Making Education

All chapters in this book have engaged with prospects, theorising and possibilities for future-making education. Standing as we are on an Earth whose vanishing face is challenging what we have known and believed to be true, education is called upon to undertake the formidable task of reconfiguring its aims and expectations: moving out from the job of offering knowledge and truth to seek to enable leaners to find out their own, many truths, valuing the diversity and richness of experience. In this sense, future making is not conceived as making a product, in the manner of a bricklayer laying the blocks and foundations for a new Earth in which to retreat and find shelter. In this view, the focus is too simply located on the labouring hands, leaving everything else out of sight. Such is the danger of viewing STEAM education as a new chimera, drawing its force from the assertive and extraordinary power of the combination of science and technology. On the contrary, the invitation and the challenge of this book is to show readers the force of Deleuze's "minor" movement, which is more tentative, ordinary and hesitant; an approach that opens spaces – like the water flowing through the rocks – for dominant discourses to erode and collapse and for silent gestures to bring new signs, to perform new forms of relating, thinking and communicating. A future-making education is a widening out of possibilities for appraising and attending to our presence and our purpose in the world.

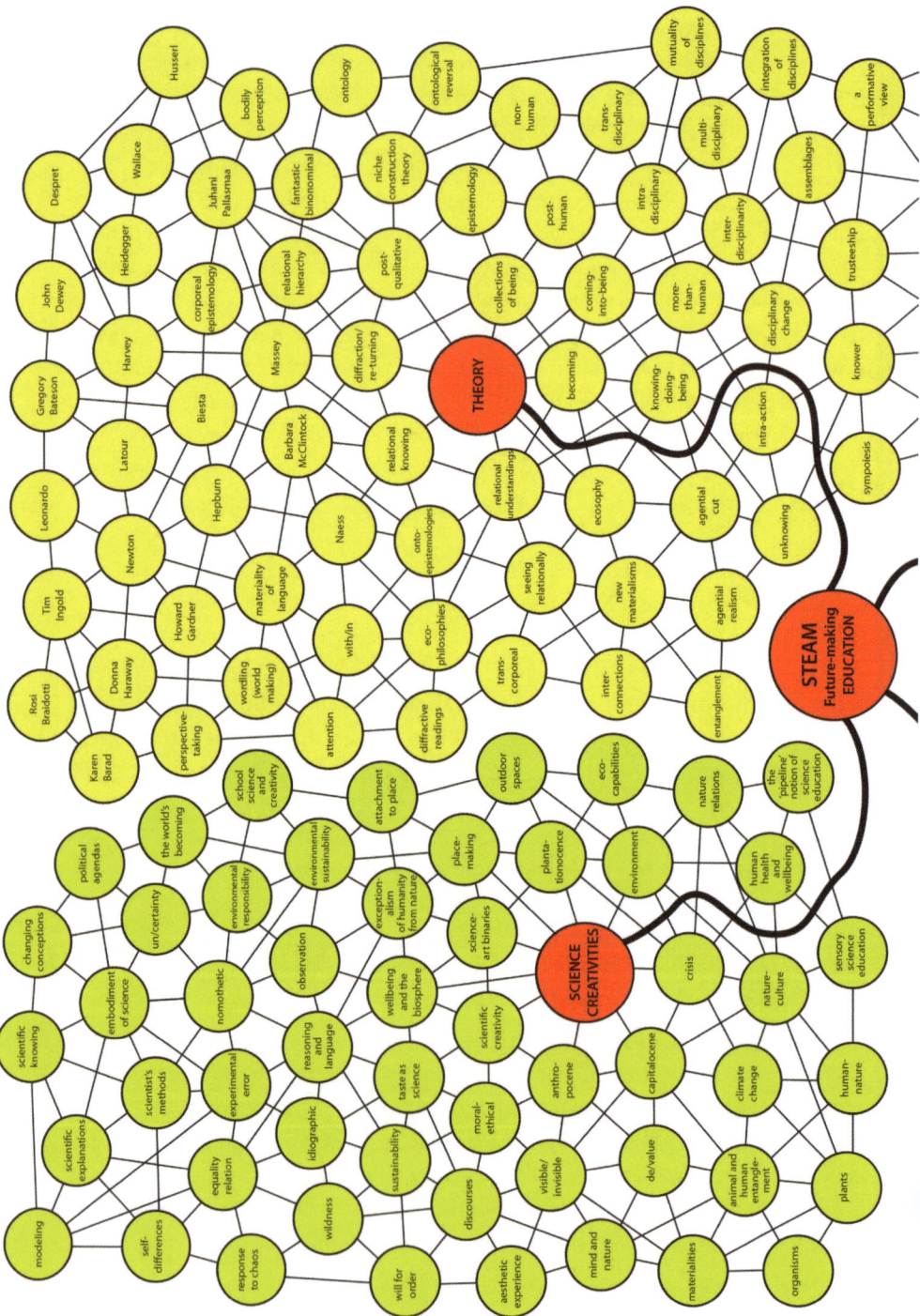

A rhizomatic cross-hatch of woven thematic threads created in the process of the collective authoring of this book reconfiguring the textual interconnections between science and arts creativities

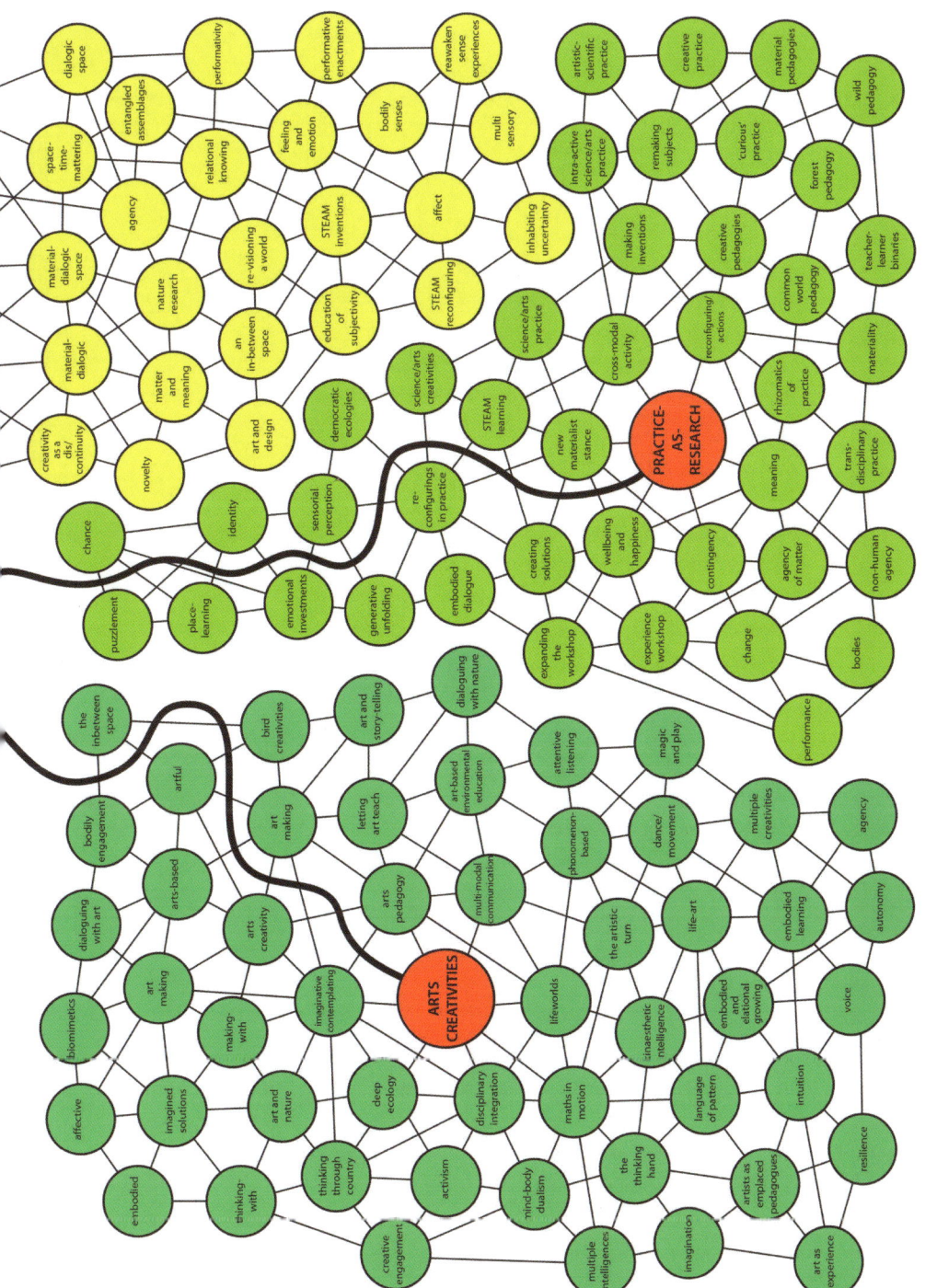

An ordinary day
Norman MacCaig

I took my mind a walk
Or my mind took me a walk –
Whichever was the truth of it.
The light glittered on the water
Or the water glittered in the light.
Cormorants stood on a tidal rock
With their wings spread out,
Stopping no traffic. Various ducks
Shilly-shallied here and there
On the shilly-shallying water.
An occasional gull yelped. Small flowers
Were doing their level best
To bring to their kerbs bees like
Ariel charabancs. Long weeds in the clear
Water did Eastern dances, unregarded
By shoals of darning needles. A cow
Started a moo but thought
Better of it ... And my feet took me home
And my mind observed to me,
Or I to it, how ordinary
Extraordinary things are or
How extraordinary ordinary
Things are, like the nature of the mind
And the process of observing.

References

Barad, K. (1999). Agential realism: Feminist interventions in understanding scientific practices. In M. Biagioli (Ed.), *The science studies reader* (pp. 1–12). New York, NY: Routledge.

Barad, K. (2007). *Meeting the universe halfway: Quantum physics and the entanglement of matter and meaning.* Durham, NC: Duke University Press.

Coleman, R., & Ringrose, J. (2013). Introduction: Deleuze and research methodologies. In R. Coleman & J. Ringrose (Eds.), *Deleuze and research methodologies* (pp. 1–22). Edinburgh: Edinburgh University Press.

Colucci-Gray, L., Burnard, P., Trowsdale, J., Cooke, C. F., Davies, R., & Gray, D. S. (2017). *BERA research commission reviewing the potential and challenges of developing STEAM education through creative pedagogies for 21st learning: How can school curricula be broadened towards a more responsive, dynamic, and inclusive form of education?* Full Report ResearchGate. doi:10.13140/RG.2.2.22452.76161

Deleuze, G., & Guattari, F. (1987). *A thousand plateaus: Capitalism and schizophrenia.* London: Continuum.

Haraway, D. (1988). Situated knowledges: The science question in feminism and the privilege of partial perspective. *Feminist Studies, 4*(30), 575–599.

Haraway, D. (1997). *Modest_Witness@Second_Millenium Female-Man_meets_ oncoMouse: Feminism and technoscience.* New York, NY: Routledge.

Haraway, D. (2016). *Staying with the trouble: Making kin in the Chthulucene.* Durham, NC: Duke University Press.

Hickey-Moody, A. (2016). Manifesto: The rhizomatics of practice as research. In A. Hickey-Moody & T. Page (Eds.), *Arts, pedagogy and cultural resistance: New materialisms* (pp. 169–192). London: Rowman and Littlefield.

Stengers, I. (2007). Diderot's egg: Divorcing materialism from eliminativism. *Radical Philosophy, 144,* 7–15.

What Knowledge Do We Need for Future-Making Education?

Tim Ingold

STEM is an acronym. An acronym is not just a short cut. It is also a device that enables us to speak of things, or of persons, without naming them. To name someone, or something, is to call them up, to bring them into living presence, to dwell on them, and to join our lives with theirs. Say the word "science", not casually but with deliberation, pause on it for a while, and it is as though you were afoot in a landscape of knowledge, stretching like a range of mountains for as far as the eye can see, ripe for exploration. Say the word "technology", with the same care, and an entire history of human endeavour opens up before you, from the tool-making of our earliest ancestors to today's information systems. Say "engineering", and you are with Archimedes and Leonardo, with the great inventors who brought us steam power and aviation, all intent on harnessing the protean forces of nature and putting them to human use. Finally, say "mathematics", and you enter an enchanted world of pure form, with an incomparable beauty, and a certain mystique, all of its own. With the acronym, however, all this remains behind locked doors. There is, in its enunciation, no trace of affect. No vistas open up. Short-circuiting the name, the acronym also short-circuits any feeling we might have for that of which we speak. It rouses no passions, no recollections, no spectres from the past. It betokens nothing but clean, detached instrumentality.

STEM, then, is more than shorthand for a congeries of disciplines with long and complicated names that we lack the patience to spell out in full. It is an index of the wholesale takeover of these disciplines, in the name of research and development, and their subordination to the logic and interests of global capital. As such, STEM has no past, no history. There are histories of science, technology, engineering and mathematics, but there is no history of STEM. Rather, in the name of interdisciplinarity, STEM cuts across the histories of knowledge, much as internationalism cuts across the histories of nations. And having no past, STEM also has no future. Or more precisely, its future can only be one that turns existing models into reality, projections into fact. This is a future incubated in cavernous, glass-walled enclosures ranging from research laboratories to corporate headquarters, or even giant domes devoted to the

© KONINKLIJKE BRILL NV, LEIDEN, 2020 | DOI: 10.1163/9789004421585_024

simulation of natural ecosystems, their closely guarded and strictly controlled interiors masquerading as open access, disguising secrecy as transparency. The acronym is like a key-code that unlocks the door to the incubator. Only those in possession of the code can enter. They will be the masters of a new universe, one that promises untold wealth and aimless luxury for the few that make it into its glass palaces, while dismissing the remaining inhabitants of a ravaged and depleted planet as surplus to requirements.

Science, technology, engineering and mathematics are of course human endeavours. But they are also fundamentally humanistic. They have long been driven by an ideal of improvement, and by the thought that it is for every generation to build on the legacy of its predecessors. STEM, however, is a specific pathology of humanism. In responding to this pathology, and in countering its toxic side-effects, there has been a tendency to pin the blame on the victim. It is all humanism's fault, we say; it is time to move on. Death to humanism; long live posthumanism! But I wonder: do we really want to abandon humanism to a disease that could prove fatal? We surely owe it to future generations at least to attempt a cure. You do not, after all, eradicate disease by hastening the death of the patient. The pathogen, in this case, is what has come to be known as neoliberalism, an all-consuming rationality that converts every possible thing into a tradeable commodity, with a certain exchange value, on a market of global coverage. Under neoliberalism, intrinsic values – the immanent worth of things – crumble into dust. Through having been infected with this pathogen, the disciplines of science, technology, engineering and mathematics have become what they are under STEM, purely instrumental in their objectives, devoid of reverence for the phenomena they study, and dedicated to the collection and processing of mountains of data, on an industrial scale, into knowledge products potentially of commercial application.

In mistaking the disease for its victim, the prophets of posthumanism have perhaps been overhasty in pronouncing humanism's imminent demise. They should be careful what they wish for! The rationality of STEM, after all, would have us run headlong into a world of artificial intelligence and fully automated work, in which mind and reason are finally set loose from their bodily and sensuous moorings, leaving the latter – living human beings – as mere husks, destined for extinction. Inevitably, it is argued, intelligent humans will design themselves out of existence, by creating machines that will exceed those intellectual capacities by the possession of which they had once defined themselves. Far from healing the rupture, instituted in the enlightenment, between mind and world, or between reason and nature, this is to take it to such an extreme that human life itself falls through the gap. Such is the dystopian vision of outsourced minds and docile bodies offered by the champions of posthumanity in its pathogenic STEM-like form. Is that what we really want? For those of us accustomed to the comforts of relative affluence, it is a little too easy to overlook the struggles of generations past, inspired by the spirit of enlightenment and by a belief in humanity's capacity for self-redemption, against the turgid absolutism of the old regime. The benefits these struggles have brought us, from mass literacy and public health to universal suffrage and democratic governance, are all too readily taken for granted. We forget, at our peril, that these benefits have continually to be fought for and defended, lest they be lost.

Are we to put these struggles behind us? If not, then under what banner can the campaign be fought, other than that of common humanity? And how can it be fought, save through a commitment to progressive education? I admit to being perplexed by the rhetorical resort to the 'post' in posthumanism, especially coming from the mouths and pens of self-professed advocates of non-linear history. How, in the absence of a time-line, can we distinguish between before and after? Are we to think of the enlightenment as a stage that is now past, but upon which we can build, or as a wrong turning that has now to be corrected? What if it had never happened? Would posthumanists, dismissive of the enlightenment project, prefer a world without libraries, without colleges and universities, ravaged by preventable disease and ruled by populist demagogues? This is no fantasy nightmare, since we are presently seeing these things coming to pass before our very eyes, and seem to lack the mettle to prevent them. By the time we wake up to the consequences, it may be too late. And what are we to say to the millions of people around the world who still live without access to even basic education, let alone medical care and democratic representation? Are we to tell them that they have missed their chance, that the ship of enlightenment has already sailed, never to return? Are they to be left stranded, washed up by the tide of history?

It is true, of course, that as a concept and a rallying cry, humanity has had its downsides, two in particular. Both have been devastating in their consequences. The first is to have driven a wedge between society and nature, setting human history on an accelerating, upward trajectory that would leave the rest of creation in the slow lane. Assertions to this effect – that culture 'fast-tracked' humans out of their evolutionary groove – are still commonplace in mainstream scientific literature. Many scientists remain obstinately convinced of the inevitability of human progress, while turning a blind eye to the accumulations of waste rendered toxic by technologies designed to bring nature under control. Much now lies in ruins, while what remains is seriously endangered. Secondly, the idea of humanity as a universal entitlement is all very well for those empowered to lay claims to it, but for others the forcible imposition of these claims has meant enslavement, along with the loss of land, livelihood, and sometimes even life. In the history of colonialism, the flag of humanity has always been flown by the victorious, treating as less than human those who have come under its yoke. But does the lowering of the imperial flag, and the recognition of our fellowship with nature, spell the end of humanity as such? Is the very idea of the human so tainted by its association with the transcendence and domination of nature, and with the history of colonial subjugation, that we can no longer tolerate it?

Posthumanists would have it so. Their doctrine is allied with a "new materialism" that sees in the world around us neither resources to extract nor a platform on which to build but fellow travellers with whom, and which, to seek companionship. This world, they say, is "more-than-human". So it is, of course. But to acknowledge the fact hardly amounts to a revolution in philosophy! For those who actually draw a living from the land or oceans, it is simply a statement of common sense. Indeed, that the earth abounds with vitality of every possible kind, and moreover, that these other-than-human kinds have ever entered into relations with one another, and even held meanings for one another, regardless of the presence or even existence of humans, has long been obvious to everyone barring a handful of influential, western philosophers and their acolytes. The more-than-human is not a new condition, nor does it follow on from a more-than-natural condition of humanity. Nor, too, does it imply any rejection of anthropocentrism. On the contrary, it amounts to a recognition that for every one of us, the world of experience radiates from the centre where we stand to embrace others of every possible complexion, and to an acknowledgement of the debt we owe to these others for our existence as human beings. Decentring humanity would write off this debt. A humanity that had fully colonised its world, and encompassed its lands and waters, would not be at the centre but all around on the outside. This is not anthropocentrism but anthropo-circumferentialism.

This emancipation of humanity from its native Earth – even to the extent of finding other worlds to colonise – tops the agenda for STEM. Disconcertingly, it is coupled with impeccably "green" credentials, in the design of state-of-the-art facilities for managing the planet and its resources on a sustainable basis. This is its vision for the new geosocial era, dubbed the "Anthropocene", characterised by humanity's final and complete mastery of the Earth and its formative processes. But for many if not most inhabitants of the planet, the Anthropocene has inaugurated a period of profound uncertainty, coloured by anxiety over whether there will be much of a future for life on Earth, least of all for human life. Far from conferring mastery, it seems that the interventions of science, technology and engineering, aided and abetted by mathematics, have unleashed forces of a magnitude that threaten our very existence. To carry on under such conditions calls for an ecological sensibility of a quite different order: one that acknowledges the precarity of human life on an earth, or in a universe, that cares nothing for it, rather than assuming omnipotence. On the whole, humility pays off. But so does the search for human betterment. The problem lies in how to reconcile the two, and more specifically, how to introduce this reconciliation into the philosophy and practice of education. Can art ride to the rescue? Can it provide an alternative way into a future that is looking increasingly perilous? Or does art risk being sucked into the same vortex?

Possible answers cover a broad spectrum, but for convenience they may be divided into three. One is to integrate art fully within the framework of STEM, making it subordinate to the same instrumental objectives. Indeed when the acronym STEAM was first proposed, including an A for "art", it was with precisely this aim in mind. The idea was to bring art and design into the frame, as ways of thinking "outside the box", that the STEM project requires in order to satisfy its insatiable thirst for innovation. In the marketplace of knowledge, novelty is a condition for competitive advantage, and artists and designers – known as "creatives" – were tasked with coming up with the new ideas that the competition calls for, not just for designing new knowledge products, but for their advertisement. Art could make them attractive to consumers, especially the young, to whom the sense of wonder is marketed as a prize commodity. In this way of thinking, creativity and innovation mean much the same thing. They come together in the idea of what it means to be "smart", an idea that has gained extraordinary traction in recent years. It refers to an intelligence that is quick and nimble in solving problems, as well as devious, giving its possessor a competitive edge over his or her more slow-witted rivals. It is the hallmark of the successful entrepreneur, and often placed at the top in any list of attributes that a STEM-based education should inculcate in students exposed to it.

A second kind of answer posits a certain complementarity between art and STEM, allowing that art has its own raison d'être alongside and on a par with the rationale of STEM. Perhaps this would be better written as STEM + A, rather than STEAM. Here, the A stands as much for attentiveness as for art. Advocates of complementarity often appeal to the image of the divided brain, with its left side for objective analysis and logical thought, and its right side for feeling, empathy and holistic understanding. An education in art and attentiveness, then, helps with the development of the right side, tempering the dominance of the left, and leading to a better balance in students' abilities to relate to the world around them. Paying attention to their surroundings, they are more inclined to care for them, to protect them, and so to lead sustainable lives. This complementarity, however, does not trespass on the territory that STEM has already carved out for itself, and does little to challenge its rationality. On the contrary, if anything, it reproduces a persistent dualism between affective, embodied experience and the cognitive operations of a disembodied intellect, each furnished with its own distinctive style of creativity. Ironically, the former tends to be associated with the non-verbal and the latter with the verbal, even though it is above all in the bodily performance of words, in speech or writing, that the things they name are brought into affective presence, whereas nothing puts a stop to both words and feeling more than the acronymics of STEM.

The third kind of answer is more radical. This is for art to destabilise the entire project of STEM, to expose its underlying assumptions, both ontological and epistemological, to restore ways of knowing the world to ways of being in it, and in so doing, to rescue the disciplines of science, technology, engineering and mathematics from their STEM-induced stultification. It is to acknowledge them for what they really are – ongoing traditions of human endeavour and inquiry stretching deep into the past. This answer, in effect, subverts the very logic of the acronym. And if that is what we want art to do, then to call it STEAM would be not just misleading but self-defeating. For it would make no more sense, in this radical view, to add art to science than it would have done to Vitruvius, Alberti, Leonardo or Constable. For these giants of the past, in fields, respectively, of architecture, perspective, anatomy and meteorology, science and art were not separate or even separable endeavours but rather as one, in their commitment to careful observation, patient experimentation, precise description and informed speculation. This calls for an imagination, however, wholly different from that of the kind coveted by STEM. Far from closing in on smart solutions, it is an imagination that opens up to the world's ceaseless self-formation and draws its creativity from the same source. Arguably, this is the way the real sciences – and real scientists – have always worked, by feeling their way from within, guided by genuine wonder, curiosity and care.

Now if education is the means by which a society ensures its own future, then the choice between these different answers comes down to the kinds of futures they entail. Does education bring generations together in the common task of making a future for all, or does it rather seek to prepare a single-generational cohort for a future that already lies in wait for it? Here, again, the logic of STEM is uncompromising in its repudiation of the past. And without a past, STEM cannot grow into the future. Its claim, rather, is to be the future. This future, for STEM, is virtually upon us, the present already on its way out. This is why its metaphors of choice are "state-of-the-art" and the "cutting edge". Some things, of course, come with a lead time attached, of years or perhaps decades. Yet they are ready to be rolled out, the machinery to realise them up and running. And if the future is waiting, it follows that youngsters must be readied for it. This, according to its rhetoric, is what STEM education is about: preparing the coming generation for a cut-throat world in which only the smart will survive. Nothing seems more important than employability, booking a place in the new, technocratic world order. Anyone deemed unemployable is destined for the scrap-heap of redundant humanity. And with every passing year, the competition intensifies. As the future comes ever closer, time itself is compressed into the plane of instantaneity. It is the time of now.

What is the alternative? It is to see in education a means not of generational replacement but of securing the continuity of life. This is to lay the generations not over but alongside one another, like the overlapping fibres of a rope, allowing the young and the elderly – cruelly rent apart by the intrusion of an intermediate, STEM-struck generational cohort – once again to join together, as before, in the making of a common world. For they are in touch, in ways that target-driven intermediates are not, with more enduring rhythms of time wherein past and future, extending indefinitely, converge like the arms of an ellipse on the horizon of eternity. Here, imagination is not so much a power of innovation as a longing that dwells in memory. In the seasoned wisdom of the elderly, as in the curiosity of the young, there is an openness to the world, and an attentiveness to what is going on there, that hold little esteem in a system that puts all its money on smart solutions. Within such a system, the temporal drift of the elderly is dismissed as dementia, and the not-knowing of the young as ignorance. To the promoters of STEM-based education, the idea that the demented and the ignorant might together forge the future is manifestly absurd. To unite wisdom and curiosity, however, appears not only prudent but necessary for there to be a future worth living at all. This is not nostalgia, or a hankering for a lost past. It is rather a foundation for hope.

In this unification of wisdom and curiosity lies the promise of an education turned around by art. Such education, rather than teaching us about the world, allows us to be taught by it. It puts the world first, acknowledging that it is thanks to the attentive experience of habitation that we can comprehend the things and materials to be found there. Only then can we even begin to think scientifically or mathematically, change the world through engineering, or design technological solutions. Of course, we cannot think without concepts, but conceiving – even of the apparently most abstract, mathematical kind – is itself implicate in the full-bodied generation of incipient life. This conclusion, however, is not without consequences for the kind of intellectual work we call theory. For it implies that our own thinking also lies in the experiential entanglements that come from working with stuff. To weave our thinking into the more-then-human world means finding a way through its tangled mesh; it does not mean turning the world into its own picture by putting it in the frame. And if thinking in and with the world is what we truly mean by theorising, then it's time for us to step down from our academic pedestal and desist from the habit of adducing the practices we study, whether of education or anything else, merely as illustrative examples, case material or even data to support a truth that lies unassailably above and beyond the reality of which we speak. Perhaps, as theorists of education, we could all learn from a tasting our own medicine!

Index